Praise for

When **Panic** Attacks

"Few truly great books on psychotherapy have been published, and this is one of them. *When Panic Attacks* tells you how to deal with all kinds of anxiety and with most other emotional problems. It is clearly and charmingly written."

> —*Albert Ellis, Ph.D., founder of the Albert Ellis*
> *Institute and bestselling author of* A Guide to
> Rational Living

"Another masterpiece from the author who helped millions help themselves with *Feeling Good: The New Mood Therapy*. Dr. Burns's elegant writing style, compassion, and humor translate powerful psychotherapy methods into accessible, practical, and helpful tools for the vast number of individuals who struggle with anxiety."

> —*Henny Westra, Ph.D., Associate Professor and Director*
> *of the York University Anxiety Research Clinic*

"Dr. Burns has a truly unique and remarkable ability to present the most current evidence-based therapies for anxiety in a way that is engaging, compelling, easy to read, and—most important of all—useful. Readers will be able to make immediate practical use of the concepts and strategies Dr. Burns presents here. I'm sure this book will change many lives."

> —*Jacqueline B. Persons, Ph.D., Director of the San*
> *Francisco Bay Area Center for Cognitive Therapy and*
> *Associate Clinical Professor at the University of*
> *California, Berkeley*

"Besides being well written and accessible, with lots of patient narratives to spark interest, *When Panic Attacks* lays out exactly what readers need to do to feel better."

> —*Library Journal*

Also by David D. Burns, M.D.

*Feeling Good: The New
Mood Therapy*

Intimate Connections

The Feeling Good Handbook

Ten Days to Self-Esteem

*Ten Days to Self-Esteem:
The Leader's Manual*

WHEN
Panic
ATTACKS

The New,
Drug-Free
Anxiety Therapy
That Can
Change Your Life

David D. Burns, M.D.

HARMONY
BOOKS · NEW YORK

Published in the United States by Harmony Books, an imprint of
the Crown Publishing Group, a division of Random House LLC,
a Penguin Random House Company, New York.
www.crownpublishing.com

Harmony Books is a registered trademark, and the Circle colophon is a
trademark of Random House LLC.

Originally published in hardcover in the United States by Broadway Books,
an imprint of the Doubleday Broadway Publishing Group, a division of
Random House, Inc., New York, in 2006, and subsequently published in
paperback in the United States by Broadway Books, an imprint of the
Doubleday Broadway Publishing Group, a division of Random House, Inc.,
New York, in 2007. Subsequently published in paperback by
Three Rivers Press, an imprint of the Crown Publishing Group,
a division of Random House LLC, New York, in 2007.

Book design by Donna Sinisgalli

Library of Congress Cataloging-in-Publication Data
Burns, David D.
When panic attacks : the new, drug-free anxiety therapy that can change
your life / by David D. Burns.
p. cm.
Includes bibliographical references and index.
1. Panic attacks—Treatment. 2. Panic attacks—Alternative treatment.
I. Title.

RC535.B87 2006
616.85'22306—dc22
2005052260

ISBN 978-0-7679-2083-4
eISBN 978-0-7679-2389-7

Printed in the United States of America

27 26 25 24 23

First Harmony Books Edition

ACKNOWLEDGMENTS

I would like to thank my daughter, Signe Burns, for her enormous contributions to the creation of this book. Without Signe's brilliant editing and spirit, this book would have been radically different. We worked on it together for over a year—a joyous but sometimes humbling experience, because Signe's feedback was always ruthlessly honest. We had tons of fun and spent lots of time giggling uncontrollably just about the time our brains were starting to turn to mush toward the end of the day.

I also want to thank Amy Hertz for giving me the chance to write this book and to work with her new publishing imprint, Morgan Road Books. I've been knee-deep in academic research and clinical teaching at Stanford for more than ten years, and there have been many new developments in the treatment of anxiety and depression that I've wanted to share with my colleagues and with the general public. I'm especially grateful to Marc Haeringer, associate editor at Morgan Road Books, for his fabulous editing and collaboration in the creation of this manuscript.

I would also like to acknowledge many gifted colleagues whose creativity and innovation have contributed so greatly to the development and validation of the methods in this book. Of course, Drs. Albert Ellis and Aaron Beck were two of the earliest pioneers, but it's really been a team effort. Thousands of gifted clinicians and researchers worldwide have worked together to put Cognitive Behavior Therapy on the map.

Finally, I want to thank the psychiatric residents at Stanford University School of Medicine who have attended my Wednesday evening psychotherapy seminars over the past several years. This has been a dynamic personal and professional experience for me, and while I've been the teacher, I've also been the student. I've learned tremendously from all of you every single week. Your enthusiasm, compassion, and zeal have been an incredible gift!

CONTENTS

INTRODUCTION

Do self-help books actually help anyone? During the past fifteen years, Dr. Forrest Scogin and his colleagues from the University of Alabama Medical Center have conducted a series of innovative experiments designed to answer this question. The researchers randomly divided sixty patients seeking treatment for episodes of major depression into two groups. They told both groups of patients that they'd have to wait four weeks to see a psychiatrist. In the meantime, they gave each patient in one group a copy of my first book, *Feeling Good: The New Mood Therapy*, and encouraged them to read it during the waiting period. The patients in the second group did not receive the book. A research assistant called all the patients each week and administered two widely used tests that can track changes in depression.

The researchers were surprised by the results of their study. At the end of the four-week waiting period, two-thirds of the patients who read *Feeling Good* had improved substantially or recovered, even though they did not receive *any* medications or psychotherapy. In fact, they improved so much that they didn't need any additional treatment.

In contrast, the patients who did not receive *Feeling Good* failed to improve. The researchers then gave them a copy of *Feeling Good* and asked them to read it during a second four-week waiting period. Two-thirds of them recovered and did not require any additional treatment. Furthermore, the patients who responded to *Feeling Good* have not relapsed, but have maintained their gains for up to three years so far.

These were not fly-by-night studies, but peer-refereed studies published in top psychological and medical journals. The researchers concluded that *Feeling Good* "bibliotherapy" should be the first line of treatment for most patients suffering from depression because it often works faster than drugs or psychotherapy. In addition, it's incredibly cost-effective and entirely free of the troublesome side effects of psychiatric medications, such as weight gain, insomnia, sexual difficulties, or addiction.

The therapy I described in *Feeling Good* is called Cognitive Behavior Therapy (CBT), because you learn to change the negative thoughts, or "cognitions," that cause the depression, as well as the self-defeating behavior patterns that keep you stuck. Dr. Scogin's groundbreaking studies clearly show that for many individuals, CBT can be very effective in a self-help format, even without pills or the guidance of a therapist.[1]

Dozens of published studies have confirmed that CBT is also effective when administered by therapists. It's at least as good as the best antidepressant medications in the short term and is more effective in the long term. For example, in a recent landmark study conducted at outpatient clinics at the University of Pennsylvania and Vanderbilt University, 240 patients suffering from episodes of moderate to severe depression were randomly assigned to treatment with CBT, paroxetine (Paxil), or a placebo so the effects of these treatments could be compared in both the short and the long term. The results were recently published in two major papers in the *Archives of General Psychiatry*, the top psychiatric journal.[2] The findings confirmed, once again, that CBT was at least as effective as the antidepressant in the short term, but more effective in the long term.

Dr. Robert DeRubeis, the chairman of the Department of Psychology at the University of Pennsylvania, explained that CBT had more lasting effects because it gave the patients the tools they needed to manage their problems and emotions. He concluded that CBT, and not pills, should be the treatment of choice for patients suffering from moderate to severe depression. He stated: "Patients with depression are often overwhelmed by other factors in their life that pills simply cannot solve. . . . cognitive therapy succeeds because it teaches the skills that help people cope."[3]

CBT has also been shown to be effective in the treatment of anxiety. In fact, in their review of the world literature, Dr. Henny Westra, from York University in Toronto, Ontario, and Dr. Sherry Stewart, from Dalhousie University in Halifax, Nova Scotia, concluded that:

- CBT is the gold standard in the treatment of all forms of anxiety.
- CBT is more effective than any other type of psychotherapy or medication. In fact, CBT *without* medications appears to be more effective than CBT with medications.[4]

My own clinical experience is consistent with these conclusions. But here's the question: Will CBT bibliotherapy be effective for anxiety? If you're suffering from shyness, chronic worrying, panic attacks, phobias, public speaking anxiety, test anxiety, post-traumatic stress disorder, or obsessive-compulsive disorder, will this book do you any good? Some encouraging studies suggest that the answer may be yes. Dr. Isaac Marks, from the Institute of Psychiatry at the University of London, has shown that many individuals can overcome anxiety disorders using CBT techniques *without* face-to-face psychotherapy or medications. I'm hopeful that this book will prove just as effective for people with anxiety as *Feeling Good* has been for people struggling with depression. However, no book, technique, or pill will work for everyone. Some people will need the help of a compassionate and skillful therapist in addition to the methods in this book. There's no shame in that. When should you seek treatment from a mental health professional? There's no absolute rule, but these guidelines may help:

- **How severe is the problem?** If you feel overwhelmed or hopeless, face-to-face therapy can be extremely helpful.
- **Do you have any suicidal impulses?** If you have the urge to take your life, you should never rely on self-help alone. Emergency face-to-face intervention is mandatory. If you have a therapist, call him or her immediately and describe how you feel. If you have no therapist, call 911 or

go to the emergency room of the nearest hospital. Your life is too precious to play Russian roulette.

- **Do you have any homicidal impulses?** If you feel enraged and have the urge to hurt or kill other people, emergency intervention is mandatory. Don't flirt with these urges!

- **What type of problem do you have?** Some problems are harder to treat than others, and sometimes medications are indicated. For example, if you have bipolar (manic-depressive) illness with extreme, uncontrollable highs and lows, then mood-stabilizing medications such as lithium may be necessary.

- **How long have you been suffering?** If you've been working with the tools in this book for three or four weeks but your symptoms haven't started to improve, then professional guidance could help you get on track. It's the same as with anything you're trying to learn. If your tennis serve is off, you may have trouble correcting the problem on your own because you can't quite see what you're doing wrong. But a good coach can quickly diagnose the problem and show you how to correct it.

I think it's great news that so many people suffering from depression and anxiety can now be treated quickly and effectively without medications and that the prognosis for complete recovery is so positive. Whether you're seeing a therapist, taking psychiatric medications, or trying to defeat your fears on your own, the techniques in this book can be vitally important. The goal is not simply the relief of your symptoms, but a profound transformation in the way you think and feel.

PART I

The
Basics

I Think, Therefore I Fear

Practically everybody knows what it's like to feel anxious, worried, nervous, afraid, uptight, or panicky. Often anxiety is just a nuisance, but sometimes it can cripple you and prevent you from doing what you really want with your life. But I have some great news for you: You *can* change the way you feel.

Powerful new, drug-free treatments have been developed for depression and for every conceivable type of anxiety, such as chronic worrying, shyness, public speaking anxiety, test anxiety, phobias, and panic attacks. The goal of the treatment is not just partial improvement but full recovery. I want you to be able to wake up in the morning free of fears and eager to meet the day, telling yourself it's great to be alive.

Anxiety comes in many different forms. See if you can recognize yourself in any of these patterns.

- **Chronic Worrying.** You constantly worry about your family, health, career, or finances. Your stomach churns, and it seems as if something bad is about to happen, but you can't figure out exactly what the problem is.
- **Fears and Phobias.** You may be afraid of needles, blood, heights, elevators, driving, flying, water, spiders, snakes, dogs, storms, bridges, or getting trapped in closed spaces.

- **Performance Anxiety.** You freeze up whenever you have to take a test, perform in front of other people, or compete in an athletic event.

- **Public Speaking Anxiety.** You get nervous whenever you have to talk in front of a group because you tell yourself, "I'll tremble and everyone will see how nervous I am. My mind will go blank and I'll make a complete fool of myself. Everyone will look down on me and think I'm a total neurotic."

- **Shyness.** You feel nervous and self-conscious at social gatherings because you tell yourself, "Everyone seems so charming and relaxed. But I don't have *anything* interesting to say. They can probably tell how shy and awkward I feel. They must think I'm some kind of weirdo or loser. I'm the *only one* who feels this way. What's wrong with me?"

- **Panic Attacks.** You experience sudden, terrifying panic attacks that seem to come from out of the blue and strike unexpectedly, like lightning. During each attack, you feel dizzy, your heart pounds, and your fingers tingle. You may tell yourself, "I must be having a heart attack. What if I pass out or die? I can't breathe right! What if I suffocate?" You try to hang on for dear life. Before long, the feelings of panic disappear as mysteriously as they came, leaving you bewildered, frightened, and humiliated. You wonder what happened and when it's going to strike again.

- **Agoraphobia.** You're afraid of being away from home alone because you think something terrible will happen—perhaps you'll have a panic attack—and there won't be anyone to help you. You may fear open spaces, bridges, crowds, standing in line at the grocery store, or taking public transportation.

- **Obsessions and Compulsions.** You're plagued by obsessive thoughts that you can't shake from your mind, and compulsive urges to perform superstitious rituals to control your fears. For example, you may be consumed by the fear of germs and have the irresistible urge to wash your hands over and over all day long. Or you may get up and check the stove repeatedly after you've gone to bed, just to make sure you didn't leave the burners on.

- **Post-Traumatic Stress Disorder.** You're haunted by memories or flashbacks of a horrific event that happened months or even years ago, such as rape, abuse, torture, or murder.

- **Concerns about Your Appearance (Body Dysmorphic Disorder).** You're consumed by the feeling that there's something grotesque or abnormal about your appearance, even though your friends and family reassure you that you look just fine. You may think that your nose is deformed, your hair is thinning, or your body isn't shaped correctly. You may spend vast amounts of time consulting with plastic surgeons or staring into mirrors trying to correct the defect because you're so convinced that everyone can see how terrible you look.

- **Worries about Your Health (Hypochondriasis).** You go from doctor to doctor complaining of aches, pains, fatigue, dizziness, or other symptoms. You feel certain that you have some dreadful disease, but the doctor always reassures you that there's absolutely nothing wrong with you. You feel relieved for a few days, but soon you start obsessing about your health again.

If you're plagued by any of these fears, I have a question for you: What would it be worth to you if I could show you how to overcome them? Imagine, for a moment, that you had to give a talk or take an important test tomorrow, and you could go to bed tonight without that knot in your stomach, feeling confident and relaxed.

If you're lonely and struggling with shyness, what would it be worth to you to feel relaxed and spontaneous around other people so you could easily engage anyone, anywhere, in a rewarding conversation? And if you're suffering from phobias, panic attacks, or obsessions and compulsions, what would it be worth to you if I could show you how to defeat these fears for good?

These goals may seem impossible, especially if you've been struggling with anxiety or depression for years, but I'm convinced that you can defeat your fears without pills or lengthy therapy. That may not be the message that you're used to hearing. If you go to your doctor, she or he may tell you that you've got a chemical imbalance in your brain and that you'll have to take a pill to correct it. Yet the latest research confirms what my clinical experience has taught me over the years: You can defeat your fears without drugs.[1] All you'll need is a little courage, your own common sense, and the techniques in this book.

There are many theories about the causes of anxiety, but we'll focus on four of them:

- The **Cognitive Model** is based on the idea that negative thoughts cause anxiety. "Cognition" is simply a fancy word for a thought. Every time you feel anxious or afraid, it's because you're telling yourself that something terrible is about to happen. For example, if you have a fear of flying and the plane runs into turbulence, you may panic because you think, "This plane is about to crash!" Then you imagine passengers screaming as the plane crashes toward the earth in a ball of flames. Your fear does *not* result from the turbulence but from the negative messages you give yourself. When you change the way you *think,* you can change the way you *feel*.

- The **Exposure Model** is based on the idea that *avoidance* is the cause of all anxiety. In other words, you feel anxious because you're avoiding the thing you fear. If you're afraid of heights, you probably avoid ladders, high mountain trails, or glass elevators. If you feel shy, you probably avoid people. According to this theory, the moment you stop running and confront the monster you fear the most, you'll defeat your fears. It's like telling a bully "Take your best shot. I'm not running away from you any longer!"

- The **Hidden Emotion Model** is based on the idea that *niceness* is the cause of all anxiety. People who are prone to anxiety are nearly always people-pleasers who fear conflict and negative feelings like anger. When you feel upset, you sweep your problems under the rug because you don't want to upset anyone. You do this so quickly and automatically that you're not even aware you're doing it. Then your negative feelings resurface in disguised form, as anxiety, worries, fears, or feelings of panic. When you expose the hidden feelings and solve the problem that's bugging you, often your anxiety will disappear.

- The **Biological Model** is based on the idea that anxiety and depression result from a chemical imbalance in the brain and that you'll have to take a pill to correct it. Two types of medications are generally recommended: the minor tranquilizers, such as Xanax, Ativan, and Valium, and the antidepressants, such as Prozac, Paxil, and Zoloft. Your doctor may tell you that these medications represent the only truly effective treatment for depression and anxiety and that you'll need to keep taking them for the rest of your life, in much the same way that individuals suffering from diabetes will have to take insulin shots forever to regulate their blood sugar.

So we have four radically different theories about the causes and cures for anxiety. Which theory is correct? According to the Cognitive Model, you'll have to change the way you think. According to the Exposure Model, you'll have to stop running and confront your fears. According to the Hidden Emotion Model, you'll have to express your feelings. And according to the Biological Model, you'll have to take a pill.

All four theories have their advocates. I believe that the first three theories are correct, and I use Cognitive Techniques, Exposure Techniques, and the Hidden Emotion Technique with every anxious person I treat. The Biological Model is much more controversial. Although I began my career as a full-time psychopharmacologist and treated all my patients with drugs, I strongly prefer the new, drug-free treatment methods for anxiety and depression. In my experience, they're far more effective, they work much faster, and they're also superior in the long run because you'll have the tools you need to overcome painful mood swings for the rest of your life.

However, it's not an either/or type of situation. If you and your doctor feel that medications are necessary, or if you strongly prefer to be treated with an antidepressant, you can use a combination of drugs plus psychotherapy. But for the millions of people who haven't been cured by pills, as well as those who strongly prefer to be treated without them, the development of these new, drug-free methods should be good news. Let's see how they work.

The Cognitive Model

The Cognitive Model is based on three simple ideas:

1. You *feel* the way you *think*.
2. When you're anxious, you're fooling yourself. Anxiety results from distorted, illogical thoughts. It's a mental con.

3. When you change the way you *think*, you can change the way you *feel*.

The French philosopher Descartes once said, "I think, therefore I am." The techniques in this book are based on a slightly different idea: "I *think*, therefore I *fear*." In other words, anxiety results from your thoughts, or cognitions.

For example, you're probably having thoughts about what you're reading at this very moment. You could be thinking, "This is just another stupid self-help book. What a rip-off!" If so, you're probably feeling disappointed, frustrated, or even annoyed.

Or you might be thinking, "This book couldn't possibly help me. My problems are *way* too severe." If so, you're probably feeling discouraged and hopeless. Or you might be thinking, "Hey, this looks interesting, and it makes sense. Maybe it could help me." If so, you're probably feeling excited and curious.

In each case, the situation is exactly the same. Every reader is reading the same thing. Your feelings about what you're reading will result entirely from the way you're thinking, not from the words on the page.

We constantly interpret what's happening, but we're not aware that we're doing this because it's automatic. The thoughts just flow across our minds, but they have the power to create strong positive and negative emotions.

Cognitive Therapy* is based on the idea that each type of thought, or cognition, creates a certain kind of feeling. Dr. Aaron Beck, from the University of Pennsylvania School of Medicine, has called this the Theory of Cognitive Specificity. For example, if you feel sad or depressed, you're probably telling yourself that you've lost someone you love or something important to your sense of self-esteem. If you feel guilty or ashamed, you're telling yourself that you're bad or that you've violated your own personal values. If you feel hopeless, you're telling yourself that things will never change. And if you feel angry, you're telling yourself that someone is treating you unfairly or trying to take ad-

---

*Cognitive Therapy and Cognitive Behavior Therapy mean the same thing. I will use these terms interchangeably throughout this book.

vantage of you. You may also be telling yourself that the other person is a self-centered jerk.

How about anxiety, worry, panic, or fear? What kinds of thoughts lead to these feelings? Write down your ideas here before you continue reading. You may not be used to doing written exercises when you read a book. However, my goal is more than just sharing ideas with you. I want to give you some new skills that can change your life. If you don't know what kinds of thoughts cause anxiety or fear, just make a guess. Even if you're wrong, this exercise will get your brain circuits fired up. When you've made a guess, continue reading and I'll share my thinking with you.

_____

_____

_____

_____

_____

Answer

When you feel anxious, worried, panicky, or afraid, you're telling yourself that you're in danger and that something terrible is about to happen. For example, if you're having a panic attack, you may be telling yourself that you're on the verge of losing control or cracking up. If you have a fear of driving, you probably believe that you'll freeze up, lose control of the car, and cause a terrible accident.

Once you start to feel anxious, your negative thoughts and feelings begin to reinforce each other in a vicious cycle. The catastrophic thoughts create feelings of anxiety and fear, and these feelings trigger more negative thoughts. You tell yourself, "Wow, I *feel* frightened, so I must really *be* in danger. Otherwise, I wouldn't feel so terrified."

If you ask yourself about the thoughts that flood through your mind when you're feeling worried or nervous, you'll tune in to the frightening messages that trigger your feelings. The thoughts will seem completely realistic, but they're not. When you feel anxious, you're telling yourself things that simply aren't true.

This is one of the biggest differences between neurotic anxiety and healthy

fear. They both result entirely from your thoughts, but the thoughts that trigger healthy fear are not distorted. Healthy fear results from the valid perception of danger. However, healthy fear does not require treatment. If you're in
real danger, some healthy fear may keep you alive. In contrast, neurotic anxiety serves no useful function because it's not related to any real threat. The
thoughts that cause these feelings will *always* be distorted and illogical.

The Checklist of Cognitive Distortions on page 16 lists ten distortions that
can trigger feelings of anxiety, depression, and anger. You'll notice that there's
some overlap among them. Several of these distortions are especially common
when you're feeling anxious, worried, shy, or panicky. These include:

- **Fortune-Telling.** You tell yourself that something terrible is about to
  happen. For example, if you have the fear of heights and you're at the
  top of a ladder, you'll probably tell yourself, "This is *really* dangerous. I
  might fall!" If you're shy and you're talking to someone at a party, you
  may tell yourself, "I just know I'm going to say something stupid and
  look like a fool."

- **Mind-Reading.** You assume that other people are judging you or looking down on you, even when there's no convincing evidence for this.
  While registering for graduate work at Berkeley, Carrie, a transfer student, learned that there was a problem with her registration. She felt
  anxious because she told herself, "They probably don't want me here. I
  don't really belong." However, the problem was quickly straightened
  out. Later that day Carrie learned that her supervisor had changed her
  teaching assistant assignment and that she'd be teaching sophomores
  instead of juniors. She felt hurt and insecure because she told herself,
  "He probably figured out that I'm not as good as he thought I was, so he
  gave me an inferior teaching assignment."

- **Magnification.** You exaggerate the danger in a situation. A man became
  anxious when he cut himself shaving because he told himself, "Oh, no!
  It's *really* bleeding a lot! What if I have leukemia?" He couldn't shake
  this fear from his mind and insisted his doctor check him out immediately. Of course, all the lab tests came back normal.

- **Emotional Reasoning.** You reason from how you feel. You tell yourself,

"I *feel* scared, so I must *be* in danger," or "I *feel* like I'm about to crack up, so I must really *be* on the verge of going crazy."

- **Should Statements.** You tell yourself that you *shouldn't* feel so anxious, shy, or insecure, since normal people don't feel that way.
- **Labeling.** You label yourself as "a fool," "a neurotic," or "a loser."
- **Self-Blame.** You beat up on yourself for every little flaw or shortcoming, including the fact that you're anxious.

Do you recognize yourself in any of these distortions? If they sound familiar, it's a good thing, because you can change the way you *feel* when you change the way you *think*. The moment you put the lie to your distorted thoughts, your fears will disappear.

I once treated an anxious attorney who came to me for therapy toward the end of a long and brilliant career. Jeffrey was one of the most successful courtroom attorneys in Los Angeles. In fact, he'd only lost one case during his entire career. But in spite of his immense success, Jeffrey had never found any real happiness in life. He worried constantly and could never relax. One of the negative thoughts that plagued him was "What if I lose a case in court? It would be terrible!"

Jeffrey was so afraid of losing that he worked compulsively, every waking minute, seven days a week. He even gave up going on vacations because he couldn't relax or enjoy himself, but worked the entire time. Jeffrey's entire life had become a treadmill of work and worry, work and worry. He was afraid that he'd go to his grave without ever enjoying one minute of inner peace or happiness.

Jeffrey had taken numerous medications and had undergone thirty-five years of psychoanalysis, but nothing had helped with his persistent feelings of insecurity. Part of his problem, as he understood it, was that when he was five, his younger sister had died of encephalitis. One of Jeffrey's psychoanalysts told him that his feeling of inadequacy probably stemmed from a sense of guilt about her death. The analyst proposed that, deep down, Jeffrey blamed himself for his sister's death because he resented the attention she got from their parents and had often wished that she were dead. Of course, Jeffrey had nothing to do with her death, but he could remember feeling jealous of her.

Checklist of Cognitive Distortions

1. **All-or-Nothing Thinking.** You look at things in absolute, black-and-white categories. If you're not a complete success, you think you're a total failure.

2. **Overgeneralization.** You view a single negative event as a never-ending pattern of defeat. You may tell yourself, "This *always* happens," or "I'll *never* get it right."

3. **Mental Filter.** This is like the drop of ink that discolors the entire beaker of water. You dwell on one negative detail, such as an error you made, and ignore all the things you did right.

4. **Discounting the Positive.** You insist that your accomplishments or positive qualities don't count.

5. **Jumping to Conclusions.** You jump to conclusions that aren't warranted by the facts. There are two types:

   • **Mind-Reading.** You assume that people are terribly judgmental and are looking down on you.

   • **Fortune-Telling.** You tell yourself that something terrible is about to happen. "I just *know* I'm going to blow it when I take my test next week."

6. **Magnification and Minimization.** You blow things way out of proportion or shrink their importance. This is also called the binocular trick. When you look through one end of the binoculars, all your shortcomings seem as huge as Mt. Everest. When you look through the other end, all your strengths and positive qualities seem to shrink down to nothing.

7. **Emotional Reasoning.** You reason from how you feel, such as "I *feel* anxious, so I must really *be* in danger." Or "I *feel* like a loser, so I must really *be* one."

8. **Should Statements.** You criticize yourself or other people with "shoulds," "shouldn'ts," "oughts," "musts," and "have-tos." For example, "I *shouldn't* feel so shy and nervous. What's wrong with me?"

9. **Labeling.** You generalize from a single flaw or shortcoming to your entire identity. Instead of saying "I made a mistake," you label yourself as "a loser." This is an extreme form of Overgeneralization.

10. **Blame.** Instead of pinpointing the cause of a problem, you assign blame. There are two basic patterns of blame:

    • **Self-Blame.** You blame yourself for something you weren't responsible for or beat up on yourself relentlessly whenever you make a mistake.

    • **Other-Blame.** You blame others and deny your own role in the problem.

Unfortunately, this insight didn't lead to any relief. Inside, Jeffrey still felt like a "bad" person, and his analyst never told him how to overcome the problem. Although he knew that his feelings were irrational, he just couldn't shake the idea that he was a dirty and shameful person and that people would reject him if they ever found out what he was really like inside. So he spent his life trying to cover up his feelings and impress everyone. He studied hard, was a top student at the UCLA law school, and went on to become a prominent attorney.

Jeffrey had a reputation for being a tiger in the courtroom. He took on huge corporations single-handed in environmental contamination cases and always brought them to their knees. He was a highly feared adversary. But he felt extremely awkward and insecure in almost every other situation. His secretary, wife, and daughters constantly bossed him around. He worried that they'd reject him and meekly gave in to their demands.

I suggested we try the What-If Technique. This technique can help you identify the beliefs and fantasies that trigger your fears. We started with Jeffrey's thought, "It would be terrible if I lost a case in court." Our dialogue went like this:

David: Jeffrey, let's suppose you *did* lose a case in court. What would happen then? What are you the most afraid of?

Jeffrey: Then the word would spread and people would find out about me.

David: And what if people did find out about you? What's the worst thing that could happen?

Jeffrey: People would realize I'm not as good as they thought and stop sending me cases.

David: Okay, let's suppose that people *did* stop sending you cases. What would happen then?

Jeffrey: I might go bankrupt.

David: Of course, no one wants to go bankrupt. But I'd like to know what it would mean to you to go bankrupt. What would happen then? What are you the most afraid of?

Jeffrey: Then my wife and daughters would stop loving me.

David: And then?

Jeffrey: Then they'd leave me. I'd be penniless and alone.

David: And then what would happen? What's your deepest fear? What do you
    imagine?

Jeffrey: I'd end up as a homeless man, living on the streets of Los Angeles.

Jeffrey imagined himself sitting on the sidewalk, begging for spare change
as a group of attorneys he'd beaten in court walk by in their $2,000 suits. They
look at him scornfully and say, "Well, if it isn't the great Jeffrey. Look at how
pathetic he is now! What a loser!" Intellectually, Jeffrey knew that these fears
were irrational, but emotionally, he felt like the danger was real. He believed
that people really would look down on him and abandon him if he failed.

On page 19, you'll find a list of twenty-three Common Self-Defeating Beliefs (SDBs). These are the attitudes and beliefs that make us vulnerable to
anxiety, depression, and conflicts with others. Review this list and see if you
can identify a few of Jeffrey's SDBs. Remember, he starts with the thought "It
would be terrible if I lost a case in court," and ends up with the belief that he'll
be homeless, alone, and miserable. What does this fantasy tell you about his
Self-Defeating Beliefs? Put your ideas here.

1. _____
2. _____
3. _____
4. _____

Answer

Here are the Self-Defeating Beliefs that Jeffrey and I identified:

- **Performance Perfectionism.** Jeffrey believes that he must never fail or
  make a mistake.
- **Perceived Perfectionism.** He believes that other people will judge him
  as harshly as he judges himself and thinks that he has to impress everyone with his accomplishments or else they'll reject him. He doesn't
  believe that people could ever love or accept him as a flawed and vulnerable human being.
- **Achievement Addiction.** Jeffrey bases his sense of self-worth on his

Common Self-Defeating Beliefs (SDBs)

Achievement	Depression
1. **Performance Perfectionism.** I must never fail or make a mistake. 2. **Perceived Perfectionism.** People won't love or accept me if I'm flawed or vulnerable. 3. **Achievement Addiction.** My worth as a human being depends on my achievements, intelligence, talent, status, income, or looks.	13. **Hopelessness.** My problems could never be solved. I could never feel truly happy or fulfilled. 14. **Worthlessness/Inferiority.** I'm basically worthless, defective, and inferior to others.

Love	Anxiety
4. **Approval Addiction.** I need everyone's approval to be worthwhile. 5. **Love Addiction.** I can't feel happy and fulfilled without being loved. If I'm not loved, then life is not worth living. 6. **Fear of Rejection.** If you reject me, it proves that there's something wrong with me. If I'm alone, I'm bound to feel miserable and worthless.	15. **Emotional Perfectionism.** I should always feel happy, confident, and in control. 16. **Anger Phobia.** Anger is dangerous and should be avoided at all costs. 17. **Emotophobia.** I should never feel sad, anxious, inadequate, jealous, or vulnerable. I should sweep my feelings under the rug and not upset anyone. 18. **Perceived Narcissism.** The people I care about are demanding, manipulative, and powerful. 19. **Brushfire Fallacy.** People are clones who all think alike. If one person looks down on me, the word will spread like brushfire and soon everyone will. 20. **Spotlight Fallacy.** Talking to people is like having to perform under a bright spotlight. If I don't impress them by being sophisticated, witty, or interesting, they won't like me. 21. **Magical Thinking.** If I worry enough, everything will turn out okay.

Submissiveness	
7. **Pleasing Others.** I should always try to please you, even if I make myself miserable in the process. 8. **Conflict Phobia.** People who love each other should never fight or argue. 9. **Self-Blame.** The problems in my relationships are bound to be my fault.	

Demandingness	Other
10. **Other-Blame.** The problems in my relationships are always the other person's fault. 11. **Entitlement.** You should always treat me in the way I expect. 12. **Truth.** I'm right and you're wrong.	22. **Low Frustration Tolerance.** I should never be frustrated. Life should always be easy. 23. **Superman/Superwoman.** I should always be strong and never be weak.

© 2003 by David D. Burns, M.D.

achievements. He thinks that his accomplishments have to be great or else they're no good at all.

- **Approval Addiction.** He bases his self-esteem on getting everyone's approval.

- **Fear of Rejection.** Jeffrey believes that he'll be doomed to a life of destitution and misery if even a single person rejects him.

- **Pleasing Others.** Jeffrey believes that he always has to give in to the demands of his colleagues and family, even at the expense of his own needs and feelings.

- **Worthlessness/Inferiority.** Jeffrey seems convinced that he's inherently flawed and defective, so he always tries to cover up and pretend that he's much better than he really is.

- **Perceived Narcissism.** Jeffrey believes that all the people he cares about are extremely manipulative and demanding.

- **Brushfire Fallacy.** Jeffrey sees all human beings as clones who think and act in exactly the same way. He's convinced that if one person looks down on him, the word will spread and, pretty soon, everyone will look down on him and abandon him.

- **Superman.** Jeffrey believes he should always win and never lose.

You can see that in spite of all his accomplishments, Jeffrey doesn't think much of himself. He thinks he's bad and unlovable inside. At the same time, he doesn't seem to think much of his family or colleagues, either. His world, as he imagines it, is filled with judgmental and demanding people who will turn against him if he displays the slightest flaw. It's no wonder he feels so anxious!

Later on, I'm going to show you how to use a variety of methods, including the What-If Technique, to identify your own SDBs. You might try pinpointing a few of them right now, simply by reviewing the list on page 19. Circle the numbers next to the beliefs that seem to ring a bell. Although these insights can be exciting, our goal is more ambitious. We're looking for real change at the gut level. How can we help Jeffrey escape from the trap he's been in for so many years so he'll finally be able to experience the joy and self-esteem that have always eluded him?

While he was working with me, Jeffrey actually lost a case in court. It was only the second loss of his entire career. It was a small case he'd taken on pro bono as a favor to a friend, and the man he was defending really was guilty. Nevertheless, Jeffrey felt ashamed and anxious, and didn't want anyone to find out that he'd lost.

This presented us with a golden opportunity. I asked Jeffrey if he'd be willing to try an experiment to test his belief that everyone would turn against him if he failed. At the time, he was president of the California Bar Association. I suggested he could bring an index card to the next bar association meeting and keep it in his coat pocket. Then he could tell ten high-powered colleagues that he'd just lost a case in court. After each conversation, he could put a tick mark on the card to indicate whether the attorney reacted in a positive, negative, or neutral way. That way he'd find out if his colleagues would look down on him once they discovered that he wasn't perfect.

Jeffrey was extremely reluctant to do this. The idea made him intensely anxious. But he finally consented because he'd suffered for so many years and was desperate enough to try almost anything.

Jeffrey was shocked by the results of his experiment. He forced himself to tell ten attorneys that he'd lost a case in court. When I saw him the next week, he told me that five of them didn't even seem to have heard what he said. Instead, they just went on talking about themselves with great enthusiasm.

This was a relief! Jeffrey said he discovered that he'd been involved in the sixth cognitive distortion on the checklist, Magnification and Minimization. He said he'd greatly magnified his own importance in the eyes of other people and minimized how narcissistic and self-centered most attorneys were. He said that it was liberating to find out how unimportant he really was.

The reactions of the other five attorneys surprised him even more. They did not turn against him, as he expected, but poured their hearts out to him. They said it was a relief to hear that even Jeffrey lost a case from time to time. They told him about all the cases they'd lost recently and described their marital conflicts and problems with their children. Jeffrey said he felt close to his colleagues for the first time. He said that he finally felt like he actually had something to give to other people.

Jeffrey discovered that the truth was the opposite of what he'd always believed. He'd always tried to keep his weaknesses and vulnerabilities hidden because he thought they were so shameful. But in spite of all his wealth, power, and success, Jeffrey had never really gotten close to people or discovered any inner peace or happiness. In contrast, his human, vulnerable side turned out to be his greatest asset.

I call this the Acceptance Paradox. Although it's a Cognitive Therapy technique, it's also central to most spiritual traditions. For example, St. Paul was an early pillar of the Christian church. He suffered from a "thorn in the flesh." Biblical scholars don't know what this weakness was. Some have speculated that it might have been bipolar (manic-depressive) illness, sexual confusion, or stuttering. In desperation, St. Paul prayed to God to remove this thorn. But God ignored his prayers. Finally, the Holy Spirit came to St. Paul and said, "My grace is sufficient for you. For in your weakness, my strength is revealed more completely."

Jeffrey said he'd always heard of this teaching when he was growing up, but it had never made any sense to him. He said the idea that your weakness was your strength had always seemed absurd, and he'd never believed it. But now, suddenly, he comprehended what the passage really meant. He could see that his "weakness" actually was his greatest strength and his "strength" had been his greatest weakness all along. That's because the strength he'd always tried to project—the spit and polish, the fancy clothes, the incredible court-room victories—had never really brought him any peace of mind. His weakness—the feelings of anxiety and self-doubt that he'd always tried to hide—allowed him to connect with other people for the first time.

Before that session, I'd never been especially comfortable with Jeffrey. I admired him, but felt intimidated by him. He wore expensive suits and bowed formally at the start of every session. He took meticulous notes and summarized each session in detail before he left. The next session, he'd bring in meticulously typed and edited summaries for my review and approval. They read like legal documents. I sometimes wondered if he was planning to sue me! But when he had his breakthrough, he suddenly appeared human and down-to-earth. I found myself liking him much more.

One of the things I really like about Cognitive Therapy is that it complements your spiritual beliefs. No matter what your religious orientation might be, at the moment of recovery, you'll suddenly see more deeply into your own spiritual roots. This will be true even if you're not religious and don't believe in God. We all have values and beliefs that can be a source of oppression and anxiety or liberation and joy.

We could just as easily examine Jeffrey's transformation from a Buddhist perspective. Buddhism teaches that our suffering does not result from reality but from the judgments we make about reality. The Buddhists teach that there's really no such thing as success or failure, strength or weakness. These are just labels we use to judge our experiences, and these labels can be misleading and hurtful. In fact, Labeling is the ninth cognitive distortion on the checklist, and it can lead to depression, anxiety, and rage.

Buddhist teachings sometimes sound nonsensical at first. It can be hard to figure out what the Buddhists are talking about. Success is success and failure is failure. Strength is strength and weakness is weakness. What could be clearer? But when you experience a dramatic personal change, you'll suddenly understand things on a much deeper level. Jeffrey lost a case in court. Was this experience truly a "failure," as he so firmly believed? Or was it the doorway to the inner peace and joy that had always eluded him?

The Exposure Model

Jeffrey's dramatic recovery illustrates the Cognitive Model: When you change the way you *think,* you can change the way you *feel.* The Exposure Model works differently. When you're anxious, you're always avoiding something that you fear. When you confront the monster you fear the most, you'll defeat your fears.

Of course, you could argue that Jeffrey's sudden recovery resulted from exposure. When he finally opened up and told his colleagues about the case he'd lost, he confronted the monster that he'd always feared and discovered that it had no teeth.

There are many different ways to confront your fears. When I was growing up, I had a fear of blood. It wasn't much of a problem until I entered medical school. When it was time to practice drawing blood from people's arms during my second year, it dawned on me that I didn't want anything to do with it! So I dropped out of medical school for a year.

During my year off, I thought about my options and decided that I really did want to be a doctor. But I realized that sooner or later, I'd have to bite the bullet and overcome my fear of blood. Before I started my internship, I decided to work as a volunteer in the emergency room of Highland Hospital in Oakland, California, for a month. This was a major trauma center, with approximately eight thousand emergency room visits per month. Lots of the people who came into our ER were in pretty bad shape, so I figured that it would be a good place to get over my fear of blood and gore.

When I walked into the ER for the first time, I was so anxious that I felt like I was floating across the ceiling. I had no idea what to expect. But it wasn't too bad. There were two alcoholics in delirium tremens and several people with infections or fractures, but nothing bloody or traumatic.

But soon I heard sirens approaching in the distance and felt a sudden sense of dread. As the sirens grew louder, my anxiety escalated and I began to feel dizzy. Suddenly I heard several policemen and ambulance personnel shouting frantically as they ran down the hall of the ER, pushing a bloody body on a gurney as fast as they could. They headed into the major trauma room, and a dozen doctors and nurses rushed in and started working on the patient in a desperate attempt to save his life. They placed large-bore IV needles into both his arms and legs and started pumping in fluids as fast as possible, squeezing the bags of fluid with blood pressure cuffs to try to maintain his plummeting blood pressure.

I was watching from the hall and asked one of the nurses what was going on. She explained that the man was a bomber who'd been planning to blow up city hall, but his bomb had blown up in his hands while he was building it. He was barely alive. His face, chest, and arms had been badly burned, and most of the skin above his waist seemed to be missing. I could hardly stand to look at him. Then she tugged on my sleeve and said, "You've got to help."

I explained that I was just a medical student without any experience with this sort of thing and didn't know what to do. She handed me a toothbrush and said, "Get busy with this!"

I said, "This guy is on the verge of death and you want me to brush his teeth?"

She said, "No! Can't you see all those black specks in his tissue? That's gunpowder. You've got to scrub it out or it will poison him."

It was a gruesome task, because his entire chest was just a slab of raw, bloody flesh. I forced myself to scrub away with the toothbrush, with my hands in all that bloody tissue. Those were the days when we didn't routinely wear gloves, either, so I was terrified. But I couldn't stop because his life was on the line, so I had to stick with it. I was glad that he was unconscious and couldn't feel anything. After about ten minutes of sheer panic and dizziness, a strange thing happened. My anxiety started to diminish and suddenly vanished. In a flash, I was "cured" of my blood phobia.

I had stumbled across a technique known as Flooding. Instead of avoiding the thing you fear, you intentionally expose yourself to it and flood yourself with anxiety. You don't fight the anxiety or try to control it, you just surrender to it. Eventually the anxiety burns itself out and you're cured.

After that, I *loved* working in the emergency room. Blood and gore didn't faze me in the least. It always seemed like a miracle that a team of doctors and nurses could handle so many complex, life-threatening emergencies with such compassion and expertise. It was hard for me to believe that I was a part of that team, had a contribution to make, and was actually learning to be a real doctor. If I hadn't been so strongly committed to psychiatry, I might have pursued a career in surgery or emergency room medicine instead.

The Hidden Emotion Model

The Hidden Emotion Model is very different from the Cognitive Model and the Exposure Model. It's based on the idea that "niceness" is the cause of all anxiety. In fact, I sometimes think of anxiety as the "niceness disease." If you show me a hundred people who are anxious, I'll show you a hundred of the nicest people you ever met!

When I do workshops on anxiety for therapists, I usually tell them that I'd like to do a little research on my theory about niceness and anxiety and that I'm going to ask them two questions. First, I ask how many of them have struggled with some type of anxiety at some time in their life. Nearly every hand goes up.

I tell them that I want them to keep their hands in the air while I ask the second question: "How many of you consider yourselves to be basically nice people?" All the hands stay in the air, and people start giggling. Then I say, "See what I mean? There's a 100 percent correlation between niceness and anxiety!"

Of course, this is just a humorous demonstration, not real research, but it does illustrate something very basic about anxiety. When you're anxious, you're almost always avoiding a problem that's bothering you, but you're not aware of it. You push the problem out of conscious awareness because you want to be nice and don't want to rock the boat or upset anyone. All of a sudden, you feel anxious and you're not sure why. You may develop phobias or panic attacks or start obsessing about your family, your finances, or your health. Any type of anxiety can develop, but the dynamic is nearly always the same: You're upset about something, but you don't want to admit it.

The hidden problem isn't usually buried in the past but something very obvious in the here and now. You may be upset with your boss or annoyed with a friend or family member. When you bring the hidden conflict or emotion to conscious awareness, you'll suddenly understand *why* you've been suffering from anxiety, fear, or panic. When you express the feelings that you've been bottling up, often your anxiety will disappear.

During a Cognitive Therapy group at our university hospital in Philadelphia, I worked with an anxious patient named Brent who'd been admitted to the inpatient unit from the emergency room earlier that morning because he was convinced he was about to go berserk. Brent had never received any psychiatric treatment or struggled with any emotional problems in the past. He was happily married and taught biology at a local high school. He told me that he loved his work and spent nearly sixty hours a week teaching and preparing for classes. In fact, he proudly announced that the students had voted him "Teacher of the Year" every year for the past five years.

More than anything in the world, Brent and his wife wanted to raise a family of their own. They'd been trying for years, but his wife never got pregnant. She was nearly forty, and they were concerned that time was running out. Finally, in desperation, they went to the fertility clinic at our hospital, hoping the doctors there would be able to help.

While they were driving to her mother's home for a Christmas party,

Brent's wife announced that she had a special Christmas present for him. The doctor had called her that morning to inform her that she was pregnant. Brent panicked and thought he was about to lose control of the car, so he pulled over to the side of the road and told his wife that he felt too shaky to drive. She was concerned about him and offered to drive the rest of the way to the party. After a while, Brent pulled himself together, but he still felt extremely anxious.

Two days after Christmas, Brent was still struggling with waves of anxiety and panic. He went to a fast food restaurant and ordered their special Mega-Burrito to go. He explained that he didn't want any beans on the burrito and clearly said, "No beans, please," twice when placing the order, because he hated beans. The man behind the counter barely spoke English but seemed to understand. When Brent picked his burrito up, there was a different man at the cash register, so he said, "No beans, right?" The cashier nodded obligingly and spoke to the other man in Spanish. Then he said he understood about the beans and that they'd made this special burrito exactly the way he wanted. Brent paid the cashier, who handed him a bag with the Mega-Burrito inside.

When Brent got home, he sat down at the kitchen table with great anticipation, but when he opened the bag, he discovered a massive bean burrito inside. He became enraged and started to attack the burrito with his knife. He slashed it repeatedly, splattering it all over the kitchen table and walls.

Brent was a big fan of forensic detective programs on television, such as *Cold Case Files,* and was familiar with the analysis of blood spatter patterns. When he saw the burrito innards splattered all over the wall, he suddenly thought, "My God! That looks like a blood spatter pattern. What if I'm a serial killer who's about to go on a murder rampage and start slashing people to death? Maybe I'm not fit to be a father! I think I'm about to explode!"

These fears haunted Brent all afternoon. That night he could hardly sleep as he tossed and turned and obsessed about being a murderer. He even imagined this headline in the morning paper: "Local Burrito Slasher Goes on Killing Spree! Massive Manhunt Under Way!"

The next morning Brent told his wife he was cracking up and needed to be in a mental hospital in a straitjacket. She rushed him to the Stanford emergency room, where he was admitted to the locked psychiatric unit.

Brent had no history of violence or aggression and seemed like a kindly, gentle fellow. He said he'd always wanted a child of his own, and now that his dream was finally coming true, he couldn't understand why he was having such bizarre and horrible thoughts. Why was this happening?

Let's do a bit of detective work and see if we can make some sense out of Brent's fears. Here's a dedicated, hardworking high school teacher and loving husband who suddenly finds himself angrily slashing a burrito with a kitchen knife. He tells his wife that he's about to go berserk. Is something bothering Brent? Is there a hidden problem or feeling that he's sweeping under the rug?

You may not have any theories about this, and of course Brent is the only person who can tell us for sure. Even if you have no idea at all, just take a wild guess. Please don't continue reading until you've written something down. Jot down your ideas here.

_____

_____

_____

_____

_____

Answer

If you're drawing a blank, here's a hint: Think about the timing of Brent's anxiety. What was going on at the moment he began to feel so panicky? His wife had just told him that she was pregnant. Is it possible that Brent has mixed feelings about being a father? And if so, why? After all, he says he loves children and he's obviously very devoted to his students.

We'll have to put on our detective caps again. Brent also told us that he's working sixty hours a week trying to be the best teacher he can possibly be. Does he feel overwhelmed by the idea of changing diapers and taking on all the new responsibilities that go along with fatherhood? Or, to put it differently, is he feeling ambivalent? On one hand, he's always wanted a child of his own, but now that he's presented with the reality of the situation, he's getting cold feet. He feels confused and unsure about how he's going to handle it. Who's going to change the diapers at 3:00 A.M.?

I asked Brent if any of this made sense, and he said I was reading him like a book. He admitted that he did feel confused because he didn't know how he was going to keep up with everything once the baby arrived. However, he'd never expressed these feelings to his wife because he thought it wasn't normal to have negative feelings or doubts about being a father. He said he thought that a father was supposed to love his children and not feel the way he did. He was also afraid that his wife would be devastated if she found out that he felt confused, and he didn't want to upset her.

You can see that Brent's fantasies are doing the talking for him. They project this message loud and clear: "I'm not sure I'm suitable to be a father, and I have no idea how I'm going to manage everything once the baby arrives. In fact, the very thought of being a father is driving me nuts!"

Did Brent's feelings of panic mean that he didn't want to be a father or that he'd be a danger to his child? Not at all. Brent loved his wife and desperately wanted a child. He simply needed to get his feelings off his chest.

I wanted him to know that feelings of doubt were perfectly normal, so I turned to the other members of the group and asked how many of them had children. Almost every hand went up. Then I asked, "How many of you get frustrated or annoyed with your children at times?" Every hand went up. Then I said, "How many of you sometimes get so mad at your kids that you feel like killing them?" All the hands went up again, and everyone started to giggle.

I told Brent that every parent feels that way at times and that he and his wife might end up feeling a lot closer if they started to communicate with each other about all the new challenges they were facing and how they'd deal with them as a loving team. Brent's face lit up, and he said that he suddenly felt relieved, but was still concerned that his wife would be devastated if she learned about his doubts.

I said he wouldn't know until he told her, but it would be surprising if she didn't also have some doubts from time to time. I told him that she probably wasn't nearly as fragile as he thought and that talking to each other more openly actually might make their relationship more meaningful and rewarding. I pointed out that his wife was coming by for a family therapy session with the clinical social worker right after the Cognitive Therapy group; he might want to give it a try then. Although Brent said he was very nervous about opening up, he was determined to tell her how he'd been feeling.

As it turned out, she wasn't at all disturbed to learn about his feelings. She said she was already aware that he was feeling tense and felt relieved that he was finally opening up. Brent suddenly began to feel excited about the pregnancy, and his anxiety disappeared completely. He was discharged that very afternoon and didn't spend even a single night in the hospital.

So now you've learned about three powerful ways to defeat anxiety. Cognitive Techniques will help you put the lie to the negative thoughts and attitudes that make you feel anxious and depressed. Exposure Techniques will help you confront the monster that you've been avoiding. And the Hidden Emotion Technique will help you pinpoint any hidden conflicts or emotions that you've been ignoring and sweeping under the rug.

Which method should you use? All three approaches are invaluable, and I use them all with every single patient I treat. If I've learned anything in my work with individuals suffering from depression and anxiety, it's this: We're all different. You can *never* predict which method is going to work for someone, and there's no single technique that will work for everyone. It always takes some trial and error, but if you persist, you'll always find the technique that works for you.

....

Chapter 2

Are You Anxious? Or Depressed?

Most of the time, negative emotions don't come in pure packages. In fact, anxiety and depression usually go hand in hand. However, these feelings are very different from each other. Anxiety results from the perception of danger. You can't feel anxious unless you tell yourself that something terrible is about to happen. For example, if you have a fear of heights and you're hiking on a mountain trail with steep drop-offs, you'll probably feel gripped by panic because you'll think that you could slip and fall at any moment.

In contrast, when you're depressed, you feel like the tragedy has already happened. It seems like you've already fallen off the cliff and you're lying at the bottom of the ravine, broken beyond repair. You feel blue, demoralized, and down in the dumps. You tell yourself that you're worthless, that you're a failure, or that you're not nearly as good as you should be. You lose interest in life and in other people, and the activities you once enjoyed seem unrewarding. Nothing excites you anymore. You feel overwhelmed, and life seems like one long procrastination. The worst part is the hopelessness. You feel like things will never change and believe that you'll be miserable forever.

If you're depressed, you'll almost definitely feel anxious. And if you're struggling with anxiety, you may also be feeling depressed. Why is this? Scientists don't know for sure why depression and anxiety go together, but there are four competing theories. According to the first theory, most people can't distinguish different kinds of emotions. All they know is that they feel upset. By way of analogy, people who live in the desert have only one word for snow, because they rarely ever see it. Inuit, on the other hand, have many words for snow, because they deal with it constantly and need a more refined vocabulary to describe all the different kinds of snow they encounter.

According to the second theory, depression leads to anxiety. For example, if you've been depressed, you may worry about the fact that you feel defective, inferior, and unmotivated. You may be afraid that the depression will interfere with your work or personal life, that you'll never achieve your goals in life, and that you'll never feel happy again.

According to the third theory, anxiety leads to depression. There's no doubt that anxiety, shyness, worrying, phobias, and panic attacks can interfere with your work and personal life, especially when the anxiety is severe. This can be demoralizing and depressing. Some people have suffered from anxiety for years, or even decades, in spite of treatment with medications and psychotherapy. Eventually they start to feel demoralized and depressed because nothing has helped. Shame is also a central feature of anxiety. You may try to hide your symptoms of insecurity or panic, thinking that other people would look down on you or think you were weird if they knew how you really felt inside. The feelings of isolation and defectiveness can easily trigger depression because they make it so much harder to connect with others in a warm and open way.

The final theory about anxiety and depression is called the Common Cause theory. According to this theory, anxiety and depression share at least one common cause, in addition to their own unique causes. In other words, there could be something in the brain that triggers different kinds of emotions, such as anxiety and depression, at the same time. This theory makes sense to me. Most of my patients have many different negative feelings at the same time, such as depression, guilt, hopelessness, anxiety, anger, and frustration.

Let's find out how you're feeling now. Complete the four sections of the following Brief Mood Survey. The survey will only take a minute or two. Once you've completed all four sections, you can interpret your scores with the scoring keys that are referenced at the start of each section. You can take the Brief

Brief Mood Survey

Instructions. Put today's date in one of the columns to the right. Then put your score on each item in the boxes below the date, based on how you've been feeling recently. Total your score in the box at the bottom. **Please answer all of the items.**	**Put Today's Date Here**							

Score each item like this: 0 = Not at all; 1= Somewhat; 2 = Moderately; 3 = A lot; 4 = Extremely

Anxious Feelings

1. Anxious								
2. Nervous								
3. Worried								
4. Frightened or apprehensive								
5. Tense or on edge								
Total for today ➔								

Anxious Physical Symptoms

1. Skipping, racing, or pounding of the heart								
2. Sweating, chills, or hot flushes								
3. Trembling or shaking								
4. Feeling short of breath or difficulty breathing								
5. Feeling like you're choking								
6. Pain or tightness in the chest								
7. Butterflies, nausea, or upset stomach								
8. Feeling dizzy, light-headed, or off-balance								
9. Feeling like you're unreal or the world is unreal								
10. Numbness or tingling sensations								
Total for today ➔								

Depression

1. Sad or down in the dumps								
2. Discouraged or hopeless								
3. Low self-esteem								
4. Worthless or inadequate								
5. Loss of pleasure or satisfaction in life								
Total for today ➔								

Suicidal Urges

1. Do you have any suicidal thoughts?								
2. Would you like to end your life?								
Total for today ➔								

Mood Survey as often as you like to track your progress while you read this book and do the exercises. Most of my patients take it at least once a week.

The Brief Mood Survey may seem simple, but it's a valid and reliable instrument that will detect the smallest changes in how you feel. This test is not like the quizzes you see in popular magazines. In fact, research studies have shown that it's more accurate than many of the instruments currently used in research studies.

You can take the Brief Mood Survey up to eight times on a single sheet of paper. The woman in the following example was severely anxious for two weeks, with scores of 16 on June 1 and 8. Her score dropped to 10 the next week, indicating significant improvement. By June 22, her score had fallen to 6, and by the following week, it was only 3. On July 5, her score of 1 indicated almost no anxiety at all. The following week, she had a relapse, and her score shot up to 11 again. This is common. Then she used the same techniques that had helped her before, and her score dropped all the way to 0 on July 19.

Brief Mood Survey

Instructions. Put today's date in one of the columns to the right. Then put your score on each item in the boxes below the date, based on how you've been feeling recently. Total your score in the box at the bottom. **Please answer all of the items.**								
	June 1	June 8	June 15	June 22	June 29	July 5	July 12	July 19
Score each item like this: 0 = Not at all; 1= Somewhat; 2 = Moderately; 3 = A lot; 4 = Extremely								
Anxious Feelings								
1. Anxious	3	3	2	1	1	0	2	0
2. Nervous	2	2	2	2	1	0	1	0
3. Worried	4	4	3	1	0	0	3	0
4. Frightened or apprehensive	4	3	2	1	0	0	3	0
5. Tense or on edge	3	4	1	1	1	1	2	0
Total for today →	16	16	10	6	3	1	11	0

© 2005 by David D. Burns, M.D.

How to interpret your score on the Anxious Feelings test. This scale measures the emotional symptoms of anxiety. The higher the score, the more anxious you're feeling.

Scoring Key: 5-Item Anxious Feelings Test

	Score	Meaning
Normal Range	0–1	**Few or no symptoms of anxiety.** This is the best possible score. Right now you don't seem to be plagued by much, if any, anxiety or worry.
	2–4	**Borderline anxiety.** Although you only have a few symptoms of anxiety, the tools in this book could be helpful.
Clinical Range (Therapy may be indicated.)	5–8	**Mild anxiety.** This score isn't especially high, but the anxiety may be causing significant distress or discomfort.
	9–12	**Moderate anxiety.** You've answered moderately or more on at least two of the items. This is definitely enough anxiety to cause distress, and there's lots of room for improvement.
	13–16	**Severe anxiety.** This score indicates strong feelings of anxiety. You may be very uncomfortable, to say the least. The good news is that if you're willing to bring a little courage and hard work to the table, the prognosis is very positive.
	17–20	**Extreme anxiety.** You seem to be plagued by intense feelings of anxiety, and you're probably suffering a great deal. The tools in this book, as well as professional therapy, could be extremely helpful.

Your scores on this test can change rapidly. You may feel totally worried and stressed out one day and far more confident and relaxed the next. If you take this test repeatedly, you'll see how your scores change from time to time. In addition, anxiety depends a lot on the situation you're in. If you're shy but you avoid people, you probably won't experience much anxiety.

The severity of your anxiety and the prognosis for recovery are not the same. I've had many patients who felt extremely anxious but recovered quickly. In contrast, mild anxiety may require considerable patience and persistence before you overcome it. Anxiety can be frightening, but it's not dangerous, and the prognosis for improvement is bright, regardless of your score.

Research indicates that many patients with anxiety can overcome the problem on their own, using tools like the ones in this book. However, professional therapy also can be helpful, especially if you feel stuck or overwhelmed, or if your anxiety is intense. There's no rule that says you always have to tough it out on your own!

How to interpret your score on the Anxious Physical Symptoms test. This scale measures the physical symptoms of anxiety. The higher the score, the

Scoring Key: 10-Item Anxious Physical Symptoms Test

Score	Meaning
0–2	Few or no physical symptoms of anxiety
3–6	A few anxious physical symptoms
7–10	Mild anxious physical symptoms
11–20	Moderate anxious physical symptoms
21–30	Strong anxious physical symptoms
31–40	Extreme anxious physical symptoms

more physical symptoms you're feeling. Are high scores dangerous? Do they indicate that you have serious mental problems and won't be able to get better?

Not at all. The physical symptoms of anxiety are common, and certain kinds of anxiety tend to be associated with these symptoms. For example, during a panic attack, you may feel dizzy and experience shortness of breath or tightness in the chest. Most people with panic attacks indicate "A lot" or "Extremely" on these kinds of symptoms. However, there are powerful new techniques for treating panic attacks, and many patients have recovered in just a few therapy sessions or even a single session.

The physical symptoms of anxiety are not nearly as specific as the symptoms on the Anxious Feelings test. For example, if you were feeling very angry, you'd probably experience some muscle tension and rapid breathing along with a racing or pounding heart. However, these symptoms would indicate anger rather than anxiety. Similarly, you could have an upset stomach due to the flu rather than anxiety.

Some people confuse anxious physical symptoms with medical problems. For example, patients suffering from panic attacks often believe that their symptoms have a medical cause. Typically during their panic attacks they believe they're on the verge of some terrible catastrophe, such as dying or going crazy or having a heart attack. But when they go to the doctor, they learn that there's nothing medically wrong with them.

Individuals suffering from hypochondriasis also interpret benign physical symptoms, such as a headache, belly pain, fatigue, or a bruise, as a sign that they have a serious medical problem like cancer. They go from doctor to doc-

Scoring Key: 5-Item Depression Test

	Score	Meaning
Normal Range	0–1	**Few or no symptoms of depression.** This is the best possible score. Depression doesn't seem to be a problem for you at this time. If you've been depressed, this is the score you eventually want to aim for. It may take a while to get there, but if you persist, you *can* make it happen.
	2–4	**Borderline depression.** You have minimal symptoms of depression and probably only need a mental tune-up. This score usually indicates normal ups and downs. Still, a score in this range is like having a low-grade fever. The fever isn't high, but you don't have nearly as much energy and motivation as you'd like. Furthermore, if you let a borderline depression persist, often it will worsen. Although this book focuses primarily on anxiety, many of the techniques can also be very helpful for depression.
Clinical Range (Therapy may be indicated.)	5–8	**Mild depression.** You have several mild symptoms of depression or a couple stronger symptoms. Although this degree of depression is only mild, it's more than enough to rob you of self-esteem and joy in daily living.
	9–12	**Moderate depression.** This is a significant level of depression. Many people have scores in this range for months or even years at a time. Although the prognosis for recovery is very positive, the sad thing is that many depressed individuals don't realize this or believe it. They feel like they *really are* defective or inferior and believe that it's simply not in the cards for them to ever feel any real happiness or fulfillment. I hope you won't give in to that mind-set because it will operate as a self-fulfilling prophecy. Once you give up, nothing changes. Then you conclude that things *really are* hopeless. I'm convinced that every person who suffers from depression can recover and feel joy and self-esteem again.
	13–16	**Severe depression.** Individuals who score in this range usually feel incredibly down, discouraged, and worthless and nothing seems rewarding or satisfying. This degree of suffering can be overwhelming and difficult for others to comprehend. When you try to tell your friends or family how you feel, they may tell you to cheer up and look at the bright side. Of course, that kind of superficial advice-giving usually makes things worse, because you feel discounted and rejected. In fact, the prognosis for recovery from severe depression is excellent, even though it doesn't feel that way right now.
	17–20	**Extreme depression.** This degree of depression indicates almost unbelievable suffering, but the prognosis for improvement and recovery is still very positive. Although self-help techniques can be very useful, professional treatment may also be needed. It's a lot like being lost in the woods. You feel frightened because it's getting dark and cold, and you don't know how to find your way home. Often a good guide whom you like and trust can show you the path that will lead you to safety.

Scoring Key: 2-Item Suicidal Urges Test

	Meaning
Item 1	If you're feeling depressed or discouraged, elevated scores on this item aren't unusual. Most depressed individuals have some suicidal thoughts at times. These thoughts aren't usually dangerous unless you have plans to act on them. However, it would be wise to consult with a mental health professional if you have any suicidal fantasies or urges or if the feelings of depression and discouragement have lasted more than a week or two. Your life is precious, and you don't want to play Russian roulette with it.
Item 2	This item asks about suicidal urges. Any score of 1 or higher can be dangerous, and professional treatment is definitely indicated. If you have any desires to end your life, you should call 911 and seek emergency treatment immediately.

tor in search of a diagnosis because they don't realize that emotional distress, *not* a medical illness, is causing their symptoms.

How to interpret your score on the Depression test. This scale measures the main symptoms of depression, such as feelings of sadness, discouragement, inferiority, or worthlessness, along with a loss of pleasure or satisfaction in life. Higher scores indicate more severe depression.

If your score on this test is 2 or more, you may also be experiencing some of the other common symptoms of depression, such as guilt, trouble sleeping, fatigue, and a paralyzing loss of motivation to do the things you once enjoyed, such as work, hobbies, sports, or just spending time with friends or family.

Depression is one of the worst forms of suffering because it robs you of self-esteem. In addition, the feelings of hopelessness create the illusion that your suffering will go on forever. I've often said that depression is the world's oldest and cruelest con, because you fool yourself into believing things that simply aren't true. You tell yourself that you're no good, that you should be better than you are, and that you'll never experience any real joy, satisfaction, creativity, or intimacy again. Furthermore, you may be totally convinced that you're seeing the awful truth about yourself and your life.

However, the prognosis for improvement is extremely bright. In fact, recovery from depression can be one of the most joyful experiences a human being can have. Many of my patients have said it's like being born again and that they feel the happiest they've ever felt in their entire lives.

How to interpret your score on the Suicidal Urges test. Suicidal urges usually result from feelings of hopelessness. When you're depressed, you may develop the overwhelming conviction that things could never change. Then you may turn to suicide as the only possible relief from your suffering.

In fact, the feelings of hopelessness are never valid. I've had thousands of therapy sessions with seriously depressed individuals who were absolutely convinced that they were worthless and could never get better. Some of them had been depressed for decades and had taken all kinds of medications that weren't helpful. And yet they eventually recovered and experienced joy and self-esteem again. I'm convinced this is possible for you, too.

What does it mean if you scored in the "Clinical Range" on the Anxiety or Depression tests? Does it mean that you're disturbed and need to seek professional help? Not at all. Many people with scores in this range have improved or even recovered simply by using the kinds of techniques in this book on their own. However, some people will need professional guidance. If you've been struggling to overcome these problems without success, or if the feelings of anxiety and depression are causing problems in your life, then you should seek a consultation with a mental health professional. In addition, if you're experiencing suicidal thoughts or feelings, it's crucial for you to seek treatment right away from a qualified mental health professional.

How about the other side of the coin? Suppose your scores are only minimally elevated, say 2 to 4 on the Anxious Feelings test or the Depression test. Does this mean you don't need help or won't benefit from the techniques in this book? Not at all. Personally, I'd shoot for a score of 0. Don't settle for half a cup. A score of 0 can make a huge difference in how you feel.

At the same time, I don't think it's possible to feel happy all the time, and I'm not sure it would even be desirable. Life can be stressful, and we all fall into black holes of self-doubt and worry from time to time. The important thing is to know you have the tools for dealing with painful mood swings so you don't have to fear them or get trapped in them.

Chapter 3

Do You Have an Anxiety Disorder?

Anxiety comes in a variety of flavors. Some of us are chronic worrywarts. Others develop panic attacks, obsessions, phobias, or fears about their health. Many people are painfully shy or freeze up every time they have to speak in front of an audience. The chart on page 41 lists the most common forms of anxiety, along with their popular names and official diagnostic labels. The diagnostic labels come from the fourth edition of the *Diagnostic and Statistical Manual of the American Psychiatric Association*, also known as *DSM-IV*. For example, shyness is diagnosed as social anxiety disorder and chronic worrying is diagnosed as generalized anxiety disorder. Let's talk about what these diagnostic labels mean—and what they don't mean.

Let's assume that you've been worrying about things lately. Are you just a garden-variety worrywart? Or do you have an illness called generalized anxiety disorder (GAD)? Or let's say that you have a tough time in social situations because you feel awkward and self-conscious. Are you shy? Or do you have an illness called social anxiety disorder? Where does shyness end and social anxiety disorder begin? We could ask similar questions about every type of anxiety listed on the chart. For example, most of us have some insecurities about our appearance. At what point do these concerns turn into an illness called body dysmorphic disorder (BDD)?

Doctors like to use diagnostic terms, such as generalized anxiety disorder,

Your Anxiety Profile

Instructions: Check off all the types of anxiety that apply to you.

Type of Anxiety	Symptoms	(✓)	Official Diagnostic Label
1. Chronic Worrying	You constantly worry about your work, health, finances, school, or family.		Generalized Anxiety Disorder (GAD)
2. Anxiety Attacks	You suddenly feel like you're about to pass out, go crazy, die, or lose control.		Panic Disorder (PD)
3. Agoraphobia	You're afraid that something terrible might happen if you're away from home alone.		Agoraphobia
4. Fears and Phobias	You have an intense fear of something specific, such as spiders, blood, heights, driving, flying, or getting trapped in small spaces.		Specific Phobia
5. Shyness	You often feel nervous or self-conscious around other people.		Social Anxiety Disorder
6. Shy Bladder Syndrome	You feel anxious about having to use a public restroom.		There are no specific diagnostic labels for these problems. They're all considered forms of Social Anxiety Disorder.
7. Test Anxiety	You get nervous and freeze up whenever you have to take a test.		
8. Public Speaking Anxiety	Giving a talk in front of a group of people would make you feel anxious.		
9. Performance Anxiety	Performing or competing in front of an audience would make you nervous or anxious.		
10. Obsessions	You have upsetting thoughts that you can't get rid of, such as fears of losing control and harming others, confessing to a crime you didn't commit, or being contaminated by dirt or germs.		Obsessive-Compulsive Disorder (OCD)
11. Compulsions	You have the urge to perform certain rituals, such as counting things, washing repeatedly, praying, arranging things in a particular way, or repeating words silently.		
12. Post-Traumatic Stress Disorder	You're plagued by upsetting memories of a traumatic event, such as rape, death, violence, torture, or serious injury.		Post-Traumatic Stress Disorder (PTSD)
13. Health Concerns	You often worry that you have a serious medical problem or disease, even though the doctor always reassures you that everything is fine.		Hypochondriasis
14. Concerns About Your Appearance	You feel convinced that there's something abnormal or grotesque about your appearance, even though nobody else can see the defect.		Body Dysmorphic Disorder (BDD)

Note: Some people have a tendency toward anxiety and worry. If you have one type of anxiety, there's a good chance you'll have several others too.

social anxiety disorder, and body dysmorphic disorder, because it helps them think and communicate about their patients' problems in a more precise way. In addition, these diagnostic labels sometimes provide hints about what the most effective types of treatment will be. For example, the techniques that I'd use to treat your panic attacks would be somewhat different from the techniques I'd use to treat your shyness, obsessive-compulsive tendencies, or depression.

Diagnostic categories are also useful for research because you can test new treatments on clearly defined groups of patients and find out what works and what doesn't. For example, if I publish a study that demonstrates the effectiveness of my new treatment for shyness, independent investigators can try to replicate the results of my study with a similar group of shy patients to see if their patients also improve. If so, then we can say that the treatment has been empirically validated. This is how the science of human behavior marches forward. In fact, the methods I describe in this book have been tested in large numbers of studies and have been shown to be highly effective in the treatment of every form of anxiety as well as depression, in both the short term and the long term.

However, there are some troubling problems with these diagnostic labels.

- Anxiety and worry are extremely common, so we end up "pathologizing" people unnecessarily.
- You may feel defective or ashamed if your doctor tells you that you have one or more anxiety disorders. But most anxious people already feel defective and ashamed, so the diagnosis could make those feelings more intense.
- You may jump to the conclusion that you have a "brain disease" or a mental illness. As I'll explain below, this probably isn't true.
- You may feel that you're the victim of forces beyond your control and conclude that you'll need to be treated with a pill in order to get better. In most cases, this is not true, either.

If you review the diagnostic criteria for the anxiety disorders in the *DSM-IV,* you'll discover that they can be surprisingly confusing. For example, here's what you need in order to qualify for a diagnosis of GAD:

- You have to worry about things excessively, "more days than not for at least six months."
- You have to have trouble controlling your worrying.
- The worrying has to cause "significant distress" in your life.
- You have to experience the physical symptoms of anxiety, such as muscle tension.

These criteria sound perfectly reasonable until you begin to think about them critically. For example, you're not allowed to have GAD unless you've been worrying about things "excessively." How much worrying is "excessive"? Your guess is as good as mine. And why does your worrying have to last for six months before you can call it GAD? Why not four months, two months, or two days? Let's suppose that you've been worrying about things for five months and twenty-nine days. Does this mean that you *don't* have GAD? And then do you suddenly develop GAD at midnight at the end of the six months? If so, what did you have before that moment? After all, worrying that's been going on for less than six months isn't any different from worrying that's been going on for more than six months.

The other criteria for GAD are equally strange. How are you going to determine whether you have trouble controlling your worrying? Does it mean that you have trouble controlling your worrying all of the time? Or some of the time? I've never had an anxious patient who didn't have some trouble controlling their anxiety. After all, we're not exactly like robots with switches for turning our emotions on and off!

Finally, you're not allowed to have GAD unless the worrying causes "significant distress" in your life. How much distress is "significant"? And what if you worry constantly, but the worrying isn't distressing to you? After all, some people seem to like to worry. For example, you may think that your constant worrying about your children will protect them from danger and is part of your role as a loving mother. Does this mean that you don't have GAD?

Medical doctors don't diagnose real illnesses with such subjective and vague criteria. If you came into the emergency room with a high fever, coughing, and shortness of breath, and the X ray confirmed pneumonia, I'd treat your pneumonia right away. I wouldn't say, "Oh, you've only had the symptoms for two days. I'm not allowed to diagnose pneumonia unless you've had the symptoms for a week. But if you're still alive next Friday, come on back and then I can treat you for pneumonia." Obviously, that would be nonsensical. Pneumonia is pneumonia, even if it's only been present for a day, an hour, or a minute.

To my way of thinking, the *DSM-IV* diagnostic criteria for the anxiety disorders are rather nonsensical, kind of like *Alice-in-Wonderland*. You can assume that worrying turns into an illness called generalized anxiety disorder after six months, since that's the way it's officially defined in the *DSM-IV,* but keep in mind that this cutoff point is arbitrary. GAD isn't a real disease in the same sense that pneumonia is a real disease. Worrying exists, but GAD doesn't. Shyness exists, but social anxiety disorder doesn't.

Where did these diagnostic criteria come from in the first place? You may not be aware that they weren't decided on strictly scientific grounds. What actually happens is that committees of psychiatrists get together from time to time and vote on the latest versions of the diagnostic criteria. They scratch their chins and ponder about how many months of worrying are required before GAD suddenly springs to life. Six months is not "correct" in any ultimate sense—it's just the time period that the committee voted on the last time they met. They could have pulled any number out of the air, and it would have been equally valid or nonsensical. It's a little like the philosophers in the Middle Ages who argued about how many angels could dance on the head of a pin.

Why are the diagnostic criteria for the anxiety disorders so arbitrary? It's because most of the feelings that psychiatrists classify as "anxiety disorders" are simply normal feelings that we all experience from time to time. Trying to convert our feelings, which are constantly changing, into a series of "disorders" that we could "have" or "not have" leads to severe conceptual problems. You have to create arbitrary cutoff points where none exist. That's where the problem comes in. For the most part, the "anxiety disorders" are fictional entities that exist only in the minds of the psychiatrists who invent them. They're not real brain diseases.

Earlier I mentioned that most therapists have struggled with some type of anxiety, such as shyness, public speaking anxiety, phobias, or obsessions, at some time in their lives. And most have had moments when they found themselves in the dark and experienced feelings of worthlessness, hopelessness, or intense self-doubt. Therapists are human, just like everyone else. These feelings are universal human experiences. Does this mean that we all have "brain diseases"?

There's no doubt that some people experience substantially more anxiety and self-doubt than the average person, while others experience very little anxiety and almost seem to have been born happy, confident, and outgoing. Scientists don't know why some people are more anxiety-prone, but genetic and environmental factors undoubtedly play important roles. If you have a tendency to be anxious, it doesn't mean that you have a brain disease or an anxiety disorder. These all-or-nothing labels simply don't map onto human feelings in a meaningful way.

I want to be clear about what I'm saying because I don't want to throw out the baby with the bathwater:

- Anxiety and depression are real.
- These feelings can be painful and disabling.
- People who struggle with anxiety and depression deserve treatment.
- New, effective, drug-free treatments now exist, and the prognosis for full recovery is outstanding.
- It's not necessary or desirable to transform these feelings into a series of "disorders" or "brain diseases" in order to deal with them effectively.

Of course, true brain diseases do exist. Some severe psychiatric problems, such as schizophrenia and bipolar (manic-depressive) illness, undoubtedly result from a biological defect in the brain. But for the most part, these labels are arbitrary.

Still, labels carry a lot of authority in people's minds. If your doctor tells you that you have pneumonia, you have a real illness with real pathology that requires medical treatment. You believe what the doctor is telling you because the doctor has a lot of training and knowledge that you don't have. But if your doctor tells you that you have GAD, obsessive-compulsive disorder, posttraumatic stress disorder, or social anxiety disorder, she or he is simply telling you something that you already knew—namely, that you've been feeling anxious.

Once you know what types of anxiety you have and how severe the anxiety is, we can roll up our sleeves and get to work. If we take the next step and say that you have an anxiety disorder, we haven't added any new information that we didn't already have. However, we have created the impression that your anxiety results from a chemical imbalance in your brain and that a pill will cure you. We'll examine this seductive idea in the next chapter.

Chapter 4

···

Placebo Nation

The Truth About Antidepressants
and Anti-Anxiety Medications

You've probably heard that depression and anxiety result from a chemical imbalance in the brain and that the proper medication can correct this imbalance. You may even have a friend or family member who swears that Paxil or Prozac pulled them out of a mood slump. However, there are some compelling reasons to doubt that depression and anxiety result from a chemical imbalance in the brain, and some startling new studies indicate that the antidepressants may not be nearly as effective as we've been led to believe. If you're feeling curious, I'll share some information that may be disturbing to you.

You may have seen these kinds of ads on television:

"Do you feel shy around other people? You could be suffering from social anxiety disorder. Researchers believe this illness results from a chemical imbalance in the brain. And you're in luck! Medication X can correct that imbalance. Ask your doctor for a prescription today!"

Then you see an animated cartoon with smiling little serotonin molecules swimming happily across synapses and stimulating the pleasure centers in the brain. This fades into a video of a happy couple holding hands and cavorting playfully on the beach because they've recovered from their "social anxiety disorder" with the help of Medication X, and now they're madly in love. These ads are slick and seductive. They make you want to pop a pill right away. Hey, I want to cavort on the beach with that gorgeous woman, too!

Are these messages valid? Do anxiety and depression *really* result from a chemical imbalance in your brain? Do pills really represent the most effective form of treatment?

We often think that if a problem has a biological cause, it has to be treated with a pill. In contrast, if a problem has a psychological cause, we can treat it with talk therapy. However, this kind of reasoning can be misleading. Sometimes pills can be the best treatment for a psychological problem. Let's say that you get a headache because you've been under stress. You reach for an aspirin, and it works like a charm. Within an hour, your headache is gone. So even though your headache resulted from a psychological problem, you treated it effectively with a pill. This doesn't mean that the pill corrected an aspirin deficiency in your brain. Aspirin was just the quickest and easiest way to get over your headache.

On the other hand, psychotherapy is often the best treatment for a biological problem. Many research studies suggest that genetic factors play a significant role in depression and many forms of anxiety. For example, some investigators are convinced that a blood phobia is almost entirely genetic. Obviously, whatever we inherit has to be biological, so a blood phobia must have a biological cause, at least in part. However, you may recall that I overcame my blood phobia in just a few minutes when I was working on a horribly bloody patient in an emergency room just before I started my internship. In this case, I treated a biological problem with a psychotherapeutic technique called Flooding. So the real question is this: What's the best way to get over depression and anxiety—drugs, psychotherapy, or a combination of the two?

According to the chemical imbalance theory, drugs definitely represent the best treatment for anxiety and depression. This theory has been around for a long time. In fact, it goes all the way back to Hippocrates, the father of modern medicine. He called depression "melancholia" because he thought it resulted from some kind of black poison secreted by the gallbladder. Melanin is a black pigment, and *cholia* refers to the gallbladder. Today, scientists are still looking for some type of chemical imbalance that causes depression and anxiety, but they're looking in the brain rather than the gallbladder.

The chemical that's received all the attention is called serotonin, one of the many chemicals that transmit electrical signals between the nerves in the brain. Many psychiatrists believe that depression and anxiety result from too little serotonin in the brain and that mania (states of extreme euphoria) results from too much. If so, medications that boost brain serotonin levels should have antidepressant and anti-anxiety effects. In fact, you could think of serotonin as the happiness molecule.

Following my psychiatric residency training at the University of Pennsylvania School of Medicine, I did several years of research on the chemical imbalance theory. During that time, I published research studies in peer-reviewed journals, wrote chapters for psychopharmacology textbooks, and lectured at scientific meetings throughout the United States and occasionally abroad. I was fortunate to win the A. E. Bennett Award, one of the world's top awards for basic psychiatric research, for my work on brain serotonin metabolism.

In the 1970s, my colleagues and I did a variety of experiments to test the theory that depression results from a serotonin deficiency in the brain. Our results simply were not consistent with this theory. For example, in one study, we boosted brain serotonin levels in depressed veterans by giving them massive daily supplements of L-tryptophan, an essential amino acid that rapidly crosses into the brain, where it's converted to serotonin. However, their moods did not improve at all. We published this study in the *Archives of General Psychiatry*, one of the top research journals.[1] I also reviewed the entire world literature on brain serotonin but couldn't find one shred of compelling evidence that a deficiency of serotonin, or any chemical imbalance in the brain, caused depression, anxiety, or any other psychiatric disorder. To this day, I'm still not aware of any studies that have ever validated the chemical imbalance theory.

The antidepressants that began to come out in the late 1980s, like Prozac, were called SSRIs (selective serotonin reuptake inhibitors) because they had extraordinarily potent effects on the brain serotonin system. If the serotonin deficiency theory was valid, these new drugs would undoubtedly have vastly superior antidepressant and anti-anxiety effects. In other words, patients who take SSRIs should recover quickly, because these drugs have potent effects on the brain serotonin system. But this hasn't been the case. In fact, the latest studies raise serious questions about whether these new antidepressants have *any* true antidepressant effects at all, above and beyond their placebo effects.

Many neuroscientists no longer consider the chemical imbalance theory of depression and anxiety to be valid. Instead they're doing research on the neural circuits in the brain, not focusing so much on chemical balances and imbalances. After all, the brain is not a hydraulic system, like the brakes in your car. Instead, it's a sophisticated and enormously complex information-processing system, kind of like a supercomputer that can think and feel. But one difference between the brain and a computer is that the brain creates new brain cells and new electrical circuits every day. In fact, every morning when you wake up, you're a slightly different person, since your brain has changed during the previous twenty-four hours.

Lots of people who suffer from depression or anxiety still believe that their mood problems result from a chemical imbalance in their brains, and that's understandable. You may believe this because your doctor told you it was true or because you heard it on television. But if your doctor tells you that you have a chemical imbalance in your brain, she or he may be confusing a theory with a fact. Most doctors are hardworking and well-meaning, and they want to do their best for you and for all their patients. But they've also heard the chemical imbalance theory over and over again.

This theory is fueled more by drug company marketing than by solid scientific proof. Billions of dollars of annual profits from the sale of antidepressant and anti-anxiety medications are at stake, so drug companies spend vast amounts of money promoting the chemical imbalance theory. They also subsidize a large proportion of the budget of the American Psychiatric Association and underwrite an enormous amount of research and education at medical schools.

Of course, supporting research and education is not a bad thing, but money buys influence, and the drug companies are focused on marketing their drugs. Academic research should be all about getting to the truth. Drug company research is all about selling new products.

As a physician, I'm not supposed to make claims that I can't document. If you've been feeling fatigued lately and I suspect that the problem results from iron deficiency anemia, I'll order some blood tests to find out. If the tests confirm my diagnosis, I'll give you a prescription for some iron supplements, and you'll soon be feeling perkier. But if I tell you that your depression or panic attacks result from a chemical imbalance in your brain, then I'm telling you something that can't be proven, because there is no test for a chemical imbalance in the human brain.

Some people find this hard to believe because the chemical imbalance theory has been so widely popularized and promoted. For example, you may have seen brain scans of people who were depressed or anxious in popular magazines or on TV. The researchers probably pointed out that the brain scans of people who were depressed were different from the brain scans of people who'd recovered and were feeling happy again. Some people think these images prove that a chemical imbalance in the brain causes anxiety and depression. In fact, this type of reasoning has been used to "prove" that a whole host of emotional and behavioral problems, including depression, anxiety, and even attention deficit hyperactivity disorder, are brain diseases that need to be treated with pills.

Scientists are justifiably excited about the new neuroimaging techniques, such as MRI (magnetic resonance imaging) and SPECT/PET (single photon/ positron emission computed tomography), because they allow us to peek into the living brain for the first time. The images indicate patterns of blood flow and oxygen utilization throughout the brain. They show that different parts of the brain use more blood and oxygen when they're more active. As a result, by assessing the amount of blood flow and oxygen use, researchers can get an indirect assessment of the brain regions that are more active during different behavioral and emotional states.

However, patterns of blood flow in the brain are a far cry from conscious thoughts and feelings. The brain images don't tell us anything about what's normal or abnormal and cannot be used to detect any kinds of "chemical imbalances." They also don't tell us anything about cause-and-effect relationships in the brain. They only show us that the brain is alive and well and doing its thing. If you're feeling sad, your brain may show one pattern; if you're feeling happy or excited, it may show another. But these pictures don't allow us to say that feelings of sadness, happiness, or excitement are brain diseases, and they don't tell us how the brain creates these feelings. In fact, we don't yet even know how the brain creates consciousness, much less abnormal states of consciousness such as depression, rage, or a panic attack.

Regardless of what causes depression and anxiety, the practical issue is how we're going to fight these problems. Most people think that medications represent the most effective treatment. In fact, this is the official position of the American Psychiatric Association, and the vast majority of physicians in the United States think it's the gospel truth.

As mentioned in Chapter 1, two types of medications are usually recommended for anxiety and depression. These include the minor tranquilizers, such as Xanax, Ativan, and Valium, and the antidepressants, such as Prozac, Paxil, or Zoloft. The minor tranquilizers are also called benzodiazepines, and they do have potent anti-anxiety effects. Let's say you're worrying and having trouble getting to sleep, so you take a .25 mg tablet of Xanax. If you've never taken a benzodiazepine before, it will work like a charm. You'll fall asleep almost immediately and wake up the next morning feeling relaxed and refreshed. It's like a miracle pill.

Does that mean that the Xanax corrected a chemical imbalance in your brain? No. It just means that the Xanax helped you relax and fall asleep. A couple stiff drinks would probably have the same effect, but they wouldn't be correcting a chemical imbalance in your brain, either!

Unfortunately, there's a downside to the Xanax solution. If you begin taking that drug or any of the benzodiazepines regularly, the odds are high that you'll become physically dependent on them within approximately three weeks. Then when you decide to stop taking them, you'll experience withdrawal effects, including severe anxiety and insomnia. The longer you take these drugs and the higher the dose, the more intense and prolonged the withdrawal becomes. However, these are the very problems that you took the medication for in the first place. Then you and your doctor may conclude that you haven't recovered and need to keep taking the drug. That's how people get hooked on the benzodiazepines. In fact, some experts have stated that withdrawal from Xanax can be as difficult as withdrawal from heroin. That's why I almost never prescribe the benzodiazepines for anxiety or depression.

Of course, there are exceptions to every rule, and sometimes these drugs can be incredibly helpful. For example, let's say you have to have a colonoscopy, and the doctor offers to give you an intravenous benzodiazepine to help you relax during the procedure. By all means, go for it! You'll be on cloud nine, and you'll absolutely *love* the colonoscopy. In fact, you'll probably want to have one every week! But if you're suffering from anxiety, insomnia, or depression, the benzodiazepines definitely aren't the way to go.

The antidepressants have also been heavily promoted for anxiety and depression. Everyone's heard about Prozac, and the antidepressants have one big advantage over the benzodiazepines: They're not addictive. But how effective are they? What do the latest data show?

Before I can answer this question, we'll need to discuss something called the placebo effect. This is the improvement that results from taking a sugar pill that has no active ingredients. Imagine this scenario: A man who's been feeling worthless and discouraged for several months seeks treatment from his local psychiatrist. The doctor explains that he's suffering from depression and that it results from a chemical imbalance in his brain. The doctor reassures him and gives him a prescription for an antidepressant that will correct the imbalance.

Four weeks later, the man reports that he's feeling much better. He's sleeping better, his mood has lifted, and he's productively involved in life again. He and his psychiatrist attribute his dramatic improvement to the antidepressant. Is this sound reasoning? Can we reasonably conclude that:

- His depression resulted from a chemical imbalance in his brain?
- The antidepressant corrected this chemical imbalance?
- His improvement resulted from the antidepressant?

Although many people will draw these kinds of conclusions, the man's improvement doesn't provide convincing evidence for any of them. All we can say for sure is that he was depressed and now he's feeling better. That's great, but we don't know what caused his depression or what triggered his improvement. His improvement could have resulted from the passage of time, unexpected events that lifted his mood, the fact that he became more active, the medication, *or* the placebo effect.

Why is the placebo effect so important? Our expectations can have powerful influences on the way we think, feel, and behave. If you're convinced that something will help, there's a good chance that it will help, even if it has no real effects at all. Let's say that you and I work as marketing executives for a pharmaceutical company. One day, at a press conference, we announce the synthesis of a wonderful new antidepressant called Placebin. We emphasize the superior antidepressant effects of the new drug and explain that it has few or no side effects and virtually no toxic effects. In fact, we're so excited by this new breakthrough drug that we're going to give Placebin to a million depressed people absolutely free of charge in a huge, nationwide clinical trial. There's tremendous enthusiasm for Placebin, and our company's stock goes up by more than $1 billion overnight.

Of course, we don't tell anyone that our new drug is just a placebo, with no active chemical ingredients. How many patients who take Placebin will recover?

Numerous research studies have shown that if you give an inert placebo to people who are suffering from depression, at least 30% to 40% of them will recover. This means that within a few weeks, 300,000 to 400,000 of the patients in our clinical trial will recover. They'll swear by the drug and tell all their friends how great it is. Some may even appear on *Oprah* and provide glowing testimonials about how Placebin corrected the chemical imbalance in their brains and changed their lives. The airwaves will be flooded with ads for this remarkable new medication, and hundreds of thousands of people will rush to their doctors to get prescriptions for it. Controversial books will appear, asking whether it's ethical to prescribe such powerful "happiness pills."

But, of course, Placebin didn't really do anything for anyone. It was the patients' expectations, not the pills, that caused them to get better. The patients actually healed themselves but didn't realize it. Hope is the most potent antidepressant in existence.

The placebo effect creates tremendous confusion about how and why medications and psychotherapy work. You can create any kind of kooky new treatment for depression or anxiety, and if you can convince people that it works, it will be effective for some patients, even if it involves blatant quackery. As a result, you may conclude that your treatment has potent antidepressant or anti-anxiety effects when it doesn't. This type of deception has been going on for thousands of years. In the old days, snake-oil salesmen capitalized on the placebo effect when they sold their magical elixirs. They also capitalized on people's demands for quick and easy miracle cures for whatever ailed them.

Now, you may be thinking, "Well, this is all rather academic, because we know that the antidepressants do work. They've been validated in numerous scientific studies and approved by the Food and Drug Administration." In fact, the situation isn't nearly as clear-cut as you might think. Recent studies suggest that all of the currently prescribed antidepressants may have few, if any, real therapeutic effects above and beyond their placebo effects. For example, in a recent multiuniversity study funded by the National Institute of Mental Health, 320 patients with major depression were randomly assigned to treatment with the herb St. John's wort, sertraline (Zoloft), or a placebo. The investigators wanted to find out, for once and for all, whether St. John's wort had any antidepressant effects, so they compared it to a "real" antidepressant on one hand and an inactive placebo on the other.

Neither the Zoloft nor the St. John's wort fared very well. Although 32% of the patients who received the placebo recovered, only 25% of the patients who received Zoloft and 24% of the patients who received St. John's wort recovered.[2] This study clearly showed that St. John's wort had no antidepressant effects above and beyond its placebo effects. I suspect the poor results with St. John's wort were widely publicized because the pharmaceutical industry wanted people to stop taking it and start taking antidepressants instead. However, the drug companies didn't publicize the fact that the antidepressant didn't fare any better than the St. John's wort. Neither the Zoloft nor the St. John's wort had any real antidepressant effects above and beyond their modest placebo effects!

That was one of the best studies of antidepressants ever conducted, and the results were not consistent with the widely held notion that the chemicals called antidepressants actually have strong and specific antidepressant effects. Were these results just an aberration of some type? In their review of the world literature, as well as all the data that's been submitted to the Food and Drug Administration (FDA) by drug companies over the past several decades, Dr. Irving Kirsch, from the University of Connecticut, and his colleagues have concluded that these results are actually very typical. Their analyses indicate that the differences between antidepressants and placebos are minimal at best and that at least 75% to 80% of the effects we attribute to antidepressant medications result from their placebo effects.[3]

The figure on the top of page 57 illustrates the problem. It's a schematic representation of the types of data that drug companies have submitted to the FDA to gain approval for their new antidepressants. In these studies, thousands of patients with moderate to severe depression were randomly assigned to treatment with a placebo or an antidepressant.[4] Their scores on the Hamilton Rating Scale for Depression averaged 25. The higher the score on the Hamilton Scale, the worse the depression. As you can see, a 25-point reduction in scores would be needed for full recovery. The patients who received the antidepressant experienced a 10-point reduction in their depression scores; those who received a placebo experienced an 8-point reduction.

There are three striking things about these results. First, neither the antidepressant nor the placebo was especially effective. This is particularly disconcerting when you consider the fact that these are the kinds of results you'll find in the *most* favorable studies that drug companies have conducted.

Second, the difference between the drug and placebo groups was only 2 points. This is the most improvement you could attribute to the drug itself, and it's extremely small, especially considering the fact that a 25-point reduction would be needed for full recovery. Some researchers have suggested that such a tiny effect probably does not justify prescribing antidepressants, given the significant side effects, toxic effects, and hazards associated with these agents.[5] A psychotherapy technique that caused only a 2-point improvement in depression wouldn't make my top 100 list! That's because dozens of techniques can cause huge changes in patients' moods very quickly.

Finally, 8 of the 10 points of improvement in the drug group, or 80%, clearly resulted from the placebo effect, not from the drug itself. I want to be crystal clear about what this means, because it's important, and it may seem confusing if you're not used to thinking about research studies. If you're feeling depressed and I give you a placebo, but I tell you that you're receiving a real antidepressant, you'll experience an 8-point improvement in depression, on average. If, instead, I give you a "real" antidepressant like Prozac, you'll experience a 10-point improvement in depression, on average. This means that 80%

Antidepressants versus Placebos: The "Best" Studies

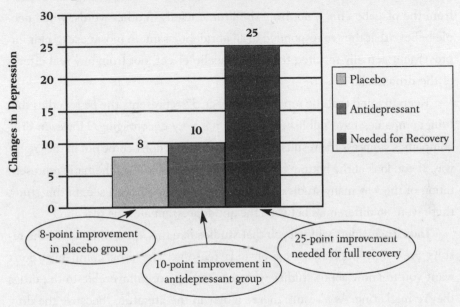

Antidepressants versus Placebos: A Typical Study

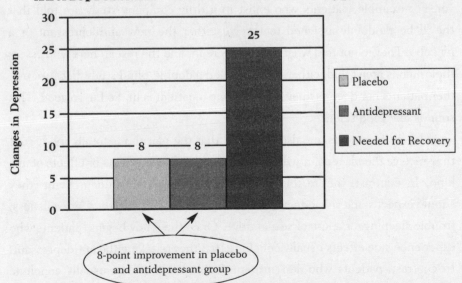

of the improvement you experience when I give you Prozac will actually result from the placebo effect, not from the Prozac itself. In other words, when people believe that they've responded to an antidepressant, in most cases, their improvement actually resulted from the placebo effect, not from any real effects of the drug itself.

Keep in mind that the top figure on page 57 represents the *best* studies that drug companies have published, and it's not very encouraging. However, drug companies suppress the results of many studies that don't come out in the "right" way. If you look at the bottom figure on page 57, you'll see a schematic representation of the way many studies actually come out. As you can see, in this study, there were *no* differences between the antidepressant and the placebo.

Industry insiders will tell you that studies like this are common, but the results are rarely published—for obvious reasons. The drug companies don't want you to know about studies with results that are unfavorable to the drugs they're marketing. As a result, there's a bias in the literature, because the drug companies are extremely selective about what they'll publish. This leads to false perceptions about the effectiveness of antidepressants; the published studies nearly always seem to favor the medication over the placebo.

Drug companies use all sorts of tricks to try to stack the deck in their favor. For example, patients who enlist in a drug company study are told that they'll be randomly assigned to receive either the new antidepressant or a placebo. They're not told what group they're in, and the researchers who assess their moods aren't told, either. This is called a double-blind study, because neither patients nor doctors knew which group a patient is in. So far, so good. This sounds like good science.

However, patients are also informed that the placebo is totally inert, so if they receive the placebo, it will have absolutely no side effects or effects of any kind. In contrast, they're told that if they receive the antidepressant, they should expect some side effects, such as upset stomach, diarrhea, nervousness, trouble sleeping, or a loss of sexual drive. Once the study begins, patients who experience side effects usually conclude that they're taking the antidepressant. In contrast, patients who don't experience any side effects usually conclude that they're in the placebo group. If you ask patients which group they think they're in, they'll be correct as often as 80% of the time. And if you ask the researchers who monitor their progress, their guesses usually will be correct, too.

This means that the studies aren't really double blind, because both patients and researchers know very well who's receiving the antidepressant and who's receiving the placebo. Patients with side effects generally conclude that they're getting the powerful new antidepressant, so they become more hopeful and optimistic. As a result, their depression scores may improve. In contrast, patients who think they're only getting the placebo may feel discouraged because they tell themselves, "Darn it! I ended up in the placebo group. A placebo can't help me. This always happens to me!" As a result, their depression scores may worsen. This can create an artificial but statistically significant difference between the drug and placebo groups, even when no real difference exists.

These studies have many other serious flaws, as well, flaws that are particularly egregious because they are easily solvable. For example, the drug companies could use active placebos rather than inactive placebos. If the drug they're testing causes sedation, they could use an antihistamine like Benadryl for the placebo, because this medication makes you feel sleepy. Or if the drug they're testing causes feelings of speediness, nervousness, and diarrhea, like Prozac, they could use caffeine for the placebo. That way, the patients would have a much harder time figuring out what group they're in.

Why don't the drug companies correct these flaws in their research methods? This is a case where the needs of marketing clash with the needs of science. If a drug company can come up with two studies that demonstrate a statistically significant difference between their new drug and a placebo, they'll receive FDA approval to market the drug. The value of their stock will instantly escalate, so there's a huge financial incentive to make these studies come out in the "proper" way.

Recent studies of antidepressants have been even more troubling. The fact that all of the new antidepressants seem to cause significant increases in the rates of completed suicide in children has been well publicized. The FDA recently has required so-called black box warnings for these drugs—labels reserved for the most dangerous drugs.[6] But you may not have heard that the same link between antidepressant use and suicide exists with adults.

Dr. David Healey, from the University of Wales College of Medicine, recently used the Freedom of Information Act to obtain all the data in the Food and Drug Administration on adults who were randomly assigned to SSRI antidepressants, such as Prozac, or placebos, in worldwide drug company studies. He discovered that the suicide rates in the patients who received antidepressants were nearly three times higher than the rates in patients who received placebos.[7] If these drugs really had antidepressant effects, why would they cause such striking *increases* in suicide rates in both children and adults? You could even argue that antidepressants shouldn't be prescribed for anyone who's feeling depressed! (You can review an article about the increased risk of suicide in patients taking SSRI antidepressants online at www.ohri.ca/newsroom/02172005.asp)

These studies suggest that true antidepressant medications may not yet exist. Chemicals like Prozac and Paxil are called antidepressants, but their true antidepressant effects seem underwhelming at best. Many people find these studies hard to swallow and simply cannot believe them at first. We all know someone who's said, "Prozac really worked for me. It saved my life." But remember that at least 30% to 40% of the people who receive a placebo will say exactly the same thing.

My clinical experience over the years has been consistent with the new research. As I mentioned, I started out doing brain research and psychopharmacology at the Affective Disease Research Unit at the University of Pennsylvania School of Medicine. During that time, I gave out antidepressants by the bucketful. A few of my patients were helped a lot, and some were helped a little, but many weren't helped at all. These experiences were sharply at odds with what I heard when I attended the annual American Psychiatric Association conventions or continuing education symposia sponsored by drug companies. I kept hearing that 80% of depressed or anxious patients could be treated successfully with antidepressants, and I couldn't understand why my clinical experiences were so greatly at odds with the party line. I knew that I wasn't doing a poor job prescribing the medications. We had one of the finest psychopharmacology teams in the world.

Even during my pure psychopharmacology days, I was looking for some type of psychotherapy to supplement the pills I was prescribing. However, when I first heard about Cognitive Behavior Therapy (CBT), I wasn't particularly impressed. I knew that my patients constantly bombarded themselves with negative thoughts, such as "I'm hopeless. I'll never get better!" but I didn't believe they could recover simply by learning to change the way they were thinking. It sounded too much like Dr. Norman Vincent Peale's *Power of Positive Thinking*. Depression and anxiety seemed far too serious and severe for such a simplistic approach.

But when I tried these methods with some of my more difficult patients, my perceptions changed. Patients who'd felt hopeless, worthless, and desperate began to recover. At first, it was hard to believe that the techniques were working, but I could not deny the fact that when my patients learned to put the lie to their negative thoughts, they began to improve. Sometimes they recovered right before my eyes during sessions. Patients who'd felt demoralized and hopeless for years suddenly turned the corner on their problems. I can still recall an elderly French woman who'd been bitterly depressed for more than fifty years, with three nearly successful suicide attempts, who started shouting "Joie de vivre! [joy of living] Joie de vivre!" one day in my office. These experiences made such a strong impact on me that I decided my calling was in clinical work rather than brain research. After considerable soul searching, I decided to give up my research career and become a full-time clinician.

Over the years, I've had more than 35,000 psychotherapy sessions with depressed and anxious patients, and I'm every bit as enthusiastic about CBT as when I first began learning about it. However, today the therapy is substantially more powerful and refined than when my colleagues and I were just beginning to develop it in the mid-1970s. Over the past three decades, many research studies have validated the effectiveness of CBT in the treatment of depression and anxiety. In fact, CBT has become the most extensively researched form of psychotherapy ever developed and is now the most widely practiced form of psychotherapy in the United States.

For example, in the introduction to this book, I referred to the recent study by Drs. Henny A. Westra and Sherry H. Stewart. They reviewed the entire world literature on the treatment of anxiety with medications or CBT and concluded that CBT, not pills, works best, and recommended it as the gold standard for the treatment of all the anxiety disorders.[8] In another superb review of the world literature, Dr. David Antonuccio and his colleagues compared CBT with medications in the treatment of depression. They concluded that CBT, not medication, is the treatment of choice for depression in children, adolescents, and adults.[9] Recent studies indicate that CBT does not offer just a quick fix for mood problems, but appears to be superior to antidepressant medications in the long term, as well.[10]

These studies are completely consistent with my clinical experience. I did careful Relapse Prevention Training with every patient prior to discharge, and I can count on two hands the number of patients who returned for help with relapses after they'd completed treatment. In addition, most of them required only one or two sessions to nip the relapse in the bud and get back to feeling good again. I think this fact is extremely promising, given the chronic and relapsing nature of depression and anxiety when patients are treated with drugs alone.

Should you try to use CBT on your own? Or should you try to find a good therapist to work with? In the introduction, I referred to recent research studies by Dr. Scogin and his colleagues at the medical center of the University of Alabama. Their studies have clearly shown that many people who are feeling depressed or anxious can use CBT techniques effectively on their own, without medications or psychotherapy, simply by reading a book like this and doing the exercises I describe.[11] This type of treatment is called bibliotherapy. I think Dr. Scogin's research is encouraging and important, because millions of people cannot afford therapy or can't locate a good therapist near their home. However, this doesn't mean that everyone can, or should, try to do it on their own. Many people with more severe problems will need the guidance and support of a mental health professional. There's no shame in that. Sometimes a little TLC and skillful guidance can make all the difference in the world!

Pills or Skills? Dr. Burns's Prescription

- Genetic and environmental factors undoubtedly play a huge role in how we think, feel, and behave, but there's no convincing evidence that depression and anxiety result from a chemical imbalance in the brain. Scientists don't yet know what causes depression and anxiety.

- It's not reasonable to claim that drugs are the most effective treatment for depression or anxiety. This claim has been made by the American Psychiatric Association and has been widely publicized by the pharmaceutical industry, but it's not consistent with the latest research, which raises serious questions about the safety and effectiveness of the antidepressants and the benzodiazepines. The research also indicates that CBT, not pills, is the most effective treatment for depression and all the anxiety disorders, both in the short term and in the long term.

- There are exceptions to every rule. Medications can be helpful or even lifesaving for some people who suffer from severe depression or anxiety, but should be combined with CBT for the best effect.

- Some severe psychiatric disorders, such as schizophrenia and bipolar illness, will require medications, but CBT can also help.

- Long-term treatment with antidepressants usually isn't necessary. Once you've recovered completely from an episode of depression or anxiety, you probably can taper off your antidepressant medication if you've been treated with CBT or have learned to use the techniques in this book.

- Many people can learn to use these techniques successfully on their own, without the help of a therapist. But a good therapist can speed your recovery, especially if your problems are severe.

- Regardless of whether you're receiving medications, psychotherapy, or a combination, or simply working with these techniques on your own, you should monitor your moods at least once a week with the Brief Mood Survey on page 33 to see whether you're improving. The only valid goal of any therapy is to get well.

- Avoid the benzodiazepines, such as Xanax, Valium, Ativan, and others, because they're addictive.

- Avoid polypharmacy (combining multiple drugs) whenever possible. Dangerous drug interactions can occur, and patients often end up feeling drugged and overmedicated.

- If you are taking an antidepressant, watch for the development of suicidal impulses, and seek help immediately if they occur. (Of course, the same advice pertains to people who aren't taking antidepressants.)

- Never make any drug decisions on your own. Always consult with your doctor first. Teamwork and trust are the keys to good therapy.

Chapter 5

···

What Would It Be Worth If I Could Show You How to Change Your Life?

Anxiety and depression are the most common mental health problems throughout the world, and they create tremendous suffering. They can rob you of self-confidence, productivity, and peace of mind. They can also create conflicts in your relationships with other people. But I have some great news for you. You *can* change the way you feel without drugs or lengthy therapy. I'm going to show you how to use many powerful techniques that can help you defeat your fears and overcome feelings of depression. In many cases, you can achieve these results much faster than you might think.

However, there's no free lunch. Simply reading about these techniques won't be effective. Understanding is useful, but it won't cure anxiety or depression. If you want to change your life, you're going to have to pick up these tools and use them. You'll have to do three specific things:

1. You may have to give up certain hidden benefits of the anxiety and depression. This will involve a loss.
2. You'll have to confront the monster you fear the most. This will take some courage and determination.
3. You'll have to do some written exercises. This will require active effort.

You may not believe that real change is possible, but if it were, would you want that result? Would you be willing to change your life right now if I could show you how?

Let's find out by doing a thought experiment. Imagine that you and I were having a therapy session, and there was a magic button on my desk. If you pressed the button, all your problems would suddenly disappear with absolutely no effort on your part, and you'd walk out of today's session feeling wonderful. Would you press that button?

The obvious answer is "Yes, of course I'd press that button!" But many people have the opposite reaction. They're reluctant to press the button. Even though their suffering is real, they have mixed feelings about change, so they cling to the status quo. Traditionally, therapists have called this puzzling phenomenon "resistance." In this chapter, you're going to learn how to pinpoint the hidden forces that may be keeping you stuck. Once you expose these hidden forces to the light of day, often they'll lose their power to defeat you.

I once treated a young man named Sam who worked at a fast food restaurant in Washington, D.C. One night, two armed gunmen broke in and robbed him at gunpoint just as he was locking up. Then they locked him in the restaurant's walk-in freezer and left him there to freeze to death before they ran off with the money. The next morning, the manager discovered Sam huddled and shivering in the freezer, barely alive and badly traumatized.

Months later, Sam came to me for treatment with all the classic symptoms of post-traumatic stress disorder. He'd recovered physically but was still consumed by intense feelings of anxiety and rage. Vivid, terrifying memories of the incident popped into his mind unexpectedly. These flashbacks made Sam feel panicky, helpless, and vulnerable. He also had fantasies of getting revenge on the men who robbed him.

Sam was miserable every waking minute of every day and desperately wanted to get his life back. I told Sam that even though he'd been through a terrifying and humiliating experience, the prognosis for full recovery was bright. I explained that his negative feelings resulted from the frightening thoughts and vivid fantasies that were constantly flowing across his mind and told him that many powerful new techniques could help him change the way he was thinking and feeling. With a little luck and hard work, his anxiety and anger might even disappear completely.

I thought Sam would be thrilled to hear that message, but instead, he insisted that my techniques couldn't possibly help and began fighting me tooth and nail. I suddenly felt more like his enemy than his ally. Sam was miserable and desperate for relief, but when I offered to help him, he started arguing with me.

Why was Sam resisting me? Think about it for a moment and jot your ideas below. Cover up my answer with a sheet of paper so you won't be tempted to read it before you've completed this exercise.

_____

_____

_____

_____

_____

Answer

Although Sam was suffering, I wondered if he thought that his anxiety and anger were helping him in some way. If so, this might explain why he was resisting me. To find out, I suggested we try a Cost-Benefit Analysis (CBA), a motivational technique that will help you pinpoint the forces that keep you stuck. You list all the advantages and disadvantages of a thought, feeling, or habit that's causing problems for you. Then you balance the advantages against the disadvantages so you can make a more enlightened decision about whether you want to change or not.

I asked Sam if he could think of any advantages of feeling constantly anxious and angry. As you can see on page 68, Sam came up with quite a few advantages. First, he believed that his anxiety would keep him vigilant and protect him from further harm. This is a common belief among individuals who struggle with anxiety. I call it "Magical Thinking." It's the idea that even though your anxiety is painful, it's protecting or helping you in some way.

There were also some hidden benefits of Sam's anger. It showed that Sam was strong and not about to let a couple of thugs push him around and get away with it. His revenge fantasies showed that he had a sense of pride and self-esteem and wasn't going to let two sadistic gunmen walk all over him.

The advantages of Sam's anxiety and anger made it clear why he was resisting treatment. He wasn't being irrational, ornery, or stubborn, and he wasn't trying to defeat me. From his perspective, he felt like he was simply being responsible, moral, manly, and realistic.

Then I asked Sam if he could think of any disadvantages of constantly feeling anxious. Was there a price he was paying for feeling that way? As you can see from his Cost-Benefit Analysis, Sam listed some pretty compelling disadvantages, such as the fact that he felt miserable every waking minute of every day. He also questioned the notion that his anxiety would protect him from danger or help him cope more effectively in the unlikely event that he was robbed again.

Was there also a downside to Sam's anger? It dawned on Sam that the gunmen didn't even know he was angry, so he was only punishing himself with his constant rage and revenge fantasies. It was *his* life that was going down the drain, not theirs.

I asked Sam to weigh the advantages of the constant anxiety and anger against the disadvantages on a 100-point scale. Did the benefits or the costs feel greater? Even though he'd listed more advantages, Sam decided that the disadvantages were greater, so he put a 70 in the circle on the right and a 30 in the circle on the left. Sometimes one strong disadvantage will outweigh several advantages, or vice versa.

As a homework assignment, I suggested that Sam might want to go to the local police station and ask if they had any tips on how to avoid being mugged or robbed, since he lived in a dangerous neighborhood. The officer at the desk gave him a brochure with eight excellent safety tips on how to avoid being attacked. Sam was surprised to discover that "constant worrying" was not one of the recommended methods. When I saw Sam the next week, he'd had a real change of attitude. His resistance had disappeared, and we began working together as a team. After just a few sessions, Sam's anxiety and anger disappeared completely and he was ready to terminate his treatment.

Sam's story illustrates how resistance works. On some level, you may not want to recover, even if recovery requires absolutely no effort on your part. Of course, for each person and problem, the reasons for resisting change will be somewhat different. For example, if you suffer from test anxiety, you may con-

Sam's Cost-Benefit Analysis

Describe the attitude, feeling, or habit that you want to change: Constantly feeling angry and worrying about getting robbed.

Advantages	Disadvantages
1. If I'm constantly vigilant, I'll be less likely to get robbed again. I'll be on the lookout in case anyone tries to pull a fast one.	1. I feel miserable every waking minute of every day.
2. My anxiety seems realistic, since people get mugged and robbed in this neighborhood all the time.	2. Anxious people probably get mugged just as often as people who feel happy and confident. In fact, if you're anxious and insecure, you may be more likely to become a target.
3. My anger shows that I'm strong and that these losers can't just walk all over me and get away with it.	3. The chances of being robbed at gunpoint again are small.
4. I have the *right* to be angry, because what they did was wrong.	4. The worrying won't help me if I do get robbed again.
5. My feelings of rage show that I have a strong value system.	5. The gunmen who robbed me don't know I'm angry, and they definitely don't care about my feelings, so I'm the only one who's suffering. I'm really only punishing myself.
6. I can feel sorry for myself, since I was a victim.	
7. If I'm on the lookout, I might spot them one day, and I can have them arrested.	
8. I can fantasize about getting revenge on them.	

(30)   (70)

stantly worry that your mind will go blank or that you'll freeze up when you take your final exam. But you may also believe that the anxiety is the price you have to pay to do really good work. You may think that the constant worrying will motivate you to work hard and do your best. There is a grain of truth to this. A small amount of anxiety can be motivating, but you rapidly reach a point of diminishing returns. Too much anxiety can cripple you. I've found that I do my best work when I'm feeling relaxed and confident, not when I'm worried or anxious.

Alternatively, you may want to overcome your fears but may not want to do what you're going to have to do to get the job done. The price of recovery may seem too high. There's one thing that every anxious individual will have to do—

that he or she absolutely won't want to do—to get well. Do you remember what it is? Put your ideas here before you continue reading.

_____

_____

_____

_____

_____

Answer

You may have guessed the answer right away. If you want to overcome your anxiety, you're going to have to face your fears and confront the monster you fear the most. For example, if you're suffering from claustrophobia, I might ask you to allow yourself to be trapped in a small, confined space, say a closet, until you're flooded with anxiety. Would you do it?

Of course, exposure to the thing you fear isn't the only tool we're going to use. I'm going to teach you forty powerful ways to defeat your fears. Most of the techniques we'll use aren't frightening. In fact, they can be exciting. But exposure will be an important part of our treatment plan, and it will be scary at first. It always requires tremendous courage and determination.

I once treated a thirty-one-year-old man named Trevor who hadn't had a date in over five years. This was surprising to me, because he was a tall, handsome fellow, and he seemed quite friendly and charming. I wanted to be sure I was sizing him up correctly so I decided to check it out with my daughter, who was helping out in the front office of my clinic that summer. I reminded her that I couldn't tell her anything about my patients, but had she noticed Trevor or had any impressions of him? She said that she definitely had noticed him and that he was drop-dead gorgeous. In fact, she said that he looked like a model from _GQ_ magazine.

Why was such a handsome, personable fellow having so much trouble getting a date? It turned out that Trevor had a tendency to sweat a great deal and felt intensely self-conscious because he was convinced that any woman would be disgusted when she saw the circles of sweat on his shirt under his armpits. He was so worried about sweating that he'd become almost housebound, especially during the summer months.

Trevor said he was tired of being lonely and wanted to get his social life in gear. I asked what it would be worth to him if I agreed to show him how to do this. He said he was desperate and would do practically anything to make that happen. That was the message I was hoping to hear. I told Trevor that I wanted to schedule a double session with him so that we could go outdoors and do some Shame-Attacking Exercises, instead of just talking in the office. I explained that when you do a Shame-Attacking Exercise, you do something foolish in public on purpose so you can see that the world doesn't really come to an end. I warned Trevor that the Shame-Attacking Exercises would probably be frightening, but might help him overcome his fears.

The following Tuesday, Trevor showed up at 2 P.M. for his double session. It was August in Philadelphia, and it was especially hot and humid that day. As we were leaving the hospital to do our Shame-Attacking Exercises, I stopped by the clinical lab, borrowed a plastic squirt bottle, and filled it with water. Once we were outside, I told Trevor that we were going to jog to the local convenience store to work up a little sweat. He looked nervous but agreed, so off we went.

When we arrived at the store a few minutes later, we were both pretty sweaty. I told Trevor I wanted to squirt his armpits with water to make it look like he was totally soaked in sweat. I said that I also wanted to pour water on his head so it would look like sweat was literally dripping from his face. Once he was soaked, I wanted him to go inside the store and stand near the cash register, where everyone could see him. Then I wanted him to place his right hand on the back of his head with his elbow pointed to the side so his sweaty armpit would be completely exposed, point to his armpit with his left hand, and say, loudly enough so everyone in the store could hear him: "Boy, it sure is hot today! Look at me! I'm sweating like a pig!"

Trevor was terrified and couldn't believe what I was asking him to do. He insisted that he couldn't possibly do it because everyone in the store would be totally grossed out when they saw how sweaty and disgusting he was. I reminded him that he'd promised to do whatever it took, even if it was frightening. I told him that this was the price he had to pay if he really wanted to defeat his fears and change his life.

We debated the merits of the Shame-Attacking Exercise for several minutes. Should he or shouldn't he? Finally Trevor said, "Okay, if you think it's so easy, I'd like to see *you* do it!"

I said, "Sure, no problem." I squirted my armpits and face with copious amounts of water and went into the store with water dripping from my head. I put my hand on the back of my head, pointed to my armpit, and loudly declared how hot and sweaty I was. The people in the store didn't seem terribly interested and just went about their business. It was almost as if I were invisible.

Then I noticed a homeless man sitting on the sidewalk next to the front door of the store, quacking like a duck. People weren't paying any attention to him, either!

I went back outside and told Trevor it was his turn. He looked terrified, swallowed hard, and went for it. Once again, no one seemed repulsed or shocked by his sweaty armpits. The only difference was that he was so handsome that several people in the store started talking to him. It was as if they'd found a long-lost friend! Trevor could barely believe what had happened.

Then we jogged to several other stores in the neighborhood, taking turns doing our Shame-Attacking Exercises. People seemed amused by our sweaty antics; no one seemed put off. Many people chatted with us about how hot it was. This was a revelation to Trevor. He was shocked that we kept getting such friendly reactions from everyone.

We finally ended up in a boutique that sold fashionable women's sportswear. I noticed an attractive young woman giving Trevor the eye, but he was totally oblivious and didn't seem to be aware of her. I told him to approach her, put his hand on his head, point to his armpit, and make his sweaty proclamation again.

He became intensely resistant and insisted that he couldn't possibly do that because she'd be totally grossed out. I told him that this was exactly what he had to do if he wanted to gain liberation from his fears. This would be his graduation exercise. I promised I wouldn't ask him to do any more Shame-Attacking Exercises if he'd just do it this one last time.

He reluctantly approached her, pointed to his armpit, and shyly commented about how sweaty he was. She didn't seem at all concerned about his sweat but seemed extremely pleased that he was talking to her. Soon they were deeply engrossed in conversation. After a few minutes, she suggested that it might be fun to get together for coffee sometime. Trevor looked dumbfounded and said it sounded like a great idea. She said, "Then you'll need my phone number so you can give me a call." She scribbled it on a piece of paper, pressed it into the palm of his hand, and said, "Call me soon!" Trevor walked out of that store on cloud nine. He was speechless.

Why were the Shame-Attacking Exercises so effective? Trevor discovered that his negative thoughts were completely off base. The moment he stopped believing what he'd been telling himself, his shyness was ancient history.

Many experts believe that Exposure Therapy always works like this. In fact, it's not the exposure, per se, that ends your fears. Instead, your anxiety vanishes the moment you put the lie to the distorted thoughts that triggered it in the first place. Unfortunately, it's never easy to confront your fears, and there's psychological novocaine that will numb the terror you feel when you do.

So far, we've talked about giving up the hidden benefits of your negative feelings and facing your fears. But there's something else you're going to have to do if you want to overcome your anxiety and develop greater self-esteem. I'm talking about the written exercises. They are the keys to your success. If you do them, it will be hard to fail. If you resist them, it will be hard to succeed.

I've asked you to do a number of written exercises already. Did you do them? Or did you skip over them and continue reading? If you want tangible results, these exercises will be invaluable.

In the next chapter, you're going to learn how to use the Daily Mood Log, the backbone of the therapy. The Daily Mood Log will help you pinpoint and change the thoughts that trigger anxiety and depression. However, it will require consistent effort, and you can't do it in your head. Numerous published studies, as well as my own clinical experience, have underscored one important fact: Depressed and anxious individuals who don't do self-help assignments between sessions usually don't improve. Sometimes they even get worse. In contrast, the people who roll up their sleeves and work hard are the ones who experience the most rapid and lasting improvement. I want you to be one of them.

Many people resist the written exercises. They don't want to pick up a pen or pencil because they don't think it's necessary. They get into a passive mindset. They want the magic without the hard work. But genuine emotional change requires effort and practice.

I once treated an intensely unhappy woman named Eileen who consistently "forgot" to complete the Daily Mood Log between sessions. During her sessions, she complained about all the people in her life who'd let her down, but she was reluctant to pinpoint any specific problems she wanted to work on. One day, Eileen said, "Maybe I like feeling anxious and depressed."

I told Eileen that she was probably on to something and suggested we could list all the advantages of being depressed and anxious and all the disadvantages of getting better. This is similar to the Cost-Benefit Analysis that Sam did, but it's a paradoxical approach. We're examining only the factors that are keeping Eileen stuck and ignoring the benefits of recovery.

Eileen came up with many advantages of being miserable, including:

- When I'm upset, I get lots of attention from my husband.
- I don't have to cook or do any housework. He does everything for me.
- I don't have to go out and look for a job, which frightens me.
- I can play the role of victim and feel sorry for myself.
- I can complain about all the people who don't love me enough, especially my father and my brother.
- I can be angry all the time.
- I can feel special.
- I can frustrate Dr. Burns and show him that he can't control me or tell me what to do.
- I can justify drinking and taking tranquilizers whenever I want.

Eileen also listed many disadvantages of getting better. They included:

- I'll have to work hard doing the psychotherapy homework assignments between sessions.
- I'll have to stop drinking and maybe even attend AA meetings.
- I'll have to cook and do housework.
- I might have to look for a job.
- There won't be any reason to meet with Dr. Burns anymore.
- I won't feel special anymore. I'll be ordinary, just like everyone else.

- I'll have to develop relationships with people, and that will be anxiety-provoking.
- I'll have to do all the things I've been putting off.
- I won't be able to complain about all the people who have wronged me.
- I'll lose my sense of identity as a victim.

I told Eileen that her depression was clearly a good thing. I said I was greatly relieved to see that there were so many advantages of the depression and so many disadvantages of recovering, especially since she was a full-fee patient and usually scheduled a double session with me every week. Even though we tended to fight and argue during the sessions, I said she was one of my favorite people to fight with, and I'd miss her greatly if she recovered and we couldn't meet again. I added that I hoped she'd keep "forgetting" to do the homework assignments so that we could keep working together for years to come.

When Eileen returned for her session the next week, she reported that she'd worked with the Daily Mood Log every day for at least thirty minutes. She'd also stopped drinking and had already attended two AA meetings. She said she was feeling much better and thought she'd be ready to terminate treatment soon. Although Eileen's suffering was real, she'd resisted the treatment for years. Her resistance to the written homework assignments was really a reflection of her fears that the treatment might work and that she'd have to say good-bye to an old and faithful friend.

Many people are like Eileen. They have one foot in the water and the other foot on the shore. On the one hand, they desperately want to change their lives, but at the same time, they resist change. For each of us, the reasons for resisting change will be a little different. No matter what the problem is, you'll always have to give up certain hidden benefits and pay a price if you want to change your life.

As you can see from the examples in this chapter, effective treatment doesn't consist of simply lying on the couch and expressing your feelings or trying to understand where your fears came from in the first place. It means working together collaboratively. So now I need to hear from you. How would you answer these three questions?

- If you could push a magic button and make all your anxiety, depression, or anger disappear *right now,* would you push that button?
- Are you willing to confront the thing you fear the most, even if it's tremendously anxiety-provoking at first?
- Are you willing to do some written exercises while you read this book, even though it will require some hard work?

If you can say yes to all three questions, the end of your anxiety may be just a stone's throw away!

....

Chapter 6

The Daily Mood Log

During a recent workshop in New York, I asked for a volunteer who'd be willing to work on a personal problem in front of the group. A therapist named Marsha raised her hand and explained that she needed help with her constant worrying about her twenty-six-year-old daughter, Leslie. Marsha described herself as a "Jewish mother" and said that her compulsive worrying embarrassed her and sometimes annoyed Leslie.

Marsha explained that Leslie had struggled with her weight ever since she was a child. When she reached adolescence, the problem got worse. Dieting didn't work, and Leslie became morbidly obese. As a last resort, Leslie had recently undergone stomach-stapling surgery, with outstanding results. She'd already lost more than seventy pounds and was feeling terrific. Still, Marsha constantly worried about Leslie and had thoughts like these all day long: "Did Leslie remember to take her medicines? Is she drinking plenty of fluids?" She'd get so nervous that she'd call and check up on Leslie several times each day.

Although Marsha's obsessive worrying and compulsive calling were intrusive, Leslie usually reacted with a sense of humor and tolerance. Marsha said they had a solid, loving relationship.

It isn't difficult to understand Marsha's feelings, because any loving parent worries at times. However, Marsha's worrying was excessive since Leslie was responsible and doing fine. Marsha said she felt embarrassed because she was a mental health professional and worked with anxious parents every day. She said she felt like a fraud because she gave them lots of advice but didn't seem to practice what she preached. She was frustrated with herself.

I asked Marsha to fill out a Daily Mood Log. The Daily Mood Log is based on the idea that when you change the way you *think,* you can change the way you *feel.* You'll find a blank copy on pages 78 and 79. There are five steps.

Step 1.   **Upsetting Event.** Write a brief description of the upsetting event at the top of the Daily Mood Log. Choose any moment when you were feeling anxious or upset.

Step 2.   **Emotions.** Circle the words that describe how you were feeling at that moment, and rate each feeling on a scale from 0% (not at all) to 100% (extreme). Put these ratings in the "% Before" column.

Step 3.   **Negative Thoughts.** Pinpoint the negative thoughts that are associated with each feeling. Ask yourself questions like this: "When I feel guilty, what am I thinking? What thoughts are flowing across my mind?" Or "When I feel anxious and worried, what am I telling myself?" For example, if you're feeling depressed, you may be telling yourself that you're worthless or unlovable. Indicate how much you believe each thought on a scale from 0% (not at all) to 100% (completely). Put these ratings in the "% Before" column.

Step 4.   **Distortions.** Identify the distortions in each negative thought, using the Checklist of Cognitive Distortions at the bottom of the second page of the Daily Mood Log.

Step 5.   **Positive Thoughts.** Challenge each negative thought with a new thought that's more positive and realistic. Indicate how much you believe each positive thought on a scale from 0% (not at all) to 100% (completely). Put these ratings in the "% Belief" column. Now rate your belief in your negative thoughts again, and put the new ratings in the "% After" column.

The first step is extremely important because all of your problems will be embedded in any single moment when you were feeling anxious or upset.

Daily Mood Log

Upsetting Event: _____

Emotions	% Before	% After	Emotions	% Before	% After
Sad, blue, depressed, down, unhappy			Embarrassed, foolish, humiliated, self-conscious		
Anxious, worried, panicky, nervous, frightened			Hopeless, discouraged, pessimistic, despairing		
Guilty, remorseful, bad, ashamed			Frustrated, stuck, thwarted, defeated		
Inferior, worthless, inadequate, defective, incompetent			Angry, mad, resentful, annoyed, irritated, upset, furious		
Lonely, unloved, unwanted, rejected, alone, abandoned			Other (describe)		

Negative Thoughts	% Before	% After	Distortions	Positive Thoughts	% Belief
1.				1.	
2.				2.	
3.				3.	
4.				4.	
5.				5.	

Negative Thoughts	% Before	% After	Distortions	Positive Thoughts	% Belief
6.				6.	
7.				7.	
8.				8.	

Checklist of Cognitive Distortions

1. **All-or-Nothing Thinking.** You view things in absolute, black-and-white categories.

2. **Overgeneralization.** You view a negative event as a never-ending pattern of defeat: "This *always* happens!"

3. **Mental Filter.** You dwell on the negatives and ignore the positives.

4. **Discounting the Positive.** You insist that your positive qualities don't count.

5. **Jumping to Conclusions.** You jump to conclusions not warranted by the facts.
   - **Mind-Reading.** You assume that people are reacting negatively to you.
   - **Fortune-Telling.** You predict that things will turn out badly.

6. **Magnification and Minimization.** You blow things out of proportion or shrink them.

7. **Emotional Reasoning.** You reason from your feelings: "I *feel* like an idiot, so I must really *be* one."

8. **Should Statements.** You use shoulds, shouldn'ts, musts, oughts, and have tos.

9. **Labeling.** Instead of saying "I made a mistake," you say, "I'm a jerk," or "I'm a loser."

10. **Blame.** You find fault instead of solving the problem.
    - **Self-Blame.** You blame yourself for something you weren't entirely responsible for.
    - **Other-Blame.** You blame others and overlook ways you contributed to the problem.

When you learn how to change the way you were thinking and feeling at that moment, you'll understand the solution to all your problems.

Marsha's Daily Mood Log appears on page 81. As you can see, Marsha described the upsetting event simply as "Worrying about Leslie during the workshop." I asked Marsha to identify and rate her negative feelings. The Daily Mood Log lists ten categories of emotions. The first category is "Sad, blue, depressed, down, unhappy." Marsha circled the word "sad," and estimated this feeling at 100% in the "% Before" column, because she was feeling profound sadness. She also circled anxious, guilty, ashamed, inadequate, incompetent, lonely, embarrassed, discouraged, stuck, irritated, and overwhelmed. The strongest feelings were "stuck" and "overwhelmed," which she estimated at 200%. These feelings were off the charts!

Next, Marsha recorded these three thoughts in the Negative Thoughts column:

1. I *shouldn't* be so silly and stupid and worry so much about Leslie.
2. I *should* be able to let go. After all, I'm a psychologist, so I shouldn't be so neurotic.
3. I may screw up and lose Leslie's respect because I'm so overcontrolling.

As you can see on page 81, the ratings in the "% Before" column indicate that Marsha believed the first two negative thoughts 100% and the third one 50%. Marsha really has two problems. First she worries, and then she beats up on herself because of the worrying.

We know that Marsha is motivated because she courageously volunteered for a demonstration in front of her colleagues. But things aren't always as obvious as they might at first appear. Could she have mixed feelings about letting go of her relentless worrying and self-criticisms? Can you think of any reasons why Marsha might resist change? Put your ideas here. Even if you're drawing a complete blank, just take a guess.

_____

_____

_____

_____

Marsha's Daily Mood Log

Upsetting Event: Worrying about Leslie during the workshop.

Emotions	% Before	% After	Emotions	% Before	% After
Sad, blue, depressed, down, unhappy	100%		Embarrassed, foolish, humiliated, self-conscious	60%	
Anxious, worried, panicky, nervous, frightened	100%		Hopeless, discouraged, pessimistic, despairing	90%	
Guilty, remorseful, bad, ashamed	90%		Frustrated, stuck, thwarted, defeated	200%	
Inferior, worthless, inadequate, defective, incompetent	75%		Angry, mad, resentful, annoyed, irritated, upset, furious	25%	
Lonely, unloved, unwanted, rejected, alone, abandoned	90%		Other (describe) overwhelmed	200%	

Negative Thoughts	% Before	% After	Distortions	Positive Thoughts	% Belief
1. I *shouldn't* be so silly and stupid and worry so much about Leslie.	100%			1.	
2. I *should* be able to let go. After all, I'm a psychologist, so I shouldn't be so neurotic.	100%			2.	
3. I may screw up and lose Leslie's respect because I'm so overcontrolling.	50%			3.	
4. It would be so hard to lose another child.	100%			4.	
5. I was responsible for Elisa's death. I was selfish and let her down.	100%			5.	
6. I better not screw up again!	100%			6.	

Answer

Marsha might resist letting go of her anxiety and self-criticisms because:

- She may feel like worrying is central to her role as a loving mother. She may feel like she's protecting Leslie.
- She may have the superstitious belief that something terrible will happen if she stops worrying.
- She may think that all the guilt and self-criticism will help her overcome the problem.
- She may think that her negative thoughts are absolutely true.
- The constant worrying may keep her from facing some other problem she's been ignoring, such as loneliness or a problem in her marriage.

Of course, this is all speculation, and we won't know for sure until we ask Marsha. I said, "Marsha, if I could show you how to overcome your anxiety *today*, so that you'd stop worrying about Leslie completely, would you do it?"

Marsha said she would definitely do it if I could show her how. I wanted to make absolutely sure, so I asked the question slightly differently. "But wouldn't that be dangerous? After all, if Leslie *does* forget to take her medicine or drink plenty of fluids, you'll be there to remind her. But if you stop worrying, you might not make that call. Furthermore, all the worrying shows what a concerned, loving mother you are."

Marsha said she could see what I was driving at, but pointed out that Leslie was very responsible and didn't need the constant reminders. Then she became quiet and hung her head. In a soft voice, she said, "But it would be so hard to lose another child." On the verge of tears, Marsha explained that she had another daughter, Elisa, who was born with hydrocephalus, a swelling of the brain that results from a blockage of the cerebral ventricles. Shortly after Elisa was born, a neurosurgeon had to place a shunt in her brain to bypass the blockage and prevent fatal brain swelling.

Despite this problem, Elisa developed normally and was bright and well adjusted. She studied hard in high school and enrolled at Cornell University as a premedical student. On parents' day, Marsha drove to Ithaca from her home in Manhattan to visit Elisa. Elisa was thrilled to see her mother but complained of headaches and nausea. Marsha asked if she'd cleaned the shunt recently, since any blockage could cause these symptoms.

Elisa reassured Marsha that the shunt was fine. Marsha was exhausted from the long drive, but asked Elisa if she wanted to go out to dinner. When Elisa said she had to study for an important test the next day, Marsha was relieved because she was looking forward to unwinding at the hotel.

Marsha became quiet again. I could see tears welling up in her eyes, but she was holding back. It was so quiet that you could hear a pin drop in the room. Then she blurted out, "Elisa died that night!" and began to sob uncontrollably.

After she wept for a little while, I asked Marsha if she'd had any trouble grieving Elisa's death. She nodded. I asked if she felt guilty about Elisa's death. She nodded again and said that she felt she'd been selfish and that if she'd simply stayed with Elisa a little longer, she could have saved her life. She said she felt like she'd let her daughter down and wanted to make sure she didn't make the same mistake again.

I asked Marsha to add these additional negative thoughts to her Daily Mood Log. As you can see on page 81, she believed them all 100%.

I asked Marsha what thought she wanted to work on first. She selected the fifth thought, "I was responsible for Elisa's death. I was selfish and let her down." On the following chart, use checks to indicate which distortions are present in this thought. Refer to the definitions of the cognitive distortions on page 79 when you do this exercise. Identifying the distortions in a negative thought is more of an art than a science, so you don't need to worry about getting it exactly right.

Distortion	(✓)	Distortion	(✓)
1. All-or-Nothing Thinking		6. Magnification or Minimization	
2. Overgeneralization		7. Emotional Reasoning	
3. Mental Filter		8. Should Statements	
4. Discounting the Positive		9. Labeling	
5. Jumping to Conclusions • Mind-Reading • Fortune-Telling		10. Blame • Self-Blame • Other-Blame	

Answer

I think you could make a good case for all ten distortions.

Distortion	(✓)	Explanation
1. All-or-Nothing Thinking	✓	Marsha is telling herself that Elisa's death was all her fault, but a host of factors contributed to it.
2. Overgeneralization	✓	Marsha is overgeneralizing from her behavior that night to her entire sense of identity. She was exhausted and wanted to rest the night that Elisa died, so she concludes that she's a selfish human being.
3. Mental Filter	✓	She ruminates about the "error" she made and thinks about all the ways she failed Elisa.
4. Discounting the Positive	✓	Marsha discounts all the sacrifices she's made for both of her daughters over the years.
5. Jumping to Conclusions • Mind-Reading • Fortune-Telling	✓	Marsha thinks she should have been able to predict what was going to happen and save her daughter's life (Fortune-Telling). Of course, if she'd known that Elisa was in danger, she would have intervened. Marsha is also saying that she let Elisa down (Mind-Reading), but there's no reason to suspect that Elisa ever felt like her mother let her down.
6. Magnification or Minimization	✓	Marsha magnifies her own importance and minimizes the fact that Elisa was extremely responsible and self-reliant.
7. Emotional Reasoning	✓	Marsha *feels* guilty, so she assumes that she *is* guilty.
8. Should Statements	✓	Marsha is telling herself that she *should* have done something different that night.
9. Labeling	✓	She labels herself as "selfish."
10. Blame • Self-Blame • Other-Blame	✓	Marsha blames herself for Elisa's death.

On page 85, you can see how Marsha listed the distortions in all the negative thoughts on her Daily Mood Log. She used abbreviations like MF for Mental Filter and DP for Discounting the Positive.

What do you gain from identifying the distortions in your negative thoughts? First, you'll see that the negative thoughts aren't nearly as realistic as you thought. Remember, Marsha believed most of her negative thoughts 100%. But how realistic can a thought be when it contains so many distortions? Second, the distortions will give you some guidance about how to put the lie to the

Marsha's Daily Mood Log

Upsetting Event: Worrying about Leslie during the workshop.

Emotions	% Before	% After
(Sad) blue, depressed, down, unhappy	100%	
(Anxious) worried, panicky, nervous, frightened	100%	
(Guilty) remorseful, bad, (ashamed)	90%	
Inferior, worthless, inadequate, defective, (incompetent)	75%	
(Lonely) unwanted, rejected, alone, abandoned	90%	

Emotions	% Before	% After
(Embarrassed) foolish, humiliated, self-conscious	60%	
Hopeless (discouraged) pessimistic, despairing	90%	
Frustrated, (stuck) thwarted, defeated	200%	
Angry, mad, resentful, annoyed, (irritated) upset, furious	25%	
Other (describe) (overwhelmed)	200%	

Negative Thoughts	% Before	% After	Distortions
1. I *shouldn't* be so silly and stupid and worry so much about Leslie.	100%		MF, DP, ER, SH, LAB, SB
2. I *should* be able to let go. After all, I'm a psychologist, so I shouldn't be so neurotic.	100%		SH, LAB, SB
3. I may screw up and lose Leslie's respect because I'm so overcontrolling.	50%		MR, FT, SH, LAB
4. It would be so hard to lose another child.	100%		FT
5. I was responsible for Elisa's death. I was selfish and let her down.	100%		AON, OG, MF, DP, MR, FT, MAG/MIN, ER, SH, LAB, SB
6. I better not screw up again!	100%		FT, ER, SH, LAB, SB

Positive Thoughts	% Belief
1.	
2.	
3.	
4.	
5.	
6.	

thought. I'm going to show you how to use many techniques that will help you put an end to feelings of anxiety, panic, and depression. Once you've identified the distortions in a thought, you can make some educated guesses about which techniques to try first.

Because Marsha's fifth negative thought clearly involved Self-Blame, I decided to try the Double-Standard Technique first. This technique capitalizes on the fact that many of us operate on a double standard. When we're upset, we rip ourselves to shreds. But if we were talking to a dear friend with the exact same problem, we'd be far more objective and compassionate. I asked Marsha what she'd say to a friend whose daughter had died under similar circumstances. Would she say, "You were responsible for your daughter's death. You were selfish and you let her down"?

Marsha seemed shocked and said she'd *never* talk to a dear friend like that. I asked what she'd say instead. Marsha replied: "I'd tell her that she's not God, and she can't be there to help her children at every moment. I'd remind her that if she'd known her daughter needed help that night, she would have been there for her, just as she'd been so many times in the past. I'd also remind her that she'd always been a very kind and giving individual and a very devoted mother, and that it wasn't very realistic to label herself as selfish."

I asked Marsha if she was just being nice to her friend or speaking the truth. She said her statement was absolutely true. I asked her to write it down in the Positive Thoughts column of her Daily Mood Log, directly across from the fifth negative thought. You can see on page 87 that she wrote, "If I'd known Elisa needed my help that night, I would have been there for her, just as any loving mother would have been." I asked Marsha to rate how much she believed this thought. She put 100% in the "% Belief" column because the positive thought seemed absolutely true to her.

I pointed out that the positive thought seemed to contradict the negative thought. On the one hand, she's telling herself that she was selfish and that she was responsible for Elisa's death. But on the other hand, she knows that she would have done anything to save her daughter's life. You can't believe opposite things at the same time, so she'd have to give up her belief in either the negative thought or the positive thought.

Marsha said the negative thought no longer seemed realistic. I asked her

Marsha's Daily Mood Log

Upsetting Event: Worrying about Leslie during the workshop.

Emotions	% Before	% After		Emotions	% Before	% After
Sad, blue, depressed, down, unhappy	100%	15%		Embarrassed, foolish, humiliated, self-conscious	60%	0%
Anxious, worried, panicky, nervous, frightened	100%	5%		Hopeless, discouraged, pessimistic, despairing	90%	0%
Guilty, remorseful, bad, ashamed	90%	5%		Frustrated, stuck, thwarted, defeated	200%	0%
Inferior, worthless, inadequate, defective, incompetent	75%	0%		Angry, mad, resentful, annoyed, irritated, upset, furious	25%	0%
Lonely, unloved, unwanted, rejected, alone, abandoned	90%	0%		Other (describe) overwhelmed	200%	0%

Negative Thoughts	% Before	% After	Distortions
1. I *shouldn't* be so silly and stupid and worry so much about Leslie.	100%	10%	MF, DP, ER, SH, LAB, SB
2. I *should* be able to let go. After all, I'm a psychologist, so I shouldn't be so neurotic.	100%	10%	SH, LAB, SB
3. I may screw up and lose Leslie's respect because I'm so overcontrolling.	50%	5%	MR, FT, SH, LAB
4. It would be so hard to lose another child.	100%	0%	FT
5. I was responsible for Elisa's death. I was selfish and let her down.	100%	5%	AON, OG, MF, DP, MR, FT, MAG/MIN, ER, SH, LAB, SB
6. I better not screw up again!	100%	0%	FT, ER, SH, LAB, SB

Positive Thoughts	% Belief
1. My constant worrying probably isn't necessary, but it's not silly or stupid. It's a sign of love and concern.	100%
2. Even psychologists are permitted to have feelings.	100%
3. It would be desirable to stop worrying and calling Leslie so often, but I'm not going to lose her respect if I show compassion and concern for her.	100%
4. This seems extremely unlikely. Leslie is doing fine.	100%
5. If I'd known Elisa needed my help that night, I would have been there for her, just as any loving mother would have been.	100%
6. This is awfully harsh and makes me feel like I'm walking on eggshells all the time. I didn't "screw up" in the first place.	100%

to indicate how strongly she now believed it, from 0% to 100%. You can see that she crossed out the 100% in the "% Before" column and put 5% in the "% After" column, indicating that she no longer believed the fifth negative thought.

If a positive thought is going to change the way you feel at the gut level, it has to fulfill two conditions:

- **The Necessary Condition.** The positive thought must be 100% true or nearly 100% true, or it won't help. Rationalizations and half-truths won't change the way you think and feel.
- **The Sufficient Condition.** The positive thought has to put the lie to the negative thought. Remember, when you change the way you *think,* you can change the way you *feel.*

Marsha's positive thought was absolutely valid. It also put the lie to her negative thought, and she no longer believed that her selfishness had caused Elisa's death. This means that the positive thought fulfilled the necessary and sufficient conditions for emotional change. In fact, Marsha experienced a sudden wave of relief and no longer felt guilty and ashamed about her daughter's death. I asked if she thought the guilt she felt about Elisa's death and her constant worrying about Leslie were related. In other words, was she constantly worrying about Leslie so she could make absolutely sure that she didn't lose a second daughter in the same way?

Although this motive might seem obvious to you, it came as a complete surprise to Marsha. Even though she was a psychologist, she'd never thought about this possibility. We sometimes have great insight into other people's problems but a blind spot when it comes to our own.

This insight cast her worrying in a different light. Instead of viewing it as a compulsive neurosis that she should get over, she saw it as an expression of love for both of her daughters. I also asked whether all the guilt and shame might have been the stumbling block that had prevented her from grieving Elisa's death and letting go. Marsha nodded and began to weep again.

Unresolved feelings, such as anger or guilt, sometimes interfere with the grieving process. These feelings make it difficult to say good-bye to the person who died, so the death becomes frozen in time. But now that Marsha was no longer feeling guilty, she could finally experience the profound feelings of sadness and loss that had been bottled up for so many years.

After she cried, Marsha felt a dramatic uplift in her mood. At this point, I asked if she could challenge the other thoughts on her Daily Mood Log. As you can see on page 87, she came up with convincing positive thoughts that seemed to contradict all the negative thoughts that had been plaguing her. The numbers in the "% Belief" column were all 100%. As you can see in the "% After" column, her belief in the negative thoughts went down substantially, indicating that the positive thoughts fulfilled the necessary and sufficient conditions for emotional change.

To find out if she was feeling better, I asked Marsha to reevaluate her negative emotions on a scale from 0% (not at all) to 100% (extreme). As you can see in the "% After" column in the Emotions section, all her negative feelings improved dramatically. She still felt some sadness and a touch of anxiety and guilt, but this was perfectly normal. After all, she'd just been thinking about the death of her daughter.

I asked Marsha if she'd ever discussed her feelings about Elisa's death with Leslie. This had never occurred to her, and she decided to have the discussion that very evening, immediately after the workshop.

It only took forty-five minutes for Marsha to put an end to years of worrying and guilt. I don't mean to imply that everyone will experience relief in forty-five minutes! But I'm convinced that every person who suffers from anxiety or depression can be helped just as much as Marsha was.

There were several keys to her recovery. First, Marsha focused on one specific moment when she was feeling anxious. Second, she pinpointed exactly how she was feeling and recorded the negative thoughts that were causing all the worrying, guilt, and shame on the Daily Mood Log. That allowed both of us to see exactly what she was telling herself. We're all different, and we all think about things differently. One of the great things about the Daily Mood Log is that it reflects your unique thoughts and feelings.

Third, we uncovered the hidden emotions that were fueling Marsha's fears about Leslie. At first, she didn't realize that she was worrying about Leslie because of all the guilt and shame she still felt about Elisa's death. She'd never been able to come to terms with the loss because the feelings of guilt and shame had blocked her grieving.

Fourth, Marsha was willing to take a chance and confront the devil she'd been avoiding. She'd been afraid of the memories and feelings because they were so painful to her. But when she brought them out into the light and tackled them head-on, recovery was only moments away.

Finally, when she put the lie to her negative thoughts, she forgave herself and allowed herself to grieve. At that moment, she experienced profound relief and recovered. When you experience enlightenment at one moment of your life, there will nearly always be a dramatic shift in all of your perceptions about yourself and the world.

The Daily Mood Log may seem simple, but it's a very sophisticated tool for changing how you think and feel. It will be the cornerstone of your treatment, as well.

Next I'll review the five steps and highlight the most common mistakes that people make at each step. Why not get started on your own Daily Mood Log now? You can use the blank one on pages 78 and 79 while you review these steps. Remember to do it on paper. Trying to do it in your head simply won't work because your negative thoughts will chase each other around in endless circles. Don't worry about writing in your book. You'll find another copy of the Daily Mood Log on pages 420 and 421. Feel free to make copies for your personal use.

Step 1. Upsetting Event

At the top of the Daily Mood Log, write a brief description of one moment when you were feeling upset. Make sure the problem you describe is specific as to person, place, and time. It can be any moment when you felt down, worried, or panicky. Good questions to ask yourself include:

- What time of day was it?
- Where was I?
- What was going on?

Remember that all your problems will be embedded in any single moment when you were suffering. When we pinpointed the negative thoughts and feelings that Marsha was having during the workshop, we understood the cause of all of her worrying. And when she changed the way she was thinking and feeling at that moment, she experienced a profound change that affected her entire life.

One of the most common errors people make at Step 1 is trying to work out their problems in their head. As I've said, this won't work. You'll just go around in circles because your negative thoughts and feelings will seem so overwhelming and convincing. Your task will be far easier if you record your negative thoughts and feelings on paper. Then you can focus on them one at a time.

This advice might seem like common sense, but many people ignore it. They'd rather just talk about the problems in their lives. Of course, we all need a listening ear when we feel upset. But if you want to change your life, sooner or later you'll have to focus on one specific moment when you were upset. The key to all of your suffering will be embedded in that single moment.

This is quite different from traditional therapy, where you talk on and on in a general way to a therapist who listens attentively and occasionally nods and says, "Tell me more." The idea with traditional therapy is that if you talk about your feelings and explore your past for long enough, eventually some type of profound change will occur. This model of therapy is portrayed in virtually every movie and television show about therapy, such as *Good Will Hunting* and *Ordinary People*. I loved those movies, and they certainly make the traditional model of therapy look inspiring. But in my experience, unstructured talk therapy has a tendency to drag on endlessly, and nothing ever really changes. If you have a friend or family member who's been in psychotherapy for years and years, you probably know what I'm talking about.

If you've been suffering from feelings of anxiety, insecurity, or depression, I want you to be able to wake up in the morning and say, "It's great to be alive." To achieve that goal, you'll have to pick up the Daily Mood Log, roll up your sleeves, and get to work.

Step 2. Emotions

After you've described the upsetting event, circle all of the words that describe how you feel, and rate each feeling on a scale from 0% (not at all) to 100% (extreme). Put your ratings in the "% Before" column. When you complete the Daily Mood Log, you can rate your feelings again in the "% After" column, the way Marsha did on page 87.

It's important to identify and rate your negative emotions because specific kinds of feelings result from certain kinds of negative thoughts. Doing this will make it easier to identify your negative thoughts in Step 3. From the Daily Mood Log, the emotions are:

- **Anxiety, nervousness, or worry.** You tell yourself that you're in danger and that something terrible is about to happen.
- **Panic.** You tell yourself that you're about to die, suffocate, pass out, lose control, or go crazy.
- **Embarrassment.** You tell yourself that you looked like an idiot in front of other people.
- **Shyness.** You tell yourself that other people will see how nervous and insecure you feel and look down on you.
- **Loneliness.** You tell yourself that you're unlovable and doomed to be alone forever.
- **Depression.** You tell yourself that you're a failure or that you've lost something important to your sense of self-esteem.
- **Hopelessness.** You tell yourself that your problems will never be solved and that your suffering will go on forever.
- **Guilt.** You tell yourself that you're a bad person or that you've violated your own value system.
- **Shame.** You tell yourself that other people will see how bad, defective, or flawed you are and look down on you.
- **Inferiority.** You tell yourself that you're not as good as other people or not as good as you should be.
- **Frustration.** You tell yourself that other people or events should be the way you expect them to be.

- **Anger.** You tell yourself that other people are self-centered jerks who are treating you unfairly or intentionally taking advantage of you.
- **Feeling Trapped.** You tell yourself that you have to give in to the demands of your spouse, lover, friends, or family.

Step 3. Negative Thoughts

Record the negative thoughts that flow across your mind when you feel upset. Ask yourself questions like this: "When I'm feeling hopeless and discouraged, what am I telling myself? When I'm feeling panicky, what messages am I giving myself?"

List them in the Negative Thoughts column of your Daily Mood Log and rate how strongly you believe each thought, from 0% (not at all) to 100% (completely). Put your ratings in the "% Before" column. Here are some tips to keep in mind at the Negative Thoughts step.

- Use complete sentences. Don't put "go crazy" in the Negative Thoughts column, because it doesn't mean anything. Instead you could write, "I'm on the verge of going crazy."
- Keep each negative thought reasonably short. One sentence is usually enough. It's difficult to work with long, rambling thoughts.
- Try to avoid rhetorical questions like "Why am I so anxious all the time?" or "What's wrong with me?" That's because you can't put the lie to a question. However, you can easily transform a rhetorical question into a negative thought like "I shouldn't be so anxious all the time," or "There must be something wrong with me."
- Don't put descriptions of your feelings in the Negative Thoughts column. Avoid statements like "I'm worried about my exam" or "I feel panicky right now." Record your feelings in the Emotions section of the Daily Mood Log. If you describe your feelings in the Negative Thoughts column, you'll get frustrated because you can't disprove a feeling. However, you can put the lie to the distorted thoughts that cause the negative feeling.
- Make sure the negative thought does not involve the description of an event. For example, "Trisha rejected me and I feel miserable" does not

belong in the Negative Thoughts column because it's the description of an event (Trisha rejected me) and a feeling (miserable). Record the event at the top of the Daily Mood Log, and list your emotions (lonely, hurt, angry, inferior, rejected, discouraged, and miserable) directly underneath. In the Negative Thoughts column, you can record the thoughts that cause these feelings, such as:

1. "It's all my fault." 100%
2. "No woman will ever love me." 100%
3. "I'll be alone forever." 100%

Step 4. Distortions

Record the distortions in each negative thought in the Distortions column. As you can see on page 79, the box at the bottom of the Daily Mood Log lists the definitions of all ten distortions, so you can just review the list after you've recorded your negative thoughts. Usually you'll find many distortions in each thought.

Remember that when you list the distortions on your Daily Mood Log, you can use abbreviations to save time. For example, you can use MAG for Magnification, LAB for Labeling, SH for Should Statements, and SB for Self-Blame.

Step 5. Positive Thoughts

Generate more positive and realistic thoughts that will put the lie to your negative thoughts. Ask yourself, "Can I think about this problem in a more positive and realistic way?" Remember the necessary and sufficient conditions for emotional change:

- **The Necessary Condition.** The positive thought must be 100% true.
- **The Sufficient Condition.** The positive thought must put the lie to the negative thought.

Step 5 will be difficult. If it were easy to put the lie to your negative thoughts, you wouldn't need this book in the first place! Make sure that you indicate how strongly you believe each positive thought in the "% Belief" column and then re-rate your belief in the corresponding negative thought.

If you're like the many people I've worked with over the years, your initial efforts won't be very effective for one of two reasons. Either the positive thoughts won't be 100% true, so they'll fail to fulfill the necessary condition for emotional change, or they won't put the lie to the negative thoughts, so they'll fail to fulfill the sufficient condition for emotional change. Don't worry about that! That's exactly the way it's supposed to be right now. I'm going to show you how to use an array of powerful techniques that will help you put the lie to the negative thoughts that make you feel anxious, worried, panicky, inadequate, or depressed. I'll also show you how to select the techniques that are the most likely to work for you, now and for the rest of your life.

PART II

The
Cognitive Model

Chapter 7

Uncovering Your Self-Defeating Beliefs

Cognitive Behavior Therapy is based on the idea that depression, anxiety, and anger result from distorted negative thoughts in the here and now. This theory explains why we feel the way we do, but it doesn't address several important questions:

- Why are some people so vulnerable to painful mood swings, while others seem to be naturally happy and confident all the time?
- Why are different people vulnerable to different kinds of problems? For example, some of us fall apart whenever we're criticized, while others fly into a rage whenever someone cuts them off in traffic.
- What explains the timing of episodes of depression, anxiety, or anger, and what triggers these problems in the first place?

This is where Self-Defeating Beliefs (SDBs) come in. Your attitudes and personal values explain your psychological vulnerabilities. Once you've pinpointed your SDBs, you'll know exactly why you get upset and when you're likely to get upset in the future.

There are two basic types of SDBs: Individual SDBs and Interpersonal SDBs. Individual SDBs are usually self-esteem equations that tell you what you need to be or do in order to be a worthwhile human being. The basic formula is "I need X in order to feel happy and fulfilled." X could be perfection, achievement, love, or approval. Here are some examples of Individual Self-Defeating Beliefs:

- **Perfectionism.** You believe you should always try to be perfect. Whenever you fail or fall short of a goal, you beat up on yourself relentlessly and tell yourself that you're not as good as you should be.
- **Perceived Perfectionism.** You think you have to impress everyone with your talent or accomplishments to get them to like and accept you. You believe that your friends and colleagues won't respect you if they discover that you're flawed or vulnerable.
- **Achievement Addiction.** You base your self-esteem on your intelligence, talent, accomplishments, or productivity.
- **Approval Addiction.** You think you need everyone's approval in order to be worthwhile. You get defensive and feel threatened whenever anyone criticizes you or disapproves of you.

Interpersonal Self-Defeating Beliefs lead to conflicts with other people. Usually they're expectations about what happens in close, intimate relationships. They shape our understanding of what we have to do to be loved and respected and how other people will treat us. Here are a few examples.

- **Blame.** You believe that you're innocent and the person you're not getting along with is to blame for the problems in your relationship.
- **Truth.** You feel convinced that you're right and the other person is wrong.
- **Entitlement.** You believe that people should think, feel, and behave the way you expect them to. When they don't, you get angry and frustrated.
- **Love Addiction.** You believe that the only true happiness comes from being loved by someone you care about. You think you'll be doomed to feelings of emptiness and worthlessness if you're ever rejected or alone.

- **Submissiveness.** You believe that you have to meet everyone else's needs and expectations, even if you make yourself miserable in the process. Love becomes a form of slavery because you feel that you always have to give, give, give in order to be loved.

- **Perceived Narcissism.** You believe that the people who care about you will be self-centered, exploitative, and fragile. You feel that you can never be open and spontaneous or tell them how you really feel inside because they'll fly off the handle and reject you.

- **Conflict Phobia.** You believe that anger, conflict, and disagreements with other people are dangerous and should be avoided at all costs.

Many people don't understand the difference between a negative thought and an SDB. It's actually pretty simple. Your SDBs are *always* present, but negative thoughts surface only when you're upset.

For example, let's say you have an Achievement Addiction. This means that you base your self-esteem on your productivity, status, intelligence, or accomplishments. As long as things are going well in your studies or career, you'll feel reasonably happy and contented. But you'll be vulnerable to painful mood swings whenever you fail or fall short of your goals. At that point, your mind will be flooded with negative thoughts such as "I'm such a loser. Why did I screw up like that? I shouldn't have made that mistake!"

Your vulnerabilities may be different. For example, if you have a Love Addiction, you'll feel reasonably happy and fulfilled as long as you're involved in a loving relationship with someone you care about. But if you feel alone, rejected, or unloved, you may fall into a severe depression because you'll feel worthless.

Identifying your Self-Defeating Beliefs is more than just an exercise in self-awareness. When you modify these beliefs, you'll be far less vulnerable to painful mood swings in the future. You'll enjoy greater creativity, productivity, joy, and intimacy.

You can pinpoint your own SDBs with the Downward Arrow Technique. Select a negative thought from your Daily Mood Log and draw a downward arrow underneath it. The arrow is a form of shorthand for questions like these:

"If this thought were true, why would it be upsetting to me? What would it mean to me?"

When you ask yourself these questions, a new negative thought will pop into your mind. Write it down directly under the arrow, and draw another arrow underneath it. Ask yourself the same kinds of questions again. If you repeat this process several times, you'll generate a chain of negative thoughts. When you review these thoughts, you can easily pinpoint your Self-Defeating Beliefs.

I'll show you how it works. A young man named Rasheed was studying to be a pilot and was anxious about his upcoming Federal Aviation Administration (FAA) examination. Even though Rasheed was at the top of his class, he constantly felt nervous and tense because he was asking himself, "What if I flunk the test?"

You may recall from Chapter 6 that it's a good idea to convert a rhetorical What-If question into a statement when you put it in the Negative Thoughts column of your Daily Mood Log. Then you can challenge the thought more easily. You can see how Rasheed put "I might flunk the test" on his Daily Mood Log on page 103.

I asked Rasheed to put a downward arrow directly underneath this thought and said, "Rasheed, we know you're a top student, so you'll probably do very well on the test. But let's assume the opposite. Let's imagine that you really *did* flunk the FAA test six months from now. What would that mean to you? Why would it be upsetting?"

He said, "Then I'll look bad in front of my buddies."

I told him to write this down under the arrow and put another arrow underneath it. Then I asked, "And then what? Let's suppose that you flunk the test and look bad in front of your buddies. What would that mean to you? Why would that be upsetting to you?"

He said, "Then they'll lose respect for me." I told him to write that down and put another arrow underneath it. We repeated this process several more times and eventually ended up with the thought, "That would mean I was worthless."

You're generally done with the Downward Arrow Technique when you come up with a thought like this:

Rasheed's Daily Mood Log

Upsetting Situation or Event: Thinking about my FAA test in six months.

Emotions	% Before	% After	Emotions	% Before	% After
Sad, blue, depressed, down, unhappy	50%		Embarrassed, foolish, humiliated, self-conscious	0%	
Anxious, worried, panicky, nervous, frightened	85%		Hopeless, discouraged, pessimistic, despairing	80%	
Guilty, remorseful, bad, ashamed	25%		Frustrated, stuck, thwarted, defeated	50%	
Inferior, worthless, inadequate, defective, incompetent	90%		Angry, mad, resentful, annoyed, irritated, upset, furious	0%	
Lonely, unloved, unwanted, rejected, alone, abandoned	80%		Other (describe)		

Negative Thoughts	% Before	% After	Distortions	Positive Thoughts	% Belief
1. I might flunk the test.	100%			1.	
2.				2.	
3.				3.	
4.				4.	
5.				5.	
6.				6.	
7.				7.	
8.				8.	

Rasheed's Downward Arrow Technique

Negative Thoughts	% Before	% After	Distortions	Positive Thoughts	% Belief
1. I might flunk the test.	100%			1.	
2. Then I'll look bad in front of my buddies.	100%			2.	
3. Then they'll lose respect for me.	100%			3.	
4. That would mean I'd wasted all my time and money.	100%			4.	
5. Then everything I've lived and worked for will go down the drain.	100%			5.	
6. That would mean I was a failure.	100%			6.	
7. That would mean I was worthless.	100%			7.	

- That would mean I was worthless.
- That would mean life was not worth living.
- Then I could never feel happy again.

You can see the entire chain of negative thoughts that Rasheed and I generated on page 104. Review these thoughts and see if you can identify a few of Rasheed's Self-Defeating Beliefs. The list of twenty-three Common Self-Defeating Beliefs on page 106 will help you. List several of Rasheed's SDBs here before you continue reading.

1. _____

2. _____

3. _____

4. _____

Answer

Here are the SDBs Rasheed and I came up with:

- Perfectionism
- Perceived Perfectionism
- Approval Addiction
- Achievement Addiction
- Spotlight Fallacy
- Brushfire Fallacy

These beliefs are extremely common in people who suffer from performance anxiety. Rasheed's worrying did not result from the fact that he had to take the test but from the way he was thinking about it. He seems to base his self-esteem on his achievements and on getting everyone's approval. He's very perfectionistic and assumes that his classmates will be just as judgmental and critical as he is. He feels as if he's performing under a bright spotlight, having to impress his friends to get them to like him. He also thinks they're like clones who will react in exactly the same way, so if one of them looks down on him, they all will. Of course, these attitudes put him under tremendous pressure.

Although SDBs always contain a grain of truth, they tend to be pretty mis-

Common Self-Defeating Beliefs (SDBs)

Achievement	Depression
1. **Performance Perfectionism.** I must never fail or make a mistake. 2. **Perceived Perfectionism.** People won't love or accept me if I'm flawed or vulnerable. 3. **Achievement Addiction.** My worth as a human being depends on my achievements, intelligence, talent, status, income, or looks.	13. **Hopelessness.** My problems could never be solved. I could never feel truly happy or fulfilled. 14. **Worthlessness/Inferiority.** I'm basically worthless, defective, and inferior to others.
Love	**Anxiety**
4. **Approval Addiction.** I need everyone's approval to be worthwhile. 5. **Love Addiction.** I can't feel happy and fulfilled without being loved. If I'm not loved, then life is not worth living. 6. **Fear of Rejection.** If you reject me, it proves that there's something wrong with me. If I'm alone, I'm bound to feel miserable and worthless.	15. **Emotional Perfectionism.** I should always feel happy, confident, and in control. 16. **Anger Phobia.** Anger is dangerous and should be avoided at all costs. 17. **Emotophobia.** I should never feel sad, anxious, inadequate, jealous, or vulnerable. I should sweep my feelings under the rug and not upset anyone. 18. **Perceived Narcissism.** The people I care about are demanding, manipulative, and powerful. 19. **Brushfire Fallacy.** People are clones who all think alike. If one person looks down on me, the word will spread like brushfire and soon everyone will. 20. **Spotlight Fallacy.** Talking to people is like having to perform under a bright spotlight. If I don't impress them by being sophisticated, witty, or interesting, they won't like me. 21. **Magical Thinking.** If I worry enough, everything will turn out okay.
Submissiveness	
7. **Pleasing Others.** I should always try to please you, even if I make myself miserable in the process. 8. **Conflict Phobia.** People who love each other should never fight or argue. 9. **Self-Blame.** The problems in my relationships are bound to be my fault.	
Demandingness	**Other**
10. **Other-Blame.** The problems in my relationships are always the other person's fault. 11. **Entitlement.** You should always treat me in the way I expect. 12. **Truth.** I'm right and you're wrong.	22. **Low Frustration Tolerance.** I should never be frustrated. Life should always be easy. 23. **Superman/Superwoman.** I should always be strong and never be weak.

leading. In the first place, Rasheed was at the top of his class, so it wasn't very likely that he would flunk the test. A certain percentage of the students who take the FAA exam do flunk the first time they take it, but they're allowed to take it again, so Rasheed's catastrophic thinking wasn't realistic. It wasn't true that his career would be ruined or that his life would go down the drain if he didn't pass the test on his first try. In addition, Rasheed's classmates are probably far more accepting than he imagines and much more concerned about their own performance than his.

I suggested that he might ask several of his friends if they'd be disappointed in him if he flunked the test and had to take it again. He learned that they were worrying about the test as much as he was and were relieved to discover that he felt the same way, since he always seemed so confident. Ultimately Rasheed passed his test with flying colors on his first try.

The Downward Arrow Technique is easy to learn and can quickly provide you with a wealth of valuable information about your own attitudes and beliefs. Always start with a negative thought on your Daily Mood Log. It doesn't make any difference what thought you choose, so select one that's interesting to you. Draw a downward arrow under it and ask yourself, "If that were true, what would it mean to me? Why would it be upsetting to me?" A new thought will pop into your head, and you can jot it down under the arrow.

If you repeat this process several times, eventually you'll come to the bottom of the barrel. Now review the list of Common SDBs on page 106. Your SDBs usually will be obvious. This exercise will help you understand why you're vulnerable to the kinds of mood problems that have been bothering you. Of course, insight alone will not be enough. In the next chapter, I'll show you how to develop a more rewarding personal value system.

....

Chapter 8

How to Modify a Self-Defeating Belief

How do you change a Self-Defeating Belief (SDB)? There are three steps:

1. **Do a Cost-Benefit Analysis (CBA).** This is always the first step. You won't feel motivated to change the belief until you see that the disadvantages are greater than the advantages.
2. **Revise the Belief.** See if you can come up with a new belief that preserves all the advantages but eliminates the disadvantages.
3. **Test the Belief.** Often you can do an experiment to see if the SDB was realistic or valid in the first place. This is where you transform intellectual understanding into real emotional change at the gut level.

Step 1. The Cost-Benefit Analysis

Let's work through these three steps together. I've listed the belief "I should always try to be perfect" at the top of the CBA on page 109. Can you think of any advantages of this mind-set? Ask yourself, "How will this attitude help me? What are the benefits of thinking this way?" List them in the Advantages column. Then ask yourself how this mind-set will hurt you. What are the disadvantages of trying to be perfect? Is there a downside? What price will you pay for believing this? List the costs of perfectionism in the Disadvantages column.

Perfectionism Cost-Benefit Analysis

Describe the attitude, feeling, or habit that you want to change:
I should always try to be perfect.

Advantages	Disadvantages

Remember to list the advantages and disadvantages of trying to be perfect or basing your self-esteem on being perfect. Don't list the advantages and disadvantages of *being* perfect. There probably aren't any disadvantages of being perfect, but that's not an option!

Complete the CBA now. List all the advantages and disadvantages of trying to be perfect. When you're done, weigh them against each other and put two numbers that add up to 100 in the circles at the bottom. If the advantages are greater than the disadvantages, the number in the left-hand circle will be greater. If the disadvantages are greater, the number in the right-hand circle will be greater. Remember that one strong advantage sometimes outweighs many disadvantages, and vice versa. When you're done, review the completed CBA on page 111.

The man who completed the CBA on page 111 decided that the disadvantages of trying to be perfect outweighed the advantages, so he put a 35 in the circle on the left and a 65 in the circle on the right. However, the results will be different for everyone. If the advantages of a belief are greater, it means that the attitude is working for you, so there's probably no reason to modify it or give it up. If the disadvantages are greater, it means that the belief isn't working very well for you. In this case, you can revise it.

Step 2. Revise the Belief

Once you realize that SDBs always have a healthy and an unhealthy side, the job of modifying them becomes easier. You don't have to feel like your personal values are totally irrational or ridiculous, and you don't have to give up all of your beliefs. Instead, you can do a little mental tune-up, so you can get rid of the downside of any SDB while maintaining what's positive about it.

Let's assume that the disadvantages of trying to be perfect are greater than the advantages. What could you tell yourself instead of "I should always try to be perfect"? Put your ideas here before you continue reading.

_____

_____

_____

_____

_____

Perfectionism Cost-Benefit Analysis

Describe the attitude, feeling, or habit that you want to change:
I should always try to be perfect.

Advantages	Disadvantages
1. I'll work hard.	1. My perfectionism may create lots of stress and worry.
2. When I do great work, I'll feel terrific.	
3. I won't settle for mediocrity and end up with a second-rate career.	2. When I fail or make a mistake, it will feel devastating.
4. My exceptionally high standards will show that I'm a very special and extremely talented person and that I'm a cut above other people. After all, we wouldn't expect someone who's just average to be perfect!	3. My perfectionism may prevent me from being creative and taking risks, since I'll be afraid of failure.
5. My perfectionism gives me an easy way to measure my self-esteem.	4. It will be hard to learn from criticism because I'll feel threatened and defensive. My self-esteem will always be on the line.
6. Other people will admire me because I'm so hardworking and conscientious.	5. I often do my best work when I'm relaxed and not trying so hard.
	6. I may lose sight of the bigger picture because I'll focus too much on all the small details.
	7. I don't get along very well with other people when I get perfectionistic and demanding.
	8. People seem to like me more when I express an interest in them, not when I'm trying to impress them with my own accomplishments.
	9. I may procrastinate because every task will seem overwhelming.
	10. I'll never feel like I've succeeded because I'll never really be perfect at anything. There will always be room for improvement.

35   65

Answer

There are lots of ways to revise any SDB, including perfectionism. Here's one approach:

> There's nothing wrong with trying to do outstanding work, but if I try to be perfect, I'll be setting myself up for lots of stress, worry, and disappointment. When I make a mistake or fall short of a goal, I don't need to feel ashamed or worthless. There's always room for improvement. I can decide to view my mistakes as opportunities for learning and personal growth.

> If you adopted this attitude, you'd lose nothing except for a lot of stress, strain, and self-doubt. You might end up being even more productive and creative because you'd feel more relaxed and your self-esteem wouldn't always be on the line.

Step 3. Put the Belief to the Test

Revising the SDB leads to intellectual change and gives you something to hang your hat on, but, deep down, you still may believe that the SDB is true. For example, even though you realize that your perfectionism makes you depressed and anxious, you may still feel that you should try to be perfect. You may also believe that something terrible will happen if you stop beating up on yourself every time you fall short of your goals. Step 3 leads to change at the gut level. You put the SDB to the test so you can find out if it was ever valid in the first place.

In my *Feeling Good Handbook,* I described a chronically anxious medical school professor named Nate who suffered from low self-esteem and feelings of inadequacy. One day, Nate brought me a copy of his curriculum vitae (CV). I was blown away. He'd listed over sixty pages of research publications, prestigious awards, and keynote addresses he'd given at major conferences around the world. I asked Nate how he reconciled his low self-esteem with all of his accomplishments. He said that every time he looked at his CV, he felt discouraged and told himself that his colleagues' research studies were far more rigorous and important than his own. He said his own papers seemed "soft" and consisted primarily of theoretical work, rather than hard-core laboratory research with real tissue. He said: "Dr. Burns, no matter how much I accomplish, it never seems good enough. I feel like I climb and climb to get to the top of the highest mountain. But once I arrive at the top, instead of feeling a sense of accomplishment, I see an even higher mountain in the distance and my heart sinks because I have to start hiking again. Where's the reward? When's the pay-off ever going to come?"

Perfectionism was clearly one of Nate's SDBs. He told himself, "If I can't do something perfectly, it's not worth doing at all." Although he could see that this attitude was making his life miserable, he was reluctant to let go of it. He thought that without his perfectionism, he'd have to settle for a life of mediocrity.

I suggested that Nate could use the Pleasure/Perfection Balance Sheet to test this belief. As you can see on page 115, I told him to write "If I can't do something perfectly, it's not worth doing at all" at the top of the sheet, and asked him to list several activities with the potential for pleasure, learning, personal growth, or accomplishment in the left-hand column. I encouraged him to include a wide range of activities, not just things related to his work.

I told him to predict how satisfying and rewarding each activity would be, on a scale from 0% (not at all satisfying) to 100% (totally satisfying). I emphasized that he should make these predictions on paper *before* he did each activity. After he completed each activity, he could record how satisfying and rewarding it turned out to be, using the same scale.

I also asked Nate to rate how *perfectly* he did each activity on a scale of 0% (the worst possible rating) to 100% (absolute perfection). That way he could find out:

- If it was true that he only enjoyed the things he did perfectly.
- How his predicted satisfaction levels compared with his actual satisfaction levels.
- Which activities were the most and the least rewarding.

The next week, Nate had some interesting results to share with me. One of his activities was giving the welcoming lecture to the incoming class of medical students. Nate gave this lecture every year because he was considered to be the most charismatic speaker at the medical school.

Nate predicted that the lecture would be 70% satisfying, but his actual sat-isfaction was only 20%. This was surprising, since he'd received a thirty-second standing ovation, and he'd rated his perfection level for the talk at 90%.

I asked Nate why his satisfaction rating was so low. He explained that he always got standing ovations, so he routinely timed them. The previous year, the medical students had stood and cheered for more than a minute at the end of his talk. This year, they only stood and cheered for half a minute. Nate felt disappointed and started worrying that he was over the hill.

I thought, "Give me a break! I give lectures all the time and I've never once gotten a standing ovation. And this guy is complaining because his standing ovation was only thirty seconds long!"

The second entry on Nate's Pleasure/Perfection Balance Sheet was equally intriguing. On Saturday afternoon, he'd discovered that a pipe in his bathroom had broken and flooded the floor. Nate decided to try to fix it himself instead of calling a plumber. His predicted satisfaction level was only 10%, since he wasn't very good at fixing things around the house and had never before tried to do any plumbing.

He had to make several trips to the hardware store to buy tools and parts and to get tips on how to do it, so he didn't get the pipe fixed until 10:00 P.M. He ex-plained that any plumber could have fixed the pipe in five minutes, so he rated his perfection level at 5%. But his satisfaction level for this activity was 100%. In fact, he felt exhilarated. Nate said it was the most satisfying thing he'd done in years.

I said, "Nate, your whole problem is that you chose the wrong profession. You should have been a plumber!"

The result of Nate's experiment was not consistent with his belief that things weren't worth doing unless he did them perfectly. It dawned on him that there were many sources of satisfaction in his life that he'd overlooked, such as taking a walk through the woods with his wife, even though neither of them were world-class hikers, playing squash with his son, even though neither of them were champions, or just going out with his family for ice cream cones on a warm summer evening.

This experiment had a significant impact on Nate's feelings of self-esteem and on his career. He told me that his feelings of anxiety and inferiority de-

Nate's Pleasure/Perfection Balance Sheet

Belief: If I can't do something perfectly, it's not worth doing at all.

Activity	Predicted Satisfaction (0%–100%)	Actual Satisfaction (0%–100%)	Perfection (0%–100%)	Notes
1. Give welcoming lecture to new medical school class	70%	20%	90%	I got my usual standing ovation, but the students only stood and cheered for 30 seconds.
2. Fix broken pipe in bathroom	10%	100%	5%	It took a long time, and I made many mistakes, but I did it!
3. Play squash with Joe	75%	90%	40%	We didn't play especially well, but we had a great time.
4. Jog	50%	85%	50%	It was just an average jog today, but at least I did it.
5. Take family downtown for ice cream	60%	90%	50%	We had a lot of fun together.
6. Prepare draft of paper for research journal	50%	50%	75%	I created a decent outline, but it doesn't seem like a very exciting paper.
7. Take a walk through the woods with Sally on Saturday	50%	100%	25%	We weren't champion hikers, but we had a fabulous time.

© 2003 by David D. Burns, M.D.

creased and that his productivity actually increased because he was no longer so worried about having to do everything so perfectly.

Your SDBs may be very different from Nate's, but the basic process of revising and testing them will be similar. Once you've identified an SDB that seems to be causing problems for you, you can do a CBA. If the disadvantages of the belief are greater than the advantages, try to modify the belief so you can get rid of the disadvantages while maintaining the advantages. Then you can test the belief to see if it was true. The type of experiment you do will depend on the belief you're testing and the types of situations that upset you. In Chapter 1, you saw how an attorney named Jeffrey tested his Perceived Perfectionism by telling ten colleagues that he'd just lost a case in court.

Let's practice the three steps in modifying an SDB. Pick one SDB from the following list that interests you.

- **Love Addiction** (CBA on page 117). I can't feel truly happy or fulfilled without love. If I'm rejected or alone, I'm bound to feel worthless and miserable.
- **Perceived Perfectionism** (CBA on page 119). Other people won't love or respect me if they see that I'm a flawed human being.
- **Entitlement/Blame** (CBA on page 121). People should be the way I expect them to be.

Now complete a CBA for the belief you've chosen, using the CBA form on the page listed in parentheses. Ask yourself how the belief will help you and how it will hurt you. Once you've listed all the advantages and disadvantages you can think of, put two numbers that add up to 100 in the circles at the bottom to indicate which list feels more compelling.

Remember to list the advantages and disadvantages of the *belief*. Let's say that you're working on the Love Addiction. List the advantages and disadvantages of basing your self-esteem and capacity for happiness on being loved. Do *not* list the advantages and disadvantages of *being* loved. There aren't any disadvantages! At least, there aren't any that I can think of.

But if you base your self-esteem on other people's love, there will be lots of positive and negative consequences. On the positive side, you'll feel happy and

Love Addiction Cost-Benefit Analysis

Describe the attitude, feeling, or habit that you want to change: I can't feel truly happy or fulfilled without love. If I'm rejected or alone, I'm bound to feel worthless and miserable.

Advantages	Disadvantages

Love Addiction Cost-Benefit Analysis

Describe the attitude, feeling, or habit that you want to change: I can't feel truly happy or fulfilled without love. If I'm rejected or alone, I'm bound to feel worthless and miserable.

Advantages	Disadvantages
1. When I feel loved, I'll feel great.	1. I'll feel depressed whenever I'm alone.
2. If I believe that true happiness and self-esteem can come only from someone else's love, I won't have to assume responsibility for my own happiness.	2. I may seem needy and push people away.
	3. Rejection will be devastating.
3. Most people agree that you can't feel truly happy or fulfilled without being loved, so my beliefs will be similar to lots of other people's.	4. I'll be overly sensitive to conflicts and disagreements with other people. Instead of listening, I'll get defensive, because I'll feel so threatened. My sense of self-esteem will always be on the line.
4. This belief seems true, so I feel like I'm being honest.	5. If I believe that self-esteem is based on snagging a partner, I may be trying to get someone else to give me something that only I can give myself.
5. I'll be a "people person" and work hard to get other people to like me.	
6. I can blame other people for my unhappiness.	6. Other people will control my moods and self-esteem.
7. I can feel like a victim and pity myself when someone rejects me.	7. I'll always be in a one-down position, having to chase the other person. This will give them too much power over me, and they may lose respect for me.
8. This belief will keep me motivated to date and socialize.	
9. The fantasy of a prince (or princess) who will sweep me off my feet and make all my dreams come true feels romantic and exciting!	

Perceived Perfectionism Cost-Benefit Analysis

Describe the attitude, feeling, or habit that you want to change: Other people won't love or respect me if they see that I'm a flawed human being.

Advantages	Disadvantages

© 2003 by David D. Burns, M.D.

Perceived Perfectionism Cost-Benefit Analysis

Describe the attitude, feeling, or habit that you want to change: Other people won't love or respect me if they see that I'm a flawed human being.

Advantages	Disadvantages
1. I'll work hard to impress people.	1. I'll feel like I have to be perfect to be loved.
2. People like winners, so when I do a good job, people will respect and admire me.	2. I won't be open with other people.
3. I won't have to share my feelings or tell people how I really feel inside.	3. I may get defensive whenever someone criticizes me, because I'll feel like I always have to be right. This may trigger more conflict because the other person will get frustrated and feel like I never listen.
4. I won't have to risk rejection.	
5. I can hide my weaknesses and present a polished image to the world.	4. People won't get to know the real me.
6. I can feel like a victim and secretly resent people for being so judgmental and not accepting me the way I really am.	5. I'll feel anxious whenever I'm around other people.
7. I'll always appear calm and in control.	6. I'll keep people at a distance.
8. I'll feel like I'm being honest and facing the truth about life, because people can be very rejecting when someone screws up.	7. I won't achieve the kind of intimacy that I want.
	8. I may sell people short and make assumptions about them that aren't really true. They may be more accepting than I think.
	9. It takes an awful lot of time and energy trying to be so perfect all the time. It's draining.
	10. People seem to like me better when I'm more spontaneous and not trying so hard.
	11. I may secretly resent the fact that people seem to be so judgmental and demanding.

Entitlement/Blame Cost-Benefit Analysis

Describe the attitude, feeling, or habit that you want to change: People should be
the way I expect them to be.

Advantages	Disadvantages

Entitlement/Blame Cost-Benefit Analysis

Describe the attitude, feeling, or habit that you want to change: People should be the way I expect them to be.

Advantages	Disadvantages
1. I'll feel morally superior.	1. I'll feel angry, frustrated, and stressed out most of the time.
2. I can keep people at a distance. I won't have to get close to them.	2. It will be hard to resolve conflicts and disagreements because I'll always have to be right. This will put the other person on the defensive.
3. I can blame people for the problems in my relationships with them.	
4. I won't have to examine my own role in the problem.	3. My friends may get turned off by my negative attitude and my constant complaints about other people.
5. This belief protects me from feeling vulnerable. I can fly into a rage instead of feeling hurt or disappointed when things don't go my way.	4. I'll be in a sour, cynical mood most of the time.
	5. I won't feel very joyous or creative.
6. I'll feel convinced that I'm right and other people are wrong.	6. Anger can be draining and exhausting.
7. I can have fantasies of revenge and justify aggressive behavior.	7. I'll be frustrated because other people will get stubborn when I start blaming them. They'll insist everything was my fault.
8. Anger is empowering and exciting. It gives me a sense of who I am and what I stand for.	8. I'll have lots of enemies.
9. I can tell my friends what a jerk and a loser the other person is.	9. I may develop health problems like high blood pressure or a heart attack.
10. I'll stick up for myself. I won't let other people push me around.	10. The fact is, the world won't be the way I expect it to be, no matter how angry or demanding I get.

worthwhile if you feel loved. On the negative side, rejection may be devastating, and your neediness may drive people away. I'm sure you can think of even more advantages and disadvantages. Once you're done with your CBA, review the completed CBA for that belief on the page that follows it. I haven't filled in the two numbers in the circles at the bottom, because these evaluations are highly personal and there's no "correct" answer. Once you're done, we'll talk about how to revise any SDB that's causing problems for you.

If you enjoy doing the CBA, you may want to try the others as well. You can learn a lot from them. Sometimes it's surprising to discover how many hidden advantages and disadvantages there can be to a belief.

Let's assume that the disadvantages of the belief are greater than the advantages. You can revise the belief so that the disadvantages disappear. See if you can revise the Love Addiction belief: "I can't feel truly happy or fulfilled without love. If I'm rejected or alone, I'm bound to feel worthless and miserable." Put your revised belief here.

_____

_____

_____

_____

_____

Answer

Here's one way you could revise it:

It's not wise to rely on someone else to make me feel happy or worthwhile, since my world will collapse if they reject me. Furthermore, my neediness may drive people away and sabotage my relationships. It's great to be with someone I love, but the things I do on my own can be extremely rewarding, too.

Here's another approach that might work:

I can want loving relationships without *needing* them. Another person's love could never make me worthwhile, and their rejection could never make me worthless, either. If someone is upset with me, I can try to understand how they're feeling and ask if I did something that irritated them or hurt their feelings. If we talk things over, we may end up feeling a lot closer. If they refuse to talk about the problem and decide to reject me, it will be a disappointment, but it won't be the end of the world, and it certainly doesn't mean that I'm worthless. In fact, it would be more of a reflection on them.

When you revise an SDB, there's a great deal of room for creativity and individuality. If you revise the belief in a thoughtful way, you can have your cake and eat it, too. You won't have to give up anything you value or believe in. You'll develop a more robust and realistic value system that won't cave in on you when the going gets tough.

Once you've revised your belief, you'll want to change it at the gut level. What kind of experiment could you do to test the belief "I can't feel truly happy or fulfilled without love. If I'm rejected or alone, I'm bound to feel worthless and miserable"? Write your ideas here.

_____

_____

_____

_____

_____

_____

Answer

You could schedule activities by yourself and activities with others, and compare how rewarding and satisfying they are. Use the Pleasure-Predicting Sheet on page 125 when you do this experiment. I've listed the belief we're going to test at the top. In the left-hand column, schedule a variety of activities with the potential for pleasure, learning, or personal growth. Make sure you include activities you can do by yourself, such as jogging or straightening up your desk, as well as activities you'll do with other people, such as going to a movie or taking a walk with a friend. In the Companion column, indicate whom you intend to do each activity with. If you plan to do something by yourself, write "self" in

Pleasure-Predicting Sheet

Belief: I can't feel truly happy or fulfilled without love. If I'm rejected or alone, I'm bound to feel worthless and miserable.

Activity Schedule activities with the potential for pleasure, learning, or personal growth.	Companion Use "self" for things you plan to do alone.	Predicted Satisfaction (0%–100%) Record **before** each activity.	Actual Satisfaction (0%–100%) Record **after** each activity.

the column. Don't put the word "alone," because you're really never alone. You're always with yourself.

In the Predicted Satisfaction column, predict how satisfying and rewarding you think each activity will be on a scale from 0% (not at all) to 100% (the most). Make sure you fill out this column *before* you do each activity. After you complete each activity, rate how satisfying it turned out to be in the Actual Satisfaction column, using the same scale.

When you look at the data, you can compare your predicted satisfaction levels with the actual satisfaction you experience. Often you'll discover that many activities turn out to be far more rewarding and satisfying than you anticipated. This discovery can motivate you to do even more. You can also compare the satisfaction you get from activities you do with other people with the satisfaction you get from activities you do on your own. You may discover that some of your happiest moments come when you're alone.

I don't mean to minimize the importance of relationships with other people. However, the Pleasure-Predicting Sheet can show you that your capacity for happiness does not have to depend on other people. This idea can free you from the trap of having to rely on others for your self-esteem and paradoxically can lead to more satisfying relationships with other people.

. . . .

Chapter 9

The What-If Technique

The Downward Arrow Technique helps you pinpoint the Self-Defeating Beliefs that make you vulnerable to anxiety, depression, and problems in your relationships with other people. The What-If Technique helps you uncover a terrifying fantasy that triggers your anxiety. When you confront this fantasy, you can defeat your fears for good.

Kristin was a divorced woman who lived in Philadelphia with her two sons, who were nine and eleven years old. She came from a prominent family and was active in charitable activities. However, she'd suffered from agoraphobia for years and couldn't leave home unless she was with her children or a trusted friend.

I asked Kristin to fill out a Daily Mood Log so I could find out what she was so afraid of. The upsetting event on her Daily Mood Log was simply thinking about walking to the grocery store by herself. She felt depressed, anxious, guilty, ashamed, defective, alone, embarrassed, discouraged, and frustrated. She was telling herself, "Something terrible might happen if I walk to the store alone."

I decided to explore this fear using the What-If Technique. It's similar to the Downward Arrow Technique, but it's geared specifically to anxiety. You draw a downward arrow under a negative thought on your Daily Mood Log and ask yourself questions like this: "What if this were true? What's the worst thing that could happen? What am I the most afraid of?" A new fantasy will pop into your mind. Write it down under the arrow and draw another arrow underneath it. Continue asking yourself the same types of questions: "What if this happened? What am I the most afraid of?" If you repeat this several times, it will lead to the core fantasy that's triggering your fears.

I asked Kristin to draw a downward arrow under her negative thought and said, "Let's say you decided to walk to the grocery store on your own. What's the worst thing that could happen? What are you the most afraid of?"

Kristin said, "I might drop my handkerchief on the sidewalk without noticing that I'd lost it." I asked her to record this thought directly under the arrow and put another arrow underneath it, as you can see on page 129. This is how our dialogue unfolded:

David: Let's suppose this happened. You drop your hanky on the way to the store. What would happen then? What are you the most afraid of?

Kristin: Well, a terrible crime might be committed on the spot where I lost my hanky. Someone might get murdered there.

David: Okay, go ahead and write that down under the arrow, and draw another arrow under it. Now, let's assume that *did* happen. You drop your hanky on the sidewalk and a murder is committed at that very spot. Then what? What are you the most afraid of?

Kristin: The police might find my hanky at the scene of the crime and trace it back to me. They could use DNA sampling, for example.

David: Good. Write that down and put another arrow under it. Now let's assume that the police *did* find your hanky. What then?

Kristin: Well, they might conclude that I was the murderer and arrest me. I'd have no alibi, since I was alone.

David: Okay, let's assume that the police arrest you and bring you in for questioning and you have no alibi. What if that happened? What are you the most afraid of now?

Kristin: They might put me on trial and convict me of murder.

David: And then?

Kristin: Then they'd lock me up in prison for the rest of my life.

David: Clearly, no one would want to spend the rest of their life behind bars. But what would this mean to you? What is it about prison that's so frightening to you?

Kristin's What-If Technique

Negative Thoughts	% Before	% After	Distortions	Positive Thoughts	% Belief
1. Something terrible might happen if I walk to the store alone.	100%				
2. I might drop my hanky on the sidewalk without noticing that I'd lost it.	100%				
3. A terrible crime like a murder might be committed at the very spot where I dropped my hanky.	100%				
4. The police might find the hanky and trace it back to me.	100%				
5. They might think that I committed the murder and arrest me.	100%				
6. Then I'd be convicted of murder and would have to spend the rest of my life in prison.	100%				
7. Then my sons would have to grow up alone, without their mother.	100%				

Kristin blurted out, "My sons would have to grow up alone, without their mother. I wouldn't be there for them." She began to cry, and it seemed like we'd struck a chord.

After she had a good cry, I asked Kristin to tell me more about this fear. Of course, no mother would want to be stuck in prison and separated from her children, but this scenario seemed awfully unlikely. Why was Kristin so concerned about her sons?

Kristin explained that Tom, her eleven-year-old, had been causing problems at school. In addition, several neighbors had complained to the police that someone was breaking windows at night. A few days later, the police caught Tom throwing rocks at the neighbors' windows and threatened to send him to juvenile hall if he didn't straighten up. Kristin had also gotten reports from school that Tom was flunking his classes and getting into fights. She was annoyed with Tom but reluctant to lay down the law. She'd been trying to discipline him with love and logic, but these strategies hadn't been effective. She was also frustrated because her ex-husband spoiled the boys and didn't support her efforts to discipline them, but she hadn't expressed these feelings because she was a very *nice* person and didn't want to make waves.

There seemed to be some hidden emotions lurking behind Kristin's fears. In her fantasy, she's convicted for a crime that she didn't commit. But inside, she's really afraid that Tom is turning into a criminal. She's angry but feels guilty because she thinks it's all her fault, so in her fantasies, she's the one who ends up in prison. At the same time, she punishes Tom, because he has to grow up without his mother. Psychoanalysts call this the "masochistic solution." In other words, you can punish someone else as long as you punish yourself even more.

When Kristin sweeps her angry feelings under the rug, they resurface, disguised as frightening fantasies. You can try to ignore your anger, but it will always come out indirectly. Anxiety is nearly always the symbolic expression of how you really feel inside.

Kristin and I talked about how she could discipline Tom in a firm but loving way. She was eager to learn this skill because she was aware that her niceness wasn't getting the job done. I also taught her how to communicate more skillfully with her ex-husband so they could stop fighting and start working together as a team. Kristin's interpersonal skills and self-confidence increased considerably. Tom's teacher wrote a note to Kristin saying that there had been a marked improvement in his grades and behavior, and several months later, he was elected class president.

Although we'd resolved some of the problems that had been brewing under the surface, Kristin was still afraid to leave home alone. Sooner or later, she'd have to confront this fear. I encouraged her to leave her house alone on a Saturday morning and sit on a bench in a park several blocks from her home. I told her to sit on the bench until her anxiety went away or improved considerably, even if it took an hour or more. I said she could bring a notebook with her and record the intensity of her anxiety every few minutes on a scale from 0% (no anxiety) to 100% (sheer panic). She could also record any frightening thoughts or fantasies she was having. This technique is called Self-Monitoring.

Kristin said the assignment sounded terrifying but agreed to give it a try because she was determined to overcome her agoraphobia. I said that if her anxiety started to overwhelm her, she could distract herself by concentrating intensely on something that would require all of her attention. Kristin said she'd bring her Rubik's Cube along in case she needed it.

The big day finally came. Kristin forced herself to walk to the park and sit down on a bench. Her anxiety rose to 90%, and she was flooded with fantasies of being arrested and sent to prison. But she sat there and forced herself to endure the anxiety for nearly twenty minutes.

Suddenly she spotted a policeman about fifty feet away. Her anxiety shot up to 100%, and she had an almost irresistible urge to run home. But she remembered her promise not to leave no matter how anxious she got, so she stared at her feet and tried to make herself invisible. She could see the officer out of the corner of her eye and desperately hoped he'd leave.

Instead, he turned and began walking slowly toward her. Sheer terror! She pulled out her Rubik's Cube and started fidgeting with it. But he got closer and closer. Suddenly she saw two black shoes on the sidewalk in front of her and realized that the police officer was staring down at her, waiting.

She realized that the jig was up. She set her Rubik's Cube on her lap, looked up, and held her arms out in front of her so he could put the cuffs on. But when she looked up, she saw that it was Officer O'Reilly, an old Irish policeman she'd known ever since she was a little girl. He smiled sweetly and said, "Top o' the mornin' to ya, Kristin! It's such a beautiful day. Great to see you out and about!"

In a flash, Kristin's fears vanished. She chatted enthusiastically with Officer O'Reilly for a few minutes and then spent the next several hours walking around downtown Philadelphia, shopping and doing all the things that she hadn't been able to do for years. She said she didn't have one hint of anxiety the entire time. Her agoraphobia never returned.

Five techniques contributed to Kristin's recovery. First, we uncovered the fantasy at the root of her fears using the What-If Technique. At the same time, we exposed the frustration and anger that had been fueling her fears. This was the Hidden Emotion Technique. Finally, we combined Flooding, a form of intense exposure, with Self-Monitoring and Distraction so she could confront the monster she feared the most.

The What-If Technique will help you uncover the fantasy that's been triggering your fears, but insight alone will not be enough. Ultimately, you'll have to face your fear, just as Kristin did. The form of exposure you use will depend on the nature of your fears. We'll talk about many innovative Exposure Techniques in Part III.

....

Compassion-Based Technique

Many of us operate on a double standard. When we're feeling upset, we criticize ourselves relentlessly and rip ourselves to shreds. But if we were talking
to a dear friend with the exact same problem, we'd be far kinder and more objective. When you use the Double-Standard Technique, you decide to give up
your double standard and treat all human beings, including yourself, with one
standard that's based on truth and compassion.

Here's how it works. When you're anxious or depressed, your mind will
usually be flooded with negative thoughts about yourself and your life. You may
tell yourself that you're no good, that you've screwed everything up, and that
things will never change. Ask yourself, "How would I talk to a dear friend who
had a similar problem? Would I say such harsh things to him or her? If not,
why not?"

You may decide that you wouldn't talk to a friend like that because it would
be cruel and because those thoughts aren't realistic in the first place. If so, ask
yourself what you *would* say to your friend. Then ask yourself if you'd be willing to talk to yourself in the same compassionate way.

Several years ago, I did a three-day intensive workshop for a small group of
psychotherapists in Florida. The workshop focused on personal healing as well
as psychotherapy training. The theme was along the lines of "Physician, heal
thyself."

A marriage and family therapist named Walter explained that he'd been struggling with anxiety and depression for several months because Paul, the man he'd lived with for eight years, had found a new lover and left him. When Walter learned that Paul and his new lover were going to Hawaii to celebrate Paul's birthday, Walter felt absolutely devastated. He was so ashamed that he hadn't even told his parents that he and Paul had broken up. He put his hand on his chest and said: "It feels real heavy, right here. There's just a sense of loneliness and emptiness about the whole experience. I had a life that was very set in place and predictable. Suddenly, I don't have that, and I feel so alone. It feels so universal and final. I feel like this pain is going to go on forever, until the end of time."

My heart went out to Walter. It was difficult to see him in so much pain because he seemed like such a kind and gentle person. Of course, it's natural to feel a sense of loss when you lose someone you care about very deeply. But most of the pain of rejection results from our thoughts, not from the rejection itself. And sometimes those thoughts are extremely distorted and hurtful.

I asked Walter how he was thinking and feeling about the breakup with Paul. What was he telling himself? He said: "I feel incredibly guilty and ashamed, and it seems like it must have been my fault. Maybe I wasn't skillful enough, attractive enough, or dynamic enough. Maybe I wasn't there for him emotionally. I feel like I must have screwed up, or else Paul wouldn't have walked out on me. Sometimes I feel like a total fraud. Here I am, a marriage and family therapist, and my own relationship didn't even work out. I feel like a loser, a really, really big loser."

Walter felt sad, anxious, guilty, worthless, lonely, embarrassed, hopeless, frustrated, and angry. Most of these feelings were intense. He recorded these five negative thoughts on his Daily Mood Log:

1. I'll never be in a loving relationship again.
2. I must be impossible to live with and impossible to be in a relationship with.
3. There must be something wrong with me.

4. I totally screwed up and flushed my life down the toilet.

5. I'll end up as an old, fat, gray-haired, lonely gay man.

He believed all of these thoughts very strongly. Use checks to indicate all the distortions you can find in Walter's negative thoughts. You can refer to the definitions of the cognitive distortions on page 79.

Distortion	(✓)	Distortion	(✓)
1. All-or-Nothing Thinking		6. Magnification or Minimization	
2. Overgeneralization		7. Emotional Reasoning	
3. Mental Filter		8. Should Statements	
4. Discounting the Positive		9. Labeling	
5. Jumping to Conclusions • Mind-Reading • Fortune-Telling		10. Blame • Self-Blame • Other-Blame	

Answer

As you can see on page 136, Walter and I found all ten distortions in his thoughts.

You can see that most of Walter's suffering results from the illogical way he's thinking about the rejection. You could even say that Walter is treating himself far more harshly than Paul did. I thought the Double-Standard Technique might help because Walter seemed to be a warm and compassionate individual. I asked what he'd say to a dear friend who'd been rejected by someone he'd been living with for eight years. I said, "Would you tell him that there's something wrong with him, that he must be impossible to live with, and that he's screwed up his life and flushed it down the toilet for good?"

Walter looked shocked and said he'd *never* say something like that to a friend. I proposed we try a role-playing exercise so he could show me what he would say to a friend who was in the same predicament. I told Walter to imagine that he had a good friend named Kirk. Kirk is almost like a clone of Walter. He's also a marriage and family therapist, he's the same age as Walter, and all his strengths and weaknesses are the same as Walter's. In addition, Kirk has just broken up with his lover, Jake, after they'd been living together for eight

Walter's Distortions

Distortion	(✓)	Explanation
1. All-or-Nothing Thinking	✓	Walter is thinking about things in black-and-white extremes. He's telling himself that the relationship was a complete failure and that he's entirely to blame for the breakup.
2. Overgeneralization	✓	Walter is generalizing from the rejection to his entire self and telling himself that he's worthless, unlovable, and no good. That's why he feels so ashamed and hopeless.
3. Mental Filter	✓	Walter is focusing on all his shortcomings and filtering out his many positive qualities.
4. Discounting the Positive	✓	Walter is selling himself short and overlooking the fact that he's a warm, loyal, and compassionate individual.
5. Jumping to Conclusions • Mind-Reading • Fortune-Telling	✓	Walter is involved in Fortune-Telling when he tells himself that he'll never be in a loving relationship again and will end up fat, lonely, and alone.
6. Magnification or Minimization	✓	He's magnifying his own role in the problem and minimizing Paul's. While his willingness to examine his own role in the breakup is admirable, he's not considering the fact that it takes two to tango.
7. Emotional Reasoning	✓	He *feels* guilty, so he assumes he really *is* to blame for the breakup. He *feels* worthless, so he concludes that he really *is* a loser. He *feels* hopeless, so he tells himself that he's destined to be alone forever.
8. Should Statements	✓	Walter is telling himself that he shouldn't have any flaws or shortcomings. He also seems to believe that if he's a loving and faithful partner, then every relationship should last forever.
9. Labeling	✓	He thinks of himself as a fraud and a loser.
10. Blame • Self-Blame • Other-Blame	✓	He's blaming himself entirely for the failure of the relationship, even though he can't put his finger on anything specific that he did wrong.

years. I told Walter that I'd play the role of Kirk, and he could play himself. Here's how our dialogue went:

Kirk (played by David): Walter, can I talk to you for a minute?

Walter: What's going on?

Kirk: I don't know if you've heard the news, but Jake and I broke up about a month ago. I just found out that he's on his way to Hawaii to celebrate his birthday with his new lover. I'm devastated.

Walter: I'm so sorry to hear that. You must feel horrible.

Kirk: I *do* feel horrible. I think I've screwed up my life for good. I feel like there must be something wrong with me, and it seems like I'll never be in a loving relationship again. Does that sound reasonable?

Walter: I can imagine that it was a huge blow when Jake walked out on you, but I'm not sure I understand what you're saying. How did you come to the conclusion that there's something wrong with you or that you'll never be in a loving relationship again?

Kirk: I feel like it must have been my fault because I feel so worthless, guilty, and ashamed. I feel like I'm no good and there must be something wrong with me.

Walter: It sounds like you're being pretty hard on yourself. Did you do something that upset Jake? What do you think you did wrong?

Kirk: I can't actually think of anything. I just feel like he must have walked out on me because I wasn't good enough. Otherwise, why would he have left me?

Walter: It's unfortunate that Jake left, and my heart goes out to you. I know how devastating that can feel. But people leave relationships for all sorts of reasons. Maybe he was bored. Maybe he was angry. Maybe he was restless. Maybe he was horny and tempted by someone exciting that he met. There's a long list of possibilities. And even if there was a conflict of some type between the two of you, he was the one who walked away without trying to resolve it, not you.

Kirk: Perhaps that's true, but the fact is, he did leave me, for whatever reason, and I feel like I'll never be in a loving relationship again. I feel like my life is coming to an end and that I have nothing to look forward to but loneliness, shame, and misery for the rest of my life.

Walter: How did you come to the conclusion that you'll never be in another loving relationship again? That sounds a bit extreme. Have you ever been in a loving relationship in the past?

Kirk: Well, yes, I was just in one for the past eight years. And I've had loving relationships before that as well.

Walter: So it sounds like you've been in many loving relationships, including one that lasted eight years. Is that right?

Kirk: Yes, that's right.

Walter: Then I'm wondering if it makes sense to argue that you'll never be in a relationship again in the future. To my ear, what you're saying doesn't quite add up.

Kirk: Are you saying that since I've been in many loving relationships in the past, I'll probably be in a loving relationship again in the future, even though I feel really terrible right now?

Walter: That's absolutely right!

Kirk: Are you just saying that to make me feel good, or because it's true?

Walter: I'm saying it because it's a fact. You *have* been in many loving relationships in your life, so it seems extremely likely that you'll have another loving relationship in the future.

David (as himself again): I really agree with what you're saying, Walter. Would the same be true for you? After all, your friend, Kirk, is just like you.

Walter: Oh! I see what you mean. I guess it would have to be true for me, too.

Notice that when we did the role-playing, Walter began to argue fairly persuasively that his first negative thought, "I'll never be in a loving relationship again," wasn't very realistic. It seemed like the Double-Standard Technique was definitely working for him, but I wanted to be sure. I asked Walter if he could come up with a positive thought that would put the lie to the first negative thought on his Daily Mood Log. You can see the positive thought he came up with on page 139. This thought seemed realistic to Walter, so he put 95% in the "% Belief" column. This meant that it fulfilled the necessary condition for emotional change. In addition, Walter's belief in the negative thought went from 95% to 15%. This meant that the positive thought also fulfilled the sufficient condition for emotional change.

Negative Thoughts	% Before	% After	Distortions	Positive Thoughts	% Belief
1. I'll never be in a loving relationship again.	95%	15%	OG, MF, DP, MR, FT, MAG, ER, SH, SB	1. There's no real evidence for this. I've been in many loving relationships in the past. I feel like I'll never have another loving relationship because I'm hurting so much right now. But eventually these feelings will go away and I'll start connecting with other people again, just as I've always done in the past.	95%

Why did this sudden change occur? In the role-play, Walter was able to think about the rejection in a far more realistic and compassionate manner because he felt like he was talking to a dear friend who'd been rejected. But, of course, he was really talking to himself.

I wanted to make sure that Walter was really winning the battle with the self-critical part of his brain, so I continued the Double-Standard role-play. This time, I focused on Walter's second negative thought, "I must be impossible to live with and impossible to be in a relationship with." I argued as persuasively as I could, because I wanted to see if he could hit the ball out of the park again. Once again, I'm playing the role of Walter's friend, Kirk:

Kirk (played by David): Walter, there's another angle that I haven't told you about. What you don't understand is that I'm impossible to live with and impossible to be in a relationship with. That's the real reason I feel so bad, and that's why I'll be alone for the rest of my life.

Walter: Gosh, I'm surprised to hear you say that, because I've known you for a long time, and I've never felt that way about you. In fact, you've always been warm and open, and a loyal friend. How in the world did you come to the conclusion that you were impossible to be in a relationship with?

Kirk: Well, my relationship with Jake fell apart. Doesn't that prove that I'm impossible to be in a relationship with?

Walter: In all honesty, what you're saying doesn't make a lot of sense. In the first place, Jake was also involved in the relationship. It takes two to tango. And in the second place, you *were* involved in a reasonably successful relationship with him for eight years. So how can you claim that you're impossible to live with?

Kirk: Let me make sure I've got this right. You're saying that I *was* in a reasonably successful relationship for eight years, so it doesn't make much sense to say that I'm impossible to live with or impossible to be in a relationship with?

Walter: You've got it. Crystal clear!

At that point, Walter's face lit up, as if a lightbulb had suddenly turned on in his brain, and we both started laughing. His negative thoughts suddenly seemed absurd to him, and there was an immediate shift in his mood. I asked him to write a positive thought on his Daily Mood Log directly across from the second negative thought. As you can see on page 141, he wrote, "I was in a reasonably successful relationship with Paul for eight years." He put 100% next to this thought in the "% Belief" column. At this point, he no longer believed the second negative thought at all.

You can see how Walter put the lie to the rest of his negative thoughts. His responses to the third negative thought, "There must be something wrong with me," are interesting. He came up with three positive thoughts and believed them all 100%. The first positive thought was "Paul's behavior isn't necessarily a measure of my worth as a human being." This thought was only somewhat helpful, and Walter's belief in the negative thought only dropped to 50%. Then he wrote, "This sounds a bit extreme and unfair. Paul also contributed to the breakup." At this point, Walter's belief in the negative thought dropped to 30%. His third response was a slam-dunk. He wrote, "There are plenty of things wrong with me, and I accept that. But I have a lot to offer as well." This positive thought crushed the negative thought, so his belief in it fell all the way to 0%.

When you work on one of your own negative thoughts, you may see the same pattern. You may attack it from one angle, and it will help a little, but you'll still cling to the negative thought. Then you'll attack it from another an-

Walter's Daily Mood Log

Upsetting Event: Paul went to Hawaii to celebrate his birthday with his new lover.

Emotions	% Before	% After	Emotions	% Before	% After
Sad, blue, depressed, down, unhappy	80%	20%	Embarrassed, foolish, humiliated, self-conscious	100%	0%
Anxious, worried, panicky, nervous, frightened	100%	10%	Hopeless, discouraged, pessimistic, despairing	60%	5%
Guilty, remorseful, bad, ashamed	100%	10%	Frustrated, stuck, thwarted, defeated	100%	0%
Inferior, worthless, inadequate, defective, incompetent	90%	5%	Angry, mad, resentful, annoyed, irritated, upset, furious	50%	0%
Lonely, unloved, unwanted, rejected, alone, abandoned	100%	0%	Other (describe)		

Negative Thoughts	% Before	% After	Distortions
1. I'll never be in a loving relationship again.	95%	15%	OG, MF, DP, MR, FT, MAG, ER, SH, SB
2. I must be impossible to live with and impossible to be in a relationship with.	95%	0%	AON, OG, MF, DP, MR, MAG/MIN, ER, SH, LAB, SB
3. There must be something wrong with me.	100%	50% / 30% / 0%	AON, OG, MF, DP, MAG/MIN, ER, SH, SB
4. I totally screwed up and flushed my life down the toilet.	100%	10%	AON, OG, MF, FT, MAG/MIN, ER, SH, SB
5. I'll end up as an old, fat, gray-haired, lonely gay man.	100%	5%	FT, ER, LAB

Positive Thoughts	% Belief
1. There's no real evidence for this. I've been in many loving relationships in the past. I feel like I'll never have another loving relationship because I'm hurting so much right now. But eventually these feelings will go away and I'll start connecting with other people again, just as I've always done in the past.	95%
2. I was in a reasonably successful relationship with Paul for eight years.	100%
3. Paul's behavior isn't necessarily a measure of my worth as a human being.	100%
This sounds a bit extreme and unfair. Paul also contributed to the breakup.	100%
There are plenty of things wrong with me, and I accept that. But I have a lot to offer as well.	100%
4. I'm entitled to learn and make mistakes. By the time I'm a hundred, maybe I'll know all the answers!	100%
5. I'm going through a hard time right now, and I deserve some support. My hair is already turning gray, and I can't stop myself from aging, but the rest of the thought is a lot of horse pucky!	100%

gle, and your belief in the negative thought will go down a bit more. Then you'll come in from an entirely different angle, and suddenly you'll stop believing the negative thought altogether.

Of course, the goal is not just changing the way you think, but changing the way you feel. After Walter put the lie to all his negative thoughts, I asked him to rate how he was feeling again. Was he feeling any less upset? You can see the changes in his negative feelings in the "% After" column on page 141. His feeling of sadness fell all the way from 80% to 20%. I thought this was just about right. Walter is entitled to some feelings of sadness because he's just experienced a loss. His feelings of guilt, shame, and anxiety fell all the way to 10%, and his feelings of hopelessness dropped to 5%. The feelings of loneliness, embarrassment, frustration, and anger disappeared completely.

When people hear about rapid and dramatic changes like Walter's, they nearly always feel a bit skeptical and ask, "Will it last? Was it just a flash in the pan?" In fact, the old-time psychoanalysts discouraged rapid recovery. They discounted it as a temporary "flight into health" and thought it meant that their patients were avoiding their problems.

My thinking is different. I'm all for rapid recovery. As far as I'm concerned, the quicker the better! When do you want to get over your suffering? A month from now? A year from now? Five years from now? Or today?

The Double-Standard Technique was effective for Walter because he was a kind, compassionate person. On some level, he already knew how to defeat the negative thoughts that were making him so miserable. I just put him in touch with the loving part of his own mind. If the Double-Standard Technique had not been helpful, I would have tried other techniques.

Role-playing makes the Double-Standard Technique more dynamic, but it's not necessary. You can use this technique just as easily on your own. Simply ask yourself, "What would I say to a dear friend who had a similar problem?" If you discover that you'd be more compassionate and objective when talking to a friend, ask yourself if you'd be willing to talk to yourself in the same way. You can even write out a dialogue similar to the one I had with Walter.

No single technique will be effective for everyone, and the Double-Standard Technique is no exception. If you don't have a double standard, this technique will probably fail. Some people are every bit as hard on others as they are on themselves. The technique may also fail if you think your high standards or harsh self-criticisms are helping you. Some perfectionists have told me that they *want* to have a double standard, since they expect far more from themselves than they expect from others. They think that if they beat up on themselves when they fail or make mistakes, it will motivate them to work harder and achieve more.

If a self-critical thinking style is working for you, there's no reason to change it. But in my experience, feelings of self-blame, guilt, and inadequacy usually aren't very motivating and don't help me learn from my mistakes. Feelings of shame and guilt simply make me want to cover up my failures because I can't stand to face them. In fact, I do my best work when I'm feeling happy, relaxed, and self-accepting.

Chapter 11

Truth-Based Techniques

Prior to the time of Copernicus, people believed that the earth was the center of the universe. They were convinced that the sun orbited the earth and had strong evidence for this belief. After all, the sun rose in the east every morning and set in the west every evening.

Copernicus and Galileo challenged this notion. They claimed that people had the wrong idea and that the earth actually orbited the sun. This change in perception ultimately led to the development of modern astronomy and transformed our understanding of the universe.

Anxiety, worry, and panic also result from unrealistic beliefs. The thoughts that create these feelings are always distorted and illogical, even though they feel absolutely valid. When you use Truth-Based Techniques, you examine the evidence for your negative thoughts or test their validity by doing experiments, just like a scientist. The discovery that your negative thoughts aren't valid can be incredibly exciting because you'll develop a radical new understanding of yourself and the world.

In this chapter, you're going to learn about four techniques that can help you put the lie to the thoughts that make you anxious or depressed: Examine the Evidence, the Experimental Technique, the Survey Technique, and Re-attribution. The idea behind these techniques is "The truth shall make you free." This concept is the cornerstone of Cognitive Therapy.

Examine the Evidence

Instead of assuming that your negative thoughts are true, ask yourself, "What's the evidence for this claim? What do the facts show?" A musician named Emily was afraid of flying because she was convinced that the passengers would panic during the flight and that she'd be trampled to death in the aisle. She was aware that her fears sounded silly, but she was convinced that it might really happen.

I asked Emily if there was any evidence for this belief. How many plane tramplings had she read about in the past year? She couldn't recall a single one. How about in the entire history of aviation? Once again, she confessed that she couldn't remember any plane tramplings.

Of course, people *can* get trampled to death. It's rare but not impossible. For example, people have died at professional soccer games and rock concerts, when fans went out of control. But tramplings are not one of the more common hazards of air travel! Furthermore, more than three million people fly every day. When she thought about it, Emily had to admit that the likelihood of being trampled to death in a plane was vanishingly small—a fact she'd actually never considered.

Suppose your fear of flying results from the belief that the plane may run into severe turbulence and crash. How would you use Examine the Evidence to challenge this belief? Put your ideas here before you continue reading.

_____

_____

_____

_____

_____

Answer

You could do some online research and check it out. How dangerous is flying? How often do planes crash? What do the statistics show?

If you check the FAA website, you'll discover that the risk of being killed in an airplane crash is exceedingly small. For example, you'd have to fly every day for 22,000 years before you'd be at significant risk of dying in an accident. During 2004, not a single person died in a commercial flight in the United States, but more than 40,000 people died in automobile accidents. That's amazing when you consider the fact that there were more than fifteen million commercial aircraft flights that year. The facts indicate that commercial air travel is far safer than driving, recreational boating, or even riding a bicycle!

Examine the Evidence can be especially useful when your negative thought contains the distortion called Jumping to Conclusions. As you may recall, there are two common forms of this distortion: Fortune-Telling and Mind-Reading. Fortune-Telling is where you make frightening predictions that aren't warranted by the facts. For example, if you're afraid of flying, you may tell yourself that flying is extremely dangerous and that the probability of a crash is high. Mind-Reading is where you make unwarranted assumptions about how other people feel. For example, if you're shy, you may assume that other people don't ever feel insecure and that if they knew how nervous you felt, they'd look down on you and think you were weird.

Examine the Evidence can also be helpful for Emotional Reasoning. When you're upset, you may feel something so strongly that you think it has to be true. When you're anxious, you tell yourself, "I *feel* frightened, so I must really *be* in danger." When you're depressed, you may tell yourself, "I *feel* like a loser, so I must really *be* one," or "I *feel* hopeless, so I must really *be* hopeless." Emotional Reasoning can be very misleading because your feelings result from your thoughts, not from reality. If your thoughts are distorted, your feelings will be just as misleading as the distorted images you see in fun-house mirrors.

Your feelings can fool you. Did you ever gamble in Las Vegas? Just as you put your quarter in the slot machine, you may have told yourself, "This is my lucky quarter. I just *know* I'm going to hit the million-dollar jackpot. I can *feel* it in my bones!" Then you pulled the handle and watched the dials spin with great anticipation. What happened? Did you hit the million-dollar jackpot? That's what I mean when I say that your feelings don't always reflect the truth.

Experimental Technique

When you use the Experimental Technique, you do an actual experiment to test the validity of a negative thought or Self-Defeating Belief, in much the same way that a scientist tests a theory to find out if it's valid. The Experimental Technique is the most powerful technique ever developed for the treatment of anxiety. You've seen several examples already. In Chapter 5, you saw how Trevor used a Shame-Attacking Exercise to test his belief that women would be disgusted by his sweaty armpits. These experiments required courage, but the dividends were tremendous.

There's a subtle difference between Examine the Evidence and the Experimental Technique. When you use Examine the Evidence, you analyze data that's already available to you. It's a lot like doing library research. When you use the Experimental Technique, you test your negative thoughts in a more dynamic and dramatic fashion.

I'll illustrate the difference between these two approaches. An elementary school teacher named Kim had a driving phobia, especially when crossing bridges. She didn't like having to be so dependent on her husband and friends to drive anytime she wanted to cross a bridge. In addition, she felt ashamed of her phobia and felt that she was weak or defective. You can see Kim's negative thoughts on her Daily Mood Log on page 148.

Emotional Reasoning is one of the distortions in Kim's thoughts. She reasons from how she feels. As you can see in her first negative thought, she feels that her hands will get so sweaty and slippery from anxiety that she won't be able to hold the steering wheel if she drives across a bridge. She also feels like her legs will get so rubbery that she won't be able to push the accelerator or brake pedal, so she concludes that it will really happen. She feels like bridges are dangerous and could collapse at any moment, so she assumes that it must be true.

How could Kim use Examine the Evidence to challenge these thoughts? What do the facts show? Please put your ideas here before you continue reading.

_____

_____

_____

_____

_____

_____

Kim's Daily Mood Log

Upsetting Event: Thinking about driving over a bridge.

Emotions	% Before	% After	Emotions	% Before	% After
Sad, blue, depressed, down, (unhappy)	35%		Embarrassed, (foolish,) humiliated, self-conscious	95%	
(Anxious,) worried, (panicky,) nervous, frightened	85%		Hopeless, (discouraged,) pessimistic, despairing	80%	
Guilty, remorseful, bad, (ashamed)	50%		Frustrated, (stuck,) thwarted, defeated	100%	
Inferior, worthless, inadequate, (defective,) incompetent	65%		Angry, mad, resentful, (annoyed,) irritated, upset, furious	50%	
Lonely, unloved, unwanted, rejected, alone, abandoned	—		Other (describe) (Trapped)	90%	

Negative Thoughts	% Before	% After	Distortions	Positive Thoughts	% Belief
1. My hands are too wet and weak to hold the steering wheel.	100%				
2. My legs feel like jelly. They're so rubbery that I won't be able to use the brakes or gas pedal.	100%				
3. I'm too dizzy to focus and concentrate.	100%				
4. I'll kill innocent people.	100%				
5. The bridge is even more unstable than I am and will probably collapse.	100%				
6. What's wrong with me? I should be over this by now!	100%				

Answer

Kim could ask herself questions like these:

- Does water pour off my hands like Niagara Falls when I'm anxious? Do I often drop things, like glasses, because my hands get so slippery? Have they ever gotten so wet and slippery while I was driving that I couldn't turn the steering wheel, no matter how hard I tried? What's the steering wheel made of? Is it something really slippery, like plastic?
- Do my legs sometimes get so rubbery that I can't control them? Do I often collapse when I try to walk? Have I ever been unable to apply the brakes or press on the accelerator, no matter how hard I pushed?
- Have I ever lost control of a car and killed innocent people because I couldn't turn the steering wheel or use the brakes? How many have I killed so far?
- How many bridge collapses have I read about in my community in the past year? How about in the entire United States in the past hundred years?* How many cars go across bridges every day? How many friends or family members have I lost because they were crossing bridges that suddenly collapsed?

This type of analysis may help Kim see that she's greatly magnifying any real danger, but she may still believe her negative thoughts because she'll tell herself, "I can see that my thoughts aren't totally realistic, but I still *feel* like the bridge could collapse." In this case, we may need a more powerful technique. This is where the Experimental Technique comes in. Can you think of any experiments Kim could do to test the validity of her negative thoughts? Please put your ideas here before you continue reading.

_____

_____

_____

* Many people are familiar with the dramatic footage of the famous Tacoma Narrows Bridge disaster of November 7, 1940. The bridge shook apart due to wind-induced harmonic vibrations and poor design. However, bridge collapses in modern times are exceedingly rare.

_____

_____

Answer

Kim did many experiments to test her thoughts. For example:

• Kim brought a bucket of water into the car with her and set it on the passenger's seat when her car was parked in the driveway. She stuck her hands in the water, then grabbed the steering wheel to see if she could turn it. She was surprised to discover that she could turn it just fine, even though her hands were soaking wet.

• She kept a paper towel in the car and grabbed it from time to time while she was driving to see how much moisture it would absorb from her hands. She was surprised to find that her hands didn't seem to be at all damp or sweaty. They remained perfectly dry, even though she was quite anxious.

• She tried changing lanes several times to see if she could control the car when she was feeling anxious. She found that she had no trouble changing lanes.

• She tested her belief that her legs were too rubbery and weak to use the accelerator and brake pedal by increasing her speed by five miles an hour and then slowing down by five miles an hour. Once again, this was easy.

• She tested her belief that bridges are fragile and in danger of collapsing by walking partway across the Golden Gate Bridge near her home and jumping up and down. She stomped her feet as hard as she could and shook the girders to see if she could destabilize the bridge. Kim was surprised by how massive and solid it was.

• As a final test, she drove across the bridge and was surprised to discover that it still seemed perfectly stable. In addition, she didn't kill anyone or lose control of the car!

Kim said these experiments were frightening at first but soon began to seem funny and absurd. She could see that her negative thoughts were blatantly false and that she'd been fooling herself all along. In addition, she stopped running, confronted the monster she feared the most, and discovered that it had no teeth.

The Experimental Technique isn't a simple formula. It requires some thoughtfulness, because everyone's fears are unique. The experiments you do will have to be tailored specifically to your negative thoughts.

The Experimental Technique can be helpful for depression and anxiety, but it really shines in the treatment of panic attacks. In Chapter 1, you learned that a panic attack is an unexpected episode of overwhelming terror that strikes suddenly and reaches its peak within a few minutes. Then it disappears almost as quickly, leaving you bewildered, humiliated, and terrified that the feelings may strike again.

During a panic attack, you may tell yourself:

- "I'm having a heart attack."
- "I'm about to die."
- "I can't breathe properly. I'm going to suffocate."
- "I'm about to pass out."
- "I'm going to lose control and go crazy."

Most people experience lots of anxious physical symptoms during the attack. You may experience:

- A pounding or racing heart
- Pain or tightness in your chest
- Shortness of breath
- Dizziness or light-headedness
- Numbness or tingling in your fingers
- A lump in your throat
- The sensation of choking
- Hot flashes or cold sweats
- Trembling
- Tight, tense muscles
- Feeling like you're unreal or the world is unreal

- Nausea, butterflies in your stomach, or the feeling that you're about to lose control of your bowels

If you've ever experienced a panic attack, you know exactly what I'm talking about. Most people who suffer from panic attacks are initially convinced that they have a medical illness, such as a heart condition or a brain tumor, but there never seems to be any medical disorder that would explain the symptoms. They may rush to the emergency room during each attack and consult with numerous physicians before someone finally makes the correct diagnosis of panic attacks.

Panic attacks result from the misinterpretation of harmless physical symptoms. From time to time, most of us notice symptoms such as dizziness, tightness in the chest, or tingling fingers, but we don't pay a great deal of attention to them and they soon go away. But people who are prone to panic attacks obsess about these feelings and tell themselves that something catastrophic is about to happen. These thoughts trigger a panic attack.

For example, if you feel dizzy, you may tell yourself that you're about to have a stroke or a nervous breakdown. If you experience tightness in your chest, you may think you're about to have a massive heart attack. But, in fact, you're *not* about to have a stroke, nervous breakdown, or heart attack. Panic attacks result from a mental con. That's why the Experimental Technique can be so effective, but using it will require courage.

Terri was a happily married woman who'd suffered from severe depression and panic attacks for more than ten years. Her panic attacks always developed when she noticed dizziness, chest pain, or tingling in her fingers. Then she'd tell herself that she was suffocating and about to die from a massive heart attack, and those thoughts would trigger intense feelings of panic. She had several full-blown panic attacks every week and was suffering intensely. Her scores on the depression and anxiety tests were off the charts.

Terri had gone to doctor after doctor, including several cardiologists, but her heart and lungs always turned out to be perfectly normal. Each doctor reassured Terri that she was as healthy as an ox. But their reassurances would last only until her next panic attack a few days later. Then she'd tell herself, "Maybe this time it really *is* a heart attack!"

Eventually, one of the doctors made the diagnosis of panic disorder and referred Terri to a psychiatrist. Since then, she'd seen numerous psychiatrists who'd prescribed all kinds of pills, but nothing helped. She and her husband had four children, and wanted to have a fifth, but Terri's psychiatrist told her she'd have to wean herself off all the drugs he'd prescribed first, because they might cause birth defects. Terri was terrified about stopping the drugs, even though she knew they weren't helping her. Several days later, she spotted my book, *Feeling Good,* in her local bookstore, and noticed this wording on the cover: "The Clinically Proven, Drug-Free Treatment for Depression." She thought, "Maybe this doctor can help me," and called my office to set up an appointment.

You can see one of Terri's Daily Mood Logs on page 154. The first three negative thoughts trigger the feelings of panic. She's telling herself that she can't breathe and that she's about to pass out and die. The next three negative thoughts lead to feelings of shame, depression, and inferiority. Terri is telling herself that she *shouldn't* have these problems and that anyone who found out about them would look down on her and think she was loony or ungrateful, since her husband's career was going smoothly, her children were doing well, and there were no real problems in her life aside from her depression and anxiety.

Terri and I tried quite a few techniques that weren't effective, but she was just as depressed and anxious as ever. During our fifth therapy session, I asked Terri if she'd allow me to induce a panic attack in the office so I could show her how to put the lie to her negative thoughts using the Experimental Technique. I explained that this method was far more powerful than the ones we'd tried so far, and I thought it was time to bring in the heavy artillery.

Although Terri said this sounded like a wonderful idea, she failed to show up for her next two sessions. She called each week to say that she wasn't dropping out of therapy and really liked working with me but was terrified by the idea of having an induced panic attack in my office and wanted to know if we could try some less frightening method.

I told Terri that, ultimately, she was the boss, and I'd never force her to do anything against her will because her trust in me was absolutely crucial to our success. I explained that there were many other techniques we could use, but if she wanted to be cured, sooner or later she'd have to face the monster she

Terri's Daily Mood Log

Upsetting Event: Noticing that my fingers feel numb and that I feel light-headed.

Emotions	% Before	% After	Emotions	% Before	% After
Sad, blue, (depressed) down, unhappy	100%		**Embarrassed**, foolish, (humiliated) self-conscious	100%	
(**Anxious**) worried, (panicky) nervous, frightened	100%		(**Hopeless**) discouraged, pessimistic, despairing	100%	
Guilty, remorseful, bad, (ashamed)	100%		(**Frustrated**) stuck, thwarted, defeated	100%	
(**Inferior**) worthless, inadequate, (defective) incompetent	100%		**Angry**, mad, resentful, annoyed, irritated, upset, furious	0%	
Lonely, unloved, unwanted, rejected, alone, abandoned	0%		**Other (describe)**		

Negative Thoughts	% Before	% After	Distortions	Positive Thoughts	% Belief
1. I can't breathe properly.	100%				
2. If I stand up, I'll pass out.	100%				
3. I'm about to die.	100%				
4. There must be something wrong with me.	100%				
5. I *shouldn't* be so anxious because there's nothing wrong in my life.	100%				
6. If anyone found out about my depression and panic attacks, they'd look down on me and think I was a mental case.	100%				

© 1988 by David D. Burns, M.D.

feared the most. I pointed out that she was having many panic attacks every week anyway. It might be worth it to have one more under my supervision, and we might be able to put an end to her problem for good. I reminded her that my office was near the emergency room, so help would be just a stone's throw away in case she needed it.

Terri promised to think about it. A few days later, she called back and said she was absolutely terrified but had decided to give it a try. I scheduled a double session so we'd have plenty of time to work together.

At the beginning of the session, I induced a panic attack by having her breathe as deeply and as fast as she could for a couple of minutes. This is called hyperventilation. It leads to an increase of oxygen in the blood and creates physical sensations like light-headedness and tingling fingers. If you're prone to panic attacks, you may suddenly feel like you're on the verge of death.

To intensify the effect, I told Terri to focus on the kinds of negative thoughts she usually had during a panic attack. I said: "Notice that your chest is starting to feel tight, your fingers are tingling, and you feel like you can't breathe deeply enough. Imagine that your fingers and lips are turning blue because you're not getting enough air into your lungs. Your windpipe is closing off and we're going to have to call for an ambulance. Can you see the red light going round and round on top of the ambulance? Picture the paramedics putting you on a stretcher and giving you oxygen through a mask, but they're panicking because it isn't working. Imagine that your heartbeat is getting weaker and more erratic, and you're on the verge of a massive heart attack."

Sure enough, these statements triggered an overwhelming panic attack. Terri began sobbing and blurted out that her chest was hurting and she felt like she was about to die.

I asked, "What would you die from? A lack of oxygen in your blood?"

She said, "Yes. I feel dizzy and my fingers are tingling. I can't breathe deeply enough. My chest hurts so much. This feels so *awful,* and this *always* happens!"

I asked Terri how strongly she believed that she couldn't breathe deeply enough and was about to die, on a scale of 0% to 100%. She blurted out, "100%." Then I said, "Terri, if you really *couldn't* breathe right now, and you *were* having a heart attack, what would be one thing you could not do?"

Terri was so agitated that she could barely comprehend my question. She started sobbing and begged me to stop. She seemed so overwhelmed with terror that I was tempted to stop out of a sense of compassion. But I felt like it would be a huge mistake, because it would reinforce her illogical belief that she actually was in danger. She would have concluded, "Even my doctor thinks I'm about to die. This must really be a dangerous situation."

Furthermore, Terri was *not* about to suffocate or die. How could I get her to realize that she was fooling herself? Can you think of any experiments she could do to test her belief that she can't breathe deeply enough or that she's about to die of a heart attack? Put your ideas here before you continue reading.

_____

_____

— _____

_____

_____

Answer

I said, "Terri, if you *were* dying of a heart attack right now, and if you *were* suffocating, do you think you could exercise strenuously?" She said it would be impossible because she wouldn't be able to get any oxygen into her lungs. She said that if she even tried to stand up, she'd "pass out or something," and she pleaded with me to stop. She said that her chest hurt so badly that she felt like she was about to die.

I said, "I can see that this is very frightening to you, but I want you to stick with it. I'd like you to stand up right now so we can see if you're about to pass out. Then you can try some strenuous exercise, like running in place, so we can find out if you can't breathe properly or you're about to die."

You might think this was a risky suggestion. What if Terri actually did pass out when she tried to stand up? But remember, depression and anxiety result from distorted thoughts. Terri is fooling herself in some very profound way when she tells herself that she's about to pass out or die. From a medical perspective, do you know the cause of fainting? Fainting occurs when the heart slows down and the blood pressure drops. As a result, the heart can't pump enough blood and oxygen up to the brain. Fainting is a defense mechanism;

once a person is lying flat on the ground, the heart can pump blood to the brain much more easily because it doesn't have to pump the blood uphill. Soon there's plenty of blood and oxygen flowing through the brain again, so the person wakes up.

Is Terri in any danger of fainting? Has her heart slowed down? Has her blood pressure fallen? Is there too little oxygen in her blood?

In fact, Terri's heart is racing and her blood pressure has gone up, not down. Furthermore, she's breathing so rapidly that her blood is loaded with oxygen. Terri cannot faint, even if she tries! Fainting would be a physiologic impossibility, because her heart is racing so fast.*

Terri stood up slowly—and didn't faint. I encouraged her to start jogging in place so she could test her belief that she was having a heart attack. She started jogging very slowly, saying she felt ridiculous. I told her that it might be worth doing something ridiculous if we could put an end to her misery once and for all. She kept ruminating about her symptoms and said, "My fingers are tingling. I feel weird! I feel like I can't breathe deeply enough."

I said, "Just keep going. Can you jog a little faster?"

Terri sped up and started jogging more energetically. After a couple of minutes, she stopped and said she was too tired to continue and still was having trouble taking a deep breath.

I said, "Why don't you try a few jumping jacks?"

She said she couldn't possibly do any jumping jacks because she was too exhausted.

I said, "Why don't you try a few jumping jacks anyway?"

Terri reluctantly started doing jumping jacks. She soon found her second wind and started doing them with gusto. After another minute, she asked, "I wonder if I could really be doing this if I was having a heart attack?"

I said, "Good point! Is this what you see in the emergency rooms of hospitals? Patients with massive heart attacks standing next to their gurneys doing jumping jacks?"

* On occasion, people who are anxious do faint. For example, people with a blood or needle phobia may faint because their heart suddenly slows down and their blood pressure temporarily falls when they see a needle or something bloody. But they're not afraid of fainting, they're afraid of the needle or the blood. It's a completely different problem.

Terri suddenly started giggling, so I said, "Keep up the jumping jacks. I'm sure you'll keel over at any moment!" Then she started laughing so hard that she doubled over. I asked her how much she now believed that she was about to die of a heart attack.

She exclaimed, "Much less. In fact, I feel a whole lot better now!"

That was the first relief that Terri had experienced in over ten years of suffering. With Terri's permission, I've shown a videotape of that segment in workshops I've conducted all over the country. At the beginning of the segment, you can see Terri sobbing in sheer panic. Six minutes later, she's giggling and totally free of any feelings of anxiety or depression.

What caused this dramatic transformation in Terri's mood? Why did she suddenly feel so much better? Why did her feelings of panic and depression disappear?

Terri felt better the moment she asked, "I wonder if I could really be doing this if I was having a heart attack?" She suddenly realized that her negative thoughts couldn't possibly be valid, and the feelings of panic and helplessness vanished. This is the idea behind Cognitive Therapy: When you change the way you *think*, you can change the way you *feel*.

Some people get the wrong idea and conclude that the aerobic exercise did the trick and that jogging would be a good cure for anxiety and depression, but that would be missing the point entirely. Exercise can definitely have physical and emotional benefits, but the Experimental Technique was the real key to Terri's recovery.

The first time people recover, they may attribute it to something external, perhaps a change in the weather, getting a date, or landing a new job. They don't always see that their recovery was the direct result of the techniques they were using. This is a problem because if you don't know what helped you and why, you'll be vulnerable to relapses. You'll feel just as helpless and bewildered the next time you get anxious or depressed. In contrast, if you know exactly why and how you overcame your depression or anxiety, you can use the same method again whenever you get upset in the future. That way, you'll never have to fear anxiety or depression again.

Terri asked what she was supposed to do if she had a panic attack at home between sessions. I explained that she'd have to do her jumping jacks again. She asked, "But what if I have a panic attack while I'm driving?"

I said, "Just pull over to the side of the road so you can get out and do your jumping jacks." Terri insisted that she couldn't possibly do that because the neighbors might see her and think that she was a total nutcase. On an impulse, I jumped out of my chair, opened the office door, and walked into the waiting room. Terri couldn't see most of the room but could see that I was standing in the center. I started doing jumping jacks and carrying on in a crazy manner, shouting "I'm nuts! I'm a loony! I'm doing jumping jacks! Wheee!"

Then I walked back into the office, closed the door, and sat down. I turned to Terri and asked, in a very serious voice, "Terri, what do you think about that?"

She looked dumbfounded and said, "Dr. Burns, if you've got the nerve to make a total horse's ass of yourself in front of all your patients, that gives me the courage to do what I've got to do to beat this thing!" What she couldn't see was that the waiting room was totally empty at the time!

That session happened in 1988. I called her last summer to see if it was okay to keep showing the videotape of her session in my workshops. She said she hoped every anxious person in the United States would have the chance to see it. She was still feeling tremendous and had experienced only one panic attack since that session. It disappeared quickly when she did her jumping jacks. She proudly told me that after she had her fifth child, she'd taken up writing and had just published her first novel.

Many therapists might have concluded that Terri was going to be a difficult case. She'd failed to respond to all kinds of medications and had received lots of psychotherapy that wasn't effective. And yet, she recovered in just a few sessions once we found the technique that worked for her. In fact, I'm convinced that if someone had shown Terri how to use the Experimental Technique ten years earlier, when she had her first panic attack, she would have recovered immediately and wouldn't have had to suffer for so long.

Now that you have an understanding about how the Experimental Technique works, I'm going to ask you to be the shrink. A seventy-one-year-old woman named June came to my clinic in Philadelphia for the treatment of agoraphobia and panic attacks. June had been struggling with these problems since she was eighteen, and had been treated with drugs and psychotherapy on and off for fifty-three years. Earlier you learned that agoraphobia is the fear of being away from home alone because you're afraid that you'll have a panic attack and there won't be anyone to help you. Over time, some people with agoraphobia become housebound because they're afraid of leaving home without a trusted companion.

June commuted to sessions from New York City, where her husband owned a pharmacy. A close friend always came along with her. June had lots of personality and was quite a character. She'd arrive decked out in formal gowns, wearing lots of costume jewelry. She told me that she was a real people person. She loved people, and people loved her. She was always the center of attention at parties, almost like a stand-up comic. She'd have everyone in stitches. But she couldn't tolerate being alone because she was afraid that she'd crack up and go crazy. Although she'd never actually gone crazy, she often felt like she was on the verge of losing it.

Was June in any real danger of cracking up? People with panic attacks don't actually go crazy. They just *worry* about going crazy. People who really are psychotic, such as individuals suffering from schizophrenia, don't worry about going crazy. They're convinced they're completely sane and think that the FBI is plotting against them or spying on them with secret electronic devices. In other words, they think everyone else is nuts. So we know that June isn't in any danger of cracking up because she constantly worries about it.

But June believes that her fears are entirely realistic. What experiment could she do to find out if she really is about to crack up and go crazy? Put your ideas here before you continue reading.

_____

_____

_____

_____

_____

Answer

I asked June what would happen if she finally cracked up and went crazy right there in my office. What would it look like? She said that she'd probably be lying on the floor, like a turtle on its back, with her arms and legs flailing wildly in the air. She'd be talking in tongues, shrieking, and babbling incoherently. Then she'd get up and swirl around, singing loudly and dancing like a whirling dervish. She'd bang her head against the wall, shouting at the top of her lungs.

I said, "June, you've been afraid of this for fifty-three years. Let's find out if your fears are realistic. I want you to go for it." She seemed shocked and asked what I meant.

I said: "June, ever since you were eighteen, you've thought that you could snap at any moment, but you've never checked it out. I want you to try to drive yourself crazy right now. You can do all the things you just described. You can lie on your back on the floor and scream and babble incoherently. See if you can drive yourself crazy through forceful effort. That way, we can find out once and for all whether or not your fears are realistic."

June said, "No way, José!"

We debated the point for several minutes. I pushed her because I knew that she was resilient and trusted me. Finally, she said, "Doctor, I can see I'm not going to win this argument, so I've decided to go ahead and give it a try— but on one condition."

I said, "You've got it. What's your condition?"

She said, "You go first!"

I lay down on my back on the carpet and started flailing my arms and legs wildly and screaming incoherently. Then I got up and swirled around like a dervish, singing, shrieking, gyrating my hips, and babbling insanely. I pounded my head against the office wall and shouted, "I'm a psycho! I'm cracking up! Cowabunga!"

Every now and then, I peeked out of the corner of my eye so I could see how June was reacting. She seemed to be enjoying the show.

After a couple minutes, I sat back down in my chair and said, "Your turn!"

June got out of her chair, gingerly lay down on her back on the carpet, and meticulously arranged her gown. Then she feebly extended her right arm and leg, then her left arm and leg, and meekly said, "Ooo, ooo."

I said, "June, that won't do. This is the Olympics of psychosis. You've got to give it everything you've got. Pour your heart into it. Go for the gold. I know you can do it!"

At that point, June really got into it. She started rolling around on the floor, flailing her arms and legs wildly, shrieking, and talking in tongues. Then she got up, whirled around the office, and started pounding her head on the wall, screaming at the top of her lungs.

Her voice was far louder than I'd imagined it could be. In fact, she sounded like a booming opera singer. I remembered that my office wasn't soundproofed and wondered what my colleagues and patients would think about all the screams and shrieks coming from my office.

June kept it up for several minutes, then finally got winded and sat in her chair. I asked, "June, how are you feeling now?"

She said, "Dr. Burns, for the past fifty-three years I've been struggling to hang on to my sanity, thinking I could crack up at any moment. I've just discovered that I *can't* crack up, no matter *how* hard I try! In fact, I've *never* felt more in control than I do at this moment!"

I asked June to take the depression and anxiety tests again. Her scores were zero, indicating that her symptoms had disappeared completely. In fact, this was the first real relief she'd had in more than half a century. That was our fourth therapy session. I saw June two more times after that, but her fears didn't return. She reported that her agoraphobia was completely gone and that she could go anywhere she wanted alone, so we terminated treatment. I was sad to see her go, since she was so much fun to work with.

Although the methods I used with Terri and June might seem entertaining, I don't want to minimize how terrified these women felt at first. It's never easy to confront your fears, especially if they've tormented you for years or even decades. If you don't want to do experiments that are as extreme as the ones Terri and June did, you can try less threatening tests of your negative thoughts. Let's say that when you feel dizzy, you sometimes panic because you think you're about to lose your mind and go crazy. You could induce a panic attack by spinning yourself in an office chair until you're dizzy. However, you could decide to stop when you're only 50% panicky, instead of pushing for a full-blown panic attack. Then you could try something like counting backward from 100 by sevens out loud. You'd say, "100, 93, 86, 79, 72," and so on. This may seem challenging when you're feeling panicky, but you'll probably discover that you can do it.

Then you could try calling information to see if you can get someone's telephone number and write it down. You could also read a sentence from a book and see if you can summarize it out loud. Although you may *feel* like you're cracking up and going crazy, you'll discover that you can do these things just about as well as you ever could. This will show that you can still function normally even though you feel like you're about to crack up. Of course, these experiments will work only if you believe that you're on the verge of cracking up.

I first developed this technique in the late 1970s, but only recently has it gained popularity. Researchers report that approximately 80% of people with panic attacks recover in five to ten therapy sessions using the Gradual Exposure approach that I've just described. That's impressive when you think about how long most people have suffered with this problem and how much unsuccessful therapy they've endured.

However, the approach I used with Terri and June is called Flooding, because you flood yourself with the worst possible anxiety all at once. Flooding works faster than Gradual Exposure. In fact, one session sometimes will do the trick. However, Flooding requires more courage. Flooding and Gradual Exposure are both effective, so you can choose the approach that's more appealing to you.

Survey Technique

Researchers often conduct surveys to find out how people feel about politics or consumer products. You can use the same approach to test your negative thoughts and attitudes. A psychologist named Deborah suffered from public speaking anxiety, which was particularly troublesome because she made her living giving seminars for mental health professionals. Although she did a decent job in spite of her fears, she felt like a fraud because she thought a psychologist should have it all together.

I suggested that at the beginning of her next presentation, she could ask how many of the psychologists in the audience struggled with public speaking anxiety. She was surprised and relieved when two-thirds of the hands went up.

You can also use the Survey Technique to test the negative thoughts that trigger feelings of depression. At the start of an inpatient group at my hospital in Philadelphia, a severely depressed woman named Diane announced that she'd decided to commit suicide. She explained that she'd been treated for rapidly cycling bipolar disorder for fifteen years and had taken drug after drug, but nothing had ever helped. In fact, most of the time, her doctors had her on five different drugs at once, but she kept struggling with mood swings. It was her eighth hospitalization.

Rapidly cycling bipolar disorder is one of the most severe forms of manic-depressive illness, and it can be difficult to treat. Patients with this disorder cycle in and out of episodes of depression or mania several times every year. In spite of her struggles with the disease, Diane was married and had three children. She'd also developed a part-time consulting business designing websites, and her services were in strong demand.

I asked Diane if she was determined to commit suicide no matter what or if she was open to receiving help. She said that she was eager to receive help, if that was possible, and that she'd only decided to commit suicide because it seemed like the most logical thing to do.

Diane felt intensely depressed, anxious, ashamed, inadequate, lonely, humiliated, hopeless, frustrated, and angry, and recorded four disturbing negative thoughts on her Daily Mood Log:

1. This f __ing disease has ruined my life.
2. I'm hopeless. I'll never get better.
3. I'm a burden to my family and doctors.
4. My parents, husband, children, and doctors would be better off if I were dead.

I asked Diane which thought she wanted to work on first. She selected the fourth thought, "My parents, husband, children, and doctors would be better off if I were dead." After trying several techniques that weren't effective, I decided to try the Survey Technique. I said, "Diane, you claim that your family and doctors would be better off if you were dead. I know this may sound grotesque, but have you asked them if they want you to commit suicide?"

Diane conceded that she'd never discussed the subject with them, but that it seemed obvious that she was a burden and that they'd be better off without her. I pointed out that her husband was coming in for a family session with the social worker later that day and that it might be worth asking him, because she might be jumping to a conclusion that wasn't based on the facts. I said that since her family wasn't there in the group, she might at least ask the other patients what they thought. Did they think that her parents, children, and husband would be better off if she took her own life?

Diane protested that the people in the group probably wouldn't be honest with her. I suggested that she could ask a few of them what they thought, and then she and I could cross-examine them to find out if they were being honest or simply telling her what she wanted to hear.

Diane turned to the young woman sitting next to me and said, "Martha, do you think my family would be better off if I committed suicide?"

Tears were streaming down Martha's face as she replied: "You've got to be crazy, Diane. You don't know what you're talking about. My younger brother committed suicide five years ago. He was in the bedroom right next to mine. I heard a gunshot and found him with a gun next to him and a bullet through his head."

Martha began sobbing and described how devastated she and her parents still felt. She added: "Was my little brother a burden? You bet he was. He'd been depressed for several years, and sometimes he could be a royal pain in the ass. Did we want him to kill himself? Never! We loved him, and we wanted him to live. The burden of his depression was *nothing* compared to the burden of his death. I think about him every day, and it always breaks my heart. I don't think I'll *ever* get over it. Your family loves you, too, and if you killed yourself, it would devastate them. They'd never get over the loss."

I asked, "Diane, do you think Martha is telling you the truth or lying through her teeth?" Diane said that Martha seemed to be telling the truth.

I noticed that one of the nurses, a woman named Erika, also had tears in her eyes. I said, "Diane, why don't you ask Erika?"

Diane turned to her and said, "What do you think? Do you think I should commit suicide? Would my family be better off if I were dead?"

Erika wept and described the suicide of her son twenty years earlier. She said the unbearable feelings of grief had never diminished, that she thought about him all the time, and that she'd give anything to have him back.

Diane asked several other members of the group, one by one, what they thought. They all said the same thing. Many had friends or family members who'd committed suicide. They all described intense feelings of guilt, shame, and loss. Several thanked Diane for being so open and said she'd made it easier for them to talk about their own feelings of hopelessness and worthlessness.

I asked Diane how strongly she now believed the negative thought "My parents, husband, children, and doctors would be better off if I were dead." She said that her belief in it had fallen to 0%. In fact, it seemed so irrational that she didn't have any idea how she ever could have believed it in the first place. She wanted to know how she could talk back to her other negative thoughts, especially "This f___ ing disease has ruined my life," and "I'm a burden to my family and doctors."

I told Diane that she and I could play the roles of the two voices that were doing battle in her head. She could play the role of her negative thoughts and attack me, and I'd play the role of her positive thoughts. This technique is called the Externalization of Voices, and you'll learn more about it in Chapter 15. The dialogue went like this:

Negative Thoughts (played by Diane): Face the facts, Diane. This f___ ing disease has ruined your life.

Positive Thoughts (played by David): That sounds like All-or-Nothing Thinking. There's no doubt that this disease has been a royal pain in the ass, but I've accomplished a great deal in spite of it. I've been a good wife and mother, and I've raised three wonderful children who love me a lot. I've also been successful with my web design business in spite of my mood swings. I feel proud of what I've done.

Negative Thoughts: Well, that may be true, but you've been hospitalized eight times in the past fifteen years. That proves that you're a burden to your parents, your husband, your children, and your doctors.

Positive Thoughts: You know, you're right. I do have manic-depressive illness, and at times I *am* a burden. But you know what? I didn't choose to have this disease, so if God wants me to be a burden, so be it. I'll accept that. And I'm just going to be the best little burden I can be!

This response brought a smile to Diane's face, and she asked, "Are you saying it's okay to be a burden?"

I said: "Absolutely! If that's your fate right now, accept it. It's certainly not your fault. Your problem is not the fact that you're a burden, but the fact that you're beating up on yourself all the time and telling yourself that you shouldn't be one. The fact is, we're all a burden at times. That's just part of being human."

Diane said that a lightbulb went on in her brain. She'd never considered the idea that she could simply accept the fact that she had manic-depressive illness and that she was allowed to be a burden at times. Paradoxically, the moment Diane accepted the fact that she *was* a burden, she *wasn't* a burden anymore!

I thought it was also interesting that the manic-depressive illness itself was not the real cause of Diane's suffering. Although this disorder is thought to be biological in nature, Diane's suffering actually resulted from her distorted negative thoughts. When she put the lie to those thoughts, her depression vanished.

The Survey Technique is a good method to try when your negative thought involves Mind-Reading. That's where you jump to conclusions about what other people think or how they feel about you. Then you may get anxious or depressed and assume that the other person really is upset with you. Of course, sometimes a real conflict does exist, and you may need to talk things over with the other person to clear the air. But sometimes the problem exists only in your head. Instead of making assumptions about how other people think and feel, you can ask them and find out. This technique may seem simple, but sometimes it can be remarkably helpful.

Reattribution

Self-Blame and Emotional Reasoning are two of the most common and painful cognitive distortions. When you're depressed and anxious, you may blame yourself for problems that you're not really responsible for. But you tell yourself, "I feel guilty so I must be to blame." Sometimes the problem isn't so much that you really are to blame but the fact that you're blaming yourself. When you use Reattribution, you identify all the factors that contributed to a problem so you can develop a more realistic perspective. Then you can focus on solving the problem instead of using up all your energy beating up on yourself and making yourself miserable.

A young man named Jason was struggling with shyness. Although he was attractive and personable, he froze up whenever he was around interesting women. One Saturday morning when he was in line at the supermarket, he spotted an attractive woman checking groceries. She seemed to be smiling at him. Jason told himself it would be great if he could flirt with her when he got to the front of the line. However, he felt so awkward that he stared nervously at the counter while he paid for his groceries without saying a word to her or even looking her in the eye. He left the store feeling frustrated and humiliated. Later he told me that this type of thing happened to him all the time.

When Jason was standing in line, he thought, "If I try to flirt with her, I'll probably get shot down. That would show what a loser I am." This thought contains nearly all ten cognitive distortions, but it's a classic example of Self-Blame, because Jason is ready to rip himself to shreds if she doesn't respond positively to his attempts to flirt with her. How could Jason use Reattribution to talk back to this thought?

Let me be a bit more specific. Jason is telling himself that if he tries to flirt with her and gets shot down, it will show that he's a loser. Can you think of any other reasons why a young woman checking groceries might not respond enthusiastically to a customer who flirts with her? List several possible explanations here before you continue reading.

1. _____
2. _____
3. _____
4. _____
5. _____

Answer

There are lots of possible explanations. For example:

- She may be married.
- She may have a boyfriend.

- She may be gay.
- She may be in a bad mood.
- Customers may try to flirt with her all the time, and she may find it annoying.
- There may be a long line of customers waiting to check their groceries.
- Socializing with customers may be against store policy.
- She may feel shy or insecure.
- Jason may not be her cup of tea. She may prefer guys with a certain look or men who are older.
- Jason may seem awkward or needy.

In addition, Jason's flirting skills may not be up to speed. This wouldn't mean he was a "loser"; it would simply mean that he was inexperienced and needed more practice.

The goal of Reattribution is not to rationalize failures but to put things in a more realistic perspective. A woman named Clarisse became anxious and depressed after she broke up with a man she'd been dating for several weeks because she told herself, "It was all my fault. This always happens. I'll be alone forever." After a heart-to-heart talk with a girlfriend, Clarisse began to think about the problem differently. She told herself, "It wasn't my fault after all. Paul is a total jerk! I deserve someone better!"

This is a misuse of Reattribution because Clarisse has simply switched from the "I'm no good" mind-set to the "You're no good" mind-set. Instead of blaming herself, she's blaming the man who broke up with her. Now she'll feel angry and resentful instead of anxious and guilty.

Rather than blaming herself or Paul, Clarisse can try to pinpoint the reasons why their relationship fell apart so she can learn from the situation and grow. Does she select men who are exciting but narcissistic? Does she get too clingy too fast and drive men away with her neediness? Was she unfaithful? Did she have trouble listening or get defensive when Paul criticized her or tried to talk about the problems in their relationship? Did they have different values or interests? Does she simply need to accept the fact that the chemistry between them wasn't right? This type of information can help her develop more loving relationships in the future.

In this chapter, you've learned about four Truth-Based Techniques that can help you defeat the thoughts that trigger depression and anxiety: Examine the Evidence, the Experimental Technique, the Survey Technique, and Reattribution. Some people have asked whether they should try only one Truth-Based Technique and then move on to another category if it doesn't work. Not necessarily. For example, Examine the Evidence didn't help Terri. Although she admitted that there wasn't any real evidence that she was about to suffocate or die of a heart attack, she still believed it at the gut level. When she used the Experimental Technique and did the jumping jacks, she suddenly realized that her negative thoughts were totally absurd. At that point, her anxiety and depression vanished. The bottom line is this: The more techniques you try, the faster you'll find the one that works for you!

Chapter 12

Logical and Semantic Techniques

You've probably noticed that when you're anxious or depressed, you have a tendency to criticize yourself in extreme terms. You may tell yourself that you're a loser or insist that you shouldn't feel so anxious and insecure. If you examine the language you're using, you'll nearly always discover that you're thinking about yourself in a harsh and illogical manner. Logical and Semantic Techniques can often help you change those negative messages so you can begin to talk to yourself in a more compassionate and realistic manner.

Thinking in Shades of Gray

All-or-Nothing Thinking can cause performance anxiety, because you think that your performance has to be fantastic, or else it won't be any good at all. This type of thinking isn't very realistic, since most of the time your performance will be somewhere in between. You can reduce a lot of the pressure if you decide to evaluate yourself in shades of gray instead of black-or-white categories.

When I was first learning about Cognitive Therapy, I gave a workshop with a colleague, Dr. Aaron Beck, at the annual meeting of the Association for the Advancement of Behavior Therapy. The workshop was okay, but it didn't go as well as I'd hoped. Dr. Beck noticed that I was upset and asked what the problem was. At the time, I was still pretty perfectionistic. I told him I felt discouraged because it seemed like our workshop had been below average.

He said, "Well, David, we can thank our lucky stars for that! Remember, average is the halfway point. By definition, half of all our presentations will be below average and half will be above average. So it's great that we got this one out of the way. We can look forward to a really good one next time!" That was a tremendous relief, because it dawned on me that I didn't have to be perfect all the time and that there would always be room for improvement.

In the last chapter you read about a young man named Jason who was struggling with feelings of shyness when he noticed an attractive woman checking groceries at the supermarket. Although she seemed to be smiling at him, he felt so awkward and nervous that he left the store without saying a single thing or even smiling back. You can see Jason's Daily Mood Log on page 173. The upsetting event was "Standing in line at the supermarket." Jason felt sad, anxious, guilty, ashamed, inadequate, lonely, embarrassed, discouraged, frustrated, and mad at himself. If you've ever felt shy, you can probably identify with these kinds of feelings. The high ratings in the "% Before" column indicated that all of these feelings were fairly intense.

Jason recorded the thoughts that flowed across his mind when he was in line. They all seemed completely valid to him, so he estimated his belief in each one at 100%. Check off all the distortions you can find in his thoughts. You can refer to the definitions of the distortions on page 79 if you need to.

Distortion	(✓)	Distortion	(✓)
1. All-or-Nothing Thinking		6. Magnification or Minimization	
2. Overgeneralization		7. Emotional Reasoning	
3. Mental Filter		8. Should Statements	
4. Discounting the Positive		9. Labeling	
5. Jumping to Conclusions • Mind-Reading • Fortune-Telling		10. Blame • Self-Blame • Other-Blame	

Answer

Jason and I identified all ten distortions in his thoughts.

Jason's Daily Mood Log

Upsetting Event: Standing in line at the supermarket.

Emotions	% Before	% After		Emotions	% Before	% After
Sad, blue, depressed, down, unhappy	80%			**Embarrassed**, foolish, humiliated, self-conscious	100%	
Anxious, worried, panicky, nervous, frightened	100%			**Hopeless**, discouraged, pessimistic, despairing	90%	
Guilty, remorseful, bad, ashamed	95%			**Frustrated**, stuck, thwarted, defeated	90%	
Inferior, worthless, inadequate, defective, incompetent	95%			**Angry**, mad, resentful, annoyed, irritated, upset, furious	90%	
Lonely, unloved, unwanted, rejected, alone, abandoned	75%			**Other** (describe)		

Negative Thoughts	% Before	% After	Distortions	Positive Thoughts	% Belief
1. I don't have anything interesting to say.	100%				
2. I *never* succeed with the really good-looking girls.	100%				
3. I don't have time to deal with a relationship right now, even if I do end up having a good conversation with her.	100%				
4. I better just keep my mouth shut, since I might say something stupid and upset her.	100%				
5. People will think I'm a self-centered jerk if I try to flirt with her.	100%				
6. I *shouldn't* be so loud and obnoxious. If I'm humble and quiet, people will like me more.	100%				
7. I have no personality.	100%				
8. I must be a terrible person because I'm so concerned with superficial things like success and looks.	100%				
9. If I tried to flirt with her, I'd probably get shot down.	100%				
10. That would show what a loser I am.	100%				

Jason's Distortions

Distortion	(✓)	Explanation
1. All-or-Nothing Thinking	✓	Jason thinks about the situation in black-or-white extremes. He thinks he has *nothing* to offer and believes he'll either be a tremendous success or a total failure if he tries to flirt with her. He also believes that if he dates her, his life will be complete, but if she isn't interested, it will show that he's a total loser. No wonder he feels so much pressure!
2. Overgeneralization	✓	Jason thinks that if one person thinks he's a jerk, everyone will think so. This makes any disapproval seem extremely threatening.
3. Mental Filter	✓	Jason is dwelling on how anxious and self-conscious he feels, so he tells himself that he has no personality.
4. Discounting the Positive	✓	Jason discounts his good qualities. He's relatively attractive and intelligent and has no reason to think he'll look foolish or get shot down if he flirts with someone he's attracted to. He also discounts the fact that she seems to be smiling at him.
5. Jumping to Conclusions • Mind-Reading • Fortune-Telling	✓	Jason doesn't have any evidence that he'll get shot down or that everyone in the grocery store will look down on him if he tries to flirt with her. Will they really be shocked if he smiles and says hello to the woman checking groceries? Will they secretly admire him if he represses his feelings and acts like a monk?
6. Magnification or Minimization	✓	Jason magnifies his own importance. Do the people in line really care that much about what he does?
7. Emotional Reasoning	✓	He *feels* like he'll get shot down, so he thinks he really *will*. He *feels* like a self-centered jerk, and so he thinks he really *is* one.
8. Should Statements	✓	Jason thinks that he should always be quiet and humble and should never look foolish or get shot down.
9. Labeling	✓	Jason labels himself as "a self-centered jerk."
10. Blame • Self-Blame • Other-Blame	✓	Jason thinks that if this girl rejects him, it means that something's wrong with him. In fact, he could be extremely attractive and charming, and she still might not be interested in him.

Let's see if we can give Jason some help. His first negative thought is: "I don't have anything interesting to say." This thought contains many distortions, but it's a classic example of All-or-Nothing Thinking. Jason is telling himself that there will be one of two extreme outcomes: He'll either say something terribly clever and sweep her off her feet, or else he'll make a total fool of himself.

This mind-set makes his task pretty difficult. In the first place, he's not very experienced, so he's certainly not going to sweep her off her feet. And if he does try to flirt with her, he's convinced that all the other people in line will think he's a jerk. So no matter what happens, there will be a steep price to pay. He's placed himself in a can't-win situation with his All-or-Nothing Thinking, and it's easy to understand why he feels stuck. How could he talk back to his first negative thought, "I don't have anything interesting to say," using Thinking in Shades of Gray?

Remember, when you use this technique you stop evaluating yourself or your circumstances in extreme, black-or-white terms. Instead, you evaluate yourself or the situation in shades of gray—somewhere between 0% (total failure) and 100% (complete success). Jason feels like he has to have something terribly interesting to say to the cashier. Of course, this thought will make his mind go blank because it puts him under tremendous pressure to perform. Is there another message he could give himself that would relieve some of the pressure he feels? Put your ideas here before you continue reading.

_____

_____

_____

_____

Answer

Jason decided he could tell himself: "I probably don't need to say anything terribly clever or interesting. I could just start by smiling and saying hello, and that would be a great first step." As you can see in the "% Belief" column on page 176, he believed this thought 100%, and his belief in the negative thought went down to 25%.

Do you recall what the necessary and sufficient conditions for emotional change are? The positive thought has to be 100% true—this is the necessary

Negative Thoughts	% Before	% After	Distortions	Positive Thoughts	% Belief
1. I don't have anything interesting to say.	100%	25%	AON, OG, MF, DP, MR, MIN, ER, SH, SB	1. I probably don't need to say anything terribly clever or interesting. I could just start by smiling and saying hello, and that would be a great first step.	100%

condition—and it has to put the lie to the negative thought—this is the sufficient condition. Jason said that this positive thought did relieve the pressure he was putting on himself because he wouldn't have to try so hard.

Process versus Outcome

You can evaluate your performance based on the process—the effort you put in—or on the outcome. Both measures are important. However, your preparation and hard work are within your control, but the outcome often isn't.

For example, your grade on an important examination may depend on the kinds of questions that the teacher asks, how well the other students do, and where the teacher sets the curve. The mood the teacher is in when she or he grades your examination may also play a role. None of these factors is within your control.

In contrast, you can control the effort you put in. For example, you can go to all the classes, take good notes, and ask the teacher about anything you don't understand. You can also do the homework assignments faithfully and carefully prepare for the exam. If you do these things, you can give yourself an A+ for your hard work, but you'll have to let the chips fall where they may, regardless of the outcome.

How could Jason use the Process versus Outcome Technique to talk back to his ninth negative thought, "If I tried to flirt with her, I'd probably get shot down"? Put your ideas here before you continue reading.

_____

_____

_____

_____

Answer

Jason could remind himself that his actions are within his control but the outcome is not. If he smiles and says hello to her, he can give himself an A+ on this assignment, no matter how she reacts, because he'll have taken that crucial first step out of the prison he's been trapped in for so long.

The Process versus Outcome Technique has been helpful to me on many occasions. As a psychiatrist, sometimes I'm confronted with challenging and stressful situations that seem beyond my control. For example, I once treated a severely depressed young woman named Rachel who'd been diagnosed with borderline personality disorder. This is an extremely difficult form of depression, with lots of manipulation and self-destructive behavior. Rachel was turbulent, impulsive, and uncooperative. She'd been treated by many therapists and had made a number of nearly successful suicide attempts.

Shortly after we began to work together, Rachel defiantly announced that she intended to commit suicide right after the session. I explained that the prognosis for improvement was positive and that if she stuck with the treatment, I was convinced she could improve a lot. I also told her that I cared about her and that it was my legal and ethical obligation to prevent her from making a suicide attempt.

Rachel insisted that I *couldn't* stop her. Suddenly she jumped from her chair and bolted toward the door. I managed to wedge myself between her and the door and attempted to restrain her as she screamed and struggled to get out. I grabbed one of her wrists and reached for the phone with my other hand so I could dial 911 for help.

Two officers arrived a couple minutes later, and I explained what was going on. They asked Rachel if she intended to commit suicide; she said she did. They took her into custody and told me that they'd contact her family and arrange for hospitalization if Rachel didn't back down from her threats. As they dragged her from my office, she shouted obscenities and screamed that I was the worst, stupidest shrink in the entire world and that she hated my guts.

I felt guilty and tremendously disappointed, and realized I'd probably never see her again. I felt like a failure, since the outcome of my treatment hadn't seemed very impressive. Still, when I evaluated my actual performance, I couldn't find any fault in what I'd done. I decided to tell myself I did a good job in a tough situation, even though it didn't turn out quite the way I wanted. I reminded myself that I might have saved her life.

Over the next several years, I thought about Rachel from time to time. Sometimes I'd tell myself, "Well, she's one patient I really screwed up with." Then I'd ask myself, "In what way did I screw up? What, specifically, did I do wrong? Is there something I should have done differently?" When I looked at the situation objectively, it seemed like I'd done the right thing, even though the outcome felt so discouraging.

Five years later, I got a call from the chief of the National Institute of Mental Health. He said, "Did you ever treat a young woman named Rachel Clark?"

My heart began to pound, and I was gripped with anxiety. I thought, "I bet she's filed an ethics complaint or a malpractice suit. He's probably calling to scold me for the bad work I did." I sheepishly admitted that I'd worked with her several years earlier, "but only for a few sessions."

He asked what treatment methods I'd used.

I explained that we'd just started using Cognitive Therapy techniques to challenge her negative thoughts, but when I told her she'd have to do psychotherapy homework between sessions, she got angry and threatened to commit suicide. As a result, she had to be hospitalized and never returned to complete the therapy. Then I asked why he was calling.

I was surprised by what he said next. He explained that the night she left my office, Rachel had been hospitalized near her parents' home in Washington, D.C. Since then, she'd been treated by eight psychiatrists, but no one had been able to get through to her, so Rachel had been referred to him. She told him that I was the only psychiatrist who'd ever helped her, and he was calling to find out what I'd done!

To this day, I'm not quite sure what it was. Perhaps it was because I'd used tough love, or because I refused to buy in to her belief that she was hopeless and worthless. I think she really became enraged that day because I was making her accountable for the first time. I was very clear that her recovery would come about only as a result of teamwork and that if she wanted to work with me, she'd have to do psychotherapy homework between sessions. *That* was the moment when she exploded.

If I'd evaluated my performance based on the fact that she had to be dragged from my office by the police, kicking and screaming obscenities and threatening suicide, I would have concluded that I'd failed miserably. But the messages I delivered that day were the ones that Rachel needed to hear, and my actions probably saved her life.

Semantic Method

When you use the Semantic Method, you simply substitute kinder and gentler language for the emotionally colorful and hurtful words you use when you're feeling upset. You may have noticed that when you're anxious or depressed, you beat up on yourself with shoulds, oughts, musts, and have-tos. Sometimes you'll direct the Should Statements toward yourself, and sometimes you'll direct them toward other people or the world in general. Self-directed Should Statements cause feelings of depression, anxiety, inferiority, guilt, and shame. For example, if you're struggling with feelings of shyness and insecurity, you may feel ashamed and inferior because you tell yourself, "What's wrong with me? I *shouldn't* feel so nervous and insecure." If you slipped up and binged when you were trying to diet, you may tell yourself, "I *shouldn't* have eaten that pint of ice cream. I'm such a fat pig! I just can't control myself." If you've been struggling with feelings of worthlessness or inferiority, you may tell yourself that you're not as good as other people or as good as you think you *should* be.

Other-directed Should Statements cause feelings of resentment and anger. For example, if you're ticked off at a friend, you may be thinking "He's such a jerk! He's got no right to treat me like that!" This is called a Hidden Should Statement because the *should* is implied. What you're really saying is "He *shouldn't* be like that!" If you get enraged when another driver cuts into your lane on the freeway, you may tell yourself something like this: "What an aggressive asshole!" This is also a Hidden Should Statement. What you're really saying is that the other driver *shouldn't* be so reckless and aggressive. It's also an example of Labeling because you're judging his entire character based on his driving. Should Statements and Labeling often go hand in hand. The Semantic Method can be helpful for both of these distortions.

When you direct Should Statements toward the world in general, you'll feel frustration. For example, if you sprain your ankle two days before a marathon you've been training for, you may get frustrated because you tell yourself, "It's unfair!" This is a Hidden Should Statement because you're implying that things should always go the way you expect them to. It's also an example of Labeling. Spraining your ankle was "unfortunate," but it's not "unfair." After all, the rock you stepped on when you twisted your ankle wasn't actually being "unfair." It was just lying there on the path, minding its own business, when you stepped on it.

Should Statements can be very difficult to get rid of because they're addictive and make you feel morally superior. In addition, you may think that something good will happen if you protest loudly enough when things don't go your way. For example, you may believe that if you beat up on yourself and make yourself miserable whenever you fall short of your goals, you'll eventually achieve something fantastic.

Many famous psychiatrists and psychologists—including Sigmund Freud—have tried to help people overcome this tendency to beat up on themselves and other people. Dr. Karen Horney, the feminist psychiatrist of the 1950s, gained fame when she wrote about "the Tyranny of the Shoulds." Dr. Albert Ellis, the noted New York psychologist, also believes that most emotional suffering results from the shoulds and absolutist demands we make on ourselves and others. He calls this tendency "musterbation."

When you use the Semantic Method, you simply substitute language that's less colorful and emotionally loaded when you think about yourself and your problems. For example, instead of telling yourself "I *shouldn't* be so shy," you can tell yourself, "It would be *preferable* if I weren't so shy." Instead of telling yourself "I *shouldn't* have made that mistake," you can tell yourself, "It would be great if I hadn't made that mistake, but I'm human, so I will make mistakes sometimes. Perhaps I can learn from the situation." As you can see, this technique is pretty simple. Instead of telling yourself "I *should have* done X" or "I *shouldn't have* done Y," you substitute an expression along the lines of "It would be preferable if I'd done X" or "if I hadn't done Y." These semantic modifications may seem small, but they can make a huge impact on the way you feel.

Should Statements aren't always irrational or self-defeating. There are actually three valid uses of the word "should" in the English language: moral shoulds, legal shoulds, and laws-of-the-universe shoulds. It's okay to say "Thou shalt not kill," because that's a moral should. It's also okay to say "You should not rob a bank," because that's a legal should. And it's okay to say "If I drop this pencil right now, it should fall toward the floor," because that's a laws-of-the-universe should.

The Should Statements that cause emotional distress don't usually fall into any of these three categories. For example, when you tell yourself, "I shouldn't be so shy," is that a moral should? It's not immoral to be shy. It's just uncomfortable. Is it a legal should? It's not illegal to feel shy. Is it a laws-of-the-universe should? When you feel shy, you're not violating any of the laws of nature. So when you tell yourself you *shouldn't* be shy, you're creating two problems for the price of one. Now you have to contend with your shyness as well as all the feelings of shame and inferiority you create when you tell yourself that you *shouldn't* be that way.

The word "should" comes from the Anglo-Saxon word *scolde*. When you use Should Statements, you're really scolding yourself or other people. When you use the Semantic Method, the goal is not really to put the lie to the Should Statement, but rather to take the sting out of it.

A woman named Regina was feeling anxious when she was planning her wedding because she was telling herself "It has to be perfect. If something goes wrong, everyone will look down on me." You may have noticed this thought contains a hidden Should Statement. This thought put her under tremendous pressure and made her feel that she and her fiancé were going to be under constant scrutiny from a judgmental audience during her wedding. Using the Semantic Method, how could Regina talk back to this thought? Put your ideas here before you continue reading.

_____

_____

_____

_____

_____

Answer

Regina decided to think about it like this instead:

I don't know what a "perfect" wedding would be like, but my fiancé and I can plan a simple and meaningful ceremony with a group of family and friends we really care about, and we can exchange vows that will be personally meaningful to us. It's not likely that anything major will go wrong, but if it does, I'm sure the people who really care about us will pitch in and help out.

This thought relieved the pressure Regina had been feeling. She simply reframed the wedding as an opportunity to make a public statement of the values that were meaningful to her and to feel close to her friends and family.

Let's Define Terms

When you're depressed or anxious, you may label yourself as "inferior," a "fool," a "fraud," or a "failure." Ask yourself what those labels mean. If you try to define what you mean by an "inferior human being," a "fool," a "fraud," or a "failure," you'll usually discover that one of four things is true:

- The label applies to all human beings.
- The label applies to no human beings.
- The label is inherently meaningless.
- The label doesn't apply to you.

For example, what's the definition of a "fool"? Is it someone who does foolish things all of the time or some of the time? If you say "all of the time," then no one is a fool, because no one does foolish things all of the time. But if you say "some of the time," then we're all fools, because we all do foolish things some of the time. No matter how you define the term, your definition will always fall apart.

This may sound like a trick with words, but it gets at something that's philosophically important. Foolish behaviors exist, but "fools" do not. Since there's no such "thing" as "a fool," you couldn't possibly be one! But if you label yourself as a fool, you'll feel anxious, inferior, and ashamed, and you'll feel like a fool—even though there is no such thing.

Many of my patients have labeled themselves as "loonies" or "nutcases" because they believe that feelings like shyness or panic are shameful, weird, or abnormal. Of course, you'll pay a pretty heavy price for labeling yourself this way. But what's the definition of "a nutcase"? Is there any such thing?

Let's say you define "a nutcase" as someone who's crazy. Then I'd ask, "What's your definition of someone who's crazy?"

You might say, "Someone with a mental disorder like schizophrenia."

Then I'd point out that people with schizophrenia suffer tremendously, but their symptoms are quite different from the symptoms of anxiety. For example, they hear voices coming from outside their heads and experience bizarre delusions. People who are struggling with feelings of shyness or anxiety generally don't have schizophrenia. Furthermore, it would be pretty cruel to label someone with schizophrenia as "a nutcase."

Let's say you define "a nutcase" differently. You say, "Well, what I really meant is that a nutcase is someone with irrational fears." Can you see any loopholes in this definition? Put your ideas here.

_____

_____

_____

_____

It's pretty easy to attack this definition. What percentage of human beings have had irrational fears at some point in their lives? When you think about it, you'll have to admit that it's pretty close to 100%. For example, you may have been anxious the first time you had to put your head underwater when you were learning to swim, but you quickly realized you could hold your breath and that it was actually fun to swim underwater. So, according to this definition, we're all "nutcases."

Let's say that you define "a nutcase" as someone who has more irrational fears than other people. Now you could ask yourself this question: "More irrational fears than all other people or some other people?" If you say "all other people," then you can't be a nutcase, because there will always be someone in the world who's nuttier than you are! But if you say "some other people," then we're all nutcases because there will always be people who are saner and less nutty than we are.

Every day, I see patients who label themselves with these kinds of thoughts:

- I'm inferior.
- I'm worthless.
- I'm a failure.
- I'm a hopeless case.

Let's focus on the thought "I'm a failure." Let's say you define "a failure" as someone who's never succeeded at anything. See if you can attack this definition. Try to show that it's meaningless, or that it applies to all human beings or to no human beings.

If "a failure" is someone who's never succeeded at anything, then there's no such thing as "a failure" because we've all succeeded at many things. You learned to talk, read, write, go to the bathroom, and so forth.

Since that definition didn't work, you decide to define "a failure" as someone who fails more than the average person. How could you attack this definition?

In this case, more than three billion human beings are "failures," since there are more than six billion of us. By definition, average is just the halfway point.

Suppose you try again. This time you define "a failure" as someone who's never accomplished anything truly spectacular. How would you attack this definition?

_____

_____

_____

_____

According to this definition, we're nearly all "failures." After all, only a tiny fraction of human beings can ever enjoy the success of an Einstein, a Beethoven, a Michael Jordan, or a Bill Gates. And furthermore, if we are all "failures," then being a failure can't be such a bad thing! We'll all have lots of company. No matter how you define this term, it will always fall apart.

The goal of Let's Define Terms is not to deny your flaws or failures. We all have to confront failure, and we all have lots of real shortcomings we need to work on. The goal of this technique is simply to free you from the shame, discouragement, and paralysis that result from hurtful and meaningless labels.

Be Specific

Performance anxiety results from the fear of failure. You tell yourself, "What if I blow it? That would be awful! I couldn't stand it!" You may tell yourself that if you fail, everyone will look down on you and it will mean that you're a failure as a human being. Of course, this thought involves Overgeneralization, because you're generalizing from your performance to your self. Overgeneralization can create anxiety as well as depression, because you'll feel like your sense of self-esteem and pride are on the line. When you use the Be Specific Technique, you stick with reality and avoid making global judgments about yourself. Instead of thinking of yourself as "a failure," you can focus on your specific strengths and weaknesses.

A University of California graduate student named Jackson came to see me for help with a lifetime of anxiety and depression. Although Jackson was doing stellar work and was ranked near the top of his class, he woke up every morning in a state of despair because he told himself:

- I can't figure out *anything!*
- I'm so dumb and incapable.

- Without my achievements, I'd just be average. There's really nothing special about me.
- Pretty soon, everybody will find out that I'm defective.

Jackson's constant self-criticisms were robbing him of any real pleasure or satisfaction in life. No matter how much he accomplished, he told himself that it wasn't good enough and that he should be doing better. During a session I supervised, Jackson described his problems like this: "I wake up every morning with a sense of doom. I tell myself that I won't ever accomplish anything worthwhile and feel like an awful, terrible person. By evening, I usually feel better, but in the morning, it seems like my whole world is about to fall apart. I get so anxious that I get short of breath. I've always based my self-esteem on my achievements, and I've gotten lots of praise for my academic work. But I've never felt like I had any intrinsic sense of self-worth. Even when things go really well, I can't seem to give myself any credit."

Jackson had recently submitted a paper to the top journal in his field, and it was accepted for publication. Instead of feeling excited, though, he felt panicky. He was absolutely certain that everyone who read the paper would see all the loopholes in his thinking and realize what a fraud he was.

Jackson told me that he'd struggled with feelings of insecurity for as long as he could remember. When he was a boy, his parents had gotten divorced. Jackson shut down emotionally and became so preoccupied with his studies that he lost interest in friends and stopped playing with other children in the neighborhood. His mother sent him to a counselor, but it didn't help.

Jackson said that he was still plagued by feelings of intense fear and inadequacy, and these feelings got fired up every time he had to meet with his supervisor. I asked Jackson what he was telling himself. He said, "I feel like my supervisor will see all the problems with my proposal and react negatively." I wanted to find out what Jackson was so afraid of so I decided to use the Downward Arrow Technique, which you learned about in Chapter 7. I asked him to write "My supervisor will see all the problems with my proposal and react negatively" on his Daily Mood Log and put a downward arrow underneath it. Here's how our dialogue went:

David: Jackson, let's assume that your supervisor does have some criticisms of your work. What would that mean to you? Why would it be upsetting to you?

Jackson: I've worked really hard on the proposal, so it would mean that my best work wasn't any good.

David: And then what? Let's assume that your best work wasn't any good. What would that mean to you?

Jackson: That would mean that there was something wrong with me.

David: And what then? Let's assume that there *was* something wrong with you? Would that be a problem?

Jackson: Oh yes, it would mean that I was a defective, incompetent human being.

You can see that Jackson's negative thoughts are loaded with cognitive distortions, but the two that really jumped out at me were Overgeneralization and Labeling. Jackson was telling himself that if his work wasn't up to speed, it would mean that he was defective. You can see that he bases his entire sense of self-esteem on his accomplishments and that if even one project goes badly, it means that he's a failure. Furthermore, he doesn't even have any evidence that his project will go poorly. So far, he's been doing great.

How are we going to help Jackson change the negative thoughts and attitudes that are making him feel so insecure? Remember that our suffering does not result from reality but from the judgments we make. In addition, these judgments are illusions. For example, there's no such thing as a "success" or a "failure." These concepts exist only in our minds.

In the following dialogue, Jackson and I will enter a nightmare world where his worst fears actually come true. Jackson will encounter a Supervisor from Hell who attacks him in all the same ways that he's been attacking himself. The Supervisor from Hell represents the part of his mind that makes him feel anxious and insecure. I'm playing the role of the Supervisor and will attack Jackson in the same way that he criticizes himself. I told Jackson to do his best and see if he could defeat me. Here's how our dialogue unfolded:

Supervisor from Hell (played by David): Jackson, I've reviewed your proposal
    and I have to inform you that it isn't any good.

Jackson: Well, you're entitled to your opinion, but I believe that my proposal
    does have merit.

There's a problem with this response. Jackson is defending himself. When
you defend yourself, you create a state of war, because the critic will feel the
urge to attack you again. In this case, the critic is really just the projection of
Jackson's own self-criticisms, so he'll end up in a battle with himself. Furthermore, his defense isn't convincing. Since the Supervisor from Hell is an expert,
Jackson's defensive response won't have any credibility.

I suggested we could reverse roles so I could model a radically different
way of responding to the Supervisor from Hell. In the next dialogue, I use Be
Specific and the Acceptance Paradox.

Supervisor from Hell (played by Jackson): Jackson, I've reviewed your disser-
    tation proposal.

Jackson (played by David): What did you think?

Supervisor from Hell: Unfortunately, it isn't any good.

Jackson: Gee, that's not what I was hoping to hear because I've been working
    hard on it, but I have no doubt that there's lots of room for improvement.
    Can you tell me about some of the things you didn't like?

Supervisor from Hell: Unfortunately, I can't. Your proposal stinks and I
    wouldn't even know where to begin. In fact, it's not just your proposal that
    I'm concerned about. It's you. I've realized that you're a defective and in-
    competent human being.

Jackson: Wow, that's some pretty harsh criticism. I want to make sure that I
    understand what you're saying. I know I have lots of flaws, but I'm not sure
    what you're thinking about when you say that I'm a defective and incom-
    petent human being. Can you fill me in on the specifics?

Supervisor from Hell: There are no specifics. You're globally defective. Do I
    have to spell it out for you?

Jackson: It would help me a lot if you could.

Supervisor from Hell: I've already told you. There *are* no specifics! Weren't you listening? If you had half a brain, you'd know what I was talking about!

Jackson: I apologize if I seem dense. Are you saying that there aren't any specific problems with my proposal or my life that you could mention?

Supervisor from Hell: No, stupid! I've told you that you have *so many* deficiencies that I wouldn't know where to begin. It would be like trying to clean out the New York sewer system with a spoon.

Jackson: Boy, that definitely sounds like an unpleasant task, but I have to admit that I still don't have a clear idea of what you're thinking about. It sounds like you're annoyed with me, and there's definitely a sharp edge in your voice. I'm still trying to understand what you're saying because I have great respect for you and for your expertise. Did I focus on the wrong questions in my proposal? Did I propose the wrong methods to try to answer those questions? Did I select a bad topic? Was my writing unclear? I feel like I need something to hang my hat on.

Supervisor from Hell: I told you already. You stink. Your ideas stink. Your work stinks. Enough said! Good-bye!

Jackson could see that no matter what he said, he couldn't get to me with his vague, global attacks. He realized that the real goofball was the Supervisor from Hell, not himself. Interacting with someone like this might be a bit disconcerting, but Jackson could see that the Supervisor from Hell was clearly the one who needed help.

Let's imagine that the Supervisor from Hell had come up with a specific criticism, such as "Your proposal is way too long." Then Jackson could say, "Good point. I'll cut it down. How many pages would you recommend?"

Jackson and I did a role reversal, to make sure that he could defeat the Supervisor from Hell. He did a great job, and I couldn't get to him. At the end of the session, he was feeling a lot better.

You don't need another person to use this technique. Writing out a dialogue with an imaginary critic instead of role-playing with a friend can be just as effective.

The main idea behind this technique is to move from vague overgeneralizations about your worth as a human being to specific flaws or defects. A specific criticism can never make you feel depressed or anxious, because it will be totally valid, partially valid, or not at all valid. If it's not at all valid, there's no reason to feel as if your self-esteem is on the line. If it's partially or completely valid, there's still no reason to feel worthless or inferior. You can simply accept the criticism and try to learn from it.

....

Chapter 13

Quantitative Techniques

Have you ever heard of biofeedback? Biofeedback is where you hook yourself up to an electronic device that constantly records a particular bodily function, such as your heart rate, blood pressure, brain waves, or muscle tension. The results are displayed on a television monitor. Biofeedback makes you aware of physiological activity you usually don't notice and allows you to control the activity. For example, you can learn how to slow your heart rate or reduce your blood pressure. Unfortunately, we don't yet have sophisticated electronic devices to help you monitor your thoughts, but you can achieve similar results with two quantitative techniques called Self-Monitoring and Worry Breaks.

Self-Monitoring

The Self-Monitoring Technique is really simple. All you have to do is count your negative thoughts throughout the day. If you continue Self-Monitoring for a period of time, you'll often experience a significant reduction in your negative thoughts and a marked improvement in the way you feel.

An easy way to do Self-Monitoring is to purchase a score counter like the ones golfers wear on their wrists to keep track of their scores. You can find them at golf shops or sporting goods stores, or buy them online. They're inexpensive (less than $10) and look like watches. Each time you have a negative thought, you push the button on the edge of the counter, and the number on the dial goes up by one. At the end of the day, you can record the total number of thoughts you had that day and set the counter back to zero. Usually you'll need to keep this up for a few weeks before you experience relief.

If you can't find a wrist counter, you can simply keep an index card in your pocket. Each time you have a negative thought, put a tick mark on the card. At the end of the day, tally up the tick marks and record the total.

This technique was helpful to an ophthalmologist named José who was anxious because he noticed floaters in his eyes. A "floater" is just a little speck that floats across your visual field. It's perfectly normal and usually means nothing. You may have noticed floaters in your visual field from time to time.

Each time José noticed a floater, however, he thought, "I might be going blind." This thought made him so nervous that he'd give himself an eye examination just to check things out. Of course, his vision always turned out to be perfect, and he felt temporarily relieved. But after a while, he'd notice another floater and get upset. Soon he'd be checking his vision again.

In rare cases, floaters might indicate the early stages of retinal degeneration, particularly if someone has childhood-onset diabetes. In these cases, laser surgery can be helpful. But José didn't have diabetes, and there was no reason for him to be checking his vision so often.

You might say he was a hypochondriac, except that he was both the patient and the doctor! You could also say that he was suffering from obsessive-compulsive disorder (OCD), because he had a recurring obsessive thought, "I might be going blind," and a compulsive ritual, checking his vision over and over.

José was checking his vision as often as twenty times a day at work. Sometimes he'd squeeze in a quick vision check between every patient. On weekends, he became so consumed by the fear of going blind that he'd go on a binge and check his vision over and over again all day long. This may sound wacky, but it's the way OCD works. It's like an addiction. José wasn't nuts. He was an outstanding doctor and a very gentle, caring individual. But he was being consumed by his anxiety and by the compulsion to check his vision, in much the same way that Howard Hughes, the billionaire, became totally consumed by his fears of contamination.

The upsetting event on José's Daily Mood Log was simply "Noticing a floater." He felt down, anxious, panicky, frightened, ashamed, foolish, frustrated, and annoyed. The thoughts that triggered these feelings were "I might be going blind" and "I better check my vision, just to be on the safe side." What distortions are present in these two negative thoughts? Use checks (✓) to indicate your answers below. You can refer to the definitions of the cognitive distortions on page 79.

Distortion	(✓)	Distortion	(✓)
1. All-or-Nothing Thinking		6. Magnification or Minimization	
2. Overgeneralization		7. Emotional Reasoning	
3. Mental Filter		8. Should Statements	
4. Discounting the Positive		9. Labeling	
5. Jumping to Conclusions • Mind-Reading • Fortune-Telling		10. Blame • Self-Blame • Other-Blame	

Answer

As you can see on page 194, José and I found six distortions in his negative thoughts "I might be going blind" and "I better check my vision, just to be on the safe side."

I wanted to find out if José was motivated to overcome his obsessions and compulsions, so I asked him to list all the advantages and disadvantages of checking his vision every time he saw a floater. As you can see, he listed several advantages. For example, if he kept checking his vision, he could catch any problem early and get treatment. However, there were also some disadvantages, not the least of which was the fact that the anxiety was ruining his life.

José decided that the disadvantages outweighed the advantages by a 60 to 40 margin and said that he was willing to stop examining his eyes, in spite of

José's Distortions

Distortion	(✓)	Explanation
1. All-or-Nothing Thinking		Not present.
2. Overgeneralization		Not present.
3. Mental Filter	✓	José constantly obsesses about the floaters, even though he knows they're not medically significant.
4. Discounting the Positive	✓	He discounts the fact that his vision is perfect and that there's no reason to suspect any problem with his eyes.
5. Jumping to Conclusions • Mind-Reading • Fortune-Telling	✓	He constantly worries that he's on the verge of going blind, even though he knows he's not (Fortune-Telling).
6. Magnification or Minimization	✓	He greatly exaggerates the importance of the floaters and minimizes the fact that he has perfect vision.
7. Emotional Reasoning	✓	José throws logic out the window and reasons from how he feels. He *feels* like he's about to go blind, so he assumes that he really *is* in danger.
8. Should Statements	✓	He tells himself that he *should* check his vision, even though he knows intellectually that it's totally unnecessary.
9. Labeling		Not present.
10. Blame • Self-Blame • Other-Blame		Not present.

José's Cost-Benefit Analysis

Describe the attitude, feeling, or habit that you want to change: Checking my vision many times a day.

Advantages	Disadvantages
1. It's reassuring.	1. The odds of a real problem are low.
2. I can catch any problem early.	2. The constant checking is not necessary.
3. I can get help if I need it.	3. The anxiety is ruining my life.

(40)———————(60)

the fact that there were some definite advantages. To be absolutely certain he felt this way, I said, "José, let's pretend there's a button here on the desk. If you pushed that button, all of your anxiety and worrying about floaters would suddenly disappear. Would you push it?"

"Of course, Doctor," he replied.

I said, "But then, if you get a floater, you won't check your vision, so you could end up with a serious eye problem or even go blind. Are you *sure* that you want to push that button?"

José thought for a moment and then explained he would still push the button because there was nothing wrong with his eyes. Furthermore, if he ever did have a serious eye problem—which was extremely unlikely—there'd be other symptoms as well, such as blurred vision, so there was no valid medical reason for him to check his vision over and over every day. Clearly, José was strongly motivated to do what it took to overcome this problem.

I asked José if he'd agree to stop checking his vision for an entire month, no matter how anxious he got. This is called Response Prevention, and it's extremely important in the treatment of OCD. Response Prevention means that you prevent yourself from responding to your anxiety in the way you usually do, such as checking, washing, counting, praying, arranging things symmetrically, or engaging in other superstitious rituals. José was addicted to checking his vision every time he got anxious, because the checking caused immediate feelings of relief. He'd have to stop doing this if he wanted to get over the problem. When you give up a compulsive habit, your anxiety will almost always increase for several days. This is very much like the withdrawal that addicts have to endure when they go cold turkey. But if you stick with it, your compulsive urges will generally disappear.

I also proposed Self-Monitoring. I suggested that for the next several weeks, every time he had the thought "I might be going blind," he could count it on a wrist counter. That way, he could keep track of how many times he had this thought and see if his fears diminished over time.

You can see José's progress on his Self-Monitoring Chart on page 196. The days are on the horizontal axis, and the number of obsessive thoughts he had each day are on the vertical axis. Jose recorded his thoughts about his vision every day for 22 days. As you can see, he had more than 60 thoughts the first

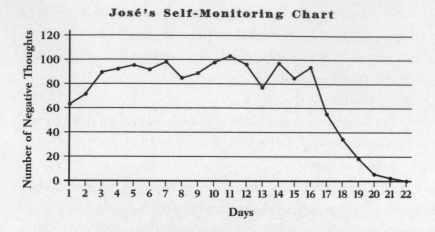

José's Self-Monitoring Chart

day. He reached a plateau of around 90 thoughts a day by the third day. On day 13, his thoughts dipped below 80 but jumped back up to 98 the following day. On day 17, his obsessive thoughts about his vision dropped below 60. They dropped below 40 on day 18. On day 20, he had only 5 thoughts about his vision, and by day 22, his thoughts about his vision disappeared entirely. José no longer believed he was going blind, and had no further urges to check his vision.

Like any intervention, Self-Monitoring has about a one-in-ten chance of being effective. If it had failed, I would have tried other techniques, one at a time, until we found one that was effective. If you'd like to try Self-Monitoring, remember that it usually takes a while before the upsetting thoughts diminish, so you should plan to stick with it for at least three weeks. You can count negative thoughts in general or a specific type of negative thought. During the first few days, the number of negative thoughts may increase as you get better and better at noticing them. Over time, they'll often diminish or disappear.

Scientists don't know why Self-Monitoring works, but it may work in the same way that meditation works. When you meditate, you concentrate on one thing. For example, you can imagine the air going slowly in through your nose and out through your mouth while you breathe slowly and deeply. At first, you may find that this is difficult, because your mind quickly wanders off to different topics, such as what you're going to do later in the day or something that's bothering you. When this happens, you simply note the distracting thought and then focus on your breathing again. You gently bring your mind back every time it wanders off.

Similarly, when you use Self-Monitoring, you simply note each distracting negative thought. Once you've counted it on your wrist counter or checked it off on your index card, you can let go of it and focus on whatever you were doing at the time it popped into your mind.

Self-Monitoring was also helpful to a carpenter named Phil who became depressed and anxious following a stroke. Phil had spells of uncontrollable crying or laughing at the slightest stimulus. Glimpsing a sunset, a baby, or even a flower would evoke sudden bouts of sobbing, and the blandest joke evoked paroxysms of uncontrollable laughter. This pattern of emotional outbursts is common after certain kinds of strokes, and it results from brain damage.

The upsetting event on Phil's Daily Mood Log was "Playing poker with my buddies and suddenly weeping." Poker was one of the things Phil enjoyed the most in life, but he was having a lot of trouble because of the unpredictable emotional outbursts. If he got a good hand, he'd start cackling uncontrollably, and if he got a bad hand, he'd start sobbing. This made it awfully tough for him to bluff, so he was understandably feeling frustrated, embarrassed, anxious, and inadequate.

His first negative thought was "I can't control myself." One of the distortions in this thought was All-or-Nothing Thinking, since he could control himself somewhat. He just couldn't control himself as well as he wanted. Phil's second negative thought was "They'll feel sorry for me and not want to play poker with me anymore." This thought is a classic example of Mind-Reading, since he's making assumptions about how his friends are thinking and feeling.

I encouraged Phil to purchase a stopwatch and keep it in his pocket. Each time he sensed he was about to burst into tears or laughter, he could start the stopwatch. Then when he began to laugh or cry, he could hit the button on the stopwatch again and record how many seconds had gone by on a small notebook he kept in his pocket.

That way, he could keep track of how long he could delay each emotional outburst, in much the same way that athletes keep track of their times when training for a competition. The idea was that even though Phil couldn't control his emotions completely, he might be able to control them a little bit. With practice, his emotional control might improve. This plan appealed to Phil since he'd been very active in sports throughout his life, and he was familiar with the idea of getting in shape through regular training. He was curious to find out if he could also master his emotional outbursts through training.

The first day, he was able to postpone the laughing or crying for only a few seconds, but by the end of the first week, he could routinely postpone it for twenty seconds. By the end of the second week, he could postpone the outbursts for nearly a minute. By the end of the third week, Phil could postpone them indefinitely.

People often ask how Cognitive Therapy can be effective if depression and anxiety result from a chemical imbalance in the brain. Don't you have to take a pill to change your brain chemistry? Phil's case provides a fairly compelling answer to that question. His emotional outbursts clearly resulted from brain damage, but a rather humble Cognitive Therapy technique quickly led to his rapid recovery from his depression and anxiety. Medications weren't necessary.

Recent brain-imaging studies have confirmed that Cognitive Behavior Therapy actually changes brain chemistry in the same way that antidepressant drugs do. I find it exciting that we now have so many powerful weapons for fighting emotional distress and that we don't always have to rely on pills.

The beauty of Self-Monitoring is that it's easy, and it often works like a charm. However, it's not effective for everybody, and more sophisticated techniques may be needed.

Worry Breaks

Worry breaks are a Paradoxical Technique. Instead of fighting your negative thoughts, you go with the flow and give in to them. You schedule one or more periods each day to feel worried, depressed, or guilty. During these times, you make yourself as upset as possible by bombarding yourself with negative thoughts. The rest of the time, you can focus on living your life in a positive, productive manner.

You can use this technique to overcome the thoughts that trigger anxiety or depression. I once treated a depressed and anxious physician named Mark who constantly bombarded himself with negative thoughts. Even though he was an excellent physician, he had thoughts like these when he was examining his patients during rounds at the hospital:

- I'm such a lousy doctor.
- Did I listen to her heart properly?
- I probably missed something important.
- What's wrong with me?
- Other doctors have a better bedside manner. I'm not very warm or friendly.
- My colleagues all seem so confident.
- Why am I so nervous and insecure? I shouldn't be having all these negative thoughts.
- My whole life is in shambles.

Mark's peers and patients regarded him as an excellent and dedicated physician, so these thoughts weren't very realistic. In addition, it wasn't productive for him to beat up on himself like this, because the feelings of guilt, anxiety, and worthlessness distracted him and interfered with his ability to concentrate on his patients. It also made it harder for him to listen while patients voiced their concerns because he was so distracted by the constant barrage of self-criticisms.

Mark couldn't very easily write down his negative thoughts while he was doing examinations, so he purchased a tiny tape recorder and kept it in the pocket of the white lab coat he wore during rounds. When he was walking from room to room, he pulled out the tape recorder and dictated his negative thoughts in a hushed voice. He didn't attempt to talk back to his thoughts. He just verbalized them, like this: "Oh, I did such a lousy job with that patient. She probably has a liver problem that I overlooked. Any other doctor could have done a better job. Even a medical student could have done better. She seemed especially upset today and I didn't even listen to what she had to say."

When he was with his patients, he tried to focus on their concerns and medical problems rather than his own negative thoughts, since he knew he could dictate them into the tape recorder the moment he was done. At the end of rounds, he went to his office, rewound the tape, and forced himself to listen to all his self-criticisms. At first, this was upsetting, but after a few days, the negative thoughts began to sound ludicrous. Before long, they began to sound so silly that he no longer believed them at all. He experienced a substantial reduction in his anxiety and depression and an increase in his feelings of self-esteem.

Worry Breaks are worth a try whenever worrying interferes with a task you're trying to complete, such as studying. Instead of fighting with your thoughts, you can simply schedule short periods of time to give in to them. During the breaks, you can:

- Write your negative thoughts on a piece of paper without challenging them.
- Sit quietly and bombard yourself with negative thoughts.
- Verbalize your negative thoughts out loud.
- Dictate them into a tape recorder, as Mark did.

The length and frequency of the Worry Breaks will be up to you. If you're studying for finals and you're feeling so anxious that you can't concentrate, you may need to schedule a one-minute Worry Break every thirty minutes, or you may find that one five-minute binge of worrying each day will be sufficient. It's strictly a matter of personal preference. If the Worry Breaks are distressing to you or don't seem helpful, don't push it. Just move on to another technique. There are many ways to defeat the negative thoughts that make you anxious.

Humor-Based Techniques

I used to conduct Cognitive Therapy groups in the inpatient unit of the Stanford University Hospital as part of my volunteer work for the medical school. The patients were suffering from the most severe forms of anxiety, depression, eating disorders, and addictions. At the beginning of each group, they often wept and expressed overwhelming feelings of hopelessness, worthlessness, panic, or frustration. Most had been in therapy for years and taken many medications, without success.

We used Daily Mood Logs and attacked the patients' negative, self-critical thoughts with the same techniques that you're learning to use in this book. Patients frequently experienced significant improvement right before our eyes, and sometimes their symptoms disappeared completely. Toward the end of the groups, the patients and I often ended up giggling uncontrollably for several minutes. Some of the most joyous and memorable experiences of my career have involved laughing and giggling with my patients.

The same is true in teaching. In my workshops, we usually spend lots of time laughing. Whenever the audience and I giggle a lot, I know we've got a great workshop going. Laughter teaches us something that words can only allude to. When you're laughing, you suddenly stop taking yourself so seriously and can see the absurdity of the fears or feelings of self-doubt that have intimidated you for so long. The laughter delivers a message of self-acceptance as well as acceptance of others.

In fact, I'm embarrassed to admit I once giggled uncontrollably for an entire session with a patient named Marie. We couldn't stop, and I was afraid that I was being terribly unprofessional. But that made the situation seem even more absurd, like a Monty Python movie, and I was practically rolling on the floor.

And what was so funny? Well, that's the awful part. When Marie came in and sat down at the start of the session, she announced that her father had just died. Good Lord! Why would a psychiatrist and a patient giggle about the sudden death of the patient's father? Now you're probably thinking that I'm really off my rocker. Well, it was actually the fifth time that Marie's father had died. Apparently, her mother tended to marry wealthy elderly men who died within a year or two of their marriage. So her mother kept getting wealthier and wealthier, and Marie had father after father. But she didn't like any of them and had barely gotten to know the last three.

Of course, she loved her real father a great deal, but he'd died of a massive heart attack when she was only fourteen years old. Now she was thirty-one, and for the past ten years, she'd had a parade of "fathers" she barely knew. She'd especially disliked the one who'd just died, so when she learned that he'd passed away, she felt happy. But that seemed totally inappropriate, and we both started giggling.

Once we started, we couldn't stop. I kept telling myself, "My gosh, you're a psychiatrist, and you're giggling about the death of your patient's father!" That idea made me giggle even more. It's a lot like when you're little and you get the giggles in church. The fact that you're supposed to be quiet and serious makes the giggling seem even funnier. And when Marie saw that I was giggling, it created a bond between us and made it easier for her to accept her own feelings.

Although the most memorable laughter occurs spontaneously during therapy sessions, three techniques intentionally capitalize on humor: Shame-Attacking Exercises, Paradoxical Magnification, and Humorous Imaging.

Shame-Attacking Exercises

If you suffer from social anxiety, you probably have an intense fear of looking foolish in front of other people. Shame-Attacking Exercises can be a potent antidote to this fear. When you do a Shame-Attacking Exercise, you intentionally do something foolish in public. You'll usually discover that most people don't look down on you and the world doesn't really come to an end. In fact, most of the time, everyone ends up having a lot of fun. This insight can be tremendously liberating. But it can be terrifying at first.

You've already seen a good example of a Shame-Attacking Exercise. You probably recall Trevor, the man with the sweating phobia. When we went into the local convenience store, pointed to our armpits, and proclaimed how sweaty we were, people's friendly responses changed his life.

I believe that Shame-Attacking Exercises were invented by Dr. Albert Ellis. Although he's over ninety years old now, he's still going strong! Dr. Ellis gives a prize to the therapist who has done the most creative and outrageous Shame-Attacking Exercise each year. Recently a psychologist from Portland took top honors. He went into a busy drugstore and asked the pharmacist, in a loud voice, "Can I buy four dozen condoms, please?"

The pharmacist nodded. Then, when everyone turned to look, the psychologist forced himself to ask, in an equally loud voice, "Do you have the little, teeny-weenie size?" Fortunately, a Shame-Attacking Exercise doesn't have to be quite that extreme to be effective.

I first learned about Shame-Attacking Exercises following a workshop I presented for Dr. Ellis's institute in New York. After my presentation, I went out to dinner at a Chinese restaurant with several of his colleagues. It was a popular restaurant, and we had to wait in a long line to be seated. The line curled around inside the restaurant, so we were standing near people who were already eating.

I told one of Dr. Ellis's colleagues that I'd heard about Shame-Attacking Exercises, but I didn't know exactly how they worked. He explained that you intentionally do something goofy in public so you can get over the fear of making a fool of yourself. He said that the only way to understand Shame-Attacking Exercises was to try one yourself, and explained that all the trainees at Dr. Ellis's institute had to do Shame-Attacking Exercises as part of their training.

I asked if he could give me an example of a Shame-Attacking Exercise that he'd done. He said it would be even better for me simply to try one while we were standing in line; then I'd know exactly how they worked. I felt a bit uneasy and asked what he had in mind. He said I could walk up to the people at one of the tables and ask them if I could sample their food. This sounded totally bizarre, and a wave of panic gripped my heart. I kicked myself and wished I hadn't asked about Shame-Attacking Exercises!

However, I felt enormous social pressure from the group I was with. They all jumped in and said that they'd all done Shame-Attacking Exercises and that I should do one, too. I could see that they weren't going to take no for an answer, so I reluctantly walked over to a table where six people were eating. Their table was covered with a variety of tasty-looking dishes. I commented on how great the food looked and asked if it tasted as good as it looked. They said it was terrific and told me that they'd been coming to this restaurant for years. I was hoping they'd spontaneously offer to let me have a taste of one of the dishes, but that didn't happen.

I looked around nervously and noticed that all my colleagues were staring at me. This was my moment of truth! So I swallowed hard, pointed at one of the dishes, and said, "I know this sounds incredibly eccentric, but I was wondering what that dish tastes like. I don't suppose you'd let me taste it, would you?"

They didn't seem at all perturbed and said, "Sure! Here, have some." Much to my surprise, they offered me a fork and encouraged me to taste the dish. I tasted it and said it was fabulous. Then they said, "Try this one, too. It's fantastic." So I tasted another dish, and it was also super. Suddenly all the people from the institute converged around the table and asked if they could try some, too. The people at the table started giving all of us samples of their food with great enthusiasm. Soon we were all giggling and having a great time, even though we didn't know the people at the table. It was one of the highlights of my trip to New York.

This experience taught me that you don't always have to be so rigid and take yourself so seriously. Most people appreciate a little goodwilled humor or eccentricity. People are bored and looking for something to spice up their day. If you act a bit goofy, in a good-natured way, most people will get a kick out of it. If you're naturally outgoing, this insight may seem trivial or obvious, but if you're shy, this discovery can be mind-blowing.

Since that day, I've done many Shame-Attacking Exercises. The next one I tried was several weeks later when I was on vacation with my family at Lake Tahoe in Nevada. Our hotel had a casino on the ground floor, and our room was on the fourteenth floor. I put on a cowboy hat, cowboy boots, a big turquoise bracelet, and dark glasses, and got on the elevator with my two children. I told them that their dad was going to teach them something important.

Once the elevator started down, I forced myself to announce the floor number at every stop. It was extremely difficult at first, and my children turned bright red. "Daaad," they said as they tugged on my sleeve and pleaded with me to stop, looking mortified.

The people in the elevator started chuckling, but I forced myself to keep it up, and the laughing got louder at each stop. By the time we got to the ground level, we were all having a great time giggling. Then the doors opened, and the people streamed out into the casino and started playing the slot machines. It dawned on me that they probably found the elevator experience mildly amusing, and it added a little spice to their day. But it wasn't very important in the bigger scheme of things.

If you're willing to try a Shame-Attacking Exercise, you're limited only by your imagination and common sense. For example, you could stand up and loudly call out the name of the street at each stop while riding on the bus or subway train. Or you could walk up to a group of people waiting to get on the bus and offer to entertain them with a song. If that seems too challenging, you could simply walk down a crowded street singing loudly and enthusiastically.

When you do a Shame-Attacking Exercise, your goal is never to do anything that would seem hostile or insensitive or that would make other people uncomfortable. When Trevor and I went into the convenience store and made the announcements about our sweaty armpits, it was harmless, and everyone seemed to enjoy our zany behavior. We weren't being disrespectful or taking advantage of anyone. However, it would have been inappropriate for us to do our Shame-Attacking Exercises in a hospital, because it would have been upsetting to patients and staff. Context is everything. The idea is simply to be a little bit outrageous and to have some fun.

Paradoxical Magnification

Instead of refuting your negative thoughts, you can buy in to them and exaggerate them. Don't try to argue with them. Instead, make them as extreme as possible. For example, if you feel inferior, you could tell yourself, "Yes, it's true. In fact, I'm probably the most inferior person in California at this time, and maybe in the entire United States." Paradoxically, this kind of absurd message can sometimes provide objectivity and relief.

A young woman named Mandy was preparing for her brown belt test in Aikido, a Japanese martial art. She felt intensely nervous for weeks before the event because she kept telling herself, "I'll really screw up in front of everybody." Rationally, she knew this was unlikely, since she'd been working hard in class and had done well on all her previous tests. Nevertheless, she couldn't stop worrying and obsessing. This was especially frustrating for Mandy because according to the underlying philosophy of Aikido, you're supposed to let go of your tension and go with the flow if you want to turn in a peak performance.

I suggested Paradoxical Magnification. Instead of struggling to be relaxed, which would backfire, Mandy could do just the opposite and spend three minutes twice a day telling herself things like this: "Not only will I screw up, but I'll undoubtedly be the worst person in the class, and perhaps in the entire country. I'll probably lose coordination and flail my arms and legs in a clumsy, foolish fashion, while my face turns beet red from nervousness. Everyone will scorn me and laugh at me. They'll not only see that my technique stinks, but that I'm a total emotional wreck, as well. Word will spread throughout the city, and soon everyone will know how dreadful I am, not only at Aikido, but at life in general."

After practicing the Paradoxical Magnification a few times, Mandy's fears began to seem absurd. She decided to set her pride aside and simply view the experience as another opportunity to practice and learn from her mistakes. Later she reported that her test was actually a lot of fun and that she received high praise from her teachers.

Humorous Imaging

When you're anxious, frightening images will often flood your mind. Using the What-If Technique, you usually can unearth the fantasy at the root of your fears. For example, if you have public speaking anxiety, you may picture the audience getting bored and falling asleep while you read your speech in a flat, uninspired tone of voice. Or, if you're afraid of dogs, you may have a frightening mental image of a dog growling and biting you. If you have obsessive worries about your health, you may imagine dying of cancer because you have a sore foot.

There are many ways to deal with these kinds of frightening images, just as there are many ways to challenge a negative thought. When you use Humorous Imaging, you substitute a funny, absurd fantasy in place of the one that's making you anxious.

Remember José, the anxious ophthalmologist who kept checking his vision because of his irrational fear that he was going blind? Although Self-Monitoring and Response Prevention were effective, there were lots of other techniques we could have tried, including Humorous Imaging. José could imagine something humorous that would highlight the absurdity of his fears.

For example, José could fantasize that he's finally gone completely blind but has courageously decided to continue his work as an ophthalmologist in spite of the fact that he can't see a thing. Word begins to spread about his incredible work, and soon newspaper and magazine articles begin to appear about the miracle doctor who continues to perform surgery even though he is totally blind. He's even invited to appear on *The Late Show with David Letterman,* where he tells a national television audience how he examines his patients' eyes with his fingertips and does complex surgical procedures with the help of his Seeing Eye dog. They show film clips of him driving the Los Angeles freeways at blazing speeds in his souped-up Porsche with his Seeing Eye dog at his side, nudging the steering wheel back and forth with his nose. If this fantasy strikes José's funny bone, he could practice imagining it whenever he begins to obsess about going blind.

Dr. Michael Yapko, an innovative cognitive psychologist and hypnotist from San Diego, tells his patients to imagine that their negative thoughts are coming from an amusing cartoon voice, like that of Elmer Fudd or Mickey Mouse. He encourages them to listen to the figure's voice berating them, rather than their own. To heighten the humorous effect, he sometimes asks them to add an even more absurd visual image to go along with the critical voice. For example, the patient might imagine that the critical voice is coming from a rectum or armpit.

The goal of this technique is to help you change your reaction to the self-critical voice in your mind, so that you're amused by it rather than hurt. Dr. Yapko points out that although the occasional presence of the negative inner voice is inevitable, its form and our responses to it are negotiable. Placing your worries in a more humorous context can serve as a natural antidote to the intense feelings of inadequacy, guilt, and self-doubt we experience when we take ourselves too seriously.

A shy woman named Nadine often noticed an attractive single attorney who'd just moved into her apartment building. I asked if she'd tried flirting with him a little. Nadine said she'd love to but felt too nervous even to make eye contact. She was afraid she'd look awkward or needy and turn him off.

I suggested that when she was talking to him, she could look directly into his eyes and imagine that he was defending a case in court in his underpants. This might lighten her mood and make him seem less intimidating. Nadine was intrigued by this idea and decided to give it a try, even though she was still pretty anxious.

The next morning, Nadine ended up alone with him in the elevator as she was leaving for work. She decided to take the plunge. She gazed into his eyes and commented on what a neat tie he was wearing. At the same time, she pictured him prancing around the courtroom in his underwear. This broke the tension and she began to giggle.

He thanked her for the compliment and asked what she was giggling about. Nadine said that she didn't know, but there was just something about him that made her feel happy. He seemed intrigued, and they were soon engaged in a lighthearted conversation. As they were getting off the elevator on the ground floor, he confessed that he'd been wanting to meet her, and asked if they might get together over a cup of coffee so they could get to know each other better. They made a date and Nadine went off to work on cloud nine.

The goal of the Humor-Based Techniques is to help you see the absurdity in your fears. When these techniques work, they can be magical and very healing. However, if you're feeling angry or upset, they could have the unintended effect of making you feel even worse. If they're not helpful, that's not a problem. Just try another technique.

Chapter 15

....

Role-Playing and Spiritual Techniques

In this chapter, we'll focus on a Role-Playing Technique called the Externalization of Voices and a Spiritual Technique called the Acceptance Paradox. My patients often say that these are the most healing and mind-blowing of all the Cognitive Therapy techniques. I almost always use these techniques together, but for teaching purposes, I'll describe them separately.

Externalization of Voices

The Externalization of Voices requires two people. The other person could be a friend, family member, or therapist. If you don't like the idea of role-playing or don't have anyone to role-play with, you can use this technique on your own, without another person. I'll show you how toward the end of this section.

Let's assume that you've been working with the Daily Mood Log, and you've recorded your upsetting thoughts in the negative thoughts column. They could be thoughts that trigger depression, anxiety, or any negative emotion you're trying to overcome. You and your partner will need your Daily Mood Log to do this effectively. One of you will play the role of your negative thoughts, and one of you will play the role of your positive thoughts. In other words, the self-critical and self-loving parts of your brain are going to engage in a battle.

When you begin, your partner can play the role of the negative voice in your mind, and you'll play the role of the positive, self-loving voice. Your partner will attack you with the negative thoughts from your Daily Mood Log. Your job is to try to defeat the critic. You can use role reversals when you get stuck.

The Externalization of Voices can be quite challenging, even a bit intimidating at first. Let's assume that you're feeling nervous because you have to give a talk at work next week, and you're bombarding yourself with negative thoughts about how you're going to screw up in front of the group. Here's an example of how the Externalization of Voices might work.

Negative Thoughts (played by your partner): When you give your talk at work next week, your mind will probably go blank and you'll look like a complete idiot.

Positive Thoughts (played by you): Actually, that's never happened. I often worry about that, but my mind has never gone blank when I've given talks at work, and I've never looked like a complete idiot. However, my public speaking skills are only average at best, and there's plenty of room for improvement.

Notice that the person in the role of the negative thoughts sounds like another person who's attacking you, but this is not what's happening. The other person is simply playing the negative part of your own mind. The fight you're having is with yourself.

In addition, the person who plays the role of the negative thoughts should always speak in the second person, "you." In contrast, the person who plays the role of the positive thoughts always speaks in the first person, "I." This rule is vitally important to the success of this technique. If you forget this rule, and the person in the role of the positive thoughts uses the second person, "you," while the person in the role of the negative thoughts uses the first person, "I," the technique will deteriorate into advice-giving and fail miserably.

For example, let's say that you've been depressed, and you feel like a loser. When you do the role-playing, you might say, "I'm such a loser." This is an error because you're speaking in the first person, "I." Now your partner will probably get confused and say something like this: "You're not a loser. You're a good person. Just think about all the people who like you and all the things that you've accomplished." This is a serious error because the other person sounds like a friend or family member who's trying to cheer you up.

This is what people usually do to someone who feels depressed or anxious. It's irritating and condescending, and it's never effective. This error resulted from the fact that the person in the role of the negative thoughts used the first person, "I." As a result, the second person playing the role of the positive thoughts used the second person, "you." Remember: *When you're playing the role of the negative thoughts, you should always say "you"; when you're playing the role of the positive thoughts, always say "I."* This will keep you on track.

The best time to use the Externalization of Voices is once you've put the lie to your negative thoughts on the Daily Mood Log using other techniques. Then you can use the Externalization of Voices to transform intellectual understanding into lasting change at the gut level.

In Chapter 10, you met Walter, a marriage and family therapist who became anxious and depressed when Paul, his lover of eight years, suddenly walked out on him and began seeing someone else. Walter was telling himself:

1. I'll never be in a loving relationship again.
2. I'm impossible to live with and impossible to be in a relationship with.
3. There must be something wrong with me.
4. I totally screwed up and flushed my life down the toilet.
5. I'll be an old, fat, gray-haired, lonely gay man.

When we used the Double-Standard Technique, Walter was able to put the lie to his negative thoughts, and his intense feelings of shame, defectiveness, and hopelessness suddenly disappeared. This is the perfect time to use the Externalization of Voices. It will help Walter cement his gains and greatly reduce the likelihood that his self-critical thoughts will come back to torment him again in the future.

In the following example, Walter will play the role of the negative part of his mind, and I will play the role of the positive, self-loving part. Although it may sound like two people arguing with each other, remember that we simply represent the two competing voices in Walter's brain.

Negative Thoughts (played by Walter): Gee, Paul walked out on you. This shows how unlovable and defective you are.

Positive Thoughts (played by David): I don't buy that. I've been in many loving relationships in my life, and I believe I'm a very loving person.

Negative Thoughts: If you were so great, then why did Paul walk out on you?

Positive Thoughts: I'd never argue that I was "so great," not by a long shot. But people leave each other for all sorts of reasons. I don't know exactly why Paul walked out on me. Maybe he was pissed off at me, or maybe he was bored and tempted by someone he met.

Negative Thoughts: Whatever. The fact remains that you're going to end up as an old, fat, gray-haired, lonely gay man.

Positive Thoughts: Well, there's definitely some truth to that. I can't prevent myself from aging or keep my hair from turning gray, and I might get fat. I don't think my sexual orientation is going to change, either. But as far as the lonely part goes, I doubt it. I do feel lonely right now, but that's natural when you've been rejected. These feelings will pass.

Negative Thoughts: You can rationalize all you want, but the fact is, you were rejected. Why don't you just face the fact that you're defective? You're no good.

Positive Thoughts: What you're saying isn't entirely clear to me, and I'm not sure how one follows from the other. In fact, I don't even know what those terms mean, "defective" and "no good." If you're thinking about some specific defects, we might have something to talk about. Believe me, I've got *plenty* of those!

Negative Thoughts: You sure do. In fact, you're impossible to be in a relationship with.

Positive Thoughts: That doesn't ring true. My friends have told me that I'm warm and open, and easy to relate to. Furthermore, I was just in a reasonably successful relationship for eight years. So what you're saying doesn't exactly make sense.

I asked Walter who was winning the battle. He said that the positive thoughts were clearly defeating the negative thoughts. He thought the negative thoughts sounded hostile and ridiculous and didn't have a leg to stand on.

When you're in the positive thoughts role, you can use any technique found in this book to fight the negative thoughts. For example, when the negative thoughts said, "You're impossible to be in a relationship with," I used Examine the Evidence. It was easy to attack that thought, because it was blatantly false. The evidence suggests that Walter isn't impossible to be in a relationship with, since he was just in one for eight years.

If you feel intimidated and fall apart when the other person is attacking you with your own negative thoughts, do a role reversal. That way, the other person can show you a more effective way of defeating your negative thoughts. Keep reversing roles until you can easily crush all of your negative thoughts.

When people try the Externalization of Voices for the first time, they typically make one of four errors:

Error 1. If the person playing the role of the negative thoughts uses the first person, "I," the person in the role of the positive thoughts will tend to use the second person, "You." This will cause the technique to fail in a big way.

Error 2. People sometimes get confused and think that this is a form of assertiveness training. They think that they're having a battle with some critical person in their life, such as their father, mother, spouse, or boss. This error will also cause the technique to fail. Remember that the person playing the role of the negative thoughts is simply a projection of your own mind. You're having a battle with yourself, and *not* with another person.

Error 3. The person in the negative thoughts role forgets that she or he is playing the negative part of *your* mind and begins to attack you with criticisms and doubts that aren't your own. This will be a waste of time, because what the person is saying won't ring true for you, and you won't be responding to your own negative thoughts. You'll be thinking, "What are you talking about? I don't have that thought!"

Error 4. Alternatively, the other person may attack you with his or her own criticisms of you. For example, your spouse might take this as an opportunity to dump on you! Then you'll get defensive and end up in a fight, and wonder why Dr. Burns thought this was such a wonderfully healing technique.

There's a simple way to avoid these errors. Hand your Daily Mood Log to the person you'll be role-playing with. Tell them to attack you by reading your negative thoughts out loud. Tell them they can use the second person, "You," so they'll sound like another person. When you're in the Positive Thoughts role, make sure you *always* use the first person, "I."

Sometimes I write the words "Negative Thoughts" on one sheet of paper and the words "Positive Thoughts" on another. The two people doing the role-playing can hold these sheets in front of them during the encounter. This helps to prevent confusion.

In spite of these precautions, it's easy to get confused at first, and you should expect it to happen. The dialogue may degenerate into a battle between two people rather than the two parts of your mind. When this happens, stop and regroup. Start over. Getting the hang of this technique takes a little practice, but it's worth the effort, because when the Externalization of Voices is done properly, the healing effects can be amazing.

If you don't have anyone to role-play with, you can do the Externalization of Voices on your own. Simply write out a dialogue on paper, just like the ones you've been reading in this chapter. Of course, you'll be playing both roles. This is almost as effective as having another person to role-play with. Several other techniques can also be effective in a role-playing format, as you'll see throughout this book.

Acceptance Paradox

If you've ever suffered from depression or anxiety, you're probably aware of how you rip yourself to shreds for all your flaws and shortcomings. Before you can feel better, you'll have to find a way to silence the relentless critic in your brain. How will you do that? There are two basic strategies: the Self-Defense Paradigm and the Acceptance Paradox. When you use the Self-Defense Paradigm, you argue with your negative thoughts and insist that they're not true. This strategy is based on the idea that your negative thoughts are deceptive and distorted, and that the truth will make you free.

The Acceptance Paradox is a spiritual technique that works in the opposite way. Instead of defending against the negative thought, you find some truth in it. You agree with it, but with a sense of humor, inner peace, and enlightenment. You actually befriend the critic in your mind. You can mix and match or blend these two styles of responding, but when the negative thoughts lead to feelings of worthlessness, inferiority, shame, or a loss of self-esteem, the Acceptance Paradox will usually be vastly more effective than the Self-Defense Paradigm.

Let's say you're feeling insecure and telling yourself that you're defective or inferior. If you used the Self-Defense Paradigm, you might remind yourself, just as a friend would, that you have lots of positive qualities and accomplishments that you can be proud of. Many people think that this type of "positive thinking" is the key to building self-esteem. In my experience, it's nearly always *in*effective, because you'll just keep yes-butting and obsessing about your flaws and shortcomings. For example, you may tell yourself, "Sure, I may have a few pitiful positive qualities, but that doesn't change the fact that I'm inferior to all those people who have accomplished so many things that are truly significant—vastly beyond anything I could ever dream of doing."

If you used the Acceptance Paradox, you might talk back to the negative thought like this: "As a matter of fact, I *do* have many defects. There's no doubt about it. I accept that." This removes the sting from the criticism and ends the debate.

Now, suppose that the inner critic relentlessly keeps trying to bash you. You can just stick to your guns, using the Acceptance Paradox, as in this example.

Negative Thoughts: It's not just that you have a few specific flaws or defects. Face it. You're globally flawed. You're a defective human being.

Positive Thoughts: You're right! It took me years to figure that out, but you got it right away. And you know something else? My defectiveness is actually one of my better characteristics!

In this case, we're pulling the teeth out of the monster's mouth and making a cosmic joke. So what if you are "defective"? Will they refuse to sell you a cup of coffee in New York? Will your friends stop hanging out with you?

The Acceptance Paradox is based on the Buddhist principle that when you defend yourself, you create an instant state of war. The moment you defend yourself, you invite another attack. Of course, the critic you're fighting is the negative part of your own brain, so you end up at war with yourself. In contrast, when you find the truth in a criticism, it loses its power over you.

Most religions, including Christianity, have emphasized that all human beings are flawed and defective. That's the human condition. The Navajos have a rule that every rug they weave must contain some defect or imperfection, or else the gods will get mad and punish them. But it's possible to experience joy and enlightenment in spite of our flawed nature. The Acceptance Paradox is one way to transform this idea into an emotional reality.

At first it may be difficult to "see" why or how the Acceptance Paradox could be helpful. Lots of people who suffer from anxiety or depression think they've *already* accepted themselves. They believe they're facing the awful truth about themselves and feel like they *really are* hopeless, worthless losers.

This is unhealthy acceptance, and it's radically different from healthy acceptance. As you can see on the Healthy versus Unhealthy Acceptance chart on page 217, unhealthy acceptance is characterized by self-hatred, despair, paralysis, hopelessness, isolation, atrophy, and cynicism. In contrast, healthy acceptance is characterized by self-esteem, joy, productivity, hope, intimacy, growth, and laughter. Healthy acceptance involves a celebration of life and a connection with other people.

In fact, we're all defective. You can view your "defectiveness" as a reason for suicide or a cause for celebration. You can accept it with joy or despair. Once you let go of the idea that you're supposed to be special, that you're supposed to have "self-esteem," and that you're supposed to live up to your ideal self and be exactly the way you think you *should* be, you'll experience freedom, joy, and enlightenment.

The distinction between healthy and unhealthy acceptance can be very hard to comprehend at first, especially when you're suffering. Writing about it is like trying to describe what it's like to see the Grand Canyon for the first

Healthy versus Unhealthy Acceptance

Healthy Acceptance	Unhealthy Acceptance
Self-esteem	Self-hatred
Joy	Despair
Productivity	Paralysis
Hope	Hopelessness
Intimacy	Isolation
Growth	Atrophy
Laughter	Cynicism

time. It takes your breath away, and words simply can't do the experience justice.

The first time I saw the Grand Canyon, I was on a camping trip with a friend from college. We arrived at the edge of the canyon late one evening but couldn't see much because it was dark. We camped out in sleeping bags next to our car. When I woke up in the morning, I realized that we'd put our sleeping bags on the ground a couple feet away from the canyon's edge. The sun was just coming up, and as I turned to look, I saw the Grand Canyon for the first time. Wow! It took my breath away. I'd heard there was a big hole in the ground, but I had no idea it would be like that!

It's the same feeling when you suddenly grasp the Acceptance Paradox. It takes your breath away! It can be a life-changing and mind-boggling experience. However, this type of understanding only springs to life during one of the role-playing exercises, such as the Externalization of Voices or the Feared Fantasy.

Let's assume that you feel inferior. Why is this? Think about how you've felt during moments of self-doubt and despair. What were you telling yourself?

You may tell yourself that you're not as intelligent, successful, or attractive as you'd like to be. You may beat up on yourself because you've made so many mistakes in life, because you haven't been a very good father or mother, or because you've failed to fulfill the dreams you had when you were growing up. Maybe you feel defective because you've been struggling with feelings of shyness or depression. Let's see if we can defeat these concerns using the Acceptance Paradox.

Imagine that the negative and positive parts of your mind are involved in a battle. You can play the role of the negative thoughts, and I'll play the role of the positive thoughts. Attack me as ruthlessly as possible and point out every flaw or shortcoming I have. Try to humiliate me.

Remember, I'm playing the role of the positive, self-loving part of your mind, and you're playing the negative part. I will try to defeat you with the Acceptance Paradox. As you read the dialogue, ask yourself who's winning the battle.

Negative Thoughts (played by you): You really aren't very intelligent, are you?

Positive Thoughts (played by David): As a matter of fact, there are lots of people who are smarter than I am. Millions of them, in fact—physicists, mathematicians, scientists, musicians, and writers. I accept that.

Negative Thoughts: Oh, so then you accept the fact that you're just a stupid, inferior person?

Positive Thoughts: Well, I've made plenty of mistakes in my life, if that's what you mean. And there are lots of people who are a lot smarter than I am. But when you say I'm stupid and inferior, that sounds pretty condemning, and I'm not exactly sure what you mean.

Negative Thoughts: That's probably because you're not too sharp. It's really pretty obvious. All those brilliant, talented, attractive people are superior to you. People like Einstein and Madonna. They're the beautiful people. You're an inferior, second-rate human being. Do you get it now? I know you don't catch on to things too quickly.

Positive Thoughts: Well, you're right, I still don't quite catch your drift on that "second-rate human being" part. Can you explain what you mean? I agree that I'm no performer like Madonna, and I'm definitely not a genius like Einstein. In fact, there are countless people with all kinds of awesome skills I don't have, and I find that exciting. There are superb electrical engineers at Intel and brilliant researchers at the National Institutes of Health. And there are all those gifted athletes who are playing in the NBA and the NFL. I don't have those kinds of skills. Is that what you meant when you said I was an inferior, second-rate human being? Or did you mean something more than that?

Negative Thoughts: Actually, it *is* a bit more than that. But I know this may be hard for you to grasp because you're such a stupid jerk. You see, our society values people with brains and achievements. People who get Nobel Prizes, for example. They're the special people, the gifted, superior ones. But you're just a peasant by comparison. You're the cannon fodder, a common foot soldier.

Positive Thoughts: Well, that's okay with me. It may sound strange, but I kind of enjoy being a common foot soldier.

Negative Thoughts: Oh, so you admit it then? You admit that you're just a lowly foot soldier?

Positive Thoughts: Definitely! In fact, most of my friends are also foot soldiers, and we have a great time hanging out and having fun together. Hey, if you only hang out with Nobel Prize winners, you may not get to hang out very often, and your circle of friends may be rather skimpy! But I may be missing something here. You seem to be implying that there's something bad or shameful about me and that there's some wonderful experience that I'm missing out on, but I can't figure out what it is or what you're referring to.

Negative Thoughts: Boy, you sure are slow! I'm trying to tell you that you don't deserve any respect, and you're not entitled to any real joy or self-esteem because you suck. You don't measure up to the lofty standards I have in mind.

Positive Thoughts: I'm sure I don't measure up to the standards of a Nobel Prize winner or someone on that level. And I've known for years that I have tons of limitations and flaws. The weaknesses you've pointed out are just the tip of the iceberg!

Negative Thoughts: How can you live with yourself? How can you stand to look at yourself in the mirror every morning, knowing how many flaws you have?

Positive Thoughts: Oh, it's easy. I just smile and say, "Good morning, flawed guy! You've got a wonderful day to look forward to! And a lot of really neat people to hang out with."

Some people see immediately how liberating the Acceptance Paradox can be, while others simply can't comprehend it at first. As one man told me, "I'm *not* going to accept my failures and shortcomings. Failure is unacceptable. It's out of the question!"

The goal of the Acceptance Paradox is not to hide or deny your deficiencies or flaws, or to settle for a mediocre and unfulfilling life, but rather to expose your flaws to the light of day so you can accept them without a sense of shame. If there's a problem you can change, you can work on it. If there's something you can't change, you can simply accept it and carry on with your life.

Chapter 16

Motivational Techniques

When you use a Truth-Based Technique like Examine the Evidence, you ask, "Is this negative thought really valid?" Truth-Based Techniques are based on the idea that "the truth shall make you free." When you use Motivational Techniques, you ask, "Is this negative thought or feeling to my advantage? What are the benefits of this mind-set? And what are the costs?"

Although anxiety, depression, and anger can involve intense suffering, they often provide us with hidden rewards that can be addictive. On the one hand, you want relief, but on the other hand, you may dig in your heels and resist change. Anthony deMello, the Jesuit mystic, has said that we yearn for change but cling to the familiar. The Cost-Benefit Analysis (CBA), Paradoxical Cost-Benefit Analysis, and Devil's Advocate Technique will help you pinpoint the hidden motivations that keep you stuck. Once you expose them to the light of day, they'll have far less power to sabotage you.

Cost-Benefit Analysis

This is one of the best Motivational Techniques of all, and it was one of the first Cognitive Behavior Therapy (CBT) Techniques I developed in the mid-1970s. It's easy to do and can be tremendously revealing and helpful. In Chapter 8, you learned how to use this technique to evaluate a Self-Defeating Belief. There are actually five different kinds of CBAs:

1. **Cognitive CBA.** You evaluate the advantages and disadvantages of a negative thought like "I'll never get better" or "I'm worthless."
2. **Attitude CBA.** You evaluate the advantages and disadvantages of a Self-Defeating Belief, such as "I should always try to be perfect" or "I need everyone's approval to be worthwhile."
3. **Emotion CBA.** You evaluate the advantages and disadvantages of a negative feeling, such as anxiety, anger, or guilt.
4. **Behavioral (or Habit) CBA.** You evaluate the advantages and disadvantages of a bad habit, such as drinking, using drugs, overeating, procrastinating, or dating a married man.
5. **Relationship CBA.** You evaluate the advantages and disadvantages of an attitude that creates problems in your relationships, such as blaming your spouse for all the problems in your marriage.

You can do any of these CBAs in a straightforward or paradoxical way, so there are actually ten different kinds of CBAs. We'll review the Straightforward CBA first, and then I'll show you how to do a Paradoxical CBA.

First, put the thought, belief, feeling, or habit that you want to change at the top of a blank CBA form, like the one on page 223. Then ask yourself, "What are the advantages of this mind-set? How will it help me? And what are the disadvantages? How will it hurt me?" List all the advantages and disadvantages you can think of in the two columns. After you complete your lists, ask yourself whether the advantages or disadvantages feel greater, and balance them against each other on a 100-point scale. Put two numbers that add up to 100 in the circles at the bottom. Your ratings should reflect how you feel.

For example, if the advantages slightly outweigh the disadvantages, you could put a 55 in the circle on the left and a 45 in the circle on the right. If the disadvantages are substantially greater than the advantages, you could put a 25 in the circle on the left and a 75 in the circle on the right. If the advantages and disadvantages come out dead even, you could put a 50 in each circle.

Let's try a Cognitive CBA together. I once treated a psychologist named

Cost-Benefit Analysis

Describe the attitude, feeling, or habit that you want to change: _____

_____

Advantages	Disadvantages

Johanna who had test anxiety. She was trying to prepare for her psychology licensure exam, but she was so overwhelmed with anxiety that she couldn't concentrate. I asked Johanna what kinds of negative thoughts crossed her mind when she was trying to study for the test. She said, "I tell myself that I'm going to study all the wrong material and flunk the test. I feel like they'll ask about all the things I don't know and none of the things I do know."

Johanna could see that these thoughts contained numerous distortions, such as All-or-Nothing Thinking, Discounting the Positive, Fortune-Telling, and Emotional Reasoning. For example, it was extremely unlikely that they'd ask about *all* the things she didn't know and *none* of the things that she did know, since the people who create the licensure examinations try to assess all the major areas of psychology in a reasonably balanced way. It seemed equally illogical to predict that she'd flunk the test, since she was one of the top students in her Ph.D. program and had never flunked a test in her life.

Although Johanna could see that her negative thoughts were distorted, she fought me tooth and nail when I encouraged her to talk back to them. She insisted that her negative thoughts were realistic and said that I just didn't understand.

I was puzzled. On the one hand, Johanna was asking for help with her test anxiety. But on the other hand, she seemed to be protecting her anxiety, almost like a mother lion guarding her cubs. What was going on? Why was she fighting me? Can you think of any ways that her anxiety might have been rewarding her? Put your ideas here before you continue reading.

_____

_____

_____

_____

_____

Answer

It dawned on me that Johanna might be reluctant to let go of the anxiety because she thought it was helping her in some way, so I suggested we try a Cost-Benefit Analysis. I asked her to list all the advantages and disadvantages of worrying about her licensure exam. As you can see on page 225, there were quite a few advantages, including "The worrying will keep me on my toes so I don't get too complacent and forget to study." I suddenly understood why Johanna was fighting me. There was some wisdom in reluctance to change, since a little bit of anxiety may motivate you to do your best.

But too much anxiety can cripple you. In fact, the second disadvantage she listed suddenly tipped the scales. As you can see, she wrote, "The constant worrying has me paralyzed. I haven't done even one minute of productive studying in the past month!" This single disadvantage outweighed all the advantages, so Johanna put a 20 and an 80 in the two circles at the bottom.

I asked her how much anxiety she thought she needed to do a good job preparing for the exam. On a scale from 0% (no anxiety) to 100% (sheer panic), she estimated her anxiety at 95%. But what was the ideal amount? Would 50% be enough? Or 25%?

Johanna said that 10% or 15% would be plenty. I told her we could work together to lower it to that level, but if she felt she was getting *too* relaxed, I

Johanna's Cost-Benefit Analysis

Describe the attitude, feeling, or habit that you want to change: Worrying about my upcoming psychology licensure examination.

Advantages	Disadvantages
1. I won't be shocked and disappointed if I do flunk.	1. I'll feel miserable every moment of every day until the exam.
2. The worrying will keep me on my toes so I don't get too complacent and forget to study.	2. The constant worrying has me paralyzed. I haven't done even one minute of productive studying in the past month!
3. I can feel angry because the test seems so unfair.	3. I'll only be punishing myself with my anger, since the people who create the test don't know or care about how I feel.
4. I can feel sorry for myself and play the role of victim.	4. The constant worrying gets tiring pretty fast.
5. My husband will try to cheer me up and reassure me that I'm going to do fine.	5. When my husband tries to cheer me up, we end up feeling annoyed with each other because I won't accept what he's saying.

(20)———————————————(80)

could show her how to replace her positive thoughts with negative thoughts, so she could generate some anxiety again!

Johanna loved this idea and suddenly became much more motivated to challenge the negative thoughts that were making her so anxious. She quickly put the lie to all of them. She felt more relaxed and started studying systematically every night. In fact, all of her anxiety disappeared within a couple days, and she began to enjoy reviewing the material. She was surprised to discover that she didn't need any anxiety at all in order to study effectively. Several weeks later, she passed her licensure exam and received one of the highest scores in the state.

The CBA can open the door to the possibility of change when you feel stuck. It's a way of giving the devil his due. Often you'll discover many good reasons *not* to change. When you bring them to conscious awareness, they'll usually lose their power over you.

Paradoxical Cost-Benefit Analysis

The Paradoxical CBA capitalizes on the fact that even though your negative thinking patterns, emotions, and habits can be exceedingly painful, they may reward you at the same time. When you do a Paradoxical CBA, you list only the advantages of the thought, belief, feeling, behavior, or habit that you're trying to change. Don't bother to list the disadvantages. Then you ask yourself, "Given all the advantages of this attitude or feeling, why *should* I change?"

Below, you'll find several negative thoughts and habits that would be good targets for a Paradoxical CBA. Choose one thought and one habit that interest you, and list all the advantages you can think of, using the form on page 227.

Negative Thoughts
- I'm inferior.
- Other people are to blame for the problems in my relationships with them.

Paradoxical Thought Cost-Benefit Analysis

List the thought you've selected: _____

_____

Advantages of Believing This Thought

1. _____
2. _____
3. _____
4. _____
5. _____
6. _____

Bad Habits

- Eating whatever I want, whenever I want
- Drinking as much as I want, whenever I want
- Procrastinating

Paradoxical Habit Cost-Benefit Analysis

List the habit you've selected: _____

Advantages of This Habit

1. _____
2. _____
3. _____
4. _____
5. _____
6. _____

When you're done, you can review my answers. These lists are not comprehensive, and you may come up with even more advantages I didn't think of.

Answers to Paradoxical CBA Exercises

Advantages of believing that I'm inferior

1. This thought explains my failures in life.
2. I can feel sorry for myself.
3. It gives me a sense of identity.
4. I won't have to take risks and try things that make me anxious.

5. I won't have to work very hard, since inferior people can't be expected to accomplish much.

6. I can secretly resent other people who accomplish more.

7. This thought seems valid, because I have no special talents and I've never accomplished anything unique or important.

Advantages of believing that other people are to blame for the problems in my relationships with them

1. I can be angry all the time.

2. I can feel morally superior.

3. Anger is empowering, so I'll feel energized, vibrant, and alive.

4. It's easy. I won't have to change.

5. This thought seems true, since other people do act like jerks.

6. I can feel innocent. I won't have to feel guilty.

7. I won't suffer the pain of examining my own role in the problem.

8. It gives me a convenient explanation for my problems getting along with others.

9. I can be hostile and do something nasty. I can put the other person down or give them the silent treatment.

10. I can act sweet and get back at the other person indirectly.

11. I can gossip and get my friends to agree that the other person is a loser.

Advantages of overeating

1. Food is an immediate reward.

2. Eating whatever I want, whenever I want, is a kind of freedom.

3. I can comfort myself with food when I'm upset or mad at someone. That way, I can avoid the problem and not get anxious.

4. I can feel sorry for myself because I'm fat.

5. I can resent those who look down on people who are overweight.

6. Dieting is a huge deprivation.

7. Exercise requires lots of effort and discipline.

Advantages of drinking

1. It feels good to get high.

2. I'll be able to relax and won't feel so awkward in social situations.

3. My favorite drink will taste so good.

4. I can treat all my emotional problems with my own special "medication."

5. I can avoid dealing with things that upset me, like arguments with my wife.

6. I can justify all kinds of aggressive or sexual behaviors I would not consider if sober.

7. When I drink, I can forget about my problems.

8. I can assert my independence and feel free to do what I really want to do. Other people can't control me.

9. My friends and I have fun drinking together.

10. I can be wild.

11. Life can be exciting.

12. It's the best way to celebrate when something good happens.

13. It's a great way to reward myself, because my life sucks. I deserve it.

14. If I quit, I'll have to go to AA meetings and hang out with all those boring people and pretend that I believe in God!

Advantages of procrastination

1. I can do something else that's more enjoyable.

2. The things I'm avoiding probably aren't that important in the long run.

3. It would be unpleasant to get started.

4. Whatever I do will only be a drop in the bucket anyway.

5. I can wait until later, when I'm more in the mood.

6. I can feel special, since special people, such as celebrities and royalty, don't have to do boring, unpleasant tasks.

7. I can get back at the person who's nagging me to do the things I've been putting off.

8. I'll have a good excuse for failing at the task I'm avoiding, such as studying or writing a paper. If I get a bad grade, I can tell myself, "Well, I didn't really try. If I had tried, I would have done great."

9. I won't have to feel bored or anxious because I can avoid all the unpleasant chores I've been putting off.

Devil's Advocate Technique

The Devil's Advocate Technique is one of the most powerful techniques ever developed to overcome bad habits and addictions. It's based on the simple but powerful idea that tempting positive thoughts make us give in to habits and addictions.

For example, while shopping at the mall, you may notice seductive fast food smells and tell yourself, "Gee, those hot, buttery cinnamon buns smell *so yummy.* I bet they taste *really good!* Mmmm. I think I'll go up and take a closer look. I can just eat a little bit to see how they taste. One little taste can't hurt. Besides, I can do some jogging and have a salad or carrots for dinner to make up for it." Once you begin to think along these lines, you end up on a slippery slope, and it becomes practically impossible to resist the urge to indulge yourself.

Notice that these thoughts are just as distorted as the thoughts that trigger anxiety and depression, but with one crucial difference: They're distorted in the *positive* direction. Some of the distortions include:

- **All-or-Nothing Thinking.** You're making the cinnamon buns sound like the most amazing and delectable gourmet treat ever created. Are they really as good as you imagine?
- **Denial.** When you're depressed, you may overlook or discount all the good things about yourself and conclude that you're a total loser. This distortion is called Discounting the Positive. When you're tempted, you may do the exact opposite. You deny or discount data that's absolutely inconsistent with what you're thinking. In this case, you're telling yourself that you'll just have *one little taste.* Is this realistic? Are you being honest with yourself? How many times have you given yourself this message in the past? Did you really stop after one little taste?
- **Fortune-Telling.** You may be making several unrealistic predictions. First, you're telling yourself how *wonderful* life will be if you can just eat one of those cinnamon buns. In fact, they're not bad, but they can be rather gooey, heavy, and sweet, and can make you feel like there's a block of cement in your stomach once you've eaten one or two of them. In addition, you may be telling yourself that you'll be struggling with dis-

appointment and deprivation forever if you don't allow yourself to have this special treat. If you don't give in, though, the temptation will probably disappear in five or ten minutes and you'll forget all about the cinnamon buns. And finally, you're telling yourself that you're going to have a salad or carrots for dinner and exercise a lot if you eat the bun. Are you *really* going to do this?

The Devil's Advocate Technique can be an effective antidote to these kinds of tempting thoughts. It involves role-playing. First, list all the thoughts you usually have before you give in to your habit. It could be the urge to drink, overeat, procrastinate, or date the wrong person. Give the list to a friend or family member, and ask that person to play the role of the devil who tempts you to give in. The other person should verbalize the tempting thoughts as seductively as possible, using the second person, "you." Your job is to see if you can defeat the devil.

For example, the devil might say, "You *really* deserve one of those tasty cinnamon buns. You've had a tough day. Mmmm. Just imagine how *wonderful* it will taste in your mouth, all sweet and buttery. Go for it!"

You could reply, "No, I'll just feel gross and bloated, and it probably won't even taste that good. I also deserve to feel thin and healthy, and I'll feel much better about myself if I don't give in to this urge."

Then your friend can tempt you again, trying as hard as possible to convince you to give in.

It can be incredibly difficult to defeat the devil, especially if your list of tempting thoughts is honest. After all, the tempting thoughts have been winning the battle for a long time. If you get stuck and can't think of a way to fight back, do a role reversal so your friend can model a more effective response.

If you don't have a friend who will role-play with you, you can write out a Devil's Advocate dialogue. Of course, you'll be playing both roles—the devil who tempts you and the part of your mind that fights back. When you're in the devil's role, make sure you try your hardest to seduce yourself into giving in. Otherwise, the technique will be superficial and ineffective. It won't have any "teeth," so to speak.

Here's an example. Let's imagine that you're struggling with the urge to procrastinate on your bookkeeping. You feel anxious because you've been putting it off, and you're way behind. The dialogue might go like this:

Devil: You know, there's really no reason to do it right now. You have more important things to do.

Self: You're right. There are lots of things I could be doing right now, but the bookkeeping has been eating away at me. If I do some work on it right now, it will be a relief, and I can start to get caught up.

Devil: No, it will just make you anxious. This isn't a good time, anyway.

Self: It may make me anxious at first, but once I get started, the anxiety will probably go away. And there will never be a "good" time, so I might as well get started now.

Devil: You can do it later on, or tomorrow, when you're more in the mood.

Self: Well, I could do it later on, but I probably won't be in the mood then, either. In fact, I probably won't ever be in the mood. If I wait until I feel like it, I'll end up waiting forever, and it will never get done.

Devil: Yes, but it will be overwhelming and stressful. You don't have enough time right now. There's just too much to do.

Self: Well, it may seem overwhelming and stressful at first, but those feelings will probably go away once I get started. Furthermore, I could just work on it for a few minutes. That would be a good first step.

Devil: That would only be a drop in the bucket. You have hours of work to do. Working for a few minutes would be a total waste of time. Besides, you need a nice cup of coffee right now. It would taste wonderful and give you some energy.

Self: It would probably be a lot more wonderful if I stopped wasting my time listening to you and got started. I can get a cup of coffee fifteen minutes from now as a reward. I hate to be insulting, but I'm afraid I can't talk to you any longer because I need to get started right now.

Devil: You'll be sorry! It's going to be awful.

Self: I don't think I'll be sorry. I might feel confused or anxious at first, because I've been listening to you and putting it off for a long time. But once I get started, it will get easier. And I'll forget all about you, too. Good-bye!

The Devil's Advocate is a Paradoxical Technique because you're tempting yourself to give in. You're not trying to persuade yourself to change. For some reason, this technique seems to increase people's determination to change and can be remarkably effective.

Very few, if any, treatment programs aimed at helping people overcome bad habits and addictions are based on this approach. Instead, they make the erroneous assumption that people *want* to change. So they show you how to achieve your goals in a systematic way and try to convince you that this or that diet or method will fix the problem. These programs nearly always fail because they don't take one vitally important fact into account: Most people with bad habits *don't* want to change. Habits and addictions are rewarding. It's fun to get high! And what could be better than eating whatever you want, whenever you want? Hundreds of years ago, that kind of pleasure was reserved for emperors and kings. Hey, it's fun to do whatever you want, whenever you want. Why *should* you change?

You may give lip service to change and tell yourself how wonderful it would be to stop drinking. But when you open the refrigerator after a stressful day and see a gorgeous bottle of beer waiting there just for you, that voice in your head will start telling you: "Mmmm! A nice cold beer would taste *so good* right now. I can almost taste it. It would be so relaxing to have a beer while I watch the game on TV. One little beer couldn't hurt. I've had a hard day, and I deserve to relax. Besides, what's the point of having to be so pure all the time, anyway?"

Similarly, if you're overweight, you probably tell yourself how *great* it would be to lose a few pounds and feel thin, sexy, and healthy. But the fact is, you don't really want to go on a stupid diet and start a daily exercise program. Food is one of life's greatest pleasures. Why give it up? After all, dieting and exercise require deprivation and discipline. Who needs that?

If you can't refute the tempting thoughts, the likelihood of success with any technique or program will be zero. After all, if you want to get into the theater, you have to buy a ticket first. But here's the good news: Once you learn to defeat those thoughts, you can make almost *any* technique or program work for you.

Chapter 17

Anti-Procrastination Techniques

Anxiety can cause lots of problems in your life, including procrastination. You may put off a task, such as writing a paper, studying, or filing your taxes, because you feel so anxious and overwhelmed every time you think about doing it. You tell yourself, "This isn't a good time. I'll wait until I'm more in the mood." But the mood never comes, and the longer you procrastinate, the more anxious and guilty you feel. You get trapped in a vicious cycle. The anxiety leads to procrastination, and the procrastination causes more anxiety.

Depression also causes procrastination. When you're depressed, you don't have any motivation or energy and you lose interest in life. Everything seems difficult and unrewarding, so you sit around and do nothing. This makes you feel even more demoralized and depressed, which causes more procrastination, so you get caught up in a vicious cycle.

In the last chapter, you learned about two techniques that can help you overcome procrastination—the Paradoxical Cost-Benefit Analysis and the Devil's Advocate Technique. In this chapter, you'll learn four more techniques that can help you break the cycle of procrastination and become more productive and creative:

1. Pleasure-Predicting Technique
2. Little Steps for Big Feats

3. Anti-Procrastination Technique
4. Problem-Solution Technique

Pleasure-Predicting Technique

You may remember Nate, the anxious professor in Chapter 8, who believed that if he couldn't do something perfectly, it wasn't worth doing at all. When Nate used the Pleasure-Predicting Sheet, he was surprised to discover that some of life's greatest rewards came from things he was just average at, such as fixing a broken pipe, taking a walk through the woods, or playing squash with his son. In contrast, some of the things he did "perfectly" turned out to be stressful and unrewarding.

You'll see a copy of the Pleasure-Predicting Sheet on page 236. In the Activity column, you can schedule activities with the potential for pleasure, learning, or personal growth. Make sure you include some activities you can do by yourself, such as "jogging" or "straightening up my desk," as well as activities with other people, like going to a movie or taking a walk with a friend. In the Companion column, indicate who you intend to do each activity with. If you plan to do something alone, put the word "self" in the column. This will remind you that you're never really alone, since you're always with yourself.

In the Predicted Satisfaction column, predict how satisfying and rewarding you think each activity will be on a scale from 0% (not at all) to 100% (the most). Make sure you fill out this column *before* you do each activity. After you complete each activity, rate how satisfying it turned out to be in the Actual Satisfaction column, using the same scale.

When you look at the data, you can learn lots of interesting things. First, you can compare your predicted satisfaction levels with your actual satisfaction levels. You'll often discover that many activities turn out to be far more rewarding and satisfying than you anticipated. This discovery can motivate you to do even more.

Many depressed people avoid doing things that used to give them pleasure because they tell themselves, "Oh, that wouldn't be any fun. I know I wouldn't enjoy that." So they sit around and do very little, and get even more depressed. Then they think, "Gee, life really is unrewarding, just as I thought." But this in-

Pleasure-Predicting Sheet

Belief: _____

Activity Schedule activities with the potential for pleasure, learning, or personal growth.	Companion Use "self" for things you plan to do alone.	Predicted Satisfaction (0%–100%) Record **before** each activity.	Actual Satisfaction (0%–100%) Record **after** each activity.

volves Fortune-Telling. They are making an unrealistic prediction, but they don't realize it because they haven't bothered to check it out.

You can also compare the satisfaction you get from activities you do alone with the satisfaction you get from activities with other people. Many people discover that some of their happiest times are when they're doing something alone. This can put the lie to the belief that the only true happiness comes from being with other people.

A writer named Raymond was having tremendous difficulties completing a proposal for his first novel. He'd sit and stare at the computer screen for hours, unable to write a single sentence. Part of the problem was that Raymond's younger brother had become a famous movie star almost overnight. Raymond was proud of him but felt a lot of pressure to accomplish something equally spectacular. He felt that it was his duty, as the oldest son, to be the most successful.

But his brother's success had set the bar almost impossibly high. Whenever Raymond and his brother hung out together, they'd eat at the most exclusive restaurants and were constantly hounded by the paparazzi and hordes of adoring fans asking for his brother's autograph. His brother was interviewed on television talk shows almost every week.

Raymond constantly daydreamed about achieving incredible success as a novelist and told himself that his life couldn't possibly be fulfilling or meaningful until he wrote "the great American novel." He was aware that his impossible goals were blocking his creativity and causing intense performance anxiety, but he couldn't let go of the idea that there really was some level of joy or satisfaction that was accessible only to the "beautiful people." He was convinced that he'd never experience any true happiness until he was at least as successful as his brother.

I asked Raymond to put this belief at the top of a Pleasure-Predicting Sheet: "I'll never feel truly happy or fulfilled until I've written the Great American Novel or accomplished something spectacular." Then he scheduled a series of activities he could do during the next week, and predicted how satisfying each one would be.

One of the activities he listed was taking his six-year-old niece to the zoo for her birthday. Raymond was very fond of her, so he predicted 70% satisfaction. As it turned out, they had a wonderful time, even though they were just doing something rather ordinary, so he gave the trip to the zoo a 99% satisfaction rating. This was totally inconsistent with his conviction that he'd never feel happy or fulfilled until he accomplished something spectacular. Raymond realized that he'd been overlooking all kinds of "ordinary" activities that he actually enjoyed a great deal. As a result, he stopped pushing so hard and began to feel more relaxed. Paradoxically, this seemed to uncork his creativity, and soon he was working like crazy on his novel.

Although the Pleasure-Predicting Technique is fairly humble, there's a profound philosophical idea behind it. Sometimes we think that we're supposed to be "special," and we get obsessed with the need to accomplish something spectacular. We may be afraid that, if we don't, we'll end up as inferior, second-rate human beings with mediocre, unfulfilling lives. Or we may get focused on other kinds of "needs," such as the need to be loved or the need for everyone's approval, and tell ourselves that we'll be miserable forever without these things.

The most memorable experiences are often quite ordinary, and every minute of every day has the potential to be deeply rewarding. The Pleasure-Predicting Technique is simply a way of transforming this idea into an emotional reality.

Little Steps for Big Feats

When you have a big project to do, you may overwhelm yourself by trying to take on too much all at once. Then you may give up and end up doing little or nothing at all. For example, if you have to write a term paper, you may tell yourself that you have to go to the library and skim twenty books on the subject in one afternoon. But that task seems so overwhelming that you end up hanging out with your friends instead of working on the paper.

Instead, you can break a complex task into a series of small steps that you can complete in a few minutes each. Then you can focus on taking one step at a time, rather than trying to do everything all at once. For example, you could approach the term paper like this:

Step 1. Ride my bicycle to the library.

Step 2. Search for some references on the computer.

Step 3. Print the list of references.

Step 4. Locate the first reference.

Step 5. Skim it.

Step 6. Write a brief summary of the main conclusions on an index card.

Once you get started, you may feel a sense of accomplishment that will motivate you to do even more. I find that I often end up working on a task for several hours, even when I'd only planned to do the first step or two.

When you think about a task you've been putting off, you may also tell yourself, "I just can't seem to get around to doing it." This makes it sound as if there were some invisible barrier or force holding you back. What you really meant is *"I don't want to."* "I can't" and "I don't want to" are not the same thing! The Little Steps for Big Feats Technique will make this distinction clear.

I once treated a depressed physician named Perry who procrastinated on getting out of bed in the morning. Instead of getting up and going to the hospital to make rounds each morning, he'd sleep in. Then he'd get up late and start rounds after lunch. This was stressful because he was constantly behind and scrambling to get caught up.

Perry explained that he'd tried everything, including using several alarm clocks at the same time. He'd place each one a little farther from his bed and set them to go off at intervals. But this exercise was useless, because he'd simply get up when the first one rang and turn them all off. Then he'd crawl back into bed and drift into a deep, satisfying sleep.

Perry had been locked into this pattern for years. He said he just *couldn't* get up in the morning and really needed my help. I told him I'd be more than happy to help him, but I wanted to be clear on the type of help he was looking for. What, exactly, was the problem he needed my help with? He said he thought he'd already made that clear. He needed help getting out of bed in the morning.

I said I'd be pleased to help him get out of bed and suggested that we could break the job down into small steps so I could find out which step he needed my help with. What would he have to do first? What would he have to do second? We came up with these six steps.

1. Open my eyes.
2. Move my right leg to the edge of the bed.
3. Swing my left leg over to the edge of the bed.
4. Sit up on the edge of the bed.
5. Stand up next to the bed.
6. Walk into the bathroom.

Then I asked Perry if he needed help with the first step. For example, did his eyelids feel heavy and sticky when he woke up? Did he forcefully try to open them, only to discover that they were frozen shut?

Perry seemed perplexed and said he'd never had any problems opening his eyes. I said, "Okay, then maybe you need help with the second and third steps, moving your right leg to the edge of the bed and swinging your left leg over there, as well. Do your legs feel especially stiff or heavy in the morning? Perhaps we could practice that part here in the office. Try swinging your left leg back and forth now, so I can watch and see what happens."

Perry seemed annoyed and said he could *obviously* move his legs over to the edge of the bed. Then I said, "Perry, I apologize if my questions seem foolish. I really do want to help you, but it still isn't clear to me exactly what you need my help with. Can you clarify that for me?"

Perry said, "Okay, what I really need help with is the fact that each morning, I turn all my alarm clocks off. Then I roll over and go back to sleep instead of getting up and getting dressed. Can you help me with that?" Suppose that you were Perry's shrink. How would you use Little Steps for Big Feats to help him get out of bed and get dressed in the morning? Put your ideas here before you continue reading.

_____

_____

_____

_____

Answer

Once again, we'd have to break the task down into tiny steps. What's the first thing Perry would have to do if he wants to get up and get dressed instead of turning off his alarm clocks and going back to sleep? Well, he'd have to move his right leg to the edge of the bed, then swing his left leg over, and so forth. This list is going to look an awful lot like the one we just completed!

Perry's real fantasy was that I'd have some magic technique that would make him *want* to get up each morning. Then the solution to his procrastination problem would be as easy and natural as breathing. But that's something I cannot provide, any more than I can make a stone float on the water or give you a winning ticket to the lottery. Perry will probably *never* want to get up in the morning when he's tired. What he'll want to do is drift off to sleep again.

Many procrastinators want to analyze *why* they procrastinate. They ask, "Why do I put things off? Why am I so unmotivated? Why can't I get out of bed in the morning? What happened in my childhood that caused me to be so lazy? Did my parents pressure me too much?" Even if you could find out why you procrastinate, would that insight really change your life? In contrast, when you simply tackle the task one step at a time, you'll often feel more motivated and stop caring about why you were procrastinating in the first place.

One of the biggest mistakes that procrastinators make is to wait for inspiration to strike. You may tell yourself, "I'll do this when I'm more in the mood. I just don't *feel* like it right now." But what comes first? Motivation? Or action?

Most procrastinators think that the motivation comes first and action follows. Extremely successful people know that it's the other way around. Action comes first and motivation follows. They don't wait around until they "feel" like doing something. They just plow ahead and do it, whether they feel like it or not.

If you wait until you "feel" like doing some unpleasant task, you'll be waiting forever. I know that I usually feel anxious when I start doing a task I've been putting off. I usually don't feel motivated until I'm well into the task. Sometimes I don't feel motivated until the task is nearly completed. The real question isn't "*Can* I do this task?" but rather "Am I *willing* to do it? What would it be worth to me to get it done?"

Anti-Procrastination Technique

This technique is similar to Little Steps for Big Feats, but it's a bit more sophisticated. You break a complex, overwhelming task down into small, easy steps and list them in the first column of the Anti-Procrastination Sheet on page 243. In the next column, you predict how difficult you think each step will be on a scale from 0% (not at all difficult) to 100% (overwhelmingly difficult). Then you predict how satisfying you think each step will be, from 0% (not at all satisfying) to 100% (extremely satisfying). Now work on the task, one step at a time. After you complete each step, record how difficult and satisfying it actually turned out to be, using the same 0% to 100% scale.

Often you'll discover that the task turns out to be much less difficult and far more rewarding than you anticipated. This will put the lie to many of your negative thoughts, such as "Oh, it's going to be *so hard*" or "I just *can't stand* working on this." The change in your mood will often motivate you to do more.

A University of Pennsylvania student named Yolanda told me that for the past two years, she'd been trying to complete a term paper to make up an incomplete in a philosophy class. Try as she might, she just couldn't seem to get the paper done. Yolanda knew that she wouldn't be eligible for graduation until she completed the paper, but every time she thought about it, she told herself that she didn't have any really creative ideas and that it was going to be way too frustrating to work on it. So she spent countless hours surfing the web, playing video games, and watching TV instead of working on the paper.

I asked Yolanda to describe what the outcome of a successful therapy session would be. If she walked out of today's session thinking, "Gee, we had a really terrific therapy session today," what would have happened?

Yolanda said, "I'd leave here feeling excited about working on my paper." What do you think about Yolanda's goal for the session? Does it sound reasonable? Put your ideas here before you continue reading.

_____

_____

_____

_____

_____

Anti-Procrastination Sheet

Task Break the task into small steps that you can complete in a few minutes.	Predicted Difficulty (0%–100%)	Predicted Satisfaction (0%–100%)	Actual Difficulty (0%–100%)	Actual Satisfaction (0%–100%)
1.				
2.				
3.				
4.				
5.				
6.				
7.				

Answer

To my way of thinking, Yolanda isn't entitled to feel enthusiastic about her philosophy paper until *after* she's started working on it and has begun to make progress. It's also conceivable that she'll complete the paper, hand it in, graduate, and *never* feel excited about it.

Procrastinators often think they're entitled to enjoy difficult or unpleasant tasks. They feel that life should always be easy and exciting, and free of frustration. Give me a break! It doesn't work that way. There's no rule that says life will always be rewarding. Some tasks, such as filling out tax forms or filing all the papers that have been piling up on your desk for the past three years, may *never* be enjoyable.

If Yolanda wants to complete her paper, she can break it down into its smallest parts and predict how difficult and satisfying each step will be on a scale from 0% (not at all) to 100% (completely). Then she can complete the first few steps, regardless of how anxious or frustrated she feels. After she completes each step, she can record how difficult and satisfying it actually turned out to be. Chances are, she will feel some guilt, anxiety, and frustration at first. But her ratings may surprise her. Over time, the negative feelings will probably diminish and the feelings of satisfaction will probably increase.

Problem-Solution Technique

Imagine that you want to get started on some task you've been putting off. It could be straightening up your desk, cleaning the garage, doing your filing, mowing the lawn, or even exercising. Briefly describe the task here.

Now tell me what day you'd like to get started on it. Write the day here.

If you wrote "tomorrow" or "next week," I'm afraid that I can't help you. I can only help you work on it today. Putting it off until tomorrow is the very essence of the problem. Would you be willing to work on it today? If the answer is yes, tell me what time you'd like to work on it. Put a specific time here.

Let's say you agree to work on straightening up your desk at 3 P.M. Ask yourself whether you'd be willing to work on it for a very limited amount of time, such as five minutes, at 3 P.M. Put a check in one of these boxes to show how you feel:

No	Maybe	Yes

If you say that five minutes would only be a drop in the bucket, I'd remind you of the old Chinese saying that the longest journeys start with a single step. If you try to do too much at first, you'll feel overwhelmed and you'll probably avoid the task. Then you'll get nothing done. But five minutes of an odious task

Problem-Solution List

Problems	Solutions
1.	1.
2.	2.
3.	3.
4.	4.
5.	5.
6.	6.
7.	7.
8.	8.

is manageable. And once you get started, there's a good chance that you'll get in the mood and end up doing more. Once you've put in your five minutes, you've completed 100% of the assignment, and you're entitled to quit without any guilt. Anything more you decide to do will be gravy.

If you agreed to work on the task for five minutes at 3 P.M., list every conceivable problem that might prevent you from getting started in the left-hand column of the Problem-Solution List. For example, you might tell yourself that you need to talk to a friend who just called, or you might tell yourself that you're not really in the mood and tomorrow will be a better day. After you list all the barriers to getting started, put the solution to each problem in the right-hand column. You won't need my help with this step, because the solutions will usually be pretty obvious. Try it now. You can see an example of a completed Problem-Solution List below.

Problem-Solution List

Problems	Solutions
1. Someone may call and I'll tell myself that I really need to talk to him or her.	1. I can tell him or her that I'm tied up but will be happy to call back a little later.
2. I'll tell myself that I need to watch the news, to make sure that nothing important is happening.	2. I can remind myself that CNN broadcasts the news 24 hours a day. I can catch the news when I'm done.
3. One of the kids might need my help with something.	3. The kids can wait five minutes. I'm not their slave!
4. I may decide that I'm not in the mood and that tomorrow will be a better day.	4. Tomorrow won't be a better day, and I won't be in the mood until I get started.
5. I may get hungry and decide that I need a snack first, so I'll have enough energy.	5. I don't need to eat before I spend five minutes straightening up my desk. It's not like the Boston Marathon, and I'm not going to faint of hunger!
6. I may decide that I have to lie down and rest for a while, so I don't get all tired out.	6. I'll feel tired and demoralized if I keep putting it off. I'll probably feel energized once I get started.
7. I may tell myself that I'd be better off if I went out and did some exercise first.	7. Exercise is great, and I can do it after I've spent five minutes straightening up my desk.
8. I may decide that it's not really as important as I thought.	8. Straightening up my desk probably isn't the most important thing in the world, but it would be terrific to get started on it.

Once my patients come up with solutions for all the problems they listed, I give them one last assignment. If they agreed to work on a task they've been putting off for five minutes at 3:00 this afternoon, I ask if they'd be willing to call and leave one of two messages on my answering machine at 3:05. They can either say "Mission accomplished" or "I stubbornly refused."

Most of the people I've worked with have agreed to make the call, but a few have refused. They said calling sounded silly or unnecessary. Over the years, every patient who agreed to call me actually completed the assignment and left the message "Mission accomplished" on my answering machine. In contrast, every patient who refused to call failed to complete the assignment. I view the call as one last test of motivation. Patients who agree to call are really telling me that they're ready, willing, and able to follow through on the assignment.

The philosophy behind this technique is fairly simple. There is no invisible barrier holding you back, and you won't need a lot of fancy footwork to solve the problem. So the real question is: Are you willing to make the call?

PART III

The Exposure Model

Chapter 18

Classical Exposure

Taking a Page from the Tibetan Book of the Dead

In the 1950s, a new form of treatment called Behavior Therapy began to compete with psychoanalysis. Behavior Therapy was based on the idea that people could learn to modify problematic feelings and behaviors quickly and directly, rather than lying on the analyst's couch and free-associating or exploring the past. Behavior therapists were aware insights about the origin of the problem usually weren't helpful. They discovered that people with anxiety often could defeat their fears through simple exposure to the thing they feared. For example, if you had a fear of snakes, your therapist might encourage you to hold a harmless garden snake in your hands. At first, you'd experience an intense flood of anxiety, but if you held the snake for long enough, the fear would eventually diminish and disappear.

Exposure to the thing the patient feared was often curative. Behavior therapists developed a variety of Exposure Techniques that now play a vital role in the treatment of all the anxiety disorders. However, I'm not a fan of the term "Behavior Therapy," because it's too vague. Almost anything could be considered a behavior. I prefer the more descriptive term "Exposure Therapy."

Exposure Therapy is based on a legend in the Tibetan Book of the Dead. According to this legend, after you die, you'll wake up in a dark place. Out of the darkness, a terrifying monster will suddenly appear. The monster will represent all the worst fears you've ever had. For each person, the monster will be different, since we all have different fears and vulnerabilities.

When the monster appears, you'll have two choices: You can try to get away, or you can surrender. If you try to get away, you will escape—but just barely—and soon you'll be lost in the dark again.

Out of the darkness, a second monster will emerge. This one will be almost as terrifying as the first, but not quite, and you'll be faced with the same choice: surrender or flee. If you try to escape, you'll succeed, but you'll soon find yourself in the dark again. Every time you escape, another terrifying monster will appear. Each monster will be slightly less terrifying than the one before, and if you run, you'll always just barely manage to get away.

According to the legend, the number of monsters you'll have to confront depends on the number of days in the month when you die. If you die in January, there will be a total of thirty-one monsters, because there are thirty-one days in January. If you run away from all the monsters, you'll be reincarnated as something very lowly, like a worm. If you surrender to one of the monsters, you'll be reincarnated at a higher level. The scarier the monster you surrender to, the greater your status in your next life will be.

In the event that you surrendered to the first and most terrifying monster, two things would happen. First, you'd discover that the monster was not real. You'd realize that it was just an illusion and that you never had anything to fear in the first place. You'd see that the monster had no teeth. This would be an incredible triumph. The discovery might also seem incredibly funny, and you'd probably start laughing because you'd realize that your fears had been the result of a gigantic cosmic joke that had persisted throughout all of your previous reincarnations.

Second, you wouldn't have to go through the life-death cycle anymore. Instead of being reincarnated, you'd be transported to a higher plane of existence, such as Nirvana. Although this is just a legend, it contains a great deal of truth. If you want to gain complete liberation from your fears, you'll have to confront the monster you fear the most. This is the essence of Exposure Therapy: Avoidance keeps your anxiety alive, and exposure will lead to the cure.

But most people who are anxious avoid the things they fear, so they never experience enlightenment or relief. If you're afraid of heights, you'll avoid high places because they make you feel dizzy and anxious. If you're shy, you'll avoid people, because you feel so insecure and inadequate. The avoidance fuels your fears, and your anxiety mushrooms. If you want to be cured, you'll have to face the thing you fear the most. There are no exceptions to this rule.

There are three basic types of exposure: Classical Exposure, Cognitive Exposure, and Interpersonal Exposure. The techniques you use will depend on the nature of your fears, as you can see in the next table. Classical Exposure involves confronting your fears in reality. These techniques are particularly effective for phobias, such as the fear of heights, blood, elevators, closed spaces, or animals. Classical Exposure Techniques also play a vital role in the treatment of obsessive-compulsive disorder and many other types of anxiety.

Selecting Exposure Techniques

	Classical Exposure	Cognitive Exposure	Interpersonal Exposure
Chronic Worrying		✓	
Panic Attacks		✓	
Agoraphobia	✓	✓	
Fears and Phobias	✓	✓	
Shyness	✓	✓	✓
Shy Bladder Syndrome	✓	✓	
Test Anxiety	✓	✓	
Public Speaking Anxiety	✓	✓	✓
Performance Anxiety	✓	✓	✓
Obsessions and Compulsions	✓	✓	
Post-Traumatic Stress Disorder		✓	
Health Concerns (Hypochondriasis)	✓	✓	
Concerns About Your Appearance (Body Dysmorphic Disorder)	✓	✓	✓

Cognitive Exposure involves confronting your worst fears in your mind's eye. Cognitive Exposure Techniques can play a vital role in the treatment of practically every type of anxiety, such as chronic worrying, panic attacks, post-traumatic stress disorder, obsessive-compulsive disorder, phobias, agoraphobia, shyness, public speaking anxiety, and body dysmorphic disorder.

Interpersonal Exposure involves confronting your fears of other people so you can overcome shyness and other types of social anxiety, such as public speaking anxiety or even interviewing for a new job. In Chapter 23, you'll see that Interpersonal Exposure Techniques can also be useful in the treatment of body dysmorphic disorder.

All forms of exposure require tremendous courage, but the results will be well worth the discomfort you'll have to endure. In this chapter, we'll focus on four Classical Exposure Techniques: Gradual Exposure, Flooding, Response Prevention, and Distraction.

Gradual Exposure

One of my psychiatric students, Dr. Anthony Mascola, was recently treating a thirty-one-year-old woman named Magdalena who had a blood and needle phobia. Magdalena's problem came to a head when her husband needed a liver transplant. She had to spend a lot of time in the hospital at his bedside while the nurses changed his dressings, took repeated blood samples, and administered intravenous fluids. Magdalena struggled with constant feelings of panic and nearly fainted on numerous occasions.

People with blood phobias sometimes faint when they're exposed to needles, blood, or gore. There's an easy way to prevent this problem. If you feel like you're about to faint, you can tighten up your arm, leg, and face muscles, as if you were working with heavy weights in the gym. Then you can relax your muscles and tighten them up again. Doing this several times will improve the blood supply to your brain and usually will prevent fainting. Some people report that the Valsalva maneuver helps as well. When you do the Valsalva maneuver, you forcefully try to exhale while keeping your mouth and nose closed. This causes a brief increase in your blood pressure, and your heart pumps out more blood.

Magdalena was very motivated to overcome her blood and needle phobia because she didn't want to get panicky and faint every time she visited her husband in the hospital. She and Dr. Mascola decided to try Gradual Exposure.

Together, they developed the following Fear Hierarchy. As you can see, they listed a variety of feared situations involving blood and needles and rated them on a scale from 1 (the least frightening) to 10 (the most frightening). The first item on Magdalena's Fear Hierarchy is simply imagining that she's waiting to have her blood drawn. This is called Cognitive Flooding. Cognitive Flooding involves imagining the thing you fear as vividly as possible and flooding yourself with anxiety, without trying to fight or control it. Cognitive Flooding is actually a Cognitive Exposure Technique, and you'll learn more about it in the next chapter.

Magdalena's Fear Hierarchy

Describe your fear: Blood and needle phobia
List the least frightening activity as Level 1 and the most frightening as Level 10.

Level	What I Fear
1	Imagine that I'm waiting to have my blood drawn. Visualize the room and the technician. Imagine the smell of the rubbing alcohol. Picture the technician applying the tourniquet and inserting the needle. Watch the test tube as it fills with blood. Yikes!
2	Write a detailed description of a time when I had my blood drawn and fainted.
3	Look at the equipment used for drawing blood during my therapy session, such as the rubber tourniquet, the test tubes, the alcohol swabs, and the needle.
4	Touch the equipment with my hands, including the needle.
5	Touch the needle to my arm with the cap still on the needle.
6	Remove the cap and touch the needle to my arm.
7	Go to the lab where blood is being drawn and watch someone having his or her blood drawn.
8	Have my blood drawn without looking.
9	Watch while my blood is being drawn.
10	Donate a pint of blood to the blood bank.

Dr. Mascola told Magdalena to close her eyes, relax, and picture the scene. He said:

Imagine that you're at the clinical laboratory waiting to have your blood drawn. Can you see the room? The phlebotomist just walked in, and he's carrying his equipment on a tray. You can see the tourniquet, the rubbing alcohol, the tubes for the blood, and the needle. He looks nervous and explains that he's a medical student.

Now he's applying the rubber tourniquet to your arm and telling you to clench your fist to make your veins pop up. He's cleaning your arm with an alcohol swab. Can you smell the alcohol? Now he's looking for a vein. He's taking the syringe out of the package. You can see the tip of the needle. He's moving it toward your arm. He's about to stick it in.

Now he's sticking your arm but he can't find a vein. He apologizes and explains that he's only done this once or twice before, and he'll have to try again.

Magdalena's anxiety shot up to 100%. Dr. Mascola continued with this technique throughout the session. At the end of the session, Magdalena still found the fantasy extremely anxiety-provoking.

Dr. Mascola instructed Magdalena to visualize the scene at home for fifteen minutes each day. After practicing on her own several times, Magdalena noticed that her anxiety became less intense. Before long, she was unable to make herself anxious when she imagined the scene.

Next, Magdalena tackled Level 2 on her Fear Hierarchy. She wrote a detailed description of a time when she had her blood drawn and fainted. She'd never allowed herself to think about this because it was so anxiety-provoking. She got anxious when she began to write about it, but her anxiety had almost completely disappeared by the time she was done twenty minutes later.

Magdalena moved up to Level 3 on her Fear Hierarchy. Dr. Mascola brought some equipment for drawing blood to the therapy session, and Magdalena looked at it without touching it. Her anxiety shot up to 100%, but after a few minutes, she could look at the equipment without much anxiety at all.

Next, Magdalena handled the equipment for several minutes (Level 4) and then let Dr. Mascola touch her arm with the capped tip of the needle (Level 5). Once again, her anxiety zoomed up to 100% but fell to nearly 0% within five minutes. Then she removed the cap from the needle and let Dr. Mascola touch the inside of her arm with the tip of the needle (Level 6). Her anxiety shot up to 100% but quickly fell almost all the way to 0% again.

Magdalena completed Level 7 on her hierarchy on her own. She went to the clinical laboratory at a local hospital and watched people having their blood drawn. The intense anxiety she felt when she walked into the clinical laboratory disappeared within twenty minutes, and she was able to watch people having their blood drawn with no anxiety at all.

At their next session, Dr. Mascola and Magdalena went to the clinical laboratory together, and she had a blood sample drawn (Level 8). For the first time in her life, Magdalena didn't faint. In fact, she decided to watch the procedure and felt relaxed the entire time (Level 9). Dr. Mascola was so excited that he called me at home to report the good news. He was elated. One of the real joys of working as a mental health professional is watching people conquer a problem that's plagued them for many years. I believe this is possible for everyone who is suffering from depression or anxiety.

Magdalena said she was ready for Level 10 on her Fear Hierarchy: donating blood at the blood bank near her home in Sacramento. This involved lying on a table for thirty minutes with a needle in her vein. Magdalena forced herself to look at the needle and watch the blood flowing from her vein the entire time. She didn't get light-headed or experience any anxiety at all.

Magdalena was overjoyed. On the way out of the blood bank, she noticed a sign saying that volunteers were needed for the local Bloodmobile. She thought, "Why not?" and signed up on the spot. That may seem surprising, given her intense blood and needle phobia, but when you conquer a fear, there's such a sense of exhilaration that the thing that terrified you so much often becomes a source of pleasure.

You can complete your own Fear Hierarchy using the blank form on page 258. List the least-threatening activity as Level 1 and the most-frightening activity as Level 10. Remember that surrender and acceptance are usually the keys to success. Try to make the anxiety as bad as you can for as long as you can at each step on your Fear Hierarchy. In most cases, the anxiety will eventually diminish and disappear. At that point, you'll suddenly realize that you've conquered the monster.

My Fear Hierarchy

Describe your fear: _____

List the least frightening activity as Level 1 and the most frightening as Level 10.

Level	What I Fear
1	
2	
3	
4	
5	
6	
7	
8	
9	
10	

Flooding

When you use Gradual Exposure, you expose yourself to the thing you fear in small steps so that it won't be quite so terrifying. In contrast, when you use Flooding, you expose yourself to the thing you fear all at once and surrender to the feelings of anxiety until they disappear.

During my sophomore year of high school, I wanted to be on the stage crew of the play *Brigadoon*. The drama teacher, Mr. Cranston, told me that people on the stage crew had to climb ladders to the ceiling and crawl around on scaffolding to adjust the lights. I told him that might be a problem for me, because I was afraid of heights. He said that I couldn't be a member of the stage crew unless I was willing to get over my fear. I asked how I could do that.

He said it was pretty simple. He set up an eighteen-foot ladder in the center of the stage and told me to climb up and stand on the top rung. I was fairly trusting, so I went up the ladder, step by step, until I was standing at the top. Then I realized that there was nothing to hang on to up there, and I was terrified! I asked what I was supposed to do next. Mr. Cranston said I didn't have to do anything except stay there until I was cured. He waited for me at the bottom of the ladder and encouraged me to stick it out.

I was absolutely petrified for about fifteen minutes. Then my fear suddenly started to diminish. A minute or two later, it disappeared completely. I proudly announced, "Mr. Cranston, I think I'm cured now. I'm not afraid of heights anymore."

He said, "That's great, David! You can come down now. It will be great to have you on the stage crew for *Brigadoon*."

I was proud to be on the stage crew and loved crawling around on the scaffolding near the ceiling, adjusting the curtains and the lights. I was surprised that something I'd feared so intensely had become so thrilling.

Why did my anxiety suddenly disappear when I was standing at the top of the ladder? Experts don't entirely understand why or how Exposure works, but we do know that when you expose yourself to the thing you fear for long enough, your anxiety will usually burn itself out. Anxiety simply can't last forever. After a period of time, the physical symptoms, such as the dizziness and butterflies in your stomach, will subside.

The perception of danger is the key to all anxiety. After I'd been standing at the top of the ladder for a while, it dawned on me that I wasn't going to fall and that I wasn't in danger. At that moment, my anxiety suddenly disappeared and the experience began to feel pleasant and exhilarating. Exposure always works by changing how you think.

If Flooding seems too overwhelming to you, Gradual Exposure is an excellent alternative. For example, if you have a fear of heights, you can simply go one or two rungs up a ladder and stay there for two minutes before climbing down. Once you feel comfortable there, you can climb up another rung or two and stay there until your anxiety goes away. Each time you practice, you can climb a little higher. Eventually you'll be able to go all the way to the top without feeling so anxious. This approach would be less traumatic than going all the way to the top on your first try.

There's been a tremendous amount of research on Flooding and Gradual

Exposure, and they're both effective. Gradual Exposure takes longer than Flooding, but it's less frightening. I prefer Flooding because you can usually get the problem taken care of right away.

Many anxious people initially resist trying either Gradual Exposure or Flooding. They point out that they've been traumatized over and over by exposure to the thing they fear, and they still feel just as anxious as ever. But there's a subtle difference between accidental and intentional exposure. When you use Exposure Techniques, you *intentionally* expose yourself to the thing you fear and decide to stick it out, no matter how anxious you get. Instead of trying to escape or control your anxiety, you surrender to it. You try to make it as bad as possible for as long as possible.

This is the exact opposite of what most anxious people do. When they accidentally confront the thing they fear, they run away as fast as they can. Many therapists fall into the same trap. They teach anxious people how to relax and control their anxiety. These strategies reinforce the idea that anxiety is dangerous and needs to be controlled. It's usually more effective to surrender to the anxiety. It's a lot like telling a bully, "Take your best shot. I'm not running away from you any longer."

A woman named Cassandra came to my clinic in Philadelphia after she and her husband read my book *Feeling Good*. Cassandra was a gorgeous woman who'd won several beauty pageants when she was in college. She was also incredibly charming and fun to talk to. Her husband had been a professional baseball player for the Texas Rangers and had landed a job as vice president of an insurance company after retiring from pro ball. Cassandra seemed to have it all, but she'd suffered from depression and anxiety for years and had a severe elevator phobia. This was a problem for her because her husband's office was at the top of a skyscraper. She'd only visited him once—by climbing up sixty flights of stairs!

At the time, we had an intensive therapy program at our clinic. People from all over the country would come for several weeks for daily sessions from a group of therapists who worked together as a team. Often we helped people overcome long-standing problems rapidly using this intensive approach.

Cassandra had received years of psychoanalysis for her elevator phobia. Her psychoanalyst had explained that the phobia had been triggered by something that was buried in her past and would require intensive, prolonged work exploring her childhood. But she'd been lying on the couch for fifteen years exploring her childhood, and she was still just as afraid of elevators as the day her psychoanalysis began. She'd also taken all kinds of medications, but they hadn't helped her, either.

At her first visit, Cassandra was apprehensive and asked if there was any hope for someone with problems as deep and severe as hers. I explained that the prognosis was extremely promising but that effective treatment for any type of anxiety always required a great deal of courage. I asked what it would be worth to her to be cured. Cassandra said she'd do practically anything to get over her fears and told me she was prepared to stay in Philadelphia for as long as necessary. She asked how long it would take. Months? Years?

I told her that everyone was different, but it often took about twenty minutes to get over an elevator phobia. She seemed surprised, to say the least, and asked how the treatment worked. I said it was actually pretty simple; all she had to do was to get on an elevator and stay there until she was cured. I explained that there was an elevator down the hall, and if she wanted to walk down there right now and get on it, I'd be happy to wait for her in my office, since I had some paperwork to catch up on. Then we'd still have time to complete her history when she came back to the office and was cured.

Cassandra seemed upset and protested that she'd come all the way from Texas to see me and was paying good money for the treatment. She said she wasn't about to go off and cure herself while I sat around doing paperwork. She said I'd have to get on the elevator and ride it with her so she wouldn't be so frightened.

I explained that this would defeat the entire purpose, because if she wasn't frightened, the treatment wouldn't work. She said, "Well, then you should at least stand outside the elevator and wait for me!"

I said, "Okay, you've got a deal."

As we walked down the hall, Cassandra said that she was feeling too frightened to get on the elevator. I asked what she was afraid of. What thoughts came to mind? She said she thought that the walls would close in and crush her, or that she might use up all the oxygen in the elevator and suffocate. I said that once she got on the elevator, she could do a couple of simple experiments to check it out. She could touch the walls and see if they seemed to be closing in on her, and she could take a couple of deep breaths to see if there was any oxygen left.

At this point, Cassandra looked panicky and said, "But don't you think I should talk some more about the origins of my fears before I try something so extreme?"

I said, "Cassandra, it's such a relief to hear you say that! That's what I was hoping you'd say. We can talk about the origins of your fears for several years if you like. I think you're a fascinating person, and you're a full-fee patient, so it will help to stabilize my practice. Heck, I might even buy a nice psychoanalytic couch for you."

That seemed to do the trick. Cassandra was trembling but said she was going to show me that she could do what she had to do and wasn't going to waste another minute talking about her childhood. She asked what she was supposed to do about all the anxiety and panic she was feeling. I explained that she wasn't supposed to do anything. I told her to try to make it as intense as possible and to try to freak out when she was on the elevator. I told her that this was the price she'd have to pay to be cured but reassured her that the anxiety wouldn't last forever, so she shouldn't try to fight it or control it in any way.

She asked, "But what if people notice that I'm hanging out in the elevator, going up and down, up and down, without ever getting off? What if they think I'm a weirdo?"

I said, "Just tell them you're being treated for your elevator phobia and that your shrink is waiting for you on the third floor. That will give you something to talk about."

Cassandra swallowed hard and stepped into the elevator. The doors closed behind her. I sat on the floor in the hall and waited, wondering what would happen. I watched the light going up to the top of the building and then down to the first floor, and then back up to the top again, with occasional stops along the way. For some reason, it always seemed to stop on the second and fourth floors.

After about twenty minutes, the elevator doors opened and Cassandra stepped out, beaming as if she'd just won another beauty pageant. She explained that she'd been in a state of panic for several minutes, but then it began to dawn on her that the walls weren't really closing in and that she could breathe just fine. Then she started chatting with two young men who were carrying boxes from the fourth floor to the second floor because they were moving to a bigger office. They asked Cassandra why she was in the elevator every time they got on. With her charming Texas accent, she explained that she was highly neurotic and was getting treatment for her elevator phobia from her shrink, who was waiting for her on the third floor while she cured herself.

The men were totally charmed. The friendly banter lifted Cassandra's mood, and before long, her anxiety disappeared completely. She stayed on the elevator a while longer because she was having so much fun talking to the young men. When she stepped out of the elevator, she told me that she had no idea how much fun it could be to hang out in elevators and flirt with cute young men!

Cassandra quickly overcame her elevator phobia with Flooding. Gradual Exposure would have been a reasonable choice, as well, but it would have taken longer. If we'd been using Gradual Exposure, I would have asked Cassandra to develop a Fear Hierarchy like the one that follows, listing the least anxiety-provoking situation as Level 1 and the most anxiety-provoking situation as Level 10. Then she could have gradually worked her way up the hierarchy, one level at a time, just as you saw in the previous section.

Cassandra's Fear Hierarchy

Describe your fear: Elevator phobia

List the least frightening activity as Level 1 and the most frightening as Level 10.

Level	What I Fear
1	Stand next to an elevator and push the button.
2	Walk in and out of an elevator without going up or down.
3	Go up one floor and get off. Walk back downstairs.
4	Go up two floors and get off. Walk back downstairs.
5	Go up one floor and get off. Wait for the elevator to return, and take it back down to the floor where I started.
6	Go up two floors and get off. Wait for the elevator to return, and take it back down to the floor where I started.
7	Go up several floors and get off. Wait for the elevator to return, and take it back down to the floor where I started.
8	Ride up and down for a full minute.
9	Ride up and down for several minutes.
10	Ride up and down on an elevator in a tall building. Stay in the elevator until my anxiety disappears completely.

That would have taken more time, because certain levels might have required repeated exposure before her anxiety disappeared completely. That's why I prefer Flooding. If you're willing to give it a try, you can often recover a lot faster.

Response Prevention

You've probably heard the expression "If you step on a crack, you'll break your mother's back." When you were a child, you may have sensed that this was superstitious nonsense, but you probably avoided stepping on cracks anyway, just to be on the safe side. Then one day, you stepped on a crack and nothing happened to your mother, so you stopped worrying about the cracks.

When you avoided the cracks, you were involved in a compulsive ritual, or compulsion. A compulsion is any repetitious, superstitious act that people engage in to ward off danger. The thought "My mother may die" is the obsession, and avoiding cracks is the compulsion. Hence the name obsessive-compulsive disorder.

Most of us experience mild obsessions or compulsive urges from time to time, but they're harmless. For example, you may have had the urge to check the mailbox after dropping a letter in, just to make sure that it didn't get stuck. You've probably also noticed that letters never do get stuck and that the checking is unnecessary. Minor compulsions usually don't have any effect on the quality of your life and don't require treatment.

But on occasion, they can be embarrassing. A life insurance salesman named Howard had the irrational thought "My family may be in danger" every time he parked his car in the garage. Then he had the urge to shout "Dark! Dark! Dark!" Rationally, he knew this was ridiculous, but he was convinced that something awful would happen if he didn't do his shouting. Aside from that, Howard was personable, happily married, and successful. His shouting ritual was just a harmless quirk.

One day, on impulse, Howard invited a colleague over for dinner after they finalized a deal. Howard offered to drive so they could talk and brainstorm about a new project on the way home. The moment Howard parked his car in the garage, he had the overpowering urge to shout "Dark! Dark! Dark!" However, he suppressed this urge so he wouldn't look like a total loony in front of his colleague.

Howard introduced his colleague to his wife, and they all sat down in the living room to have a drink. Howard grew increasingly anxious because he hadn't shouted "Dark! Dark! Dark!" when he parked the car. In spite of his rational conviction that his shouting ritual was absurd, he couldn't shake the feeling that the business deal would fall apart if he didn't go out to the garage and do his shouting. He felt so uncomfortable and distracted that he couldn't concentrate on the conversation. Eventually, he said that he'd left his appointment book in the car and had to go out and get it. Once he was in the garage, he did his shouting and felt immensely relieved. Then he went back inside to join his wife and his guest in the living room.

Howard didn't realize that they could clearly hear him shouting. His wife took him aside and whispered that they'd heard him and that his guest had looked puzzled. Howard felt profoundly embarrassed and made up a lame excuse that they'd been having problems with rats in the garage and that he had to shout every night to scare them away.

Response Prevention is the treatment of choice for any compulsive ritual. You simply refuse to give in to the compulsive urges. It's like withdrawing cold turkey from an addiction. Your anxiety will temporarily get worse, but if you refuse to give in to the compulsion, the urges will eventually disappear. There's no preparation involved. You just do it. No psychoanalysis, no fancy footwork.

How could Howard use Response Prevention to get over his compulsion to shout "Dark! Dark! Dark" every time he parks in the garage? Put your ideas here.

_____

_____

_____

_____

This problem may seem simple, but make sure you jot something down before you continue reading.

Answer

Howard simply has to refuse to give in to his urge to shout every time he parks the car in the garage. That's all there is to it. He'll get more anxious for a few days, but then the urge will disappear. Response Prevention definitely won't solve all of his problems, but it's the most effective way to overcome compulsions.

I often combine Exposure with Response Prevention for maximum effect. First, you intentionally expose yourself to the thing you fear the most. Then you resist the urge to perform your compulsive ritual.

Exposure and Response Prevention can be extremely difficult at first. If these procedures make you uncomfortable, it's a good sign. It means that you're on the right track.

It's easy to understand why so many people resist Exposure and avoid the things they fear, but avoidance always makes the symptoms worse. In contrast, when you surrender to the thing you fear the most, recovery may be only minutes away.

Exposure and Response Prevention are simple techniques that are based on common sense. It doesn't take a great deal of training or sophistication to figure out how to use them. Is it safe for you to try these techniques on your own, or should you seek the guidance of a skilled therapist first?

Research has shown that people who use Exposure Techniques on their own can recover as rapidly as people who use them under the guidance of a psychotherapist. So if you're willing to be courageous and confront your fears, these techniques can be powerful and helpful. However, if you feel overwhelmed, terrified, or hopeless, you may benefit from the help of a therapist. Sometimes a good therapist can speed your recovery by providing support and helping you find the courage you'll need to conquer your fears.

When I went to the top of the ladder my sophomore year of high school, I felt a little bit of extra confidence because Mr. Cranston was right there, encouraging me and providing moral support. And when Cassandra got on the elevator, she said she was comforted by the thought that I was waiting for her on the third floor and that I was available to help her in case she panicked or anything went wrong.

Of course, even if a therapist or friend is helping you, you'll still have to confront your fears on your own. When I was standing on the ladder, Mr. Cranston was nearby, but I was really confronting my fears alone.

Distraction

Some therapists recommend Distraction as a way of relieving some of the anxiety their patients feel during Exposure. For example, if you're feeling panicky during an airplane flight, you can concentrate on a crossword puzzle or engage the passenger next to you in conversation. If you're afraid of heights and you're climbing a ladder, you can concentrate intensely on the mechanics of what you're doing. Focus on raising your foot and putting it squarely on the next rung. Keep your eyes straight ahead. Don't alarm yourself needlessly by looking at the ground or fantasizing about falling.

You saw a good example of Distraction in Chapter 9. Kristin, the woman with agoraphobia, used Distraction when she spotted a police officer while sitting on a park bench. Instead of running home, as she desperately wanted to do, she concentrated on her Rubik's Cube. The Distraction allowed her to ride out the wave of anxiety and panic.

I don't use Distraction very often because it's an avoidance strategy that may convey the idea that anxiety is dangerous. Instead, I encourage my patients to surrender to the anxiety and try to make it as intense as possible. This paradoxical approach is often more effective.

Chapter 19

....

Cognitive Exposure

The Monster in Your Mind

The Classical Exposure Techniques in the last chapter represented the state of the art for many years. However, those techniques will work only if the thing you fear exists in reality. But what if you have a fear of flying because you think the plane will crash? You can't exactly crash a plane in order to get over your fear. And if you have a fear of lightning, you can't arrange a lightning storm to coincide with your psychotherapy.

Similarly, you can't use Classical Exposure to treat post-traumatic stress disorder (PTSD). People suffering from PTSD have experienced a horrifying, violent event, such as rape or murder, that comes back to haunt them months or even years later. For example:

- A policewoman named Jamie shot a teenage boy who pulled a gun on her during a routine traffic stop. The boy died within minutes. Months later, Jamie was still haunted by feelings of guilt and self-doubt and had horrifying memories of the event.
- A firefighter named David had to drag the body of a badly burned girl from a fire at an apartment complex. Years later, he still couldn't shake the disturbing memory from his mind.

When the thing you fear exists only in your mind's eye, as a vivid memory or frightening fantasy, more innovative forms of exposure will be needed. This is where the Cognitive Exposure Techniques really shine. They include Cognitive Flooding, Image Substitution, Memory Rescripting, and the Feared Fantasy Technique. These techniques play a vital role in the treatment of many different kinds of anxiety, such as PTSD, phobias, shyness, public speaking anxiety, obsessive-compulsive disorder, and body dysmorphic disorder.

Cognitive Flooding

When you use Cognitive Flooding, you visualize your worst fear. For example, let's say that you have claustrophobia and your worst fear is being buried alive. You could imagine being buried alive, screaming and suffocating. Try to make yourself as anxious as possible and endure the anxiety for as long as you can. Or, if you have a fear of flying, you could imagine being on an airplane that's crashing toward earth in a ball of flames. Picture the thing you fear as vividly as possible. If you become panicky, don't fight it! Instead, try to make it even worse. Eventually the anxiety will burn itself out.

Cognitive Flooding was very helpful for a woman named Theresa who developed the symptoms of obsessive-compulsive disorder after the birth of her first child. Theresa began to obsess that her baby had been switched at the hospital and was afraid that she'd ended up with the wrong baby. Intellectually, she realized that the probability of this happening was remote, but emotionally, she couldn't shake the obsession from her mind.

Theresa's son had been delivered via cesarean section. When she was in the recovery room following delivery, the doctor explained that everything had gone smoothly and that she'd given birth to a healthy son. However, he'd accidentally nicked the baby's right foot with his scalpel. He reassured her that the cut wasn't serious and would heal just fine.

Theresa was relieved when she saw that her son did have a small cut on his right foot, but soon she started obsessing and worrying that the cut might be in the wrong location. If so, this would mean that she had the wrong baby.

The doctor reassured Theresa that this was her son and that the cut was in the correct location. Still, she kept obsessing: "What if my baby was switched by mistake? That would mean that someone else has my son."

Theresa checked her son's foot over and over all day long, trying to reassure herself that this really was her baby. She became completely consumed by worrying and checking his foot.

I used many techniques to help Theresa challenge the negative thought "I might have the wrong baby," but she couldn't let go of it. I decided to try the What-If Technique. You may recall from Chapter 9 that this is an Uncovering Technique. I wanted to find out *why* Theresa was so worried about having the wrong baby.

I said, "Theresa, rationally, you know that this is your baby. But what if this wasn't your baby but someone else's? Why would that be upsetting to you? What are you the most afraid of?"

Theresa replied, "That would mean that someone else has my baby."

I asked, "And what if that were true? Why would that be upsetting to you? What are you the most afraid of?"

She said, "Well, maybe the people who got my baby are bandits. They might be kidnappers or bad people who abuse children."

At this point, I felt alarmed, because I was concerned that her fantasies might become violent, but I wanted to get to the root of her fears, so I said, "Let's suppose that were true. What are you the most afraid of? What's the worst thing that could happen?"

Theresa reluctantly described a horrible scenario where sadistic kidnappers had taken her little boy to a cabin in the desert south of the Mexican border. I asked her to describe the scene in detail. In her fantasy, she imagined that the men were holding her baby's feet, swinging him through the air and smashing his head against the wall. Then they threw him down the stairs, like a basketball, and locked his broken and bleeding body in a dark closet.

Theresa sobbed as she spoke. I asked how upset she felt on a scale from 0% to 100%. She said she felt 100% anxious, the absolute worst. The fantasy horrified her.

I was also disturbed by the fantasy and wondered if I should back off, but then I reminded myself about the basic principle of Exposure Therapy: You have to face your worst fear and endure the anxiety until it goes away. If you try to escape from the monster, your fears will intensify. So I encouraged Theresa to stick with the fantasy for as long as possible. This is how Cognitive Flooding works. We continued visualizing the gruesome fantasy until the end of the session, but Theresa's anxiety didn't improve. She was still 100% anxious.

Generally, when a technique isn't working, you can put it on the shelf and move on to another technique. But Exposure Techniques are an exception to the rule. Exposure will work *only* if the fantasy is upsetting at first. So Theresa's intense anxiety was a positive sign, even though the Cognitive Flooding was exceedingly painful for her.

As horrifying as the session had been, I felt optimistic because we were finally hitting pay dirt. I reassured Theresa that Cognitive Flooding takes time and asked if she'd be willing to stick with it, even though it was difficult to endure. She said she'd be willing to do more. I asked her to practice on her own for at least fifteen minutes every day until her next session. I knew that this would be upsetting to her and that I was asking a lot, but she'd been suffering for months and strong medicine seemed indicated.

The next week, Theresa explained that she hadn't tried the Cognitive Flooding. She said the fantasies seemed too horrible, and she'd been trying to shut them out of her mind. However, she said she'd be willing to try again during the session with my support. We spent the entire session visualizing the same horrific fantasies, but her anxiety levels remained at 100% the whole time.

At the end of the session, I emphasized the value of practice at home if she felt she could endure it. Theresa made a commitment to do the Cognitive Flooding for fifteen minutes every day, no matter how upsetting it was.

Theresa's next appointment was two weeks later. She told me that she'd practiced faithfully every day and had gotten intensely upset the first two times she tried it. The third time, however, the fantasies started to lose their credibility, and she couldn't get her anxiety above 50%. On the fourth and fifth days, the fantasies began to seem ridiculous, and her anxiety vanished.

At this point, all Theresa's doubts about her son disappeared, along with the urges to check his foot. She said that her fears about having the wrong baby seemed absurd and that she was enjoying being a new mother and felt ready to terminate therapy.

For Theresa, Cognitive Flooding seemed gruesome at first. Even I kept telling myself that there had to be an easier way and felt tempted to back off. You may feel the same way when you first try this method. It may seem too frightening. If so, this is a clue that you're probably on the right track. If you want to overcome your anxiety, you'll have to confront the devil you fear the most. Sometimes effective treatment can feel like a trip to the gates of hell. But the final result is nearly always worth the discomfort you have to endure along the way.

Image Substitution

When you feel anxious, you may fantasize about a terrible event in graphic detail. For example, if you have public speaking anxiety, you may picture yourself fumbling, feeling nervous, and looking foolish in front of the audience. By the time you get up to speak, you've worked yourself into such a state of panic that your fears actually may come true.

When I was still a psychiatric resident, I was invited to present my research on brain serotonin at NATO Advanced Study Institute on Metabolic Compartmentation in the Brain, a prestigious conference at Oxford University in England. This was my first academic presentation, and it was a great honor to be invited. However, I felt intimidated, because eighty of the world's top neuroscientists were going to be presenting their latest research.

I was particularly concerned because my findings were sharply at odds with research being conducted at one of the laboratories at the National Institute of Mental Health. I'd discovered that some of their studies on brain serotonin metabolism were seriously flawed. However, I'd heard that the director of this laboratory could be aggressive, and he'd been known to belittle scientists who disagreed with him at public symposia. I was especially apprehensive because I knew he'd be in the audience when I gave my talk.

I imagined him glaring at me disapprovingly from the front row while I mumbled nervously about my findings. In my mind's eye, I saw him stand up and start screaming at me during the question-and-answer session at the end of my talk, sarcastically pointing out all the flaws in my research. Then I pictured a grim silence from the rest of the audience as I slunk off the stage like a dog with its tail between its legs. What was even worse was that my talk was scheduled at the end of the fourth day of the conference, so I had to struggle with self-doubt for four full days, listening to these giants present their work and asking myself what I was doing there.

The night before my talk, I was in a state of panic. I can remember wandering anxiously around the Oxford campus at 3 A.M., "watching" the humiliating event unfold in my mind's eye. I spotted an owl in a tree. Even it seemed to hoot at me derisively. I couldn't sleep the entire night. By the next morning, I was exhausted. When it was my turn to speak, I walked stiffly to the podium and discovered that the scientist I'd feared was sitting in the first row, directly in front of me, exactly as I'd pictured him in my fantasies. He was staring at me with steely eyes and seemed to be frowning.

I was so nervous that I read my entire talk in a mumbly voice, rather than simply speaking spontaneously from my notes, as I had planned. At the end of my talk, I meekly asked if there were any questions. The room was dead silent. Then my adversary leaped out of his chair and started berating me, exactly as I'd imagined the night before.

When he was done, the entire room lapsed into another stony silence, and not another hand went up. After a long and embarrassing pause, the moderator said that since there didn't appear to be any questions, it was time to break for dinner. Everyone streamed out and began talking to each other as they walked, but not a single person would walk with me. I felt totally humiliated.

Although I'd felt attacked by my adversary, my negative expectations and fantasies actually had done most of the dirty work. The audience sensed my self-doubt, and I projected my work in a defensive, nervous fashion. This triggered the exact outcome that I'd feared.

On the long flight back to Philadelphia from London, I settled down enough to think about the scientist's criticisms. It dawned on me that he was full of hot air and that my research had been valid after all. His criticisms simply didn't make sense.

When I arrived home, I discussed what had happened with my colleagues. They agreed with my assessment of my adversary's criticisms. We did several new analyses that took his criticisms into account but got precisely the same results I'd presented in England. I decided it was time to submit our findings to a research journal.

Two months later, the journal's editor-in-chief called me. This was unusual, since journal editors nearly always communicate their reviews of research articles by mail. I sensed that something unusual was up and braced for further attack.

To my surprise, he told me that the scientists who'd reviewed my paper had unanimously recommended it for publication and that no revisions had been requested. He also told me that the reviewers were so impressed by the study that they wanted to submit it for the A. E. Bennett Award, an annual award for the world's top basic brain research by an investigator less than thirty-five years of age. I was dumbfounded. He advised me not to get my hopes up too high, since the world's most brilliant young neuroscientists would be competing for this award, including researchers from the very laboratory I was challenging at the National Institute of Mental Health.

Two weeks later, I received another call from the journal editor informing me that I was the unanimous winner of the award. He wanted to know whether I'd come and present my findings at the annual meeting of the Society for Biological Psychiatry in New York, where I'd receive the award. I told him I'd be thrilled to present my findings there.

The night before the award ceremony, I decided to picture the scene differently. I imagined presenting my findings in a friendly, informal, enthusiastic way and speaking spontaneously about all the unexpected twists and turns of our research while hundreds of people listened intently. I pictured a thunderous ovation at the end, with lots of people rushing to the podium to congratulate me. I didn't exactly believe these pictures but felt that they couldn't hurt.

Much to my surprise, it happened exactly as I'd imagined it! I spoke without notes, and the audience seemed to hang on every word. At the end, there was a tremendous ovation, and people rushed to the podium to talk to me. Surprisingly, my adversary wasn't among them! Why was this outcome so different? I had used Image Substitution, substituting a positive, inspiring fantasy for the frightening one that had destroyed my confidence in England.

If you want to use Image Substitution, try to tune in to the negative images and fantasies that flood your mind when you feel anxious. Let's assume that you have a fear of flying and repeatedly visualize the plane crashing in a ball of flames. Every time you notice that you're having this fantasy, substitute a peaceful, reassuring scenario. For example, you could imagine landing safely at your destination or relaxing on a beach with your family instead. You could also focus on a happy memory, such as your high school graduation or the moment your first baby was born. Any positive image will do, as long as it's appealing to you.

Memory Rescripting

If you've been a victim of a horrifying event, such as sexual or physical abuse, you may experience upsetting flashbacks and vivid memories of the event. These mental pictures are like an internal movie that accompanies your negative thoughts, and they can trigger intense feelings of panic, shame, and rage. You can edit these images in much the same way that you can change your negative thoughts.

Memory Rescripting involves a combination of Cognitive Flooding and Image Substitution. Cognitive Flooding desensitizes you to the painful memories so the traumatic event loses its power to intimidate you. Image Substitution creates a sense of mastery that helps you overcome the feelings of helplessness, so you'll stop feeling like a victim.

I once treated a young woman named Betty who suffered from a public transportation phobia. She was afraid to take any form of public transportation alone, such as planes, trains, or buses. I worked with Betty during the summer following her freshman year at the University of California in Los Angeles. She was personable and doing well in her studies and didn't seem to have any complaints other than her fear of public transportation.

Betty faithfully filled out the Daily Mood Log as part of her psychotherapy homework every day. However, she resisted any exposure to the things that frightened her. I encouraged her to get on a bus and ride it for just one block, but she said that even that was way too anxiety-provoking. She was afraid that she'd feel trapped on the bus, panic, and lose control.

During our sixth therapy session, Betty revealed something that she'd been too ashamed to tell me. When she was a little girl, the older boy who lived next door would come over and babysit for her while her mother was out. About fifteen minutes after he put her to bed, he would sneak into her bedroom, thinking she'd fallen asleep. Then he'd reach up under her nightie and fondle her.

Betty was frightened and didn't know what to do, so she'd pretend to be asleep. She felt so humiliated and ashamed that she never told her mother. What made matters worse was that he still lived next door. This meant that she had to face him whenever she went home for summer vacation or visited her mother on holidays. Although she was angry, she'd never confronted him.

I explained how Memory Rescripting works and emphasized that it might be upsetting. Betty was eager to give it a try. I told her, "Close your eyes. Relax. Visualize yourself as a little girl in your bed. Can you see yourself lying there in your nightie?"

She nodded.

I said, "Imagine that you just went to bed and you haven't fallen asleep yet. You can hear the door quietly opening. The babysitter is creeping in, trying not to make any noise. You feel anxious, because you know what's about to happen. Can you see him?"

Betty nodded again.

I asked her to describe what he was wearing and what the room looked like. She said the room was dark but he was wearing jeans, sneakers, and a Hawaiian shirt, and she could see him as he tiptoed toward her bed. I asked Betty how anxious she felt on a scale from 0% (no anxiety) to 100% (extreme anxiety). She estimated her anxiety at 90%. It's important that you allow yourself to get very upset during the Memory Rescripting. Otherwise, it won't be helpful.

I asked Betty to describe what happened next. She said he was reaching up under her nightie and fondling her. I asked how anxious she now felt. She said her anxiety level had jumped up to 100%.

Next I asked Betty if she wanted to change the scene. For example, the police could show up and arrest the babysitter, her mother could suddenly appear and rescue her, or she could invite me into her fantasy to help her.

Betty said she wanted to enter the scene herself as a large, powerful woman. She described the new fantasy in vivid detail. First, she grabbed the boy by the neck with one hand and dragged him off the terrified little girl. In her other hand, she was holding a white-hot cattle branding iron with a P on it for Pervert. Then she branded the P into his forehead while he screamed in pain. She said she could almost smell his burning flesh.

I found the fantasy upsetting, but Betty seemed to relish it. She said there was more. There was a Christmas party going on at his house next door. She dragged him into the middle of the living room, in front of his parents and all the neighbors, and forced him to shout, "I'm a sexual pervert! I abuse little girls! I need punishment!"

In the final scene of her fantasy, Betty built an open-air prison on the street in front of his house. The prison had no walls, simply bars and a stool for him to sit on. There was a sign hanging on the bars that read "Sexual Pervert," so that everyone who walked past would stare and know the truth about him.

Betty said she felt relieved, and I was glad that we were done. Her fantasy seemed pretty intense.

But then Betty described another problem that had been upsetting her and asked if we could do Memory Rescripting again. She explained that a group of fraternity boys had raped her roommate at a party in Los Angeles. Although Betty did not witness the event, her roommate had described the experience in graphic detail. Betty felt enraged and was frequently bothered by upsetting fantasies about what had happened.

Once again, I asked her to close her eyes, relax, and tell me what she saw in her mind's eye. This time, she visualized a gang of drunken frat boys dragging her roommate into a dorm room where they took turns raping her, all the while laughing and whooping it up. This fantasy made Betty intensely anxious and angry. I encouraged her to modify the fantasy in any way she wanted. Once again, she wanted to enter the scene as a large, powerful woman. But this time, she was holding a butcher's cleaver in her hand. She grabbed the boy who was raping her roommate, castrated him, and watched while he slowly bled to death.

I found this fantasy even more unsettling and was worried that the treatment might have an adverse effect on Betty. However, I'd discussed the problem of aggressive fantasies with Merv Smucker, Ph.D., a psychologist from Milwaukee who did a lot of the developmental work with Memory Rescripting. Dr. Smucker said that his patients often came up with upsetting fantasies. He recommended against censoring the fantasies, since doing so makes them seem forbidden and even more tempting. In contrast, when you let them run their course, they usually wear out and lose their ability to upset you.

Still, I was feeling a bit uncomfortable, so I told Betty that it was good that she'd gotten that upsetting fantasy out of her system, and I wondered if it was time to move on. Betty said, "Wait a minute. I'm not done yet. There are seven more boys." She described castrating each one of them in gory detail. I was totally exhausted by the end of the session and didn't know if I'd been involved in a powerful and healing intervention or psychiatric malpractice.

All my patients fill out an Evaluation of Therapy Session form in the waiting room after every session, indicating how warm and understanding I was and how helpful the session was. I was relieved to see that Betty had given me the highest possible ratings on these scales. But I still didn't know if the intervention would have any effect on her symptoms.

When Betty returned the following week, she emphasized how helpful the session had been. Then she said, "Dr. Burns, have you noticed how I've been resisting your suggestion about facing my fears and taking public transportation? Well, you might be interested in this."

She handed me a packet of tickets. I thought they might be bus tickets, since I'd been trying to persuade her to take a bus for just one block, but I could see that they were actually airplane tickets. I said, "Wow, this is terrific. Are you going to take a commuter flight from San Jose to Sacramento or something like that?"

Betty said that it wasn't a commuter flight and told me to look more closely. She had a round-trip ticket from San Francisco to Bangkok. I was dumbfounded.

Betty explained that her mother had to go to Bangkok for a week on business. She'd told her mother that I wanted her to face her fears of public transportation, so she'd decided to fly there with her. Then, instead of staying for the week, she was going to fly back immediately so she'd be alone on an airplane for fifteen hours. Betty asked, "Do you think that would be long enough, Dr. Burns?"

"More than enough, more than enough!" I exclaimed. "This is fantastic!"

I asked if she had any fears that we needed to prepare for. Betty said she was afraid that she'd have to change planes in Singapore and had disturbing fantasies of being dragged into the baggage area and raped by the Singapore mafia. She asked if we could try some more Memory Rescripting to overcome this fear.

I pointed out that we'd be using Memory Rescripting to change a frightening fantasy about something that hadn't actually happened but said it might be worth a try. Once again, she closed her eyes and described the fantasy that had been frightening her. Then she entered the fantasy as a big, strong woman, but this time, she castrated the Singapore mafia!

I saw Betty two weeks later. She'd completed her trip and was surprised because she hadn't experienced even an ounce of anxiety during the flight. In fact, she'd tried to make herself anxious on the airplane but had failed. Since returning home, she'd been taking buses and trains regularly with no problems at all.

Why was the Memory Rescripting so effective? I believe that it boosted Betty's feelings of self-confidence, because she no longer felt like a helpless victim in the disturbing fantasies and memories that had been haunting her. This gave her the courage to confront her fears of public transportation.

Memory Rescripting is a creative and potent tool that can be effective when other methods have failed. Researchers haven't yet determined whether the Cognitive Flooding or the Image Substitution part of Memory Rescripting is more important. In many cases, simply visualizing the traumatic memories and surrendering to the painful emotions will be enough. But in Betty's case, the rescripting of the fantasies seemed to empower her.

If Memory Rescripting interests you, some words of caution are in order. First, this method can be powerful, and like any form of power, it can be helpful or hurtful. If you're disturbed by memories of violence or sexual abuse, you should use this technique only under the guidance of a mental health professional.

Second, you have to be able to separate fantasy from reality. If you're struggling with suicidal or violent fantasies and have the urge to hurt somebody, including yourself, then this technique probably isn't indicated. Instead, seek professional help immediately. Don't try to fix the problem on your own. Your life is too precious. A compassionate and skillful therapist can often make all the difference in the world.

Feared Fantasy

When you use the Feared Fantasy Technique, you enter a nightmare world where your worst fears come true. There are two unusual rules in this world. First, whenever you're afraid that other people are judging you or looking down on you, they really are. In fact, their negative thoughts about you will often be even worse than you imagined. Second, they always tell you *exactly* what they're thinking. They're not polite, and they don't hold back at all.

In this nightmare world, you'll meet an imaginary critic who will rip into you in the worst possible way and attack your every weakness or shortcoming. You can respond using Self-Defense or the Acceptance Paradox. When you use Self-Defense, you argue with the critic and try to put the lie to what the critic says. When you use the Acceptance Paradox, you defeat the critic by finding truth in the criticisms. This takes the wind out of the critic's sails.

The goal of the Feared Fantasy is the same as the goal of any Exposure Technique. When you face your worst fear, you gain liberation from it and discover that you never had anything to fear in the first place.

Keep in mind that the Feared Fantasy is radically different from assertiveness training. The hostile critic does not exist in reality but is simply the projection of your own worst fears. You're really doing battle with yourself. Real people would almost never be as cruel and judgmental as the critic in your own brain.

You can either do the Feared Fantasy as a Role-Playing Technique with the help of a therapist or friend, or you can write out a Feared Fantasy dialogue. When you role-play, be sure to use role reversals whenever you get stuck, so you can learn more effective ways to defeat the hostile critic.

A woman named Monica sent me an e-mail with a question about her self-critical thoughts. She wrote:

> Dear Dr. Burns,
>
> I've suffered from depression, social phobia and panic disorder for twenty years. I also have a fear of driving. I'm using all of your books together with therapy and I'm finally getting good results.
>
> However, I wonder how different my life could have been if I'd only learned about these techniques and practiced them sooner. I constantly relive past events and think, "If only I'd done such-and-such, things could be different now."
>
> Sometimes I get depressed thinking how I've wasted my life and accomplished nothing because of twenty years of depression and anxiety. Now it seems almost too late. I struggle with the most basic things that

face normal adolescents, like career choices, getting educated, finding friends, and so on. But I'm going on forty, and I'm overwhelmed by the combination of age and inexperience.

Every sign of aging frightens me and I'm embarrassed to be so far behind in life. Do you have any ideas to counteract these thoughts? They intrude even when I'm doing positive things to change.
Thank you very much,
Monica

Monica seemed to be struggling with these negative thoughts:

- I've wasted my life and accomplished nothing because of twenty years of depression and anxiety.
- If only I'd learned about these techniques years ago, my life could be so different now.

Monica said she'd tried ten of the methods she'd read about in my books but became particularly excited when I asked if she'd ever tried the Feared Fantasy. She wrote:

I overlooked the Feared Fantasy Technique for a long time because I didn't have anyone to role-play with, but I've always enjoyed the examples in your books. I even laugh out loud sometimes. I decided to try it on paper, being both voices. It seems to resonate more than any other technique I've tried, and I'm beginning to feel a lot better. I'm waiting to see if the improvement will last. If you have any other suggestions, I'd love to hear from you. You've really inspired me!

Here's Monica's Feared Fantasy dialogue for the thought "I've wasted my life, accomplished nothing, and can't change now."

Negative Guy: Monica, I'm truly amazed at the bizarre life you've led. You've wasted your most precious years. You let the prime of your life just slip by without doing a thing. How could you let that happen?

Monica: Yes, it's true that I didn't accomplish all I desired during my young-adult years. I often get depressed over that myself. I still have a lot to work on. But considering all that's happened, I don't think I'm doing so terribly now. I'm going to therapy. I'm working on changing lifelong habits. It will take a while, but I'm fairly optimistic that I can change and do something with my life.

Negative Guy: Well, Monica, I hate to throw cold water on you, but I really see no hope. You're thirty-nine years old, and if you haven't accomplished anything yet, I don't think you ever will. You'll just have to resign yourself to your lot in life. I don't know of anyone who's led the life you have and managed to change. You're being very unrealistic. You have your head in the clouds.

Monica: Well, it may be true that you don't know anyone like me. I'm pretty unique. But I appreciate your interest in my affairs. It sounds like you think people can never change, no matter how hard they try. Is that true?

Negative Guy: Absolutely! Oh, maybe someone could change if they just had one or two of your problems. But look at you! You're a mess. No career, no relationships outside of family, no education, no place of your own, you can't even talk to people without getting anxious, you have a driving phobia, you get tired easily, and you're emotionally and physically fragile. It's a tough world out there! You'll never make it, girl. You're just dreaming.

Monica: It's true that I have no career, no relationships, and no money. Those are exactly the problems I'm working so hard to solve. I am sensitive, and it's certainly true that there are tough elements out there. But I'm not sure exactly what you're trying to say. Are you saying that only certain problems can be solved and not others? Or are you saying it's the number of problems that determines overall change? I'd like to know which problems you think are solvable and what number is the cutoff point. Is it three? Four? Twelve?

Negative Guy: I think you're missing my point. I'm not talking about numbers and statistics. I'm talking about you. You've never done anything with your life, and you never will. End of story.

Monica: Yes, I'm definitely hearing that theme in your conversation. But I'm still curious why you think I won't ever change. You said earlier that one or two of my problems might be solvable. I'd still like to know which ones. Maybe I can work on those first.

Negative Guy: Okay, I'll humor you a little. I think your problems all intensify each other. You might be able to get a job, but you're too shy. You might be able to have a place of your own, but you don't have the money. You might be able to solve the shyness, but you'd need to go out and practice, and that's where your laziness and lack of energy come in. Then there's your driving phobia and panic attacks. The list goes on and on. You're stuck in a vicious circle, between a rock and a hard place. Face it—you're doomed.

Monica: I really appreciate you taking precious time from your busy life to counsel me. But I'd still like to know why you think these problems are not solvable. All of the problems you've mentioned are very treatable by therapists using CBT techniques. Many experts have written books about how these kinds of problems *can* be solved. They can't all be wrong!

Negative Guy: Well, I guess it's the combination. You have a very bad combination of problems that's completely unsolvable.

Monica: That's very interesting. Could you tell me where you've heard about the Unsolvable Combination? Was it in a psychiatric journal or from an expert in the field of psychology or statistics? Is it some kind of Ultimate Metaphysical Law that you've discovered?

Negative Guy: I heard it from a psychiatrist. I told him about you, and he said that in forty years of practice, he's never seen a case like yours. He said he doesn't think you can be helped without medication, and even with medication, it would be very difficult, if not impossible, to cure someone as severe as you.

Monica: Psychiatrists aren't always aware of Cognitive Therapy techniques. They've been trained to prescribe medication, and that's usually their only line of therapy. I've been to two psychiatrists who told me they didn't think I could get better without medication, but I tried it and felt worse on medications than off. I've decided to go with CBT and see what happens. But I'm still interested to know why you, Negative Guy, think I'm incurable. Why do you feel so strongly that my problems are unsolvable?

Negative Guy: Okay, it's not the problems. It's you. You just don't have what it takes. Other people can solve their problems, I suppose, but you can't. If you could, you'd have done it already.

Monica: Interesting. So you're saying there's something about me that's different from other people with similar problems that makes me an extraspecial hope-less case? Could you define that particular something? What is it exactly?

Negative Guy: I can't define it. I just know it's there.

Monica: An indefinable quality.

Negative Guy: That's right.

Monica: So the thing that explains why I can never change is some indefinable quality that cannot be explained or described?

Negative Guy: Yep.

Monica: That's not much to go on. I think maybe you don't know what you're talking about after all!

Wow! I was really impressed with Monica's Feared Fantasy. I couldn't have done better myself! It was effective because she wrote down the worst criticisms she could think of. She didn't hold back. When she examined them one by one, she realized they were just a lot of hot air.

You may have noticed that the Feared Fantasy is quite similar to the Externalization of Voices you read about in Chapter 15. They both involve role-playing, and they both involve an integration of Self-Defense and the Acceptance Paradox. The main difference is that when you're using the Externalization of Voices, your partner attacks you with the negative thoughts from your Daily Mood Log, using the second person, "you." She or he does not represent a real person but simply the self-critical thoughts in your mind. So you're really doing battle with yourself.

In contrast, when you use the Feared Fantasy, your partner really does represent another person. But in this case, it's an imaginary stranger you've always feared, someone who really has all the negative thoughts about you that you imagine someone else might have. But of course, the critic is far worse than any real human being would ever be, because the critic actually says all these terrible things to you. However, the outcome of these two techniques is the same. When you find truth in the criticisms, you take all the wind out of the critic's sails, and you realize that you never really had anything to fear in the first place.

. . . .

Interpersonal Exposure

The Fear of People

Almost everybody feels shy or awkward from time to time. For most people, these feelings aren't much of a problem. But shyness can rob you of self-esteem, hold you back in your career, and prevent you from forming intimate, loving relationships.

Cognitive Therapy is based on the idea that your thoughts create all your emotions, positive and negative. If you're shy, you probably have thoughts like these in social situations:

- I don't have anything interesting to say.
- These people are out of my league.
- They won't like me. They'll think I'm boring.
- I'm the only one who feels self-conscious right now.
- If anyone knew how I felt, they'd think I was a real loser.
- Everyone can see how nervous I am.
- I shouldn't feel so nervous. I should be more relaxed.
- What's wrong with me? I must be a weirdo.

If you believe these messages, you'll feel shy and self-conscious around other people. These thoughts cause the feelings of self-consciousness and shy-

ness. Although the thoughts may seem absolutely valid when you're feeling upset, they contain many of the cognitive distortions you've been learning about.
How many distortions can you identify in these thoughts? Check off all you
can find in the following table. If you need help, review the definitions of the
cognitive distortions on page 428.

Distortion	(✓)	Distortion	(✓)
1. All-or-Nothing Thinking		6. Magnification or Minimization	
2. Overgeneralization		7. Emotional Reasoning	
3. Mental Filter		8. Should Statements	
4. Discounting the Positive		9. Labeling	
5. Jumping to Conclusions • Mind-Reading • Fortune-Telling		10. Blame • Self-Blame • Other-Blame	

When you're done, read my analysis.

Answer

As you can see on p. 287, these thoughts contain all ten distortions.

Shyness results from a mental con. When you're feeling shy, you're telling
yourself things that simply aren't true, but you don't realize it. Why does
this happen? People who feel shy aren't stupid. Why would they believe such
distorted messages? It's because the negative thoughts act as self-fulfilling
prophecies, so they appear to be true when they're not.

Let's say that you believe that other people won't like you or be interested
in you. This mind-set will make you feel anxious, self-conscious, and inhibited.
You may also feel inferior and resentful about the fact that other people seem
so judgmental and rejecting. As a result, when you're talking to someone at a
social event, you'll feel uncomfortable and constantly monitor your feelings and
behavior. You'll tell yourself: "I bet I look nervous. I just know that she can see
how shy and anxious I feel. I better try to look normal. Did I just say something
stupid? If I don't say something interesting pretty soon, she's going to get bored
and leave. But what should I say? I can't think of anything interesting to say.
Maybe I could talk about my aquarium. I think I'll ask if she likes fish."

Shyness Distortions

Distortion	(✓)	Explanation
1. All-or-Nothing Thinking	✓	You think that there are two kinds of people: the "shy" people and the "outgoing" people. But in reality, most people feel shy or anxious from time to time.
2. Overgeneralization	✓	You generalize from your shyness to your self. Instead of thinking about your shyness as a problem you can work on, you think, "There must be something wrong with *me*." The overgeneralization makes you feel like you're defective.
3. Mental Filter	✓	You focus entirely on your shyness and all your faults, and filter out what the other person is saying. This makes it practically impossible to generate any interesting conversation with someone.
4. Discounting the Positive	✓	You ignore your good qualities and tell yourself that there's nothing special or interesting about you.
5. Jumping to Conclusions • Mind-Reading • Fortune-Telling	✓	You assume that no one else feels anxious and that other people wouldn't be interested in anything you had to say (Mind-Reading). You believe that everyone can tell how awkward you feel and predict that social situations will be dreadful, humiliating experiences (Fortune-Telling). Of course, this belief functions as a self-fulfilling prophecy, so you feel convinced that your negative thoughts are totally valid.
6. Magnification or Minimization	✓	You blow your flaws way out of proportion and tell yourself that your shyness is shameful and abnormal (Magnification). You also shrink the importance of your strengths as well as what's unique about you (Minimization).
7. Emotional Reasoning	✓	You *feel* like a weirdo, so you think you must really *be* one. You *feel* like others are looking down on you, so you conclude they really *are*.
8. Should Statements	✓	You beat up on yourself and insist that you *shouldn't* feel so shy and self-conscious. This leads to feelings of shame.
9. Labeling	✓	You label yourself as a "loser" or a "weirdo." These labels make you feel abnormal, inferior, and isolated.
10. Blame • Self-Blame • Other-Blame	✓	You blame yourself and beat up on yourself because you feel shy. You may secretly blame other people as well, because you imagine that they're very judgmental and rejecting and would never like or accept you.

This inner dialogue distracts you and prevents you from interacting with the other person in an animated, natural, spontaneous manner. You're so preoccupied with yourself and your own anxiety that you don't tune in to what other people are saying and you don't express any real interest in them. This makes you appear odd, self-absorbed, and boring. You may also look tense and unhappy because you're not emotionally connected with the person you're talking to. Pretty soon, the other person gets uncomfortable and tells you that he or she needs to talk to someone on the other side of the room.

Of course, this is exactly what you thought was going to happen, so you tell yourself that you were right all along. You conclude that you *really are* a boring person and that other people *really aren't* interested in you. You feel like a victim, and it never occurs to you that the entire scenario was the direct result of your own distorted thinking. You forced the other person to treat you in the exact way you dreaded.

The same thing occurs with public speaking anxiety. If you imagine that you're going to do a poor job, and you feel anxious because you think that the audience will get turned off and feel bored or antagonistic, that's exactly what will happen. Of course, there's a positive side to the equation. You can learn to relate to other people in a warmer and more dynamic fashion, and you have far more power than you think.

In this chapter, you'll learn about five Interpersonal Exposure Techniques that can help you transform your social life from rags to riches: Smile and Hello Practice, Flirting Training, Rejection Practice, Self-Disclosure, and the David Letterman Technique. In Chapter 14, you learned about Shame-Attacking Exercises, which could also be classified as Interpersonal Exposure Techniques.

Smile and Hello Practice

When I was a little boy, my father took me to see the movie *War of the Worlds*. When we were walking back to the car after the movie, I noticed that he said hello to almost everyone who walked past us on the street, and most of them said hello back.

I was surprised and asked him how he'd gotten to know so many people. He told me that he didn't know any of them and explained that it was okay to say hello to people you don't know. He encouraged me to do it, too, so I also started smiling and saying hello to the people we passed. I trusted my father and thought this was the natural thing to do.

Of course, almost everybody smiled back and said hello. After all, I was just a little boy walking with my father. Furthermore, I was cross-eyed and had to wear thick glasses, so I was kind of goofy-looking. They were probably amused and maybe they thought I was cute. At any rate, it was pretty good anti-shyness training.

If you suffer from shyness, you can do the same thing. You can force yourself to smile and say hello to ten strangers every day. Usually you'll discover that people are much friendlier than you expected.

If you feel too insecure to tackle this assignment, you can start with something easier. You can start by smiling and saying hello to inanimate objects, such as plants or lamps. Then you can practice on cats and dogs you encounter when you're out walking. Once you feel comfortable smiling and saying hello to animals, you can move on to human beings.

Start with strangers who seem nonthreatening. For example, you can smile and say hello to an elderly man waiting at a bus stop. Chances are, he'll appreciate it, and you may even make his day. You'll discover that when you smile and say hello to people in a genuine and cheerful way, often your energy brightens them up, and they'll reflect the positive energy back to you. Before long, you'll find that you can say hello to anyone.

However, if you're shy, this technique may seem extremely threatening at first. I once treated a likable but painfully shy young man named Roger. Roger was from India and worked for a biotechnology firm in Philadelphia. He was extremely self-conscious and convinced that everyone could see how shy and awkward he felt. Grocery stores were sheer misery for him. When he was standing in line, waiting to check his groceries, he'd stare at the floor and try to make himself invisible because he felt so awkward and out of place.

Roger often watched talk shows on late-night television. He thought that most Americans were as outgoing and sociable as talk show hosts like David Letterman and Jay Leno. He was even convinced that total strangers in grocery store lines constantly chatted and made witty jokes with each other. He had no real evidence for this because he was always staring at the floor, but he was pretty sure it was true. Of course, Roger couldn't think of a single witty thing to say when he was standing in line. When it was his turn to check his groceries, he'd pay and leave as quickly as possible, feeling certain that every person there was judging him and could see how shy and awkward he felt.

Roger also felt uncomfortable when he was walking down the street. He was convinced that people looked down on him because of his dark skin and long hair. Sometimes he'd get so mad about how unfair it all was that he'd look up and give someone a dirty look, as if to say "Gotcha! I caught you looking down on me!" Of course, the angry expression on his face alarmed the person he was staring at, so that person did look surprised. This convinced Roger that people *really were* looking down on him and that he'd caught them in the act.

I proposed an experiment that might help Roger put his negative thoughts to the test. I suggested that when he was in a grocery store line, he could force himself to raise his eyes up from the floor and look around to see what was really going on. Then he could count how many people were chatting with strangers in an animated manner and how many were minding their own business. Roger reluctantly agreed to try this experiment the next time he was in a grocery store.

The following week, he reported that it had been extremely difficult to stop staring at the floor, because he felt intensely self-conscious and didn't want to attract any attention. But when he forced himself to look around, he was surprised to discover that none of the people in line were chatting or telling witty jokes. Instead, most of them were staring off into space or reading the *National Enquirer* they'd just borrowed from the magazine rack. They weren't making clever comments to the person who checked their groceries, either. They just said, "How much is it?" or "Thank you," and were on their way.

We were off to a great start but weren't home yet, as Roger was still having trouble connecting with other people. I suggested he try Smile and Hello Practice next. I told Roger to smile and say hello to at least twenty strangers during the next week. He could choose people he saw on the way out of my office, strangers walking down the street, or people shopping in the mall. I advised him to keep track of how many people responded to him in a negative, neutral, or positive manner. That way, he could test his belief that people were judging him and looking down on him.

He wasn't at all enthusiastic about this assignment and resisted intensely, making up all kinds of excuses about why he "couldn't" or "shouldn't" have to do it. He said it was way too anxiety-provoking and insisted that people would think he was some kind of weirdo. When he left the office, he made a half-hearted promise to "try," but it was clear that he had no intention of following through.

The next week, Roger confessed that he hadn't done the Smile and Hello Practice. He explained that he just *couldn't* smile at strangers because he was too nervous. He insisted that his smile would look fake. I told him that wouldn't be the end of the world and created a game called "Smile on Command." I told Roger that we could take turns shouting "Smile!" Whenever the other person said that word, we had to put a smile on our faces and say "Hello," no matter how anxious or phony we were feeling.

This exercise was hard for me, too. I've always felt inhibited about having to smile on command because when I was little, I had a crooked smile and was often teased about it. But the game was a lot of fun. Every time I shouted, "Smile!" Roger would produce a ridiculous, fake-looking smile and say, "Hello there." He looked so silly that it made me giggle. Then Roger would laugh and suddenly his "fake" smile became completely genuine. If you want to try this exercise with a friend or family member, I think you'll find it amusing.

In spite of our success with this game, Roger resisted the Smile and Hello Practice for several more weeks. He kept making up excuses about why he couldn't or shouldn't have to do it. I knew that if I could just get him to loosen up and interact with people, it would go a long way toward helping him break out of his shell. He was actually quite charming and likable, but he wasn't giving himself a chance.

At the time, my wife was working in my clinic as part of her clinical psychology training. She was also treating Roger in separate sessions. We decided to meet with him together and lay down the law as a team. We told Roger that this was the treatment we were offering and that he must do it. We were firm and wouldn't take no for an answer. Perhaps it was a bit like two parents doling out "tough love." Roger reluctantly agreed to do it, even though he was sure it would be horribly humiliating and anxiety-provoking.

When he came in for his session the next week, he was on a high. He said he'd smiled and said hello to many people and was surprised that nobody had given him any dirty looks. In fact, most of the people had smiled back in a friendly way. He'd even gotten into animated discussions with several people. This blew his mind, and he felt exhilarated. He said he didn't feel at all shy anymore but was talking to people like crazy all day long. Roger felt so good that he decided to terminate his treatment within a couple weeks.

I wondered if the results would last or if his sudden improvement was just a flash in the pan. Several years later, Roger called and asked if he could come in for a tune-up session. He was concerned about a career decision and needed some help sorting out his options.

I was very happy to see him again and asked how he'd been doing. He said that his shyness was ancient history and that he was totally uninhibited and chatted with people everywhere all day long. He'd even started going out dancing and had become a social butterfly. He'd dated lots of wonderful women and now had a steady girlfriend whom he adored.

When I present Roger's case in professional workshops, therapists often ask, "Would you still have used Smile and Hello Practice if Roger had been an unpleasant, awkward fellow? What if people really had rejected him?" I believe that the treatment should always be tailored to each person's unique circumstances. Roger was charming, so it seemed likely that he would have a positive experience when he did the Smile and Hello Practice. If I'd been working with someone different, I might have used different techniques. I'd never intentionally set anyone up for humiliation or failure.

Smile and Hello Practice may also work differently in different parts of the country. In California, I say hello to strangers all the time, and I usually get positive responses. But in New York City, it would be different. A colleague and I once said hello to forty strangers in fifteen minutes while walking around Rockefeller Plaza, and not a single person acknowledged us! If you keep this limitation in mind, Smile and Hello Practice can often be a lot of fun.

Flirting Training

Most of the shy and lonely patients I've treated never learned how to flirt. They usually seem overly serious when they're trying to get to know someone they're interested in. In contrast, some people seem to have the gift of gab. They can connect with almost anyone in a lighthearted, affectionate way that sets others at ease. Researchers don't know for sure whether some people are born with this talent or whether they learn it when they're growing up. By the same token, it's unclear whether some people are born with the tendency to be shy, or whether painful experiences when we're growing up lead to shyness.

Animal models support both possibilities. Researchers have discovered that some pointer dogs seem to have a "shyness" gene that makes them terrified of humans from the very moment they're born. When puppies with the shyness gene see a human being for the first time, they run and hide, shaking and trembling in terror. Puppies without the shyness gene are naturally friendly and outgoing. The first time they see a human being, they eagerly run up to the person, wagging their tails excitedly and hoping to be petted. If it works the same way in humans, you could argue that shyness is inherited.

On the other hand, you're probably familiar with the problem of feral cats that were raised in the wild, without human contact. Unless they're adopted as kittens, they develop a deep distrust of people. If they're adopted later on, they may never completely outgrow their fear of humans or become as affectionate and trusting as cats that are born into loving homes. I know from experience, because we have a feral cat, as well as two we adopted when they were six weeks old, and the differences are profound. So you could also make a strong case that shyness is learned.

Regardless of what causes shyness in humans, I'm convinced that good interpersonal skills can be learned. If you struggle with shyness, there's a tremendous amount you can do to overcome this problem and get your social life in gear.

What is effective flirting? It's hard to give a precise definition, but here are a few approximations:

- You make people feel special and admired. You praise them for what they've done and how wonderful they are, but you do it in a lighthearted way. You get them to talk about themselves without trying to focus a lot of attention on yourself. As a result, they'll often conclude that *you're* special, even if you don't say much of anything about yourself.

- You tease the other person in a friendly way, in much the same way that an older sibling might tease a younger sibling that she or he is proud of. Often this creates an atmosphere of fantasy and fun that makes the other person feel curious and intrigued.

- You use positive body language, including looking into the other person's eyes or touching them on the arm affectionately while talking in an animated way.

Of course, these techniques have to be used skillfully and thoughtfully. In some situations, it would be inappropriate to touch the other person, and touching could seem intrusive in any situation if it's done in a clumsy or aggressive manner.

I once treated an elementary school teacher named Annemarie who came to Philadelphia for several weeks for treatment in our intensive program. Annemarie was struggling with chronic feelings of unhappiness and loneliness. She explained that she had few friends and spent nearly all of her free time preparing for her classes. She was a wonderfully dedicated teacher, but life just didn't feel very exciting or rewarding. She was pleasant and attractive but seemed a bit stiff.

I asked Annemarie what she was hoping to achieve in therapy. If we had a magic wand, what would happen? How would her life change? She said she wanted to have more fun in life.

I wanted to find out exactly what she had in mind, so I asked, "What day would you like to start having fun?"

She said, "How about today?"

"Good," I replied. "When would you like to start having more fun? During the session or after the session?"

I was relieved when she replied, "After the session."

I asked what she was planning to do after the session. It was Friday afternoon, and she said she was going to take the Metroliner from Philadelphia to New York to visit a friend for the weekend.

I asked, "If the trip to New York turned out to be incredibly fun, what would have happened? What's your fantasy?"

She seemed embarrassed and awkwardly explained that if her fantasy came true, several gorgeous guys would flirt with her on the train. She said that she was shy and lonely and hadn't had a date in years.

I knew from personal experience that the train would be packed with yuppies commuting back to New York. Annemarie was charming and attractive, so I knew my job would be easy if I could persuade her to break out of her shell. I said, "I suspect that there will be lots of cute guys on the train, and one of my specialties is teaching lonely women how to wrap men around their fingers. But there's a catch."

She asked, "What's the catch, Dr. Burns?"

I said, "You'll have to agree to do what I tell you to do, and it might make you extremely anxious at first. If you have any doubts at all, we can work on something else instead."

Annemarie told me that she was tired of having a life that was so serious and dull and that she'd do whatever it took, as long as it wasn't illegal or unethical. That was the answer I was looking for.

I explained that the first secret of flirting was to remember that it's just a game. It's for fun. If you take it too seriously, you'll fail because the magic won't be there. Lots of people feel bored with their lives and want a pleasant distraction. If they sense that you're playing with them in an affectionate way and that you're not desperately serious, they'll like you more. But if they feel like you're needy or chasing them, they'll reject you. That's because of the Burns Rule: "People only want what they can't get. They never want what they can get."

One way to flirt is to give the person you're talking to a compliment. However, compliments nearly always work better if you come across in a playful, good-natured, affectionate way and don't sound overly serious. In fact, if the compliment is a little bit insincere, it sometimes works even better. I know that this advice flies in the face of conventional wisdom, but bear with me.

I told Annemarie that she was a bit too serious and needed to come across in a more mischievous, lighthearted way. I explained it like this:

Let's assume that you start a conversation with a really cute guy you're sitting next to on the train, and it dawns on you that he's a total airhead. He always hears about how handsome he is, and he's bored by that message. So instead, you can tell him that he's got a really interesting mind and that you just *love* the way he thinks about things. If you want to be a little bit over the top, you can add that he probably hears that from people *all the time*.

Now, we know that he doesn't really hear that message all the time. In fact, he's probably never heard it before. He'll be intrigued, and he'll quickly be eating out of your hand. But don't get hooked on him. He has to realize that you're not chasing him. Be like a butterfly and talk to someone else. Remember the Burns Rule: "People never want what they can get. They only want what they can't get."

Let's say that the guy sitting on the other side of you is a total egghead. He's dumpy-looking, but he's on his way to present his latest research to the New York Academy of Science. You can strike up a conversation with him and compliment him on some feature of his appearance. For example, you could say this in a very sincere, admiring tone of voice: "There's something about your eyes that's so intense, but I bet you hear that from women *all the time*."

Now, you and I know that he doesn't hear that all the time. In fact, he's probably never heard that before, even from his mother! He'll probably blush and get excited, and he'll definitely remember you for a long time.

Now the good-looking airhead will be thinking: "What's wrong with *my* blue eyes? That guy's a total nerd. I want her to talk to *me* again."

The most important thing to remember is that adults are basically children who grew up and got serious, but underneath, we all still want to play and have fun. We all want a little fantasy in our lives. Flirting is just a game you play. You mean it, and yet you don't.

Annemarie and I did some role-playing in the office so she could practice flirting. She was a natural. All she really needed was the permission to be flirtatious and outgoing. She had lots of Southern charm, and I could see that she was going to be terrific.

She agreed to flirt with at least three guys on the train that afternoon. Then she got anxious and asked, "What if someone sees me flirting and looks down on me? What if I flub up, or people think I'm some kind of shameless, fallen woman?"

To help her overcome her fears, I suggested we try the Feared Fantasy. That's one of the Cognitive Exposure Techniques you read about in the last chapter. I explained that we'd enter an *Alice-in-Wonderland* nightmare world where her worst fears would come true. In this world, the passengers on the Metroliner really do look down on her because she's been flirting shamelessly with attractive men. In addition, these passengers tell her exactly what they think about her and don't pull any punches.

I explained that I'd play Annemarie's role and that she could play the role of a hostile passenger. I told her to verbalize what the hostile passengers might be thinking and try to humiliate me. I told her she could be as brutal as she wanted and say horrible things that people would never really say to each other. I explained that the hostile passengers actually represented her own worst fears and rigid standards. Our dialogue went like this:

Hostile Passenger (played by Annemarie): Hey, I just saw you flirting with three different guys. Are you desperate, or some kind of slut, or what?

Annemarie (played by David): A little bit of both, actually. I've been lonely and preoccupied with work, so I decided to break out of my shell and start to open up more. Also, I've been taking slut-training lessons from my shrink in Philadelphia, and I'm glad you noticed. Perhaps the training is paying off!

Hostile Passenger: Well, if I were you, I wouldn't admit it. I mean, you look totally shameless. You're making a complete fool out of yourself.

Annemarie: You are so right. I'm getting more shameless by the minute. And you know, I'm having a ball.

Hostile Passenger: You can do whatever you want, but don't forget that everyone is watching you and looking down on you because of your low moral standards and outrageous behavior.

Annemarie: That's okay, actually, because it's these cute guys I'm interested in. And they don't seem judgmental at all. Who knows, I might even get a date with one of them.

Hostile Passenger: You'll never get a date that way because you look totally lame. Your flirting techniques suck.

Annemarie: I know there's plenty of room for improvement because I'm just learning the ropes. Tell me, what approach do you recommend? What has worked for you? Perhaps I could give your flirting techniques a try.

Annemarie could see that she wasn't going to get my goat. She said she realized that the passengers on the train probably wouldn't really care if she was flirting. But even if someone was critical of her, she could live with it.

When I saw Annemarie on Monday, she was beaming. She told me that the Metroliner had been loaded with attractive young men. She felt nervous and awkward, but forced herself to start a conversation with an average-looking fellow who was standing next to her. She learned that he was an actuary. He seemed unbearably boring, but she blew a little smoke in his face and told him that his work sounded incredibly important and exciting. She said he must be awfully intelligent to be able to do something like that.

He was thrilled and began to pour out his life story to her. A few minutes later, she started flirting with an attractive young actor, and soon he was eating out of her hands, too. He asked for her number and invited her to attend the opening of an off-Broadway play he had a small part in. He said he hoped they could get together while she was in New York. Annemarie was amazed and told me that she felt like she had a new secret weapon.

When you begin your Flirting Training, you can select people who aren't particularly threatening. In fact, you can even begin with animals, just as with Smile and Hello Practice. I do this all the time, and it works like a charm. For example, if I see a dog on the sidewalk, I pet it and say the most outrageous things: "Oh, you're such a handsome fellow. I've never seen a dog with such an intelligent and friendly face!" Dogs love the attention, and they're remarkably uncritical. Their owners are usually pretty pleased, as well. Of course, if it's a snarling rottweiler, you might want to pass!

Next, you could try flirting with people who aren't objects of romantic interest. Most people are looking for a little sunlight to brighten their day. You can practice making friendly, admiring comments to people who are almost guaranteed to respond positively, such as the bellman at the hotel, a police officer who's walking down the street, the flight attendant on the plane, a fellow who's shopping for clothes at the mall, or someone who's working out at the gym. Once you feel comfortable, you can start to flirt with people you're more interested in. However, the goal of this technique is not to get a date but simply to engage people in friendly, lighthearted exchanges and make them feel good. This mind-set will reduce a lot of the pressure you feel. Paradoxically, you may actually end up getting a date, even though your goal was quite different.

Rejection Practice

If you're afraid of rejection, you can try to accumulate as many rejections as possible in order to learn that the world doesn't come to an end. For example, when he was a young man, Dr. Albert Ellis, the well-known New York psychologist, asked two hundred women for a date during a two-week period. All but one turned him down, and she failed to show up!

Although he didn't get a date, he conquered his fears of rejection and ultimately developed a robust social life. In fact, he eventually became renowned for his expertise on romance and dating and for many years wrote a sex advice column for a popular men's magazine.

Although I'd never heard of Dr. Ellis when I was a medical student, my friend Spyder and I stumbled across the same technique. Spyder lived in the garage behind a house I was renting with friends. He was a good-looking drummer who was looking for a band to hook up with. He was also painfully shy, a problem I shared.

In an attempt to conquer our fears, we'd walk around the streets of Palo Alto and San Francisco for hours at a time, taking turns approaching attractive young ladies and trying to get to know them. If it was Spyder's turn, I'd spot a good-looking young lady, and he'd have to approach her and try to get a date. If it was my turn, he'd select someone and I'd have to do the same thing.

Our experience was similar to that of Dr. Ellis. We got shot down every time. I think it was because we were both overly serious and sincere and still a bit on the nerdy and desperate side. But we did overcome our fears of rejection, and that turned out to be the first step in developing far more exciting social lives.

Self-Disclosure

Instead of shamefully hiding your feelings of shyness or nervousness in social situations, you disclose them openly. This technique requires a good sense of self-esteem to be effective.

Shortly after I opened my clinical practice in Philadelphia, my wife and I purchased a home in the suburb of Gladwyne. Most of the homes in Gladwyne are large and expensive. We didn't have a lot of money, so we bought the least expensive home in the neighborhood.

Our daughter, Signe, often played with a little girl named Penelope, who lived near us. One day my wife asked me to pick Signe up from Penelope's house. I was wearing a crummy old T-shirt and dirty Levi's. I jumped into our old rusted-out Fiat and drove to Penelope's house. The driveway was so long that the house was completely hidden from the road. As I drove up, I realized that Penelope lived in a mansion. I walked up to the massive front door feeling pretty intimidated.

I rang the bell and waited. Suddenly the front door opened, and a gorgeous woman appeared. She looked like a model from the cover of *Vogue*. She was slim and tan, and dressed in beautiful clothing and jewelry. She introduced herself as Penelope's mother. I felt anxious and nervously said, "I'm here to pick up my daughter, Signe."

"Oh, please come in," she said. She ushered me into a foyer that was the size of our living room. It had a high ceiling, and the walls were decorated with huge paintings in ornate gold frames, like the ones you might see at the Louvre in Paris. She picked up on the fact that I was feeling uneasy and asked, "Is something wrong?"

I said, "As a matter of fact, I've never been in a house as impressive as this one, and I feel a bit intimidated."

She said, "Isn't that rather neurotic? I heard that you were a shrink!"

"Oh yes," I replied, "I'm *very* neurotic! When you get to know me better, you'll see that this is just the tip of the iceberg!"

She laughed and I immediately felt more relaxed. My wife and I soon became good friends with her. Although she seemed to have everything going for her, I later learned that her life wasn't quite as glamorous as it appeared, and she was struggling with the same kinds of conflicts and challenges that we all have to confront at times.

I'd used Self-Disclosure. You simply disclose your shyness instead of trying to hide it and look "normal." The simple acknowledgment of my anxiety paradoxically made it disappear, whereas any attempt to hide my shyness would have made it worse.

However, Self-Disclosure may not be quite as easy as it sounds. I once treated a brilliant young man named Joseph who was admitted to Harvard University at the age of fourteen. He graduated with high honors four years later, but was painfully shy and had never had the chance to develop any social skills with kids his own age. He was particularly shy around attractive women and was certain that any woman who knew how shy he felt would reject him.

Joseph had blossomed into a charming and handsome young man, and I thought it was a shame that he was so isolated and afraid to date. I encouraged him to acknowledge his shyness when he was talking to women, rather than trying so hard to cover it up all the time. But he refused to do this. He was convinced I was nuts and insisted that he'd look totally lame and get rejected if he did that.

Joseph's resistance to Self-Disclosure was classic. When it's time to confront the monster you fear the most, many people panic and run off in the opposite direction as fast as they can. I knew that as long as Joseph kept trying to hide his shyness, the awkward feelings would intensify, but he fought me tooth and nail and insisted that I didn't know what I was talking about.

After several weeks of resisting, Joseph finally agreed to do an experiment to test what I was saying. He'd been doing some consulting work for an insurance company in Philadelphia and had noticed an attractive blond secretary who seemed to be giving him the eye a lot. However, he'd never dared to talk to her because he felt so nervous.

He agreed to ask her out, but he'd never been on a date and was afraid she'd say yes, and then he wouldn't know what to do. I said he could just take her out to dinner at a restaurant in Chinatown called the Riverside. My family and I went there almost every week because the food was fantastic. Then he and his date could go to a movie. But I told him he would have to disclose his shyness during the date. That way he'd find out if his fears were justified.

Joseph said it was going to be awfully difficult, but he'd force himself to do it this one time, just to prove how wrong I was.

The young lady seemed enthusiastic when he asked her out and accepted the invitation to dinner and a movie. While they were eating, Joseph felt self-conscious and kept trying to act "normal" so she wouldn't notice how uncomfortable he felt, but he couldn't think of anything to talk about. There were several long, awkward silences. She asked if anything was wrong.

He couldn't endure the tension any longer and told her he had something to confess. She looked alarmed and asked what the problem was. He told her that he sometimes felt shy and tongue-tied when he was around a really beautiful woman and had to apologize because he was feeling that way right now.

He was sure she'd reject him on the spot. Instead, she said, "Oh, I've been looking for a sensitive man like you for the longest time! I'm so tired of all these macho guys who are always hitting on me."

Joseph couldn't believe his ears!

After dinner, she asked if he wanted to skip the movie and go back to her apartment, "just to talk and have a glass of wine." They ended up making love and spent the night together. When Joseph came back for his next therapy session, he exclaimed, "I'm a believer! I'm a believer!"

Self-Disclosure is based on the idea that your shame, and not your shyness, is the real enemy. Without the shame, shyness can actually be an asset because it can make you seem more vulnerable and attractive. But if you're shy, you probably won't believe that, because the shyness and shame are so tightly intertwined in your mind.

Of course, there's some art involved. If you disclose your shyness in a self-effacing way, it may backfire because you'll make the other person uncomfortable. They may feel sorry for you or think they're supposed to reassure you. For example, you wouldn't want to say: "Oh, I'm so horribly shy that I can't stand to be around other people. To be honest, I'm a social outcast without a friend in the world, except, of course, for my dog, and he only puts up with me because I feed him. I'm so lonely that I can't stand it any longer. Will you be my friend?"

Obviously, that's tongue-in-cheek, but it sounds needy and subtly hostile, and the other person will be turned off. Self-Disclosure is a powerful tool because you won't have to hide your awkward feelings anymore, but it will be most effective if you express yourself in a relaxed and self-accepting way.

David Letterman Technique

If you're shy, you probably suffer from the Spotlight Fallacy. In social situations, you may feel like you're performing onstage under a bright spotlight and have to impress people to get them to like you. This is stressful because it puts you under intense pressure to come up with something interesting to say. The harder you try, the more awkward and less spontaneous you feel.

Most people are far more interested in talking about themselves. Paradoxically, the best way to impress someone is to put *them* in the spotlight. Get them to talk about themselves while you listen admiringly. This makes you an audience member instead of a performer—a much easier role for sure.

I call this the David Letterman Technique because you capitalize on the same techniques that successful talk show hosts use when they interview guests. They always keep the spotlight on the other person and rarely talk about themselves. This brings out the best in their guests and makes for a dynamic and relaxed conversation.

How do you do this? Instead of trying to impress the other person by saying something interesting or talking about yourself, you can use the Five Secrets of Effective Communication. Although I initially developed these techniques as a way of dealing with interpersonal conflict, you can also use them to develop fascinating conversations in social situations. Here's how they work.

1. **Disarming Technique.** Find truth in what the other person is saying, even if it seems totally absurd or ridiculous. People love it when you agree with them.
2. **Thought Empathy and Feeling Empathy.** Try to see the world through the other person's eyes. When you use Thought Empathy, you paraphrase the other person's words and reflect back what was said so the person can see that you were listening and got the message. For example, you might say, "Wow, you just said X, Y, and Z. Is that right? I'd love to hear more about that." The other person will get excited and will

probably have more to say on the topic, since you appear to be a receptive audience.

When you use Feeling Empathy, you comment on how the other person might be feeling, given the words he or she used. For example, if the person was expressing strong opinions about how unfair some new company policy is, you could say, "Wow, you've got a darn good point, and I can imagine you might be pretty ticked off about it, too." This statement also illustrates the Disarming Technique, because you've agreed that the statement has merit. Thought and Feeling Empathy usually are much more effective if you can combine them with the Disarming Technique.

3. **Inquiry.** Ask simple questions to draw the other person out. You could say, "I'm really intrigued by what you're saying. Can you tell me a little more about that?"

4. **"I Feel" Statements.** You express your own thoughts and feelings. This may be unnecessary because most people are so eager to talk about themselves.

5. **Stroking.** You compliment the other person. Convey respect or admiration. Find something genuinely positive to say about him or her.

You can remember these techniques more easily if you remember the acronym, EAR. As you can see on the chart on page 305, EAR stands for Empathy, Assertiveness, and Respect. If you use these techniques skillfully, you can usually get the other person to do most of the talking. Paradoxically, if you express an interest in others, they'll often end up feeling impressed with you.

When I was a medical student, we were all afraid of a secretary named Clarisse who worked for the chairman of the Department of Medicine. She was a bit caustic and wielded a lot of power, and if you got on her bad side, she could make your life miserable. One day I had to ask Clarisse a question about one of my clinical rotations. She seemed annoyed, so I blurted out something like this: "You know, Clarisse, I really admire the way you run this department. You're incredibly organized and efficient. I'm always singing your praises, and I wish I had that kind of skill."

She melted like butter and always treated me like a prince after that. She

Five Secrets of Effective Communication (EAR)

E = Empathy

1. **The Disarming Technique (DT).** Find some truth in what the other person is saying, even if it seems totally unreasonable or unfair.
2. **Empathy.** Put yourself in the other person's shoes and try to see the world through his or her eyes.
  • **Thought Empathy (TE).** Paraphrase the other person's words.
  • **Feeling Empathy (FE).** Acknowledge how the other person probably is feeling, based on what he or she said.
3. **Inquiry (IN).** Ask gentle, probing questions to learn more about what the other person is thinking and feeling.

A = Assertiveness
4. **"I Feel" Statements (IF).** Express your own ideas and feelings in a direct, tactful manner. Use "I Feel" Statements, such as "I feel upset," rather than "you" statements, such as "You're wrong!" or "You're making me furious!"

R = Respect
5. **Stroking (ST).** Convey an attitude of respect, even if you feel frustrated or angry with the other person. Find something genuinely positive to say to the other person, even in the heat of battle.

© 1991 by David D. Burns, M.D. Revised 2001.

probably felt frustrated with her life and may not have heard a kind word in a long time. Although I'd only used one of the techniques, Stroking, it turned my relationship with Clarisse completely around.

If you want to learn to use the Five Secrets of Effective Communication in real-life situations, you'll have to practice. Just reading about them won't be enough. You'll need to do some written exercises as well as a bit of role-playing.

Imagine that you're feeling shy and having trouble thinking of anything to say to the person you're talking to. Write down one thing that she or he might say that you'd have trouble responding to. Then write down a response that utilizes two or three of the Five Secrets of Effective Communication. For example, let's say that you're at a party, and you've just met an unbelievably boring fellow named Jarvis. You're struggling to think of something to say and feeling nervous. When you ask Jarvis what kind of work he does, he says, "I study dust for a living."

How would you respond to Jarvis? Write down what you might say below. After each sentence, indicate in parentheses what techniques you used, using the abbreviations on the chart. For example, if you use the Disarming Technique, you can put "(DT)" at the end of the sentence. Don't continue reading until you've written out your response.

_____

_____

_____

_____

_____

Answer

There are many ways you could respond to Jarvis. Here's one approach:

> You study dust? (TE; IN) That's intriguing. (ST) I've never met anyone who studied dust before, but I'll bet that dust can be fascinating. (ST) In fact, I recently saw a science show on the Discovery Channel, and they said there are regions in the universe where there are incredible dust showers that consist entirely of diamonds. (IF) What kind of dust do you study? (IN)

As you can see, I used four of the Five Secrets of Effective Communication in my response, and I put the techniques I was using in parentheses after each sentence. No matter what the other person says, you can always find a way to make the conversation interesting if you use these techniques and keep the spotlight on the other person.

Now I'd like you to try again. Imagine that you're talking to someone at a cocktail party and feeling shy. Write down one thing that someone might say to you. Make sure you pick something that you'd ordinarily have trouble responding to.

_____

_____

_____

_____

_____

Now write down what you'd say next. Remember to use the Five Secrets of Effective Communication. Put the techniques you're using in parentheses after each sentence.

_____

_____

_____

_____

_____

Once you've tried this written exercise several times, you'll begin to see how easy it is to set other people at ease and trigger animated discussions with anybody, anywhere, anytime. Then you can practice with a friend or family member using role-playing. Ask her or him to play the role of someone you're trying to talk to, and you can play yourself. After the person makes one brief statement, respond using the Five Secrets. Now ask the person to grade you. Did you get an A, B, C, or D? Ask what he or she liked and disliked about your response.

If you didn't get an A, do a role reversal and say the same thing to the person that he or she just said to you. After the person responds, grade her or him. If you reverse roles several times, usually you'll find that you can generate an excellent response.

Here are a couple tips to remember when you're doing the role-playing. It usually works best if you limit it to one exchange at a time. In other words, ask the other person to make one comment, and then you can respond. Now ask the person to critique you. This allows your partner to highlight what you did right and what you did wrong. Then you can do a role reversal and see if your partner can come up with a more effective response. Continue doing role reversals until you come up with a response that's effective.

Feel free to make two copies of the Five Secrets of Effective Communication on page 305 so you'll each have a copy to refer to during the role-playing. That will make it easier to respond and to provide helpful, specific feedback for each other. Once you've practiced several times, you'll be ready to use the Five Secrets in real time. Remember to start with people who aren't threatening, such as children, and then work your way up to situations that are more challenging. I think you'll be surprised to discover how easy it is to relate to other people when you get the knack of shining the spotlight on them.

The Five Secrets of Effective Communication can be incredibly helpful in a wide variety of anxiety-provoking situations, including public speaking. Many people with public speaking anxiety are afraid that someone in the audience will put them on the spot and ask a hostile or difficult question. If you use the Five Secrets of Effective Communication, you can turn the most hostile criticism to your advantage instantly, and you'll never have to be afraid of any question, no matter how confrontational the person sounds.

I once gave a lecture on brain serotonin at the Baylor College of Medicine in Houston. About five hundred psychiatrists were in the audience. The talk was well received, but a psychiatrist in the back row began berating me during the question-and-answer session. He proclaimed that his own groundbreaking research had proven that a certain vitamin cured depression and insisted that I was involved in a conspiracy with the drug companies to suppress his discovery. He angrily shouted that he wouldn't stand for it.

I really felt on the spot! Tension swept across the audience instantly, and five hundred pairs of eyeballs were staring at me. I resisted the urge to defend myself. Instead, I told him that he had an excellent point and said his criticism of the profession was absolutely valid. I emphasized that many researchers protect their own territory and aren't really open to new ideas that contradict the party line. I pointed out that throughout medical history, important breakthroughs often had emerged from small labs such as his where creative mavericks pursued their own ideas and ultimately triumphed. I encouraged him to approach me after my lecture so I could learn more about his research.

He looked as pleased as punch and quieted down immediately, and the Q&A period continued smoothly. The audience seemed to appreciate my kind response to the heckler. In fact, so many hands went up that I didn't have the chance to answer all of the questions. The positive response to my lecture was overwhelming.

After the lecture, a large and enthusiastic crowd rushed to the podium with questions and comments. I noticed the heckler pushing his way through the pack and braced myself for more attack. But when he got to the front, he grabbed my hand and excitedly started shaking it and congratulating me. He loudly proclaimed that my lecture was by far the best he'd ever heard on brain chemistry and asked if he could obtain copies of my slides to use in his own lectures!

Why was my response so effective? I'd simply used the Disarming Technique and Stroking, two of the Five Secrets of Effective Communication. I disarmed the heckler when I agreed that research is often more political than scientific and that people who didn't promote the party line were sometimes unfairly locked out. When I characterized him as a creative and courageous maverick, he softened because he suddenly felt validated and viewed me as his ally rather than his enemy.

The Five Secrets of Effective Communication can help with public speaking anxiety in two different ways. First, your anxiety will go down because you'll realize that you have a fabulous way of handling *anything* that people might say to you during presentations. Second, if someone does ask a nasty or difficult question, and you use the Disarming Technique and Stroking skillfully, the audience will respond positively because they'll see that it's safe for them to ask questions, as well. This will lift the morale of the entire group.

PART IV

The Hidden
Emotion Model

....

Chapter 21

The Hidden Emotion Technique

Sweeping Your Problems Under the Rug

I once treated a young woman named Alicia who suffered from recurrent panic attacks at work. Shortly after graduating from high school, Alicia got married and took a job working for a man who was starting a business as a soda pop wholesaler.

Alicia's panic attacks seemed to strike whenever her boss walked past her desk. Feelings of nausea would sweep over her, and she'd have the urge to vomit. She often had to go to the lounge and lie down for a while. Sometimes she got so sick that she'd have to go home. Alicia went to several doctors to find out what was wrong, but everything seemed normal. There didn't seem to be any medical explanation for her symptoms.

Alicia also experienced panic attacks when she was at home, especially when her husband was away on business trips. She'd get panicky and call him in a state of utter terror. She sounded so desperate that sometimes he had to cut his trips short to rush home and take care of her. Alicia loved him and felt guilty about causing so many problems for him.

Aside from her panic attacks, Alicia seemed to be happy and well adjusted. She told me that everything else in her life was just fine. She loved her work and admired her boss. He frequently praised her and told her what a tremendous asset she was to the company.

Alicia's panic attacks seemed to come from out of the blue and didn't make any sense to me. Why was this happening? I worked with Alicia using a variety of CBT Techniques. These methods were helpful but brought only partial relief. Alicia's anxiety improved but didn't disappear.

During our seventh therapy session, Alicia asked me if cognitive distortions, such as All-or-Nothing Thinking, could apply to family problems. I asked what she meant. She explained that when she was growing up, her parents labeled her as the "good daughter." She always tried hard to please her parents and teachers, got straight As, was an outstanding athlete, got along well with everybody, and was elected class president in her junior and senior years. She was independent and responsible, the kind of person you could always rely on to get the job done right.

In contrast, her parents labeled her sister, Joanie, as the "bad daughter." Joanie was wild and rebellious. She often stayed out late and got into trouble. When Alicia thought about it, she said that these labels weren't very realistic. She said that Joanie clearly wasn't "bad." She also got excellent grades and had lots of friends. Now she was happily married and was a loving mother with two beautiful baby daughters.

In addition, Alicia acknowledged that she didn't always feel as "good" as everyone thought. Sometimes she felt rebellious and also wanted to be wild, like Joanie. But she felt like she wasn't allowed to rebel because she had to play the role of the good daughter. She said that these labels were pretty misleading because she and her sister were similar in many ways.

I asked Alicia if she thought the insight about the good and bad daughter labels might have anything to do with her panic attacks. She paused and then confessed that she actually hated her work, but thought she wasn't allowed to feel that way because everyone expected her to be so responsible all the time, like the good daughter. She said she didn't want to spend her life selling soda pop and really wanted to quit, but was afraid she'd disappoint her husband, boss, and parents.

I said, "Alicia, if we could wave a magic wand and make all your dreams come true, what would you be doing?" She said she'd fantasized about designing women's clothing ever since she was a little girl but had never had the courage to pursue her dream. She didn't even know if it was realistic but was dying to give it a try.

Alicia also said that she'd never really had any time just to loaf and have fun. She'd always worked during her summer vacations, even when she was in high school, and had never taken time off just to enjoy life because she felt like she wasn't supposed to.

Alicia decided to tell her husband and boss how she felt. As it turned out, they weren't at all angry. In fact, they were very supportive. She decided to resign and spend a couple of months relaxing. Then she wanted to pursue the career she'd always dreamed about.

Alicia's panic attacks vanished instantly, and she terminated therapy. She wrote to me six months later to let me know how grateful she was for my help and to tell me that she'd never had another panic attack. She'd taken her first real vacation and had absolutely loved her time off. Then she'd gotten excited about going back to work. After a bit of networking, she landed a job as an apprentice to a woman who designed women's sportswear. She said it was the fulfillment of a lifelong dream and she was loving every minute of her new life.

Notice that Alicia's panic served as a substitute for assertiveness. Her panic was her way of saying "Something's wrong in my life. This job is not for me." But she was afraid to admit how she really felt, so she got what she wanted indirectly, by playing the sick role. Her symptoms of panic and nausea enabled her to stop working and go home. But nobody was allowed to get mad at her, since she seemed to be genuinely ill.

At first, I thought that Alicia's dramatic recovery was an isolated phenomenon, but I began to see the same pattern in more and more of my patients. It wasn't limited to patients with panic attacks but occurred in every conceivable type of anxiety, including chronic worrying, phobias, obsessive-compulsive disorder, hypochondriasis, and performance anxiety, to name just a few. Eventually I realized that approximately 75% of my anxious patients were sweeping some problem or feeling under the rug. When we brought the problem to the surface and addressed it, the anxiety nearly always disappeared, just as it did with Alicia.

I decided to call this the Hidden Emotion Technique. This technique is based on the idea that when you're anxious, often there is some problem or feeling that you're avoiding because you don't want to upset anyone or hurt their feelings. You may be angry with a friend or want something that you think you shouldn't want. Pretty soon you're feeling anxious, and you're not even aware of the problem that triggered the anxiety in the first place. The problem you're ignoring is usually something incredibly obvious that's bothering you *right now.* It's about as subtle as an elephant standing right next to you, yet you don't notice that it's there.

The Hidden Emotion Technique sounds deceptively simple, but it's not nearly as easy as it sounds. That's because you probably won't be aware of the problem that's bugging you when you feel anxious. At first, nearly all the anxious people I've treated have insisted that everything was just fine, except for the darn anxiety. It usually takes some time and good detective work before the problem surfaces.

Why do anxiety-prone individuals deny or "forget" their problems? I believe it's because most people who suffer from anxiety are overly nice. I'm convinced that niceness is the cause of nearly all anxiety. In fact, if you're struggling with anxiety, I'll bet you a dollar to a dime that you're a very nice person. Your "niceness" results from these kinds of Self-Defeating Beliefs:

- **Pleasing Others.** You feel as if you have to please everyone else, even at the expense of your own needs and feelings.
- **Anger Phobia.** You feel that you're not allowed to be angry, or you may think that anger is dangerous and must be avoided at all costs. When you're irritated or annoyed with someone, you act nice, push your feelings under the surface, and tell yourself that you shouldn't feel the way you do.
- **Conflict Phobia.** You avoid conflict because you feel that you have to get along with everyone all the time.
- **Emotional Perfectionism.** You think you should always feel happy, cheerful, and optimistic about your life, your work, and other people.
- **Emotophobia.** This is the flip side of Emotional Perfectionism. Emotophobia is a term I coined that means "the fear of negative emotions." You believe you should always be in control of the way you feel and

never allow yourself to feel anxious, vulnerable, lonely, jealous, annoyed, or inadequate.

These Self-Defeating Beliefs are all slightly different ways of saying the same thing: namely, that you tend to be overly nice and you're not always in touch with how you really feel. When you get upset, you automatically push the problem out of your mind. Pretty soon you're so consumed by anxiety that you forget all about the problem that was bothering you in the first place.

Researchers don't know why anxious individuals have this tendency to ignore problems. It's not simply a matter of being psychologically naive. I'm pretty psychologically savvy, yet I sometimes overlook obvious conflicts or problems that are bugging me. Although anxiety-prone people are often unassertive, this usually isn't the issue, and assertiveness training doesn't correct the problem. The problem is that they don't even know how they feel.

When I ask anxious individuals if something's bothering them, they usually say no. They reassure me that they love their spouses, get along with all their friends and colleagues, and enjoy their work—but they just need help with the constant worrying or panic attacks. They're not being dishonest. They simply don't realize what the problem is. They can't put their finger on it.

Weeks later, when the real problem surfaces, they say, "Oh, that! Well, yes, that *was* bothering me all along. Of course."

The problem may result from the way our brains are wired. It's almost as if there's a part of the brain that knows exactly what the problem is, but the part of the brain that's consciously aware can't access the information.

If you're feeling anxious, the Hidden Emotion Technique is definitely worth a try. There are two steps:

1. **The Detective Work.** This is the hardest part. You have to put on your thinking cap and try to figure out who or what is really bothering you. Bringing the problem to conscious awareness can be extremely difficult. You may tell yourself that you don't have any problems except for the anxiety itself. But sooner or later the problem usually does surface. The problem will usually turn out to be something that's bugging you in the here and now, not something that's buried in the past. In addition,

it nearly always will be something that's pretty obvious, such as hating your job, being upset with a friend, or wanting to do something different with your life. It generally won't be a deep, complicated psychological problem, like an Oedipal complex.

2. **The Solution.** Once you've identified the problem that's bugging you, you'll have to express your feelings and do something about it. When you solve the problem, your anxiety will frequently diminish or disappear.

Over time, you'll get better at tuning in to how you really feel, but you may always have a tendency to sweep your feelings under the carpet when you're upset. Then you'll feel anxious again. But once you realize what's really going on, your anxiety will become more of an asset than a liability. It's really your body's way of telling you "Hey, you're upset about something. Check it out."

Now I want you to be the shrink and use the Hidden Emotion Technique to help three patients who've been suffering from anxiety. Although you may be very different from any of these patients, these exercises will make it much easier for you to use this powerful technique to overcome the fears that have been plaguing you.

Remember that the Hidden Emotion Technique involves two steps:

1. Identify the problem or feeling that's bugging you.
2. Express your feelings and take steps to resolve the problem.

The Woman Who Thought She Was About to Die

We'll start with someone you've already met. You probably remember Terri, the woman who suddenly recovered from years of relentless panic attacks and depression when she did jumping jacks during a panic attack in my office. Even though she recovered completely, I was curious about why she developed this problem in the first place, so I asked about the first panic attack she'd had ten years earlier. What was going on at the time?

Terri explained that she and her husband had just arrived in Jamaica for a much-needed vacation. They'd been looking forward to the trip and had been saving for nearly a year. Terri's parents had agreed to take care of the children while they were gone so they could have a relaxing trip without the kids.

Terri and her husband were so excited to be vacationing that they'd invited another couple to join them. After they landed in Jamaica, they jumped into a taxi and headed to the hotel. Along the way, Terri was chatting with the other woman about all the exciting things they were planning to do. As they were talking, the other woman said how grateful she was that Terri and her husband had generously agreed to pay for the entire vacation—the plane tickets, the food, the hotel, the taxi, and even the tips. That came as quite a shock because Terri and her husband weren't wealthy and had never offered to pay for the other couple's expenses.

Of course, Terri was exceptionally "nice" and didn't want to upset anyone, so she didn't say a thing. Instead, she started hyperventilating. Soon she began to feel dizzy and short of breath, and her chest started to hurt. She panicked and blurted out, "I think I'm about to die!"

The taxi driver rushed them to an emergency medical clinic where they administered oxygen. Of course, this was the worst thing they could have done because Terri already had too much oxygen in her blood from her rapid breathing. Her symptoms worsened, and the doctor advised Terri to get on the next plane back to the United States so she could be treated at a major medical center.

The taxi driver drove them back to the airport immediately, and they all took the next plane back to the United States. By the time they got to an emergency room, Terri's panic attack was long gone, but their vacation was ruined. She began to have panic attacks almost every week and went from doctor to doctor in search of a cure. She soon began to feel discouraged and depressed because the terrifying attacks were becoming more and more frequent, and no one seemed to know how to help her.

Now I want you to use the Hidden Emotion Technique. Think about what was going on in the taxi at the moment Terri's first panic attack developed. What message did her symptoms project to the other woman? How do you think Terri was feeling? Even if nothing comes to mind, I want you to take a guess. When you're done, I'll share my thinking with you.

_____

_____

_____

_____

_____

Answer

Terri was extremely upset when she learned that the other couple expected her and her husband to pay for the entire vacation. However, she didn't verbalize these feelings or even realize how annoyed she felt because she was too "nice." Instead, her symptoms did the talking for her. Indirectly Terri was saying, "I won't pay!" She was also saying, "You make me sick" and "You ruined my vacation, so I'll ruin yours!" But by adopting the sick role, she could act innocent and no one was allowed to get mad at her. After all, it looked like she was on the verge of death.

You can see how clever our anxiety can be! Terri's symptoms had powerful and immediate effects on the people she was upset with. Does this mean that she was being passive-aggressive and manipulating everybody? Not at all. If you're prone to anxiety, you often don't realize how you're feeling, so the feelings you're trying to ignore come out indirectly, disguised as anxiety. Some people start worrying when they get upset. Others develop phobias. Some, like Terri, get panic attacks. Others get obsessive-compulsive symptoms. Scientists don't know why the brain chooses one form of anxiety over another. Once you get anxious, you may get so preoccupied with the weird and frightening symptoms that you're feeling that you completely lose track of the problem that was bothering you in the first place.

Terri said this interpretation made perfect sense to her. She said that in retrospect, she could see that negative feelings had probably triggered nearly all of her panic attacks over the past ten years. Her attacks often seemed to strike right after she'd had a conflict or argument with someone, such as her children. She loved her children very much, but sometimes they misbehaved and got into trouble. Terri usually tried to reason with them instead of laying down the law. Then they'd keep misbehaving, and Terri would start to hyperventilate, which triggered a panic attack. This allowed her to project this message to her children: "You're killing your poor mother with your bad behavior. You'd better stop right now!"

Anxiety almost never strikes unexpectedly, even though it always feels that way at the time. There's usually some problem or conflict that you're avoiding, but you don't realize it because you're so good at automatically pushing your negative feelings out of conscious awareness.

The Woman Who Couldn't Stop Worrying

Marci was a seventy-one-year-old Florida woman who'd been plagued by chronic worrying for more than fifty years. None of the treatments she'd received had ever helped her at all. She and her husband came to my clinic in Philadelphia for several weeks to participate in our intensive therapy program.

Although the focus of Marci's worrying changed from time to time, the pattern of compulsive worrying was always the same, and once she started worrying about something, she just couldn't stop. Recently she'd been worrying about her two sons, Tim and Freddy. Both sons were divorced and had recently remarried and moved to California. They loved to hike, and every time Marci saw television reports about mud slides or earthquakes in California, she started worrying about them. Sometimes she'd imagine that they'd been involved in a terrible accident or an earthquake while they were hiking in the wilderness. In her mind's eye, she'd picture them pinned under boulders with their legs crushed, screaming in pain as they slowly bled to death.

Marci also worried about Ralph, her seventy-eight-year-old husband. He played tennis every day and his doctor had recently given him a clean bill of health. Still, Marci worried about him constantly and didn't know why. For example, when preparing dinner one evening, she imagined him suddenly collapsing on the floor from a massive heart attack. In this frightening fantasy, she'd call 911, kneel by his side, and pound on his chest in a desperate attempt to jump-start his heart while he slipped into unconsciousness and died. These fantasies popped into her mind unexpectedly all day long.

Why was this happening? When you use the Hidden Emotion Technique, you try to identify some feeling or conflict you've been sweeping under the rug. Do you have any theories about Marci's worrying? Why does she constantly imagine that her husband and sons are dying? What's triggering these fears? What's going on behind the scenes?

Remember that "nice" people are usually the ones who have problems with anxiety. What are Marci's symptoms telling us about how she feels inside? Put on your detective cap again and look for the clues. Here are some hints.

- The hidden problem or feeling is something in the here and now. It's not a conflict that's buried in the past.
- The hidden problem is incredibly obvious. It's about as subtle as an elephant standing right next to you—but you're just not noticing.
- The problem isn't mysterious, like an Oedipal complex or an existential struggle about the meaning of life. It's a common problem we can all identify with.
- The anxiety usually is a symbolic representation of the conflict or problem that's bugging you. It's your brain's way of communicating your repressed feelings indirectly.

In fact, anxiety is a lot like a waking dream. People who are anxious are like artists and poets who communicate feelings indirectly, with images and metaphors. Remember Alicia, the woman who got panicky and nauseated every time her boss walked past her desk? Her symptoms were simply her way of saying, "I don't want to be here anymore." But she was too "nice" to admit that she wanted to resign, and she didn't want to hurt her boss's feelings. So she "showed" him how she felt through her symptoms.

What are Marci's fears telling us? What's bothering her? Put your ideas below. If you're drawing a blank, just make a guess. Please don't continue until you've listed at least one possibility.

_____

_____

_____

_____

_____

Answer

You may have guessed that Marci is afraid of being alone or abandoned, because in her fantasies, her husband and sons all end up dying. That's a great guess, but it's a little off target. Initially you may make a number of wrong guesses when you use the Hidden Emotion Technique, and that's okay. When I'm working with patients, I ask, "Could it be this?" or "Could it be that?" Usually my guesses aren't valid, but sooner or later, patients suddenly "remember" what's bothering them, and then we understand the anxiety from a completely different perspective. When you think about what's triggering your own anxiety, you probably won't be able to hit the bull's-eye right away, either. But if you keep your mind open, the hidden problem or feeling usually will dawn on you.

In case you're still not sure about what's bothering Marci, here are a few hints. Ask yourself these questions.

- What happens to Marci's husband and sons in her fantasies?
- Who creates these fantasies?
- What do these fantasies tell us about how Marci might be feeling? What kinds of feelings might trigger these kinds of fantasies?

Notice that in her fantasies, Marci's sons die slow, horrible deaths. So in a sense, Marci is killing them off over and over. What feeling might she be harboring? If you guessed that she has some unexpressed anger toward her sons, you get the Sigmund Freud Award!

I first met with Marci the afternoon that she and her husband arrived in Philadelphia. When she described her worries about her husband and sons, I asked if she might have some negative feelings toward them that she hadn't expressed. I pointed out that she kept killing them off in her fantasies every day and wondered if she might feel annoyed or even angry with them.

Marci explained that she loved both of her sons dearly but confessed that she didn't like the women they'd recently married. However, she didn't want to come across like the wicked witch or the evil mother-in-law, so she'd simply stuffed away her feelings and pretended that everything was perfect. But inside, the feelings were eating away at her.

I asked if she also had some angry feelings toward her husband, since she was killing him off in her fantasies, too. Had they been arguing or fighting recently? Marci told me that she and her husband never argued or fought. In fact, they'd never exchanged angry words even once in more than fifty years of marriage.

I couldn't believe what I was hearing. I said, "Do you mean to tell me that you've never once felt any annoyance or anger toward your husband?"

She replied, "Doctor, I didn't say that. I said that we've never argued or exchanged angry words. I didn't say I never felt upset with him!" She explained that when she was growing up, she'd never seen her parents disagree about anything and that they taught her that people who truly loved each other should never fight or argue. Marci confessed that she often felt annoyed with her husband but didn't think she should express those feelings, so she stuffed them away.

However, anger is one feeling that *always* gets expressed, one way or the other. You can try to ignore it, but it will simply come out indirectly. Marci's anger was disguised as constant worrying that her sons and husband were about to die. But in her fantasies, their deaths always result from something beyond her control, such as an earthquake or a heart attack. That way, Marci can kill them off but remain in the role of the innocent, loving wife and mother. She doesn't have to notice that she's the one who's creating the fantasies and doing the killing!

Pinpointing the hidden cause of your anxiety is crucial, but usually, insight alone won't lead to a cure. In order to feel better, you'll have to express your feelings or solve the problem that's bothering you. Marci and I talked about how she could express her feelings in a tactful, loving way, so that she could be more open and honest with her sons and husband without sounding hostile or critical or alienating them. We practiced these skills using role-playing and she did a good job.

After the session, she went back to her hotel room and decided to call both of her sons and tell them how she'd been feeling. She said these were the best conversations she'd ever had with them, and her worrying about them disappeared.

The next morning, Marci appeared with her husband and asked if he could join us for the session. She said that they probably could benefit from some communication training, as well. I used a marital therapy method called the

One-Minute Drill. This exercise helps couples express negative feelings and listen to each other in a loving way, without getting defensive. Marci and her husband liked the exercise. Before long, they were communicating intimate feelings that they'd never shared with each other. They cried and hugged and said they felt closer than they'd ever felt before. At the end of the session, Marci said that all her worrying had vanished and she finally felt completely free of anxiety for the first time in more than fifty years.

I told Marci that the good news was that she was finally cured of her chronic worrying. I said that the even better news was that the worrying probably would come back over and over again for the rest of her life. Why is that the even better news? What will it mean when Marci gets anxious? Put your ideas here before you continue reading.

Answer

Most people think that anxiety is a bad thing, not a good thing. But I have the opposite point of view. No one can feel happy all the time. We all have our share of heartbreak and disappointment from time to time. Sooner or later, Marci will get upset again, and when she does, she'll probably sweep her feelings under the rug and start worrying again. Although she'll probably get much better at recognizing and expressing negative feelings, such as anger, she may never get to the point where she can do this consistently in real time. For some people, the tendency to sweep negative feelings under the rug is automatic. It happens before they know what hit them.

But Marci won't need to be concerned about that anymore. Why? Because whenever she starts worrying, it will simply be her body's way of telling her that she's upset or annoyed with someone. Once she pinpoints the problem and expresses her feelings, her worrying will disappear again. Viewed from this perspective, Marci's worrying is actually an asset, because her anxiety is a signal that there's a problem that she needs to deal with.

The Hidden Emotion Technique may seem simple, but it can be challenging. It's not always easy to tune in to the problem or feeling that's bugging you. Usually, considerable persistence is necessary before the problem you've been covering up jumps into conscious awareness. In the meantime, you may think that this technique doesn't apply to you. Keep your mind open and think about the people you know and the activities you're involved in. Ask yourself, "Is something bothering me that I've been ignoring? Am I mad at someone? Am I upset about something?"

Sooner or later, the hidden feeling or problem usually will surface. When it does, you'll understand your anxiety in a radically different way and you'll have a powerful new tool for defeating it.

The Pathologist Who Feared Cadavers

Now that you've worked through a couple of Hidden Emotion exercises, I'm going to give you a slightly more challenging case. I once treated a pathology resident named Corey who sought treatment for obsessive-compulsive disorder, a problem he'd struggled with on and off since childhood. Recently his symptoms had flared up and were threatening his career. Corey explained that while he was doing an autopsy several weeks earlier, a small piece of the cadaver's spinal column snapped off, flew into the air, and lodged in his eye. He quickly removed it and his eye didn't seem injured, but he started worrying that he might have contracted Creutzfeldt-Jakob disease, an infectious and horrible form of dementia. It's the human version of mad cow disease, and everyone who gets it dies within six months.

Rationally, Corey knew that the man he was dissecting had died of a heart attack and didn't have Creutzfeldt-Jakob disease. Still, his anxiety was overwhelming, and he developed a contamination phobia along with compulsive slowness. He began to wear two sets of gowns and gloves for every autopsy and meticulously made sure that no flesh was exposed. He even started wearing a NASA space helmet to protect his face! It took him more than an hour to get dressed before each autopsy.

Corey also started spending more and more time doing his autopsies to "ensure correctness." Before long, he'd slowed down to a snail's pace and couldn't finish any of his dissections, even after hours and hours of intense effort. Partially dissected bodies began piling up in the morgue, and the other pathology residents started complaining that they couldn't complete their autopsies because there wasn't any room.

When I asked Corey if anything was bothering him, he insisted that everything was fine. He explained that he was happily married and got along very well with all the other residents in his program. In addition, he told me he'd known he was going to be a pathologist ever since he was a little boy. He said that everything in his life was great, aside from his symptoms, but he was concerned that he might have to leave the training program if he couldn't do something to turn the situation around.

Corey's symptoms may seem odd, but this is a classic case of OCD. Now it's time for our detective work. Is something bugging Corey that he's not telling us about? Do you believe him when he says there are no problems in his life? Or is he trying to tell us something? What hidden feeling or problem could Corey be struggling with? Put your best guess here.

_____

_____

_____

_____

_____

Answer

Of course, Corey is the only one who can tell us for sure what's going on. We can only make educated guesses. But if you're still in the dark, ask yourself these questions:

- Does Corey seem to enjoy his work?
- Does he really have positive feelings toward the other residents in his program? What's the impact of his obsessive-compulsive symptoms on them?

Corey and I used a variety of CBT techniques with only partial success. After five or six sessions, his anxiety had improved about 50%, but he was still struggling. Every time we met, I asked him if there were any problems that he hadn't told me about. Was something bugging him? He always insisted that everything was fine, except for the OCD.

At the beginning of the eighth session, things took an unexpected turn. Corey brought me an advertisement from a local medical newsletter. Apparently, a teaching hospital down the road needed an emergency room resident beginning in a few months. Corey seemed excited.

I said, "Corey, why are you so excited? You told me that you always wanted to be a pathologist."

He replied, "No, my *father* always wanted me to be a pathologist. If you want to know the truth, I *hate* pathology. I've always wanted to be an emergency room doctor."

Then he admitted something else. He was Jewish, but he was working in a fundamentalist Christian hospital. He felt there was some subtle anti-Semitism among the staff. For example, he sometimes thought he got the short end of the stick in terms of the on-call schedule and rotations, but he always acted polite so that his colleagues and supervisors wouldn't get annoyed or label him as a complainer.

Suddenly Corey's symptoms made perfect sense. His contamination phobia and obsessive slowness were his way of saying, "I can't stand dissecting dead bodies. I don't want to spend my life doing this!" At the same time, he was making life miserable for all the other residents in the program and getting back at them indirectly by playing the role of an innocent victim of OCD.

Of course, Corey will have to express the feelings he's been hiding and do something about the problem that's bugging him. After the session, he drove to the hospital that had placed the ad and submitted an application for the position. He had excellent credentials, and the director of the program accepted him on the spot. Then he drove back to his own hospital and met with the director of residency training. Corey explained that he'd be resigning at the end of June because he'd decided that pathology was not for him. He also expressed his concerns about the religious bias he'd encountered. The two of them had a good heart-to-heart talk, and Corey felt relieved.

When I saw him the next week, Corey was jubilant. He explained that his fears of contamination had vanished and that he'd gotten caught up on all his autopsies. In fact, he said he could do autopsies faster than any other resident in the program. He was excited about his new career plans and felt ready to terminate therapy.

I love the Hidden Emotion Technique, not only because it's a powerful treatment tool, but also because it makes anxiety understandable, so it no longer seems strange, weird, or mysterious. Anxiety doesn't strike out of the blue, without rhyme or reason. Instead, it evolves in a human context. The real fear underneath most anxiety is the fear of your true emotions and feelings. When you use this technique successfully, you'll not only overcome your anxiety, but you'll gain a much deeper appreciation of who you are and what it means to be a human being.

PART V

Selecting the Techniques That Will Work for You

Chapter 22

The Recovery Circle

Failing as Fast as You Can

So far you've learned about many kinds of Cognitive Techniques, Exposure Techniques, and the Hidden Emotion Technique. These techniques can help you put the lie to the negative thoughts that trigger anxiety and depression. Look at the complete list of all of these tools, "40 Ways to Defeat Your Fears," on page 334. It should be reassuring to see that you have so much firepower available, but at the same time, it may feel overwhelming or confusing. How can you figure out which technique is going to work for you?

The answer to this question is not necessarily straightforward. You might think that some techniques will work for chronic worrying and that other techniques will work for feelings of inferiority, phobias, shyness, panic attacks, or obsessive-compulsive disorder. While there's some truth to this idea, it's not quite that simple. The technique that works is almost always unexpected.

For example, in Chapter 11, you saw how a woman named June overcame fifty-three years of panic attacks and agoraphobia when we used the Experimental Technique. When she discovered that she couldn't make herself go crazy, no matter how hard she tried, her feelings of panic finally disappeared. Prior to that, I'd tried more than ten techniques that hadn't been effective.

If I'd known that the Experimental Technique was going to work so well

40 Ways to Defeat Your Fears

Cognitive Model	Motivational Techniques
Uncovering Techniques 1. Downward Arrow Technique 2. What-If Technique	20. Cost-Benefit Analysis (CBA) 21. Paradoxical CBA 22. Devil's Advocate
Compassion-Based Technique 3. Double-Standard Technique	**Anti-Procrastination Techniques** 23. Pleasure-Predicting Sheet
Truth-Based Techniques 4. Examine the Evidence 5. Experimental Technique 6. Survey Technique 7. Reattribution	24. Little Steps for Big Feats 25. Anti-Procrastination Sheet 26. Problem-Solution List
	Exposure Model
Semantic Techniques 8. Semantic Method 9. Let's Define Terms 10. Be Specific	**Classical Exposure** 27. Gradual Exposure 28. Flooding 29. Response Prevention 30. Distraction
Logic-Based Techniques 11. Thinking in Shades of Gray 12. Process versus Outcome	**Cognitive Exposure** 31. Cognitive Flooding 32. Image Substitution 33. Memory Rescripting
Quantitative Techniques 13. Self-Monitoring 14. Worry Breaks	34. Feared Fantasy
Humor-Based Techniques 15. Shame-Attacking Exercises[a] 16. Paradoxical Magnification 17. Humorous Imaging	**Interpersonal Exposure** 35. Smile and Hello Practice 36. Flirting Training 37. Rejection Practice 38. Self-Disclosure 39. David Letterman Technique
Role-Playing Technique[b] 18. Externalization of Voices	**Hidden Emotion Model**
Spiritual Technique 19. Acceptance Paradox	40. Hidden Emotion Technique

[a] This technique could also be classified as an Interpersonal Exposure Technique.
[b] Other techniques that work well in role-playing include the Double-Standard Technique, the Acceptance Paradox, Devil's Advocate, the Feared Fantasy, Flirting Training, and the David Letterman Technique.

for June, I would have tried it first. But it's very difficult to make those kinds of predictions because two people with the same kind of anxiety often respond to completely different techniques. In this chapter, I'm going to show you how to select the techniques that will work for you. Always start by filling out a Daily Mood Log. Do you remember what the five steps are? See if you can list them here before you look at the answers.

Step 1. _____

Step 2. _____

Step 3. _____

Step 4. _____

Step 5. _____

Answer

These are the five steps:

Step 1. Describe the upsetting event. This can be any moment when you were feeling upset.

Step 2. Circle your negative feelings and rate them on a scale from 0% (not at all) to 100% (the worst).

Step 3. Record your negative thoughts, and indicate how strongly you believe each one, from 0% to 100%.

Step 4. Identify the distortions in each negative thought.

Step 5. Substitute thoughts that are more positive and realistic. Indicate how strongly you believe them, from 0% to 100%. Now rerate your belief in each negative thought again.

The fifth step is the most important one, because that's where you defeat your fears. However, it's also the most difficult step, because you'll usually be convinced that your negative thoughts are absolutely valid. It's easy to put the lie to someone else's negative thoughts but much harder to see how you're fooling yourself.

After you've completed the first four steps, choose one negative thought that you'd like to work on first, and put it in the middle of a Recovery Circle, like the one on page 340. The circle is like a trap you're in. As long as you believe the thought in the center, you'll feel anxious and depressed. You'll see that there are sixteen arrows with boxes at the ends. Each arrow represents a different way to escape from the trap and put the lie to the thought that's upsetting you.

Select a variety of techniques from the list of 40 Ways to Defeat Your Fears and put the name of one technique in each box around the Recovery Circle. It's best to list at least fifteen techniques because we don't know which one is going to work for you. The more techniques you list, the more firepower you'll have available to help you put the lie to the negative thought in the middle of the circle.

How will you know which techniques to put in the boxes? That's easy. Just go through the detailed list of 40 Ways to Defeat Your Fears starting on page 356. This list includes brief explanations of how each technique works and will make your job much easier. If a technique looks promising, write the name of that technique in a box. We'll talk more about this topic later on in this chapter.

Right now, you don't have to worry too much about which techniques you select or how each technique is going to work. Just make sure that you select a lot of techniques. If the negative thought in your Recovery Circle makes you feel anxious, make sure that you include techniques from all three categories: Cognitive Techniques, Exposure Techniques, and the Hidden Emotion Technique. Here's a good mix: include at least twelve to fifteen Cognitive Techniques, two or three Exposure Techniques, and the Hidden Emotion Technique.

When you've listed at least fifteen techniques on your Recovery Circle, you can try them out, one at a time, until you find the one that works for you. If a technique doesn't help, move on to the next one on your Recovery Circle. Your goal should be to fail as fast as you can so you can get to the technique that does work for you as quickly as possible.

Why is it necessary to try so many techniques? It's because most of the techniques you try won't be effective, but that isn't a problem because so many others are available. If you understand this before you start working on the negative thought, you won't have to feel frustrated or upset when a technique doesn't work. On average, you'll have to try at least ten to fifteen techniques before you find the one that puts the lie to your negative thought. That's why the Recovery Circle is so important. You'll have all the tools you need to overcome practically any kind of negative feeling, including depression, anxiety, and anger.

I wish I could tell you that there is one incredible technique that works for everybody, and for every kind of negative emotion. That would make life simple. Promoters are always trying to sell us on the idea that one simple technique will cure whatever ails us. One year we're told that aerobic exercise, like jogging, is the answer. The next year we hear that mindfulness meditation is the ultimate antidote to stress. For decades it was psychoanalysis. Then it was St. John's wort. But there is no cure-all, and there never will be. The Recovery Circle represents a radically different approach. You create a powerful treatment program that's individualized to your specific problems.

Let's see how it works. You probably remember Jason, the young man who was feeling shy when he was standing in line at the supermarket, thinking about the attractive young woman who was checking groceries. Even though she seemed to be smiling at him, he was too anxious to smile back or even look at her. One of his negative thoughts was "I have no personality."

This thought will make Jason feel so anxious and insecure that he'll probably lose the race before he ever gets out of the starting gate. If he really believes that he has "no personality," he'll feel awkward, needy, and insecure if he does try to talk to her. This will turn her off, and then he'll conclude that he really doesn't have any personality.

Jason's negative thought isn't terribly realistic, either. In fact, he was charming, bright, energetic, and creative. He also had a great sense of humor. What are the distortions in his thought "I have no personality"? Check off all the distortions you can find in the following table. The definitions of the distortions appear on page 428, in case you'd like to review them.

Distortion	(✓)	Distortion	(✓)
1. All-or-Nothing Thinking		6. Magnification or Minimization	
2. Overgeneralization		7. Emotional Reasoning	
3. Mental Filter		8. Should Statements	
4. Discounting the Positive		9. Labeling	
5. Jumping to Conclusions • Mind-Reading • Fortune-Telling		10. Blame • Self-Blame • Other-Blame	

Answer

Jason and I found all ten distortions in his thought "I have no personality."

Distortion	(✓)	Explanation
1. All-or-Nothing Thinking	✓	Jason thinks that he either has a terrific personality or no personality at all. This isn't very realistic because no one is all one way or the other. Sometimes we're relaxed and personable. Other times we feel tense and awkward. Most of the time we're somewhere in between.
2. Overgeneralization	✓	Jason is generalizing from one situation to his entire self. So if he feels awkward and self-conscious when he's standing in line at the supermarket, he concludes that he must have no personality at all.
3. Mental Filter	✓	Jason is focusing on all the times when he's felt anxious and self-conscious in social situations and filtering out all the times he's felt relaxed and personable.
4. Discounting the Positive	✓	Jason discounts all his good qualities. In fact, he's reasonably attractive and intelligent and has no reason to think he'll look foolish or get shot down if he flirts with someone he's attracted to. He also discounts the fact that the cashier seemed to be smiling at him.
5. Jumping to Conclusions • Mind-Reading • Fortune-Telling	✓	Jason is assuming that the cashier will think he has no personality, but he has no evidence for this (Mind-Reading and Fortune-Telling).
6. Magnification or Minimization	✓	Jason minimizes the fact that he can be quite charming and appealing when he feels relaxed.
7. Emotional Reasoning	✓	He *feels* like he has no personality, so he concludes that he *really is* boring and inept.
8. Should Statements	✓	Jason thinks that he should have a bubbly, outgoing personality. He constantly compares himself with his ideal self and with other people, and thinks he *should* be like that.
9. Labeling	✓	Instead of telling himself that he feels shy and awkward, which is perfectly normal, Jason is telling himself that he has no personality. He's labeling himself in a destructive way.
10. Blame • Self-Blame • Other-Blame	✓	Jason is putting himself down because he feels shy and anxious.

I asked Jason if there was another message he could give himself that would be more positive and more realistic. He said he could tell himself, "I have a great personality." I told him to write this down in the Positive Thoughts column of his Daily Mood Log and indicate how much he believed it. As you can see in his "% Belief" column, he believed it only 20%, because he knew that he felt uncomfortable around girls and didn't have much experience talking to them. His positive thought failed to fulfill the necessary condition for emotional change because it wasn't 100% true. As you can see in the "% After" column, he still believed the negative thought 100%.

Negative Thoughts	% Before	% After	Distortions	Positive Thoughts	% Belief
7. I have no personality.	100%	100%	AON, OG, MF, DP, MR, FT, MIN, ER, SH, LAB, SB	7. I have a great personality.	20%

This is where the Recovery Circle comes in. Jason wasn't able to put the lie to his negative thought on his own, so we'll need to use some of our techniques. Write his negative thought in the middle of the Recovery Circle on page 340. See if you can list at least fifteen techniques that might help him put the lie to this thought. You can refer to the summary of 40 Ways to Defeat Your Fears on page 334 or the list with brief descriptions of each technique, on pages 356 to 363. Put the name of one technique in each box around the circle. When you're done, turn to pages 342 to 345 and I'll tell you about the techniques that Jason and I selected.

Answer

You can see the Recovery Circle that Jason and I completed on page 342. Don't worry if your own list of techniques is different. As long as you selected at least fifteen techniques, you'll be in good shape.

Examine the Evidence was the first technique we tried. I asked Jason if there was any evidence that he *did* have a good personality. He said, "I can be very funny and relaxed when I'm at home, hanging out with my family." I asked

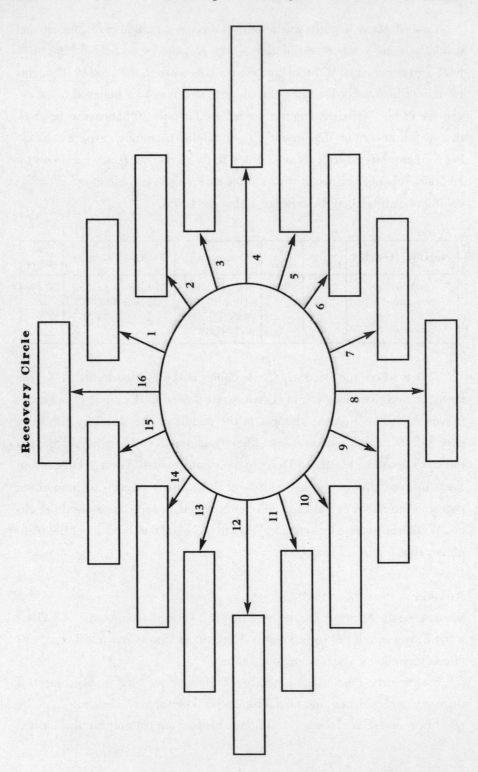

Recovery Circle

him to write this down in the Positive Thoughts column of his Daily Mood Log.
As you can see in the "% Belief" column, he believed this thought 100%.

Negative Thoughts	% Before	% After	Distortions	Positive Thoughts	% Belief
7. I have no personality.	100%	100%	AON, OG, MF, DP, MR, FT, MIN, ER, SH, LAB, SB	7. I have a great personality.	20%
		95%		I can be very funny and relaxed when I'm at home, hanging out with my family.	100%

This positive thought didn't fulfill the
necessary condition for change
because Jason only believed it 20%.

This positive thought didn't fulfill the
sufficient condition for change.
Although it was 100% true, it didn't
put the lie to the negative thought.

However, if you look in the "% After" column, you'll see that Jason's belief
in the negative thought only went down to 95%. This minimal reduction tells
us that he still believes the negative thought. That's because the positive
thought is really a form of condemnation through faint praise. Jason explained
that his experiences with his mother and brother didn't count because he felt
awkward and tense whenever he was around girls his own age. In this case, the
positive thought fulfilled the necessary condition for emotional change, because it was 100% true, but it didn't fulfill the sufficient condition, since it
barely reduced Jason's belief in the negative thought.

Now we've got a problem. When I asked Jason if he could challenge the
negative thought, he came up with a positive thought that wasn't effective.
Then we tried Examine the Evidence, but he still couldn't put the lie to the
negative thought. He was still convinced that he had no personality. What
should we do next? Put your ideas here before you continue reading.

_____

_____

_____

_____

_____

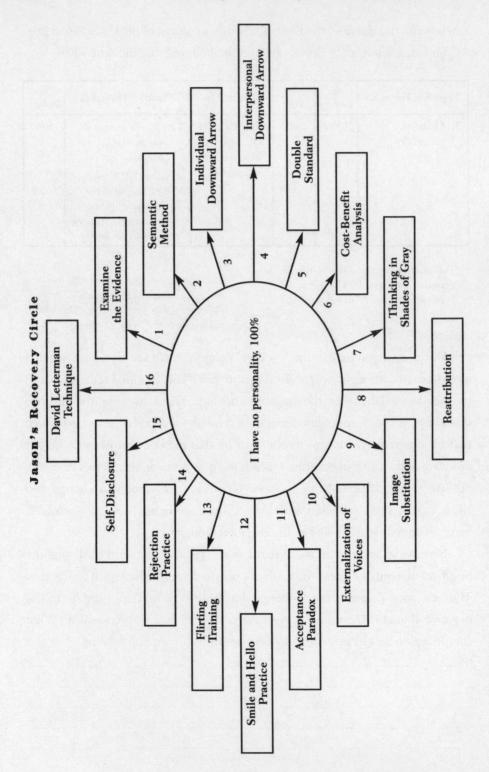

Jason's Recovery Circle

David Letterman Technique

Examine the Evidence

Semantic Method

Individual Downward Arrow

Interpersonal Downward Arrow

Double Standard

Cost-Benefit Analysis

Thinking in Shades of Gray

Reattribution

Image Substitution

Externalization of Voices

Acceptance Paradox

Smile and Hello Practice

Flirting Training

Rejection Practice

Self-Disclosure

I have no personality. 100%

Answer

When a technique doesn't work, just move on to the next technique on your Recovery Circle. If it were easy to put the lie to negative thoughts, people would never have to struggle with depression or anxiety in the first place. Fortunately, we have plenty of other techniques to try.

The distortions in your negative thought often will provide you with some ideas about which techniques to try, because certain techniques can be especially effective for certain kinds of distortions. Jason's thought "I have no personality" is a hidden Should Statement because he's telling himself that he *should* have a bubbly, outgoing personality and say something terribly clever to the cashier. This puts him under tremendous pressure. It's also unrealistic, because most of us feel somewhat nervous and awkward when we're just starting to date. I certainly did! You're not going to feel terribly funny or spontaneous at first, because you're not sure what to expect. This doesn't mean that you're defective or that you have no personality; it just means you're inexperienced.

The Semantic Method is the next technique on our Recovery Circle. Often it's helpful for Should Statements. I asked Jason if he could give himself a less insulting message when he was feeling nervous. Could he think about his awkward feelings in a kinder, gentler way? Jason came up with this positive thought: "I have a pretty good personality when I'm feeling relaxed. My real problem is shyness and not a lack of personality."

I asked Jason to put this thought in the Positive Thoughts column of his Daily Mood Log and indicate how strongly he believed it. As you can see in the "% Belief" column, he believed it 100%. In addition, it reduced his belief in the negative thought to 25%, as you can see in the "% After" column. This meant that the positive thought fulfilled the necessary and sufficient conditions for emotional change.

How far should you try to reduce your belief in a negative thought? This will depend on the type of negative thought you're working on. Sometimes you can reduce your belief in a negative thought all the way to 0%. In Jason's case, I thought the reduction to 25% was sufficient. That's because he does feel awkward in social situations, so the negative thought contains some truth. In

Jason's first attempt at a positive thought wasn't effective because he didn't really believe it.

Negative Thoughts	% Before	% After	Distortions	Positive Thoughts	% Belief
7. I have no personality.	100%	100%	AON, OG, MF, DP, MR, FT, MIN, ER, SH, LAB, SB	7. I have a great personality.	20%
		95%		I can be very funny and relaxed when I'm at home, hanging out with my family.	100%
		25%		I have a pretty good personality when I'm feeling relaxed. My real problem is shyness and not a lack of personality.	

Jason came up with this positive thought when we used Examine the Evidence. Although he believed it, it wasn't effective because it didn't reduce his belief in the negative thought.

Jason came up with this positive thought when we used the Semantic Method. It was effective because he believed it 100%, and it reduced his belief in the negative thought to 25%.

the future, that will probably change, but for now, he's taken a huge step forward.

Once Jason put the lie to this negative thought, his mood began to lift, and he was soon able to put the lie to all of his negative thoughts. Look at his completed Daily Mood Log on pages 346 to 347. As you can see, the intensity of all his negative feelings fell to 20% or less, with the single exception of his anxiety, which only went down to 50%.

Why did Jason's anxiety only go down to 50%? Although a 50% reduction in anxiety is actually fairly good, we're looking for much more than that. We want Jason's feelings of shyness and anxiety to go all the way down to 0%. This won't happen until he does something else. What will the next step be? Put your ideas here before you continue reading.

_____

_____

_____

_____

_____

Answer

Armchair exercises will get you only so far when you're trying to overcome anxiety. To get to the next level, Jason will need to use the Interpersonal Exposure Techniques that we listed on his Recovery Circle, such as Smile and Hello Practice, Flirting Training, Rejection Practice, Self-Disclosure, and the David Letterman Technique. He'll definitely have his share of rejections and successes along the way, just like anyone else, but once he faces his fears, soon his painful shyness will be just a memory.

Now it's time for you to give it a try. Start with the blank Daily Mood Log on pages 348 and 349. At the top, write a brief description of *one* moment when you were feeling upset. Circle all the emotion words that reflect your feelings and indicate how strong each feeling is on a scale from 0% (not at all) to 100% (extreme). Now list your negative thoughts and indicate how strongly you believe each one on a scale from 0% (not at all) to 100% (completely). After you've identified the distortions in your negative thoughts, using the list at the bottom of the Daily Mood Log, you'll be ready for the Recovery Circle.

Select one thought you want to work on first, and put it in the middle of the blank Recovery Circle on page 351. List at least fifteen techniques you could use to put the lie to this thought. When you're selecting techniques, you can use the one-page list of 40 Ways to Defeat Your Fears on page 334 or the longer list beginning on page 356. Put the name of one technique in each box around the circle. If you come up with more than sixteen techniques, use the second Recovery Circle on page 352.

Are there any guidelines you can follow when you're selecting techniques? I've tried to steer you away from this idea as much as possible. Formulas can

Jason's Daily Mood Log

Upsetting Event: Standing in line at the supermarket.

Emotions	% Before	% After	Emotions	% Before	% After
Sad, blue, depressed, down, unhappy	80%	0%	Embarrassed, foolish, humiliated, self-conscious	100%	20%
Anxious, worried, panicky, nervous, frightened	100%	50%	Hopeless, discouraged, pessimistic, despairing	90%	10%
Guilty, remorseful, bad, ashamed	95%	0%	Frustrated, stuck, thwarted, defeated	90%	15%
Inferior, worthless, inadequate, defective, incompetent	95%	15%	Angry, mad, resentful, annoyed, irritated, upset, furious	90%	15%
Lonely, unloved, unwanted, rejected, alone, abandoned	75%	20%	Other (describe)		

Negative Thoughts	% Before	% After	Distortions	Positive Thoughts	% Belief
1. I don't have anything interesting to say.	100%	25%	AON, OG, MF, DP, MR, MIN, ER, SH, SB	1. I probably don't need to say anything terribly clever or interesting. I could just start by smiling and saying hello, and that would be a great first step.	100%
2. I *never* succeed with the really good-looking girls.	100%	35%	AON, OG, ER, SH	2. That's because I never give myself the chance!	100%
3. I don't have time to deal with a relationship right now, even if I do end up having a good conversation with her.	100%	0%	DP, SH	3. This is ridiculous. I'd love to have a relationship with a girl I really liked!	100%
4. I better just keep my mouth shut, since I might say something stupid and upset her.	100%	20%	MR, ER, SH	4. There's no evidence for this. But I'll probably say stupid things lots of times in my life, and it won't be the end of the world.	100%

Jason's Daily Mood Log (continued)

Negative Thoughts	% Before	% After	Distortions	Positive Thoughts	% Belief
5. People will think I'm a self-centered jerk if I try to flirt with her.	100%	25%	AON, MR, FT, MAG, ER, SH, LAB, SB	**5.** That's not very likely. Most people in the store won't be all that interested in what I do. And even if they did disapprove of my flirting, what are they going to do to me? Throw stones? Scorn me? Have me arrested?	100%
6. I *shouldn't* be so loud and obnoxious. If I'm humble and quiet, people will like me more.	100%	10%	MR, FT, ER, SH, LAB, SB	**6.** You can flirt without being loud and obnoxious. But would it be the end of the world if I got shot down or made a fool of myself?	100%
7. I have no personality.	100%	25%	AON, OG, MF, DP, MR, FT, MIN, ER, SH, LAB, SB	**7.** I have a pretty good personality when I'm feeling relaxed. My real problem is shyness and not a lack of personality.	100%
8. I must be a terrible person because I'm so concerned with superficial things like success and looks.	100%	10%	AON, OG, SH, LAB, SB	**8.** Most young men are attracted to sexy, good-looking women. After all, I'm not training to be a Buddhist monk!	100%
9. If I tried to flirt with her, I'd probably get shot down.	100%	25%	DP, MR, FT, ER, SH, SB	**9.** I probably won't get shot down if I smile and say hello in a friendly, low-key way. But if I did get shot down, I'd survive. In fact, if I got shot down a few times, it would be a good thing, because it would mean I was confronting my fears. I won't get shot down forever, and sooner or later, I'll get a date.	100%
10. That would show what a loser I am.	100%	0%	AON, OG, MF, DP, MAG, ER, SH, LAB, SB	**10.** There are lots of reasons why a girl might shoot me down if I tried to flirt with her. It could be because I'm inexperienced, because she already has a boyfriend, or because I'm not her cup of tea. None of these things would make me "a loser."	100%

Daily Mood Log

Upsetting Event: _____

Emotions	% Before	% After	Emotions	% Before	% After
Sad, blue, depressed, down, unhappy			Embarrassed, foolish, humiliated, self-conscious		
Anxious, worried, panicky, nervous, frightened			Hopeless, discouraged, pessimistic, despairing		
Guilty, remorseful, bad, ashamed			Frustrated, stuck, thwarted, defeated		
Inferior, worthless, inadequate, defective, incompetent			Angry, mad, resentful, annoyed, irritated, upset, furious		
Lonely, unloved, unwanted, rejected, alone, abandoned			Other (describe)		

Negative Thoughts	% Before	% After	Distortions	Positive Thoughts	% Belief
1.				1.	
2.				2.	
3.				3.	
4.				4.	
5.				5.	

Negative Thoughts	% Before	% After	Distortions	Positive Thoughts	% Belief
6.				6.	
7.				7.	
8.				8.	

Checklist of Cognitive Distortions

1. **All-or-Nothing Thinking.** You view things in absolute, black-and-white categories.

2. **Overgeneralization.** You view a negative event as a never-ending pattern of defeat: "This *always* happens!"

3. **Mental Filter.** You dwell on the negatives and ignore the positives.

4. **Discounting the Positive.** You insist that your positive qualities don't count.

5. **Jumping to Conclusions.** You jump to conclusions not warranted by the facts.
   - **Mind-Reading.** You assume that people are reacting negatively to you.
   - **Fortune-Telling.** You predict that things will turn out badly.

6. **Magnification and Minimization.** You blow things out of proportion or shrink them.

7. **Emotional Reasoning.** You reason from your feelings: "I *feel* like an idiot, so I must really *be* one."

8. **Should Statements.** You use shoulds, shouldn'ts, musts, oughts, and have tos.

9. **Labeling.** Instead of saying "I made a mistake," you say, "I'm a jerk," or "I'm a loser."

10. **Blame.** You find fault instead of solving the problem.
    - **Self-Blame.** You blame yourself for something you weren't entirely responsible for.
    - **Other-Blame.** You blame others and overlook ways you contributed to the problem.

be very misleading, and it's always hard to predict which techniques will work the best for any person or problem. However, the tables on pages 353 and 354 will give you something to hang your hat on. They provide hints about how to select the most effective techniques based on:

- **The distortions in your negative thought (page 353).** Different distortions respond to different kinds of techniques. For example, some techniques work well for thoughts that involve All-or-Nothing Thinking, whereas other techniques are more geared toward thoughts that involve Fortune-Telling, Mind-Reading, Should Statements, or Self-Blame.
- **The type of problem you're working on (page 354).** Different types of anxiety, such as shyness, panic attacks, post-traumatic stress disorder, or obsessive-compulsive disorder, also respond to different types of techniques. In addition, the techniques that are helpful for anxiety will be different from the techniques that are helpful for depression, a relationship problem, or an addiction.

Check marks on the tables indicate that the category listed at the top of the column might be worth a try. A box that is grayed out indicates that this category would be an especially good choice. For example, the table on page 353 indicates that the Semantic Method usually works extremely well for Should Statements. The table on page 354 indicates that if you're suffering from shyness, the Interpersonal Exposure Techniques will be important. You could also try an Uncovering Technique like the What-If Technique or the Interpersonal Downward Arrow, a Motivational Technique like the Cost-Benefit Analysis, a Spiritual Technique like the Acceptance Paradox, or a Cognitive Exposure Technique like the Feared Fantasy.

However, don't be too literal about following these guidelines when you select techniques, because we can't predict what will work for you. That's what makes this approach so fascinating, flexible, and powerful.

One disclaimer is necessary. Just writing the description of a feeling in the middle of a Recovery Circle, such as "shy" or "depressed," won't do you any good at all. There are no techniques you can use to attack feelings like shyness, panic, and depression. Instead, focus on one specific moment when you were

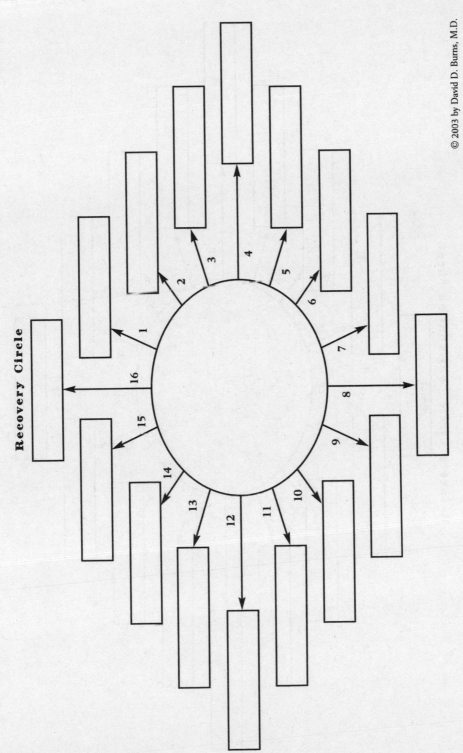

Recovery Circle

Recovery Circle Continuation Sheet

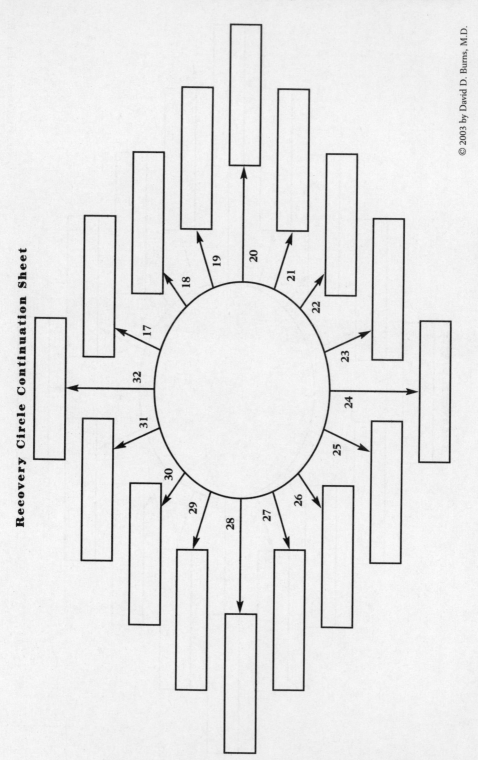

Selecting Techniques Based on the Distortions in Your Negative Thought

Distortions	Uncovering	Compassion-Based	Truth-Based	Semantic	Logic-Based	Quantitative	Humor-Based	Role-Playing	Spiritual	Motivational	Anti-Procrastination	Classical Exposure	Cognitive Exposure	Interpersonal Exposure	Hidden Emotion
	Cognitive Techniques											**Exposure Techniques**			**Hidden Emotion**
1. All-or-Nothing Thinking	✓	✓	✓	✓	✓			✓	✓	✓					
2. Overgeneralization	✓	✓	✓	✓				✓	✓	✓					
3. Mental Filter	✓	✓	✓	✓	✓	✓		✓	✓	✓					
4. Discounting the Positive	✓	✓	✓	✓		✓		✓	✓	✓					
5. Jumping to Conclusions															
• Mind-Reading	✓	✓	✓	✓		✓	✓	✓	✓	✓	✓	✓	✓	✓	✓
• Fortune-Telling	✓	✓	✓				✓	✓	✓	✓	✓	✓	✓	✓	✓
6. Magnification and Minimization	✓		✓	✓	✓	✓	✓	✓	✓	✓	✓	✓	✓		
7. Emotional Reasoning	✓	✓	✓	✓		✓	✓	✓	✓	✓	✓	✓			
8. Should Statements	✓	✓	✓	✓	✓		✓	✓	✓	✓	✓				
9. Labeling	✓	✓	✓	✓		✓	✓	✓	✓	✓	✓				
10. Blame															
• Self-Blame	✓	✓	✓	✓			✓	✓	✓	✓					
• Other-Blame	✓	✓	✓				✓	✓	✓	✓					

Selecting Techniques Based on the Problem You're Working On

Your Problem	Uncovering	Compassion-Based	Truth-Based	Semantic	Logic-Based	Quantitative	Humor-Based	Role-Playing	Spiritual	Motivational	Anti-Procrastination	Classical Exposure	Cognitive Exposure	Interpersonal Exposure	Hidden Emotion
	Cognitive Techniques											Exposure Techniques			Hidden Emotion
Chronic Worrying	✓	✓	✓			✓		✓		✓		✓	✓		✓
Panic Attacks	✓	✓	✓					✓	✓	✓		✓	✓		✓
Agoraphobia	✓	✓	✓					✓		✓		✓	✓		✓
Fears and Phobias	✓	✓	✓					✓	✓	✓		✓	✓		✓
Shyness	✓	✓	✓	✓	✓		✓	✓	✓	✓		✓	✓	✓	✓
Performance Anxiety and Public Speaking Anxiety	✓	✓	✓	✓	✓		✓	✓	✓	✓		✓	✓		✓
Obsessions and Compulsions (OCD)	✓	✓	✓			✓		✓		✓		✓	✓		✓
Post-Traumatic Stress Disorder (PTSD)	✓	✓						✓	✓	✓			✓		✓
Hypochondriasis	✓	✓	✓					✓		✓			✓		✓
Body Dysmorphic Disorder (BDD)	✓	✓	✓		✓	✓	✓	✓	✓	✓		✓	✓		✓
Depression and Feelings of Shame	✓	✓	✓			✓	✓	✓	✓	✓	✓		✓		✓
Habits and Addictions	✓			✓				✓		✓	✓				

upset and record your feelings in the emotions table of the Daily Mood Log. After you've recorded your negative thoughts, put one of them in the middle of a Recovery Circle.

Many people don't understand how the Recovery Circle relates to the Daily Mood Log. In fact, the Recovery Circle is the engine that powers the Daily Mood Log. The techniques you list on the Recovery Circle will help you generate positive thoughts. Remember that you won't feel better until you come up with a positive thought that fulfills the necessary and sufficient conditions for emotional change:

- **The Necessary Condition.** The positive thought must be 100% true.
- **The Sufficient Condition.** The positive thought must put the lie to the negative thought.

Change generally occurs in one of two basic patterns. In the first pattern, you try a variety of techniques that are all somewhat helpful, but no single technique causes a huge change in your negative thoughts and feelings. Instead, you steadily chip away using a variety of techniques, and each one reduces your belief in the negative thought a little bit more.

In the second recovery pattern, you try technique after technique, but none of them works at all. You still believe the negative thought and you feel just as anxious, worried, panicky, or depressed as ever. Suddenly you try a technique that has such a powerful effect that your belief in the negative thought drops all the way to 0%, and you recover almost immediately. I see this pattern with many of the patients I work with. That's what happened to June when she used the Experimental Technique to test her belief that she was on the verge of going nuts. When she discovered that she couldn't go crazy, no matter how hard she tried, she experienced a sudden and almost magical transformation that ended years of suffering.

What should you do if you've tried all of the techniques on your Recovery Circle, but you're still feeling stuck? This isn't unusual, and it definitely doesn't mean you're a hopeless case! Just grab another Recovery Circle and select some more techniques. Then try them out, one at a time, until you find the method that works for you. Patience and persistence will be key, because we all follow different paths to enlightenment.

40 Ways to Defeat Your Fears

COGNITIVE TECHNIQUES

Uncovering Techniques	
1. **Downward Arrow Technique (page 101)**	The Downward Arrow Technique will help you identify the Self-Defeating Beliefs that make you vulnerable to depression and anxiety. Draw a downward arrow under a negative thought and ask yourself, "If this thought was true, why would it be upsetting to me? What would it mean to me?" A new negative thought will come to mind. Write it down underneath the arrow and draw another arrow under it. Repeat this process several times. Now look at the negative thoughts you generated and review the list of Self-Defeating Beliefs on page 19 so you can pinpoint the underlying beliefs at the core of your suffering.
2. **What-If Technique (page 127)**	This will help identify the fantasy at the root of your fears. Draw a downward arrow under a negative thought and ask, "What's the worst thing that could happen if that were true?" A new negative thought or fantasy will come to mind. Write it down under the arrow and repeat the process several times. Then ask yourself, "How likely is it that this would happen? And could I live with it if it did?"
Compassion-Based Technique	
3. **Double-Standard Technique (page 133)**	Instead of putting yourself down, you can talk to yourself in the same compassionate way you'd talk to a dear friend who was upset. Ask yourself, "Would I say such harsh things to a friend with a similar problem? What would I say to him or her?"
Truth-Based Techniques	
4. **Examine the Evidence (page 145)**	Instead of assuming that a negative thought is true, ask yourself, "What's the evidence for this claim?"
5. **Experimental Technique (page 146)**	Ask yourself, "How could I test this thought to find out if it's valid?" For example, if you have panic attacks because you tell yourself you're on the verge of going crazy, you could try to drive yourself crazy by screaming incoherently, rolling around on the floor, and acting insane. That way, you can find out if your concerns are realistic.
6. **Survey Technique (page 163)**	Do a survey to test your negative thought. For example, if you think that your shyness is weird or shameful, you could ask several friends if they've ever felt shy. You'll probably discover that most people feel shy at times.

40 Ways to Defeat Your Fears (continued)

Truth-Based Techniques (continued)	
7. Reattribution **(page 167)**	If you're anxious or depressed, you may beat up on yourself relentlessly and blame yourself for your shortcomings. When you use Reattribution, you think about all the factors that contributed to the problem and focus on solving it or learning from it, instead of blaming yourself and ripping yourself to shreds.
Semantic Techniques	
8. Semantic Method **(page 179)**	The Semantic Method is especially helpful for Should Statements and Labeling. You simply substitute language that's less insulting and emotionally loaded.
9. Let's Define Terms **(page 182)**	When you label yourself as "a fool" or "a neurotic," ask yourself what those labels really mean. You'll see that there's no such thing as "a fool" or "a neurotic." Foolish and neurotic behavior exists, but fools and neurotics do not.
10. Be Specific **(page 185)**	When you use Be Specific, you stick with reality and avoid global judgments about reality. Instead of thinking of yourself as "a failure," you can pinpoint your specific strengths and weaknesses.
Logic-Based Techniques	
11. Thinking in Shades of Gray **(page 171)**	Instead of thinking about your problems in black-and-white extremes, you evaluate them more realistically, in shades of gray.
12. Process versus Outcome **(page 176)**	Evaluate your performance based on the process—the effort you put in—rather than the outcome. Your preparation and hard work are always within your control, but the outcome usually isn't.
Quantitative Techniques	
13. Self-Monitoring **(page 191)**	You can keep track of your negative thoughts and fantasies by counting them on a 3×5 card or wrist-counter like the ones golfers use to keep track of their scores. At the end of the day, record the total number of thoughts on your calendar and set the counter back to zero. If you keep this up for several weeks, often the negative thoughts diminish or disappear completely.

40 Ways to Defeat Your Fears (continued)

Quantitative Techniques (continued)	
14. Worry Breaks (page 198)	This is a paradoxical technique. You schedule specific times to feel depressed, anxious, or guilty. For example, if constant worrying prevents you from studying effectively for an exam, you might want to schedule a two-minute Worry Break each hour. During each Worry Break, you can tell yourself that you're sure to flunk. Rip yourself to shreds and make yourself as anxious as possible. Don't try to fight the feelings. You can use the rest of the hour to study and prepare for the exam. If you start to get nervous, remind yourself that you can postpone your worrying until the next Worry Break.
Humor-Based Techniques	
15. Shame-Attacking Exercises (page 202)	This technique is great for people who suffer from shyness. Instead of struggling to look "normal," you intentionally do something foolish in public, like loudly announcing the time in a crowded department store or riding a bus and shouting the name of the street at each stop. You'll discover that the world doesn't come to an end, after all. Although this technique requires great courage, it can be very liberating and enlightening. Shame-Attacking Exercises are also a form of Interpersonal Exposure.
16. Paradoxical Magnification (page 205)	Instead of struggling with your negative thoughts, you exaggerate them. Paradoxically, often they'll begin to seem absurd.
17. Humorous Imaging (page 206)	When you feel consumed with anxiety or anger, it sometimes can help to visualize something humorous. A depressed woman obsessed about the fact that she'd gotten screwed in her divorce settlement. She could barely make ends meet, and became furious every time she fantasized about her ex-husband cavorting with his new trophy wife on his yacht and living in the lap of luxury. The constant feelings of anger and resentment were making her miserable. She found that picturing him at a board meeting in his underpants made her giggle. This was a useful antidote to the feelings of anger and resentment that were eating away at her.
Role-Playing Technique	
18. Externalization of Voices (page 209)	You and another person take turns playing the role of your negative thoughts and the role of your positive thoughts. The person playing the negative thoughts attacks, using the second-person "You," and the person playing the positive thoughts defends, using the first-person "I." Use role-reversals when you get stuck. Several other techniques that also work well in a role-playing format include the Double-Standard Technique, the Acceptance Paradox, the Devil's Advocate, the Feared Fantasy, Flirting Training, and the David Letterman Technique.

40 Ways to Defeat Your Fears (continued)

Spiritual Technique	
19. Acceptance Paradox (page 214)	You accept your shortcomings with tranquility and a sense of humor. The Acceptance Paradox is based on the Buddhist principle that when you defend yourself, you create a state of war. If you're defending against your own self-criticisms, you'll end up at war with yourself. In contrast, when you find the truth in a criticism, you'll take the wind out of the critic's sails. Of course, you're the critic in this case, so you end up befriending yourself. This is the most important and powerful technique of all, but it can be difficult to grasp at first. It only comes to life when you combine it with a Role-Playing Technique, such as the Externalization of Voices, or the Feared Fantasy.
Motivational Techniques	
20. Cost-Benefit Analysis (CBA) (page 221)	List all the advantages and disadvantages of a negative thought ("I'm such a loser"), Self-Defeating Belief ("I should always try to be perfect"), feeling (anger, guilt, or anxiety), or habit (drinking, using drugs, overeating, or procrastinating). You can also list the advantages and disadvantages of blaming the other person for the problems in your relationship with him or her. Ask yourself, "What are the advantages and disadvantages of this thought, belief, feeling or habit? How will it help me, and how will it hurt me?" After you list all the advantages and disadvantages you can think of, balance them against each other on a 100-point scale. Ask yourself whether the costs or the benefits seem greater, and put two numbers that add up to 100 in the two circles at the bottom of the CBA form.
21. Paradoxical Cost-Benefit Analysis (page 226)	List only the *advantages* of a negative thought or feeling. This will make you aware of the powerful forces that keep you stuck or feeling anxious. Now ask yourself, "Given all the advantages of this attitude or feeling, why would I want to change?" Once you expose all the hidden rewards, often they'll lose their power to defeat you.
22. Devil's Advocate (page 230)	List all the tempting thoughts you have just before you give in to the urge to drink, overeat, procrastinate, or date the wrong person. Give the list to a friend and ask him or her to play the role of the devil who tempts you to give in. Your friend should be as seductive as possible and say things like, "Why don't you go ahead and eat that chocolate. Mmmm, it would taste *so good!*" Your job is to talk back to the tempting thoughts and defeat the devil.

40 Ways to Defeat Your Fears (continued)

Anti-Procrastination Techniques	
23. Pleasure-Predicting Sheet (page 236)	Schedule activities with the potential for pleasure, learning, or personal growth. Predict how satisfying and rewarding each activity will be from 0% (not at all) to 100% (the most). After you complete each activity, record how satisfying it turned out to be, using the same scale. Often you'll discover that many activities are more satisfying than you predicted. You can use this technique to test certain Self-Defeating Beliefs, such as "I need love to feel happy and worthwhile. If I'm alone, I'm bound to be miserable."
24. Little Steps for Big Feats (page 238)	Instead of feeling overwhelmed by a huge task, break it down into small parts. Then you can tackle them one step at a time.
25. Anti-Procrastination Sheet (page 243)	Break a large task down into small steps and predict how difficult and how satisfying you think each step will be on a scale from 0% to 100%. After completing each step, record how difficult and satisfying it actually turned out to be, using the same scale. Often you'll discover that each step is far easier and more rewarding than you expected.
26. Problem-Solution List (page 245)	Select a specific time you're willing to get started on a task you've been putting off. Draw a line down the middle of a piece of paper, and label the two columns "Problems" and "Solutions." List all the barriers to getting started in the Problems column. Then write down how you're going to solve each problem in the Solutions column.

EXPOSURE TECHNIQUES

Classical Exposure	
27. Gradual Exposure (page 254)	When you use Gradual Exposure, you expose yourself to the thing you fear in small steps, so that it won't be so terrifying. For example, if you have an elevator phobia, you can get on an elevator, go up one floor, and get off. Once you're comfortable with that, you can ride the elevator for two floors, and gradually increase the time you spend in the elevator. You can use Gradual Exposure for any phobia, such as the fear of heights, needles, or dogs, as well as other forms of anxiety, such as shyness or obsessive-compulsive disorder.
	You can also create a Fear Hierarchy, listing the least threatening situation as 1 and the most threatening as 10. You can record the type and amount of exposure you perform each day, as well as how anxious you felt (between 0% and 100%).

40 Ways to Defeat Your Fears (continued)

Classical Exposure (continued)	
28. Flooding **(page 258)**	When you use Flooding, you expose yourself to the thing you fear all at once. For example, if you have an elevator phobia, you can force yourself to get on an elevator and ride up and down, no matter how anxious you feel, until the fear disappears. Flooding is more frightening than Gradual Exposure, but it works more rapidly. Both approaches have been used successfully in the treatment of anxiety, so you can use the approach that appeals to you.
29. Response Prevention **(page 264)**	You refuse to give in to your compulsive rituals. For example, if you have a powerful urge to check the mailbox after you drop a letter in to make sure it didn't get stuck, you could force yourself to walk away without checking it. Your anxiety will get worse temporarily, but if you refuse to give in to the urge, eventually the anxiety will disappear. This is like with-drawing cold turkey from an addiction.
30. Distraction **(page 267)**	If you feel anxious, you can distract yourself from your upsetting thoughts. For example, if you're feeling panicky during an airplane flight, you can concentrate on a cross-word puzzle or engage the passenger next to you in conversa-tion. This technique works best when paired with an Exposure Technique such as Flooding.
Cognitive Exposure	
31. Cognitive Flooding **(page 269)**	Sometimes you can't expose yourself to the thing you fear in reality. For example, if you have a fear of flying, you can't very easily crash an airplane in order to overcome your fear! However, you can confront this fear in your mind's eye using Cognitive Flooding. Visualize being in a plane crash. Make yourself as anxious as possible and try to endure the anxiety for as long as you can. *Don't fight the anxiety*. Instead, try to make it as bad as possible. Surrender to it. Eventually the anxiety will burn itself out.
32. Image Substitution **(page 272)**	Substitute a more positive or peaceful image for a frighten-ing one. If you're afraid of flying, you may visualize the plane crashing in a ball of flames. This image will create feelings of intense anxiety. Instead, you can imagine landing safely and enjoying a wonderful vacation with your family.

40 Ways to Defeat Your Fears (continued)

Cognitive Exposure (continued)	
33. Memory Rescripting (page 275)	If you've been a victim of a horrifying or traumatic event, you may be haunted by vivid flashbacks and painful memories of what happened. You can edit these images in much the same way that a movie director edits a scene in a movie. For example, if you have humiliating memories of being raped or abused, you can picture the event in your mind's eye until you feel extremely anxious. Then you can enter the scene as a powerful adult and punish the person who abused you. You may also want to talk to the child who was being abused so you can comfort him or her. Of course, in this case, your loving, adult self is really having a conversation with the child inside of you who feels hurt, betrayed, frightened, and unlovable.
34. Feared Fantasy (page 279)	You enter an Alice-in-Wonderland nightmare world where your worst fears come true. You meet an imaginary Hostile Critic who rips into you in the worst possible way, attacking all your weaknesses and flaws. You can use Self-Defense, and argue with the critic, or the Acceptance Paradox, so you can take the wind out of the critic's sails. You can also mix the Self-Defense Paradigm with the Acceptance Paradox. Although the Hostile Critic appears to be another person, he or she is really the projection of your own worst self-criticisms. You can do the Feared Fantasy as a Role-Playing Technique with the help of a therapist or friend, or you can write out a Feared Fantasy dialogue on paper.
Interpersonal Exposure (Anti-Shyness Techniques)	
35. Smile and Hello Practice (page 288)	Force yourself to smile and say hello to at least ten strangers every day. You'll usually discover that people are much friendlier than you expected.
36. Flirting Training (page 292)	You learn to flirt with people in a lighthearted, affectionate manner rather than coming across as overly serious, sincere, or heavy. This makes you seem far more playful, mysterious, and exciting.
37. Rejection Practice (page 299)	If you're afraid of rejection, you can try to accumulate as many rejections as possible so you can discover that the world doesn't come to an end. For example, instead of actually trying to get a date, you could make it your goal to get rejected ten times in one week. When I was in medical school, a friend and I went out and tried this together in Palo Alto. It was frightening at first, but turned out to be very liberating. Of course, you might end up getting a date in the process, but your goal is to collect as many rejections as possible.

40 Ways to Defeat Your Fears (continued)

Interpersonal Exposure (continued)	
38. Self-Disclosure (page 300)	Instead of shamefully hiding your feelings of shyness or nervousness, you disclose them in a relaxed, open way. The idea behind this technique is that the real problem is the shame you feel, not the shyness. Without the shame, shyness can be an asset, because it makes you appear more charming and vulnerable.
39. David Letterman Technique (page 303)	You learn to make light, casual conversation with anyone, anywhere, using the same skills that successful talk-show hosts like David Letterman and Jay Leno use. You learn to focus on the other person, using the Disarming Technique, Thought and Feeling Empathy, Inquiry, and Stroking. You put the other person in the spotlight rather than trying to impress him or her by talking about yourself. If you do this in a friendly and admiring way, the person usually will end up feeling positive about you.
Hidden Emotion Technique	
40. Hidden Emotion Technique (page 313)	This technique is based on the idea that only *nice* people develop anxiety. In fact, niceness is the *cause* of anxiety. As a result, when you feel angry or upset, you may sweep your feelings under the rug so quickly that you don't even realize what the problem is. You push the problem out of conscious awareness. Pretty soon, you're struggling with feelings of worry, anxiety, or panic, and you don't even know why.
	When you're anxious, ask yourself, "Am I focusing on my anxiety to avoid something upsetting? What's the real problem that's bothering me? Do I secretly resent my spouse, a friend, or a colleague? Am I unhappy about my job or career path? How do I really feel about what's going on in my life?" Once you bring the problem to conscious awareness, you can express your feelings or work to solve the problem that's bugging you. Often this leads to a reduction or complete elimination of the anxiety.
	The Hidden Emotion Technique can be invaluable for people struggling with hypochondriasis, chronic pain, dizziness, fatigue, or other medical complaints that seem to have no organic basis.

Chapter 23

Putting It All Together

The Woman with the Scar on Her Nose

Have you ever heard of body dysmorphic disorder (BDD)? Individuals with BDD develop the belief that something about them looks extremely ugly or grotesque. They constantly worry about their appearance and go to extreme lengths to try to correct the problem. Other people, including family and friends, usually can't see the defect and try to reassure the person that she or he looks fine. However, the person with BDD doesn't buy it, so everyone ends up feeling exasperated. This is a severe form of anxiety that's considered extremely difficult to treat.

Of course, our culture is preoccupied with beauty and physical perfection, and it's pretty tough to measure up to the impossible standards we see in *Cosmopolitan* and *GQ*. We're all aware of flaws in the way we look, but most of us accept our imperfections and carry on with our lives. But people suffering from body dysmorphic disorder take their concerns about their appearance to the extreme.

In this chapter, you're going to meet a woman named Helen who was suddenly afflicted with BDD. This was surprising because she seemed to have everything in the world going for her, and most of us might think of her as one of the "beautiful people." She was attractive and personable, had a loving husband, and was the proud mother of two wonderful little boys. She had a high-powered career and lived in a gorgeous home in Beverly Hills.

Helen had received her Ph.D. in electrical engineering at MIT. Soon after graduating, she landed a job designing computer chips for a well-known electronics company. She played a key role in the development of a popular computer chip and was handsomely rewarded for her efforts. About this time, Helen met a man named Don who taught biology at the local community college. They fell in love and soon got married. Several months later, Helen became pregnant. Just before the baby was born, she took an extended leave of absence from her work so she could raise her family.

Six years later, Helen and Don had two cute little boys, aged three and six. One evening after dinner, Don asked Helen if she had any thoughts about resuming her career. They were thinking about an addition to their home, but there was no way they could swing it on Don's salary. Helen seemed excited about the idea of going back to work.

Later that evening, while Helen was washing dishes in the kitchen, there was a small earthquake, and a piece of plaster from the kitchen ceiling fell and cut her nose. The cut bled a lot, so Don rushed Helen to the emergency room. Fortunately, the wound was superficial, and within a few weeks, it healed cleanly without a trace. However, Helen became obsessed with the idea that there was an ugly scar on her nose. When she asked Don about it, he said he couldn't see any mark on her nose at all. She didn't believe him, so she asked her parents. They said the same thing.

In spite of their reassurances, Helen became increasingly preoccupied with her nose. She couldn't let go of the idea that it looked repulsive and felt intensely anxious about it. She started spending large amounts of time every day staring into mirrors and applying makeup to cover up the imaginary scar on her nose. She was afraid to leave the house during daylight hours for fear that people would stare at her nose in disgust. She didn't even dare to go to the grocery store. Don realized that something was terribly wrong and brought Helen to the Stanford psychiatric clinic, where the psychiatric resident made the diagnosis of BDD.

Let's see if we can help Helen, using some of the tools you've learned about. Look at Helen's Daily Mood Log. The upsetting event was simply her staring into the mirror that morning, trying to cover the scar with makeup.

Helen's Daily Mood Log

Upsetting Event: Staring into the mirror this morning.

Emotions	% Before	% After	Emotions	% Before	% After
Sad, blue, (depressed), down, unhappy	75%		Embarrassed, foolish, humiliated, self-conscious	100%	
Anxious, worried, panicky, nervous, frightened	100%		Hopeless, discouraged, pessimistic, despairing	100%	
Guilty, remorseful, bad, ashamed	100%		Frustrated, stuck, thwarted, defeated	85%	
Inferior, worthless, inadequate, defective, incompetent	100%		Angry, mad, resentful, annoyed, irritated, upset, furious	60%	
Lonely, unloved, unwanted, rejected, alone, abandoned	80%		Other (describe)		

Negative Thoughts	% Before	% After	Positive Thoughts	% Belief
1. This scar spoils my face.	100%			
2. I'll never get a job.	100%			
3. People will stare at me.	100%			

Distortions

Helen felt sad, anxious, ashamed, defective, lonely, humiliated, hopeless, frustrated, and angry. The high numbers in the "% Before" column indicate that these feelings were overwhelming.

You can see that Helen recorded three negative thoughts and believed them 100%. On the next table, use checks to identify the distortions in Helen's first negative thought "This scar spoils my face." Review the definitions of the distortions on page 428 if you like. Please don't continue reading until you're done.

Distortion	(✓)	Distortion	(✓)
1. All-or-Nothing Thinking		6. Magnification or Minimization	
2. Overgeneralization		7. Emotional Reasoning	
3. Mental Filter		8. Should Statements	
4. Discounting the Positive		9. Labeling	
5. Jumping to Conclusions • Mind-Reading • Fortune-Telling		10. Blame • Self-Blame • Other-Blame	

Answer

Helen and I found ten distortions in her thought "This scar spoils my face."

I've put Helen's first negative thought in the middle of the Recovery Circle on page 369. You can think of this thought as a trap she's in. As long as she believes that there's an ugly scar on her nose, she'll feel intense anxiety. The moment she stops believing this thought, she'll feel relief.

But Helen is an intelligent woman, and lots of people have already tried to persuade her that there isn't any scar on her nose. Their efforts were completely unsuccessful. We'll need some powerful, innovative techniques to help her.

Select at least fifteen techniques that might help Helen put the lie to the negative thought, and put the name of one technique in each box on Helen's Recovery Circle. Consult the one-page list of 40 Ways to Defeat Your Fears on page 334 or the longer list with definitions that starts on page 356. Be sure to include twelve to fifteen Cognitive Techniques, two or three Exposure Techniques, and the Hidden Emotion Technique, because all three categories may contribute to Helen's recovery. The same will be true for you when you use the Recovery Circle to defeat a thought that makes you anxious.

Distortion	(✓)	Explanation
1. All-or-Nothing Thinking	✓	Helen thinks about her appearance in black-and-white extremes. Even if she had a scar on her nose, would it ruin her appearance?
2. Overgeneralization	✓	Helen generalizes from an imaginary blemish on her nose to her entire appearance.
3. Mental Filter	✓	Helen focuses on her nose and filters out anything positive about her appearance. In reality, she's quite attractive.
4. Discounting the Positive	✓	Many people have told Helen that she's extremely attractive and that they can't see the scar. She discounts this evidence and insists that they're just trying to make her feel better.
5. Jumping to Conclusions • Mind-Reading • Fortune-Telling	✓	Helen assumes that people will be shocked by her appearance, but she has no evidence for this (Mind-Reading). She also predicts that people will stare at her and get grossed out (Fortune-Telling).
6. Magnification or Minimization	✓	Helen greatly exaggerates the importance of the scar. In fact, it's invisible to other people.
7. Emotional Reasoning	✓	Helen *feels* like people will be disgusted by her nose, so she thinks they really *will be*.
8. Should Statements	✓	Helen believes that she *should always* be perfect and *should never* have any flaws. This is a "hidden should."
9. Labeling	✓	Helen thinks her face is "spoiled."
10. Blame • Self-Blame • Other-Blame	✓	Helen feels frustrated, angry, and upset and seems to be blaming her troubles on the scar on her nose.

How will you know which techniques to select for Helen? Remember that you can select techniques based on the distortions in a negative thought or on the problem you want to overcome. You may want to review the tables on pages 353 and 354. We know that Helen's negative thought contains all ten distortions and that she's suffering from BDD, so you'll have a lot of freedom in selecting techniques. As mentioned, make sure you include the Hidden Emotion Technique, because there may be some feeling or problem that Helen's sweeping under the rug. Did her sudden preoccupation with her nose

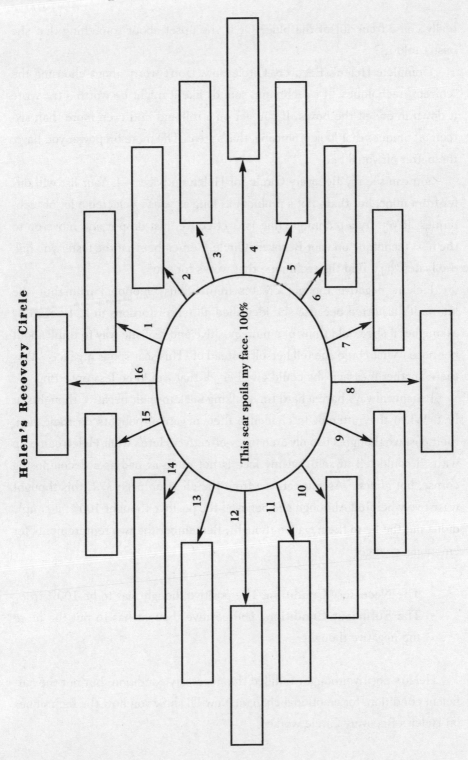

Helen's Recovery Circle

This scar spoils my face. 100%

really come from out of the blue? Or is she upset about something that she hasn't told us?

Complete Helen's Recovery Circle now. Don't worry about choosing the "correct" techniques. If a technique sounds like it might be worth a try, write it down in one of the boxes. If you get on a roll and find even more than sixteen techniques that look promising, that's great. The more firepower you have, the better off you'll be.

You can see my Recovery Circle for Helen on page 371. Your list will differ from mine, but that's not a problem as long as you've selected a lot of techniques. If you try a technique that isn't effective, just drop it and move on to the next technique on your Recovery Circle. Remember that the faster you fail, the faster you'll find the technique that works for you.

Helen's negative thought creates tremendous emotional pain, but she knows it's distorted because she identified all ten distortions in it. I began by asking her if she could think of a more positive and realistic way to think about her nose. What could she tell herself instead of "This scar spoils my face"? Was there another message she could give herself that would be less upsetting?

Patients always have a hard time talking back to their negative thoughts at first. When they attempt to challenge their negative thoughts on their own, their positive thoughts usually aren't very effective. Here's what Helen came up with: "I could tell myself that my face is not quite as bad as a decomposing corpse, but *almost*." As you can see from the chart on page 372, this thought wasn't very helpful! Although she believed the positive thought 100%, it simply didn't put the lie to the negative thought. Remember the two requirements for emotional change:

- **The Necessary Condition.** The positive thought has to be 100% true.
- **The Sufficient Condition.** The positive thought has to put the lie to the negative thought.

Helen's positive thought fulfilled the necessary condition, but not the sufficient condition, for emotional change. Now I'll show you how the techniques on Helen's Recovery Circle worked.

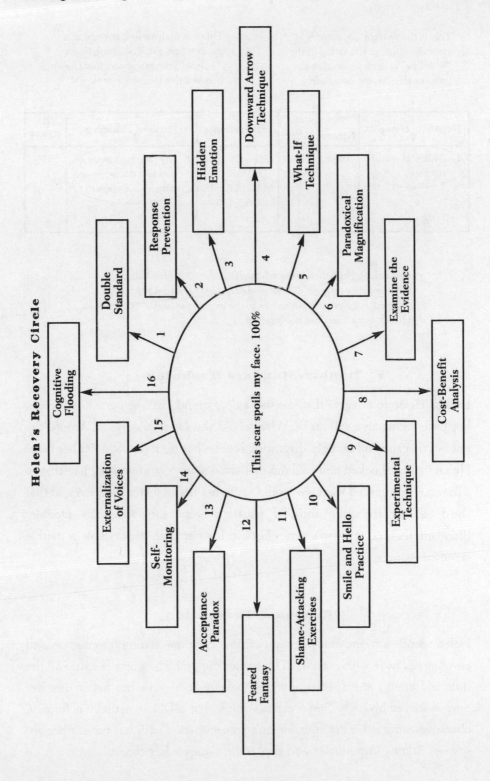

Helen's Recovery Circle

This scar spoils my face. 100%

1 — Cognitive Flooding
2 — Double Standard
3 — Response Prevention
4 — Hidden Emotion
5 — Downward Arrow Technique
6 — What-If Technique
7 — Paradoxical Magnification
8 — Examine the Evidence
9 — Cost-Benefit Analysis
10 — Experimental Technique
11 — Smile and Hello Practice
12 — Shame-Attacking Exercises
13 — Feared Fantasy
14 — Acceptance Paradox
15 — Self-Monitoring
16 — Externalization of Voices

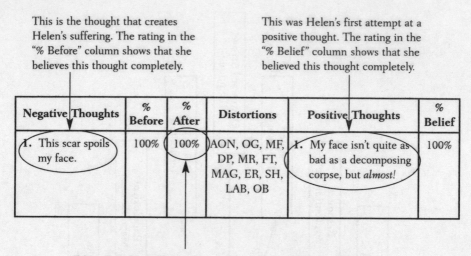

This is the thought that creates Helen's suffering. The rating in the "% Before" column shows that she believes this thought completely.

This was Helen's first attempt at a positive thought. The rating in the "% Belief" column shows that she believed this thought completely.

Negative Thoughts	% Before	% After	Distortions	Positive Thoughts	% Belief
1. This scar spoils my face.	100%	100%	AON, OG, MF, DP, MR, FT, MAG, ER, SH, LAB, OB	1. My face isn't quite as bad as a decomposing corpse, but *almost!*	100%

Although Helen believed the positive thought 100%, her belief in the negative thought did not go down. That's because the positive thought didn't put the lie to the negative thought. As a result, her anxiety did not improve.

Double-Standard Technique

I asked Helen to imagine that she had a dear friend just like herself who'd cut her nose during an earthquake. What would she say to her friend? Would she tell her that she had an ugly, disgusting scar on her nose that spoiled her face? Helen looked shocked and told me that she'd *never* say something like that to a friend. Then I asked what she would say to her friend instead. Helen said that she'd tell her friend to consider plastic surgery! Obviously, the Double-Standard Technique wasn't very effective for her. She didn't have a double standard.

Response Prevention

Helen spends a tremendous amount of time each day staring into mirrors and covering her nose with makeup. This makes the problem worse because all the time and energy she spends applying makeup reinforces her belief that her nose is incredibly ugly. Some experts think that BDD is actually a form of obsessive-compulsive disorder. Helen's preoccupation with her nose is her obsession. Staring into mirrors and applying makeup is her compulsion.

Response Prevention is the treatment of choice for any compulsion. I asked Helen to remove all the mirrors from her house and put them in her garage, facing the wall. She couldn't remove the mirror in her bathroom because it was attached to the wall, but she agreed to limit her use of it to one minute each morning when she brushed her hair. She was not permitted to look into mirrors or windows to check on her appearance for the rest of the day, no matter how anxious she got. This Response Prevention made Helen much more anxious at first, but after a few days, her urges to stare into the mirror and cover her nose with makeup became less intense.

Although Response Prevention is mandatory for anyone with a compulsion, it's usually not curative. Helen's urges to check her appearance in the mirror subsided, but her obsessive thoughts and anxious feelings did not disappear. That's because she still believed that there was an ugly scar on her nose that spoiled her face.

The Hidden Emotion Technique

Helen is an attractive, talented woman with a wonderful family and an outstanding career. Out of the blue, she suddenly developed the bizarre belief that her nose looks grotesque. Why did this happen? Is Helen upset about something that she isn't telling us? What do you think the *real* problem is? Think about it for a moment. Don't worry about coming up with the "correct" answer. Just jot down a few ideas.

1. _____

2. _____

3. _____

Answer
Ultimately, only Helen will be able to tell us if there's a hidden problem and what it is. However, we can raise a few questions about what might be bugging her.

Is Helen anxious about going back to work? The high-tech world evolves at blazing speed, and she's been out of the workforce for six years. Maybe she's secretly worried that she's rusty and over the hill, and can't cut it anymore. But if there really is an ugly scar on her nose that nobody can stand to look at, she won't have to go back to work and risk discovering that she's fallen behind.

If this is how she feels, why doesn't she just tell her husband, instead of manufacturing a delusion about her nose? Perhaps it's because Helen has been a confident, high-achieving person all her life. When she was growing up, she was always popular and a top student. She may not be used to feeling nervous or insecure, and she may be afraid that her husband would think less of her if he knew that she was feeling that way.

Is Helen angry with Don? He was the one who initiated the idea of her going back to work so they could put a new addition on their house. Helen may feel pressured and resentful, but doesn't want to express these feelings because she's too "nice." Perhaps her anxiety gives her an excuse to stay home. Then she can say, "Don, I really *want* to go back to work, but as you can see, I *can't* because I'm so crippled by fear."

Does Helen really want to stay home with the kids? Perhaps she enjoys raising her boys and feels like it would be great to be a full-time mom for a few more years. But she might find it hard to admit because she thinks she *should* be a high-achieving woman with a glamorous high-tech career *and* a family.

I was surprised that none of these possibilities rang true to Helen. She said that she genuinely wanted to return to work and felt the timing was right as far as the children were concerned. In addition, she didn't feel resentful or pressured by her husband to go back to work and wasn't concerned about being rusty or over the hill.

In many cases, the Hidden Emotion Technique is incredibly illuminating and leads to rapid improvement. But it wasn't effective for Helen, so it was time to move on to the next technique.

Downward Arrow Technique

When you use the Downward Arrow Technique, you draw an arrow under your negative thought and ask, "If that were true, what would it mean to me? Why would it be upsetting?" A new thought will pop into your mind. Write this thought down and draw another downward arrow directly underneath it. If you do this several times, you can identify the Self-Defeating Beliefs that are triggering your fears.

Put yourself in Helen's shoes and complete the following Downward Arrow Technique. I've put the questions you ask yourself next to each arrow, but feel free to modify them as you go down the chain, depending on the thought that pops into your mind. If you come up with fewer than six thoughts, or more, that's fine.

Helen's Downward Arrow Technique

Negative Thoughts

1. This scar spoils my face.

    ↓ "If that was true, what would it mean to me? Why would it be upsetting?"

2. _____

    ↓ "If that was true, what would it mean to me? Why would it be upsetting?"

3. _____

    ↓ "If that was true, what would it mean to me? Why would it be upsetting?"

4. _____

    ↓ "If that was true, what would it mean to me? Why would it be upsetting?"

5. _____

    ↓ "If that was true, what would it mean to me? Why would it be upsetting?"

6. _____

_____

You can see Helen's chain of negative thoughts on page 376, along with the questions I asked her at each level. Review her thoughts and see if you can pinpoint a few of Helen's Self-Defeating Beliefs (SDBs). Refer to the list of common SDBs on page 19 when you do this exercise.

1. _____

2. _____

3. _____

4. _____

5. _____

Helen's Downward Arrow Technique

Negative Thoughts

1. This scar spoils my face.

   ↓ "If that was true, what would it mean to you? Why would it be upsetting?"

2. People may see the scar on my nose and think I look disgusting.

   ↓ "Let's assume that happened. What would it mean to you? Why would it be upsetting?"

3. Then they'd look down on me.

   ↓ "And then what? Why would that be upsetting?"

4. Then they'd reject me. They wouldn't want to be around me anymore.

   ↓ "And if they didn't want to be around you anymore, what would it mean to you? Why would that be upsetting?"

5. Then I'd be all alone.

   ↓ "And if you were alone, what would that mean to you? What are you the most afraid of?"

6. That would mean I was worthless.

Answer

Here are the Self-Defeating Beliefs that Helen and I identified:

- **Perfectionism.** Helen believes that she must look perfect and that any tiny flaw will ruin her appearance completely.

- **Perceived Perfectionism.** She thinks that other people are extremely judgmental and will reject her if she doesn't look perfect.
- **Approval Addiction.** Helen believes that she needs everyone's approval in order to be worthwhile.
- **Fear of Rejection.** She thinks that she's bound to feel worthless and miserable if anyone rejects her.
- **Spotlight Fallacy.** Helen feels like she's under a spotlight on a stage, with everyone watching and judging her performance.
- **Brushfire Fallacy.** Helen imagines that if one person looks down on her, the word will spread and pretty soon, everyone will be gossiping and looking down on her.

It's easy to see how these SDBs fuel Helen's fears. Helen imagines a world that's filled with people who are extremely judgmental, superficial, and rejecting. She's also convinced that if one person looks down on her, everyone will. Her anxiety doesn't result from any real or imagined flaw in her appearance but from the way she's thinking about herself and the world. In addition to helping Helen put the lie to her negative thoughts in the here and now, we'll also want to help her change the SDBs that triggered her fears in the first place. That way she won't be so vulnerable to painful mood swings in the future.

You learned a little about how to change a Self-Defeating Belief in Chapters 7 and 8. Later in this chapter, I'll show you how we used the Feared Fantasy and Acceptance Paradox to challenge Helen's SDBs.

What-If Technique/Paradoxical Magnification

You may recall that the What-If Technique is similar to the Downward Arrow Technique, but you ask yourself questions like this instead: "What if this really happened? What am I the most afraid of? What's the worst thing that could happen?" The What-If Technique allows you to uncover the fantasy that's been fueling your fears. If you push this fantasy to the worst possible extreme, it will often begin to seem absurd. Here's how Helen and I used these two techniques.

David: Helen, let's suppose that you went to the Stanford Shopping Center one day without any makeup on, and people saw your nose and thought it was ugly and repulsive. Does that scenario frighten you?

Helen: Oh, yes, it sounds horrible!

David: Okay, I'd like you to focus on this fantasy. How many people do you think might be grossed out by your nose?

Helen: I'm not sure. There could be as many as a hundred.

David: Does that frighten you?

Helen: It sounds *awful*!

David: Why would it be awful? Let's say that a hundred people saw your nose and felt totally disgusted. What then? What are you the most afraid of?

Helen: They might tell their friends.

David: Okay, let's suppose that each person who saw your nose told ten friends about it. Now a thousand people know about your nose. What if that happened? Does that idea upset you?

Helen: I can't even stand to think about it!

David: I know this scenario makes you anxious, but I want you to stick with it for just a bit longer. If a thousand people agreed that your nose was the worst nose they'd ever seen, why would that be bad? What are you the most afraid of?

Helen: Well, they might tell even more people, and the word would start to spread.

David: Okay, let's assume that all one thousand people tell ten of their friends about your nose. Now there are ten thousand people in Los Angeles talking about your nose. Would that be upsetting? What would happen then?

Helen: They might tell even more people!

David: Let's examine the worst possible outcome. Assume that ten thousand people each tell ten more friends about your nose. And they all tell ten others, and so on. Now the news about your nose is spreading like wildfire throughout the Bay Area, and more than a million people are gossiping about your nose and feeling disgusted. In fact, there's so much concern that an article about your nose appears on the front page of the *Los Angeles Times* with a photo of your face taken secretly by the paparazzi through a telephoto lens. I can see the headline now: "Woman spotted at local shopping center with scar on nose. Thousands flee in terror. Parents advised to keep children indoors during daylight hours."

The last part of the dialogue is an example of Paradoxical Magnification. The goal is not to make fun of Helen, but rather to make her aware of how she's exaggerating things. Are people really going to be that judgmental and preoccupied with a tiny blemish on Helen's nose?

Once you unearth your most terrifying fantasy, you can ask yourself, "How likely is it that this will happen? How realistic are my fears?" You can also ask yourself, "If this did happen, could I live with it? Would it really be the end of the world?" It would certainly be inconvenient if Helen's nose shocked so many people. But really, who would be the loonies in this case?

Unfortunately, the What-If Technique didn't lead to any real relief for Helen. Although she could see that her worst fears seemed extremely unlikely, she was still convinced that there was an ugly scar on her nose that turned people off.

Examine the Evidence

When you use Examine the Evidence, you ask yourself questions like this: "Is there any solid evidence that supports my negative thoughts? How did I come to this conclusion in the first place?" Sometimes you'll discover that your fears are based on Emotional Reasoning, not on a realistic evaluation of the way things really are. Here's what happened when I asked Helen these questions.

David: Helen, I'm wondering how you came to the conclusion that people would be turned off by an ugly scar on your nose. Is there any solid evidence for this belief?

Helen: Well, when I look in the mirror, my face looks ugly and I get very anxious. That's the main thing.

David: It sounds like you're pretty self-critical and get upset when you look in the mirror. But I'm wondering if there's any evidence that other people also get turned off when they look at you. Has anyone asked you about the scar on your nose or noticed there'd been a change in your appearance?

Helen: No, nobody has said anything like that, but when I think about going out in public, I feel like everyone is going to stare at my nose and feel disgusted.

David: I'm sure that must be horribly stressful. I wouldn't want people to stare at me and feel disgusted, either. But I'm wondering if you have any real evidence that people actually *do* feel disgusted by your nose. When you've been out in public, have people stared at you in horror? Have any mothers look stunned or shielded their children's eyes when you walked past them?

Helen: Not exactly. I stay inside most of the time because I think my nose looks like a clown's nose or something.

David: Sometimes you can feel something very strongly, but it turns out that your feelings aren't valid. How did you come to the conclusion that your nose looks like a clown's nose? Have you had some upsetting experiences recently? What have you observed when you've been out in public?

Helen: People always act polite. They pretend like they don't notice my nose, but I have the feeling that they really do.

Helen couldn't come up with any evidence to support her belief that there was an ugly scar on her nose, other than the fact that she felt anxious and avoided going outside the house. However, she discounted the fact that no one seemed repulsed by her nose because she had such an overwhelming feeling that it really was disgusting. Examine the Evidence didn't seem to be doing the trick, so I moved on.

Cost-Benefit Analysis

Generally, we don't believe things that we have no evidence for. Why was Helen clinging to the belief that there was an ugly scar on her nose? I wondered if there might be some hidden payoffs or rewards that were fueling her anxiety. If so, it would explain why she was still stuck. If we could get them out into the open, it might relieve some of the pressure and help her think about her appearance more realistically.

To find out, I decided to try a Cost-Benefit Analysis. I asked Helen to list all the advantages and disadvantages of telling herself that there was an ugly scar on her nose that spoiled her face. How would this belief help her, and how would it hurt her? Helen's Cost-Benefit Analysis (CBA) follows. She was able to list quite a few advantages of the thought, as well as a number of disadvantages. When she weighed them against each other, she decided that the disadvantages of the thought were much greater than the advantages. Unfortunately, the CBA didn't help her very much because even though she could see that the negative thought wasn't to her advantage, she was still convinced that it was true. Clearly, it was time for a more powerful technique.

Helen's Cost-Benefit Analysis

List the attitude, feeling, or habit that you want to change: This scar spoils my face.

Advantages	Disadvantages
1. I won't have to go out on job interviews.	1. I won't be able to go back to work.
2. I can stay at home with the children.	2. I'll feel anxious and ashamed.
3. I won't have to do things that make me nervous, like grocery shopping.	3. I'll get into conflicts with my husband and parents every time they insist that there isn't a scar on my nose.
4. I can feel sorry for myself.	4. I'll feel defective.
5. I'll get lots of attention from my husband and parents.	5. I'll be afraid to interact with people.
6. I'll feel like I'm being honest, since it seems like I really do have an ugly scar on my nose.	6. I'll feel lonely and isolated.
	7. I'll be a prisoner in my own home.
30	70

The Experimental Technique/Smile and Hello Practice

The Experimental Technique involves doing an actual experiment to test the validity of a negative thought or Self-Defeating Belief. We know that there is no scar on Helen's nose. We also know that even if there were a blemish on her nose, most people wouldn't be terribly interested in it. They'll judge

Helen by how she treats them and interacts with them. But Helen doesn't realize this.

I asked Helen if she'd be willing to perform a bold experiment to test her negative thoughts. I suggested that she could go to a fashionable Beverly Hills shopping center in broad daylight and smile and say hello to twenty strangers. I told her to bring an index card with her, and after she smiled and said hello to someone, she could put a tick mark on the card to indicate whether the person responded in a positive, neutral, or negative way. That way she could put her belief that people would be grossed out by her nose to the test.

Helen was extremely reluctant to perform this experiment. She'd been hiding out in her house for weeks and was convinced that people would be shocked by her appearance. But she was determined to get well and agreed to do the experiment in spite of her fears. I offered to meet with her after she was done so we could talk about the results.

The next morning, Helen went to the shopping center and did her Smile and Hello Practice. She was amazed that fifteen of the twenty people she greeted responded in a friendly and pleasant way. Five people didn't realize that Helen was saying hello to them and ignored her. She rated them as neutral responders. No one seemed shocked or put off by her appearance.

These results were difficult for Helen to reconcile with her conviction that there was an ugly scar on her nose that turned everyone off, and her belief in the negative thought fell to 70%. This was the first time we'd made a dent in her beliefs about her nose. However, she discounted the results because she was wearing heavy makeup. She concluded that people hadn't noticed the scar but that they definitely would have been grossed out if she hadn't been wearing any makeup. If you were Helen's shrink, what would you suggest next? Put your ideas here before you continue reading.

_____

_____

_____

_____

_____

_____

Answer

I asked Helen to return to the shopping center the next day and repeat the experiment *without* any makeup on. This idea terrified her because she was certain that people really *would* stare at her nose in shock. Once again I offered to meet with her when she was through so we could discuss the results.

Helen was shocked by the results of this experiment. Almost everyone was friendly, and no one seemed repulsed by her nose. She even got into conversations with several women who were out shopping with their children. She could not reconcile this experience with her beliefs about her nose. At this point, her belief in the negative thought fell all the way to 10%, and she felt a wave of relief.

Shame-Attacking Exercises

Helen felt much better when she discovered that people were not actually disgusted by her nose. But what would happen if she *did* look foolish or if people did look down on her? Would that be the end of the world? To find out, Helen courageously agreed to go back to the shopping center one more time to do an even more outrageous experiment, a Shame-Attacking Exercise. You may recall that when you do a Shame-Attacking Exercise, you do something foolish in public on purpose so you can find out if the world really does come to an end. Shame-Attacking Exercises require tremendous courage.

Helen put on an outrageous outfit so she really would look ridiculous: a huge, feathered, purple hat she'd gotten years earlier to wear in the Mardi Gras parade in New Orleans, a flamboyant red dress with long strands of brightly colored Mardi Gras beads dangling around her neck, and sequined high-heeled shoes. This time she was *certain* that people would stare at her in disbelief when she smiled and said hello to them.

But to Helen's surprise, people still didn't react negatively. She said that they seemed even more enthusiastic and friendly, and that quite a few of the people at the shopping center looked even more outrageous than she did. After all, this is California!

While she was at the mall, Helen ran into one of her former colleagues on the chip development team. He said that they'd all been missing her and had been talking about her just a few days earlier. He said that the competition was catching up, and they needed another awesome chip to get back into the lead. He asked if she'd consider coming back and heading up their team again. Helen was overjoyed and said she'd already been thinking about a design for a new, ultra-high-speed chip. Her colleague urged her to drop by and talk to the team ASAP.

When I saw Helen the next week, she was overjoyed and ready to terminate treatment. Her fears about her nose had completely disappeared, and she'd already accepted a lucrative offer from her previous employer.

Feared Fantasy/Acceptance Paradox

Helen felt better when she discovered that her negative thoughts were false. All her anxiety disappeared. But there's a vitally important difference between *feeling* better and *getting* better.

Before we cut her loose, we'll need to do a little Relapse Prevention Training so she won't have to struggle with the same problem over and over again in the future. After all, she won't be young and gorgeous forever. Will she sink back into another mood slump a few years down the line when she starts to notice a few wrinkles and gray hairs?

To put it a bit differently, Helen still hasn't confronted her worst fear. When she did the experiments at the shopping center, she discovered that people weren't actually hostile and rejecting. But what if they were? Could she live with it?

She can't confront this fear in reality, but she can confront it in fantasy. You may recall that when you use the Feared Fantasy Technique, you enter a nightmare world where your worst fears come true. In this imaginary world, when you think people are looking down on you, they really are. And they always tell you exactly what they're thinking, no matter how brutal.

In the following Feared Fantasy dialogue, Helen is playing the role of the Mother from Hell, and I'm playing the role of Helen. The Mother from Hell is at the shopping center with her two little girls. I told Helen that in her role as the Mother from Hell, her job would be to try to cut me to shreds and humiliate me by saying the worst imaginable things about my nose, things that a real person would never actually say. Here's how it went.

Mother from Hell (played by Helen): My goodness. Did something happen to your nose?

Helen (played by David): Yes, a piece of plaster fell on my nose during the recent earthquake. There might still be a little scar there.

Mother from Hell: You call that a *little* scar? It's about as little as the Grand Canyon! Have you considered wearing a mask when you're out in public?

Helen: Gee, I've never thought about that and I don't have a mask handy right now. Is the scar upsetting you?

Mother from Hell: Upsetting? I think it's disgusting. I can't stand to look at you!

Helen: I had no idea my nose could make such an impact on people. Do you have an extra shopping bag? Perhaps I could make holes for my eyes and mouth, and cover my head while we talk, if that would make you more comfortable.

Mother from Hell: Truthfully, I think you should stay home and not show your face in public. Your nose is horrifying! Don't you realize that there are young children here in the mall? Have you thought about what might happen if they saw your nose? Turn away, children! Don't look at this awful lady's nose!

Helen: My goodness! I hadn't thought about that, either. Do you think it would be upsetting to your children to see my nose? Are they very fragile? Haven't they ever seen anyone with any kind of physical flaw or defect before?

Mother from Hell: I try to protect them as much as possible. They only go to the best schools and socialize with the best people. If they saw your awful nose, they might be traumatized and end up with nightmares.

Helen: That does sound serious. Perhaps you could shield their eyes while we talk.

Mother from Hell: Don't you be flippant! I think your behavior is outrageous. Going out in public with your nose showing is an insult to public decency. I'm going to report you to the authorities.

Helen: Please do. It sounds like a good idea. Perhaps they can warn people not to come to the shopping center on Wednesdays, because that's the day I usually come and shop. That would be great, actually, because I'd have the entire place to myself. No standing in line waiting for a salesclerk.

Now, who seems like the bigger loony: Helen, or the Mother from Hell? Helen could see that the Mother from Hell was the one who had the problem. This was a revelation to her because she'd always turned away from the monster she feared. She'd always told herself, "I can't stand to think about *that*. It's too awful!" But once she saw how easily I defeated her by using the Acceptance Paradox, she realized that there was never anything to fear in the first place.

Remember that the Feared Fantasy is *not* assertiveness training. Other people would never behave like this. When you enter the Feared Fantasy world, the monster you confront is the projection of your own self-criticisms. You're really doing battle with yourself.

Helen's first victory came when she discovered that people did not turn against her when they saw her nose. Her second victory came when she discovered that even if someone did reject her, the craziness would be with them, and not with her. This led to a shift in the Self-Defeating Beliefs that had triggered her fears in the first place, such as Perfectionism and the Approval Addiction. At this point, she was ready to terminate therapy. Her completed Daily Mood Log follows on page 387.

Helen's treatment required only six sessions, and we didn't even need to use all the techniques on her Recovery Circle. It's encouraging that the prognosis for BDD is now so bright, since it was once considered almost impossible to treat. In Helen's case, two forms of magic were operating. First, she had the necessary motivation and determination to defeat her fears. She was courageous and willing to try techniques that were frightening to her. Second, we failed as fast as we could until we found techniques that worked for her.

When people learn about Helen, they sometimes ask, "Well, what if she really did have a bizarre scar on her nose and people actually *were* shocked by how she looked?" Helen was attractive and articulate, and the experiments she performed were appropriate for her. If her problems had been different, or if the circumstances of her life had been different, I would have used a com-

Helen's Daily Mood Log

Upsetting Event: Staring into the mirror this morning.

Emotions	% Before	% After	Emotions	% Before	% After
Sad, blue, depressed, down, unhappy	75%	0%	Embarrassed, foolish, humiliated, self-conscious	100%	0%
Anxious, worried, panicky, nervous, frightened	100%	0%	Hopeless, discouraged, pessimistic, despairing	100%	0%
Guilty, remorseful, bad, ashamed	100%	0%	Frustrated, stuck, thwarted, defeated	85%	0%
Inferior, worthless, inadequate, defective, incompetent	100%	0%	Angry, mad, resentful, annoyed, irritated, upset, furious	60%	0%
Lonely, unloved, unwanted, rejected, alone, abandoned	80%	0%	Other (describe)		

Negative Thoughts	% Before	% After	Distortions	Positive Thoughts	% Belief
1. This scar spoils my face.	100%	0%	AON, OG, MF, DP, MR, FT, MAG, ER, SH, LAB, OB	1. I may *feel* like there's an ugly scar on my nose, but no one has stared at me or seemed shocked. In fact, almost everyone has been warm and friendly, even when I wasn't wearing any make-up. If someone really was shocked by my nose, I could live with it. Everybody has flaws, and most people will be more concerned with how I treat them than with any blemish on my nose.	100%
2. I'll *never* get a job.	100%	0%	AON, DP, MR, FT, MIN, ER	2. My skills are in demand, and my colleagues probably won't be all that interested in my nose.	100%
3. People will stare at me.	100%	0%	DP, MR, FT, ER	3. This isn't true. Nobody has stared at me.	100%

pletely different approach. This is one of the most important messages of this book. There are no formulas or gimmicks you can blindly apply to different problems or types of anxiety. Rather, I'm giving you a flexible, powerful, individualized approach that you can use to overcome any kind of mood problem, including the problems that are bothering you.

Chapter 24

....

Feeling Better versus Getting Better

Relapse Prevention Training

Let's say you've been working with the Daily Mood Log and Recovery Circle, and you've found some techniques that work for you. You've put the lie to your negative thoughts, and you're feeling better. If you had panic attacks, they're gone now. If you were shy, you can connect with people in social situations without feeling self-conscious and awkward. If you felt inferior or depressed, you now have self-esteem. You feel productive and creative and enjoy your relationships with other people. When you get up in the morning, you look forward to the day and tell yourself that it's great to be alive.

Feeling better is a great accomplishment. However, there's a critical difference between feeling better and getting better. *Feeling better* means that the feelings of anxiety or depression have disappeared and you feel happy and confident again. *Getting better* means that you have the tools you'll need to deal with feelings of anxiety or depression for the rest of your life.

The first time you recover, you may feel so good that it's hard to imagine that you'll ever feel bad again. You'll probably think that all your problems have been solved for good and that the feelings of joy and self-confidence will go on forever. But what's the probability that you're going to relapse in the future? Here's a hint. I define a "relapse" as one minute or more of feeling lousy—anxious, discouraged, inadequate, frustrated, or irritable. With this in mind, what do you think the probability of a relapse will be? Check the answer that you think is most likely to be correct:

	(✓)		(✓)		(✓)
0%		25%		75%	
10%		50%		100%	

Answer

Although the estimates of relapse vary, I believe that the correct answer is 100%. If you've ever struggled with anxiety or depression, sooner or later you're definitely going to feel anxious or depressed again. In fact, all human beings are going to keep relapsing forever! The Buddha said that suffering is inherent in the human condition. It's inevitable. No one can feel happy all the time, and it wouldn't even be a good thing if we could. If we were happy all the time, there'd be no contrast or challenges, and life would soon become boring because we'd feel exactly the same way all the time. According to the old Latin saying, hunger is the sweetest sauce.

Bad things happen, and we all suffer in our own unique ways. Some people get grouchy and irritable. Others get anxious and panicky. Some succumb to feelings of worthlessness and depression. Feeling lousy from time to time is as certain as the sun coming up in the morning. The main difference between people who suffer from depression and anxiety and people who don't is that the people who suffer from depression and anxiety tend to get stuck in their bad moods. That minute of feeling upset turns into an hour, the hour turns into a day, and the day turns into a week, a month, or even years of misery. People who don't suffer from depression and anxiety get upset just as often, but they know how to break out of their bad moods quickly. And that's something you can learn how to do.

An hour, a day, or even a week or two of feeling down in the dumps is perfectly acceptable. But months or years of being trapped in feelings of despair or inadequacy—that's not necessary. That's what Relapse Prevention Training is all about. I can't show you how to be happy all the time, but I can show you how to deal with your bad moods so that you won't have to get trapped by them anymore.

Once you've recovered from an episode of severe depression or anxiety and you're feeling terrific, how long do you think it will take before you experience your first relapse? Everyone is different, but take your best guess. Put a check in the table to indicate when you think a relapse is most likely to occur:

	(✓)		(✓)
1. Within a few hours		4. Within a few months	
2. Within a few days		5. Within a few years	
3. Within a few weeks		6. Never	

Answer

In my clinical practice, most of the people who've recovered from an episode of severe depression or anxiety have relapsed within a few weeks of their initial recovery. Sometimes they relapse within a few days, and sometimes it takes a month or more. But the relapse *always* occurs.

When you relapse, you may feel more depressed and anxious than you've ever felt before. Why is this? Before you recovered, you may have been struggling with depression and anxiety for a long time, so you may have given up and accepted the "fact" that you were defective and doomed to feeling unhappy forever. Then, when you recover, you can't believe how good you suddenly feel, and you may tell yourself, "Wow, my problems are gone for good! I'm going to feel like this forever. This is fantastic!"

Of course, that's the "all" side of the All-or-Nothing Thinking, and it's just as illogical as the hopelessness that results from the "nothing" side because it sets you up for a huge disappointment. When you suddenly relapse a few weeks later, the contrast with the incredibly good feelings you've been enjoying can feel unbearable. You may feel as if you got your hopes up, only to have them dashed again. It's like being slapped in the face or having the rug pulled out from under you. The pain can be intense.

I want you to know that after you've recovered, you *are* going to relapse. It's as certain as the law of gravity. Most people think that a relapse is the worst thing that could possibly happen, but it's actually the *best* thing. Do you know why? It's because you can learn to overcome it and get back to the feelings of optimism and self-esteem fairly quickly. Then you'll realize that your improvement wasn't a fluke, but the direct result of the tools you've been learning to use. Then you'll never have to fear depression or anxiety again for the rest of your life because you'll know that you can deal with painful mood swings whenever you need to. That's what I mean by *getting* better, as opposed to simply *feeling* better. This can be one of the most exciting discoveries of your life.

In Chapter 1, you learned about three models that will help you overcome anxiety and depression: the Cognitive Model, the Exposure Model, and the Hidden Emotion Model. These three models are also the keys to Relapse Prevention.

The Cognitive Model

Imagine that you've been totally free of anxiety or depression for several weeks. One morning you wake up and realize that you're feeling anxious and depressed again. How will you be feeling? What will you be thinking? If you're like the many patients I've treated over the years, you'll probably feel sad, worried, hopeless, worthless, frustrated, angry, and disappointed, and you'll be telling yourself:

- I'll *never* get better. I'm a hopeless case.
- This relapse shows that the therapy didn't work.
- My improvement was just a fluke.
- I wasn't really better. I just *thought* I was. Underneath, I was depressed the whole time.
- This therapy can't work for me. My problems are too deep.
- I'm worthless after all.
- What good are a few weeks of improvement? Now I'll be anxious and depressed for another ten years.
- This is unfair. Other people don't have to work so hard to be happy.
- There must be something wrong with me.

During a relapse, these thoughts will seem absolutely valid, and they can be devastating. Research studies indicate that many people commit suicide during relapses because these thoughts seem so convincing to them and because the pain is so overwhelming. But these thoughts are *not* valid. They're grossly distorted and illogical. If you give in to them, you'll slip back into another episode of depression or anxiety. But if you know how to put the lie to them, you can bounce back again.

If you knew for a fact that your negative feelings were only temporary and that you'd soon be feeling good again, it would make all the difference in the world. You'd just wait it out or put together a plan for coping with the problem that was upsetting you. But most depressed people feel absolutely convinced they *can't* get better, no matter what they do. Of course, this belief acts as a self-fulfilling prophecy. If you give up, nothing will change. Then you'll conclude that things really are hopeless.

What's the solution? You can prepare for the relapse *ahead of time,* when you're feeling good. If you practice talking back to your negative thoughts before the relapse occurs, it will be much easier to fight them off when the time comes.

I'll show you how this works. Imagine that you've recovered from an episode of depression or anxiety and you're feeling terrific. You know that you'll feel depressed or anxious again at some point in the future, so you're going to prepare for the relapse now. Grab a Daily Mood Log and put something like this at the top where you describe the Upsetting Event: "Having a relapse." Keep in mind that you haven't actually had a relapse yet. You're simply imagining what it will be like when you really do have a relapse.

An example of a Relapse Daily Mood Log is on page 394. After you circle and rate all the negative feelings you think you'll have during the relapse, write down the negative thoughts you think you might have and indicate how strongly you think you'll believe them. The first negative thought on the DML is "I'll *never* get better. I'm a hopeless case." I've put 100% next to it, since the thought will seem totally valid during a relapse, even if it doesn't seem particularly realistic right now.

What are the distortions in this thought? Review the definitions of the distortions on page 396, and put your answers on page 422.

Relapse Daily Mood Log

Upsetting Event: Having a depression relapse.

Emotions	% Before	% After
Sad, blue, depressed, down, unhappy	100%	
Anxious, worried, panicky, nervous, frightened	100%	
Guilty, remorseful, bad, ashamed	100%	
Inferior, worthless, inadequate, defective, incompetent	100%	
Lonely, unloved, unwanted, rejected, alone, abandoned	100%	

Emotions	% Before	% After
Embarrassed, foolish, humiliated, self-conscious	100%	
Hopeless, discouraged, pessimistic, despairing	100%	
Frustrated, stuck, thwarted, defeated	100%	
Angry, mad, resentful, annoyed, irritated, upset, furious	100%	
Other (describe) disappointed	100%	

Negative Thoughts	% Before	% After	Distortions	Positive Thoughts	% Belief
1. I'll *never* get better. I'm a hopeless case.	100%				
2. This relapse shows that the therapy didn't work.	100%				
3. My improvement was just a fluke.	100%				
4. I wasn't really better. I just *thought* I was. Underneath, I was depressed the whole time.	100%				
5. This therapy can't work for me. My problems are too deep.	100%				
6. I'm worthless after all.	100%				
7. What good are a few weeks of improvement? Now I'll be depressed for another ten years.	100%				
8. This is unfair. Other people don't have to work so hard to be happy.	100%				
9. There must be something wrong with me.	100%				

Distortion	(✓)	Distortion	(✓)
1. All-or-Nothing Thinking		6. Magnification or Minimization	
2. Overgeneralization		7. Emotional Reasoning	
3. Mental Filter		8. Should Statements	
4. Discounting the Positive		9. Labeling	
5. Jumping to Conclusions • Mind-Reading • Fortune-Telling		10. Blame • Self-Blame • Other-Blame	

Answer

As you can see on page 396, I found all ten distortions in the thought "I'll *never* get better. I'm a hopeless case."

A thought with all ten distortions in it can hardly be valid. How could you talk back to this thought? What could you tell yourself instead of "I'll *never* get better. I'm a hopeless case"? It may be helpful to ask yourself questions like these: "If I feel upset right now, does it mean that the therapy wasn't helpful? It's a fact that I'm feeling bad right now, but is it really true that I'll *never* feel better again?"

As you can see on the Daily Mood Log on page 397, I've recorded the negative thought and all the distortions in it. Your job will be to come up with a convincing positive thought. Write it down in the Positive Thoughts column, and indicate how strongly you believe it, from 0% to 100%, in the "% Belief" column. Remember the necessary and sufficient conditions for emotional change: The positive thought must be 100% true, and it has to reduce your belief in the negative thought.

Now consider the negative thought again. How strongly do you believe it now, between 0% and 100%? Put your rating in the "% After" column. When you're done, I'll show you the positive thought I came up with. But please write out your own positive thought first.

Answer

Did you actually write down a positive thought, or did you just think about it? I'd encourage you to write down a positive thought before you continue reading. This is one of the most important parts of your Relapse Prevention Train-

Distortion	(✓)	Explanation
1. All-or-Nothing Thinking	✓	This is a classic example of All-or-Nothing Thinking. You're telling yourself that the therapy either works perfectly or not at all. Shades of gray don't exist.
2. Overgeneralization	✓	You're overgeneralizing from this relapse and concluding that you'll *never* get better. You think the way you're feeling now will turn into a never-ending pattern of defeat and suffering.
3. Mental Filter	✓	You're focusing on how bad you feel now and ignoring the last three weeks, when you were feeling much better.
4. Discounting the Positive	✓	You're discounting the fact that the therapy was very helpful to you and you did get better.
5. Jumping to Conclusions • Mind-Reading • Fortune-Telling	✓	You're predicting you'll be depressed forever (Fortune-Telling).
6. Magnification or Minimization	✓	A relapse is no fun, but you're blowing it way out of proportion.
7. Emotional Reasoning	✓	You're reasoning from how you feel. You're telling yourself that you must *be* hopeless because you *feel* hopeless.
8. Should Statements	✓	There's a hidden Should Statement at work here. You're telling yourself that you *should never* have to feel upset or have any relapses.
9. Labeling	✓	You're labeling yourself as "a hopeless case."
10. Blame • Self-Blame • Other-Blame	✓	You're not blaming anyone else for the relapse. However, you may be blaming yourself, thinking that it's your fault that you had a relapse.

ing. It will only take you a minute to grab a pen and write down a positive thought.

As you can see on page 398, I rated my belief in my positive thought at 100%, and my belief in the negative thought went down to 25%. I put a line through my original estimate of 100% and put 25% in the "% After" column.

That's an excellent reduction, but if you want to push your belief in the negative thought down even more, you can try some more positive thoughts. The table on page 353, Selecting Techniques Based on the Distortions in Your Negative Thought, will provide you with lots of ideas about techniques you

Daily Mood Log

Negative Thoughts	% Before	% After	Distortions	Positive Thoughts	% Belief
1. I'll *never* get better. I'm a hopeless case.	100%		AON, OG, MF, DP, FT, MAG, ER, SH, LAB, SB		

might try. For example, the negative thought is a classic example of All-or-Nothing Thinking, so you could try a Compassion-Based Technique such as the Double Standard, a Logic-Based Technique such as Thinking in Shades of Gray, or a Motivational Technique such as the Cost-Benefit Analysis, to name just a few. It also involves Labeling, so the Semantic Method would definitely be worth a try.

Now I'd like you to identify the distortions in the rest of the negative thoughts on the Relapse Daily Mood Log on page 394. This will probably take five or ten minutes. Then see if you can challenge each negative thought with a positive one. Write your positive thoughts in the right-hand column and indicate how strongly you believe them, from 0% to 100%. Then rate your belief in the negative thoughts again and record your ratings in the "% After" column.

Right now you're probably not having a relapse, so it shouldn't be too difficult to come up with convincing positive thoughts. But when you're having a

Negative Thoughts	% Before	% After	Distortions	Positive Thoughts	% Belief
1. I'll *never* get better. I'm a hopeless case.	100%	25%	AON, OG, MF, DP, FT, MAG, ER, SH, LAB, SB	1. It's not true that I'll *never* get better, because I got better several weeks ago. In fact, every time I've felt anxious or depressed, I've always gotten better sooner or later.	100%

relapse, coming up with effective positive thoughts will be extremely hard because the negative thoughts will seem absolutely true. If you understand this and prepare for the relapse now, it will be much easier for you to put the lie to these kinds of negative thoughts later on when you are experiencing a relapse.

When you're done, you can review the positive thoughts on the completed Relapse Daily Mood Log on pages 400 to 401. This is not an exact science, and your positive thoughts will certainly be different. The main thing is to come up with some positive thoughts that work for you. You'll notice that the belief in some of the negative thoughts went down more than others. The toughest one was number 8: "This is unfair. Other people don't have to work so hard to be happy." Thoughts that contain Other-Blame can be tough to dispute because they generate feelings of anger, moral superiority, and self-pity. These feelings can be addictive. To push your belief in this thought lower than 50%, consult the technique-selection table on page 353 for additional suggestions about techniques that might help. For example, a Motivational Technique such as the Cost-Benefit Analysis would be a good one to try. How would you use this technique to challenge the thought "This is unfair. Other people don't have to work so hard to be happy"? You can review the definition of the Cost-Benefit Analysis on page 359 if you're not clear about how this technique works. Put your ideas here.

_____

_____

_____

_____

Answer

You could list the advantages and disadvantages of telling yourself that your relapse is "unfair." Ask yourself, "How will this mind-set help me, and how will it hurt me?" There are probably quite a few advantages.

- You can feel like a victim and feel sorry for yourself.
- You can feel morally superior.
- You can blame God for your fate so you won't have to feel like the relapse is your fault.
- You can feel angry.
- You may feel energized by your anger.

There are bound to be many others, as well. After you list all the advantages and disadvantages of telling yourself that the relapse is "unfair," you can weigh the lists against each other. Ask yourself whether the advantages or disadvantages of this mind-set feel greater. Draw two circles at the bottom of your lists and put two numbers in them that add up to 100 to indicate your ratings.

If the advantages of the negative thought turn out to be greater, then you probably won't need to challenge it. Telling yourself that the relapse is unfair seems to be working for you. If the disadvantages are greater, try to challenge the thought again on your Daily Mood Log.

Once you've written down effective responses to all of the negative thoughts about relapse on your Daily Mood Log, you can challenge the thoughts with the Externalization of Voices. You may recall that this is a Role-Playing Technique, so you'll need the help of a friend. Your friend can play the role of your negative thoughts, reading your negative thoughts directly from your Daily Mood Log, using the second person, "you." For example, your friend may say:

Negative Thoughts (played by your friend): You'll *never* get better. You're a hopeless case.

You can play the role of your positive thoughts and do battle with the negative thoughts, using the first person, "I." For example, you might say:

Relapse Daily Mood Log

Upsetting Event: Having a depression relapse.

Emotions	% Before	% After	Emotions	% Before	% After
Sad, blue, depressed, down, unhappy	100%	50%	Embarrassed, foolish, humiliated, self-conscious	100%	10%
Anxious, worried, panicky, nervous, frightened	100%	20%	Hopeless, discouraged, pessimistic, despairing	100%	25%
Guilty, remorseful, bad, ashamed	100%	10%	Frustrated, stuck, thwarted, defeated	100%	35%
Inferior, worthless, inadequate, defective, incompetent	100%	15%	Angry, mad, resentful, annoyed, irritated, upset, furious	100%	35%
Lonely, unloved, unwanted, rejected, alone, abandoned	100%	10%	Other (describe) disappointed	100%	25%

Negative Thoughts	% Before	% After	Distortions	Positive Thoughts	% Belief
1. I'll *never* get better. I'm a hopeless case.	100%	25%	AON, OG, MF, DP, FT, MAG, ER, SH, LAB, SB	1. It's not true that I'll *never* get better, because I got better several weeks ago. In fact, every time I've felt anxious or depressed, I've always gotten better sooner or later.	100%
2. This relapse shows that the therapy didn't work.	100%	10%	AON, OG, MF, DP, MIN, ER, SH, OB	2. The therapy did work, even though it didn't work perfectly. No one can be happy all the time. I need to roll up my sleeves and use the same techniques that helped me the first time.	100%
3. My improvement was just a fluke.	100%	10%	DP, ER	3. That's a nutty claim. My improvement was the result of the hard work I did. It wasn't "a fluke."	100%

Relapse Daily Mood Log Continuation Sheet

Negative Thoughts	% Before	% After	Distortions	Positive Thoughts	% Belief
4. I wasn't really better. I just *thought* I was. Underneath, I was depressed the whole time.	100%	10%	DP, ER	4. That's also nuts. I *did* feel better. But now I'm anxious and depressed again so I need to get back to work and challenge my distorted thoughts.	100%
5. This therapy can't work for me. My problems are too deep.	100%	20%	AON, OG, DP, FT, MAG, ER	5. The therapy was very helpful to me. Relapses are common—everyone has them.	100%
6. I'm worthless after all.	100%	35%	AON, OG, MF, DP, MAG, ER, SH, LAB, SB	6. I'm depressed, not worthless! Maybe I need to think about the problem that triggered these feelings.	100%
7. What good are a few weeks of improvement? Now I'll be depressed for another ten years.	100%	25%	DP, FT, ER, SH	7. Those three weeks of improvement were great! It was a terrific breakthrough, and a relief. Now I need to get back to work. My next improvement could last even longer. Let's take it one step at a time.	100%
8. This is unfair. Other people don't have to work so hard to be happy.	100%	50%	MR, ER, SH, LAB, OB	8. Now I'm feeling sorry for myself again. I have the right to do that, but do I really want to? It's unfortunate that I'm afflicted with a tendency toward depression, but it's not "unfair."	100%
9. There must be something wrong with me.	100%	25%	AON, OG, MF, DP, MAG, ER, SH, LAB, SB	9. Hey, I have lots of defects, but other people seem to have a lot of defects too, so I've decided to accept myself with all my warts and flaws. My real problem is bombarding myself with negative thoughts, and not my "defectiveness."	100%

Positive Thoughts (played by you): That's ridiculous. I've just had a relapse and I'm feeling upset today. This happens to everyone. I need to figure out what's bothering me and talk back to my negative thoughts again.

Remember that your friend, who's playing the role of your negative thoughts, is not really another person who's attacking you, even though it sounds that way. Your friend simply represents the negative voice in your own mind. You're really involved in a battle with yourself. If your response isn't effective, try a role reversal. That way your friend can try to model a more effective response. If you do frequent role reversals, you can often come up with effective positive thoughts fairly quickly.

To avoid confusion during the role-playing, you can write this on a piece of paper: "I am the negative thoughts. I'll use the second person, 'You.' " Then you can write on a second piece of paper: "I am the positive thoughts. I'll use the first person, 'I.' " If you hold these pages in front of you during the exercise, it will be clear that:

- One of you is playing the role of your negative thoughts and the other is playing the role of your positive thoughts.
- These are the two parts of your own mind, and you're doing battle with yourself, not with another person.
- The person who's playing the role of your negative thoughts should always speak in the second person, "You."
- The person who's playing the role of your positive thoughts should always speak in the first person, "I."

These details will be crucial to the success of the exercise. Here's an example of how the Externalization of Voices might go:

Negative Thoughts (speaking in the second person, "You"): Face it. This relapse proves that these methods couldn't possibly help you. Obviously, the therapy has failed because you're incredibly depressed and anxious right now.

Positive Thoughts (speaking in the first person, "I"): Actually, those methods were extremely helpful to me. My depression and anxiety only show that I'm having a relapse right now and that I need to get back to work with those methods again. But if I listen to your constant BS, I'll probably get discouraged and feel like giving up. So I think I'll just ignore you.

Negative Thoughts: You can try to ignore me, but you can't get away from the fact that you're a hopeless case and a worthless human being. Furthermore, the therapy never did help. You were just fooling yourself. You thought you were feeling better, but you weren't!

Positive Thoughts: Actually, I was feeling better, and I'm looking forward to working my way out of this relapse quickly so I can feel better again. I'm not "hopeless" or "worthless," but I am feeling depressed and anxious right now. Obviously, something's bugging me, and I need to figure out what it is.

Continue the dialogue until the person in the role of Negative Thoughts gives up. Switch roles as often as you need to. Don't stop until the negative thoughts have clearly been defeated.

This exercise can be extremely powerful and challenging. It isn't easy to talk back to your own negative thoughts when another person attacks you with them. So why do it? It's because this is exactly what's going to happen when you have a relapse. If you wait until the relapse occurs, your negative thoughts will seem overwhelmingly realistic and your motivation will be at its lowest level, so it will be much tougher to challenge your negative thoughts. In contrast, if you learn how to combat your negative thoughts ahead of time, when you're in a good mood, it will be much easier to put the lie to them when you're having a relapse. This may seem silly, complicated, or unnecessary, but it will give you the muscles and power you'll need to defeat the devil when the real battle comes.

You will definitely have to struggle with episodes of depression or anxiety after you recover. There's no way to prevent that. But if you pick up the tools and fight back, you usually can nip a relapse in the bud and bounce back quickly.

The Recovery Circle is also an important Relapse Prevention tool. I've emphasized that you may have to try as many as ten or fifteen techniques, and fail over and over again, before you find the one that works for you. That will require patience, persistence, and hard work. But here's some good news. Once you've found the technique that works for you, it will probably always work for you.

You probably remember Terri, the woman who was literally cured before my very eyes after I induced a panic attack during one of our sessions. When she started doing jumping jacks, she suddenly realized that she couldn't possibly be on the verge of death or suffocation, as she believed, and her panic vanished. For Terri, the Experimental Technique ended ten years of suffering. If she ever has a panic attack in the future, she'll simply have to do her jumping jacks again. She probably won't have to create another Recovery Circle, because she already knows what technique will work for her.

Besides talking back to your negative thoughts about the relapse, you'll also want to use the technique or techniques that were the most helpful to you the first time you recovered. Of course, this will be different for every person. It might be the Downward Arrow, the Double-Standard Technique, the Hidden Emotion Technique, Cognitive Flooding, the Feared Fantasy, the Acceptance Paradox, or a combination of two or three techniques.

One way to look at it is to imagine that every person, including you, has the potential for happiness, inner peace, self-esteem, and self-confidence. But sometimes it seems to be locked up in a safe, so you can't get to it. As a result, you suffer.

We're going to work together to pick the lock. We'll try one combination, but it probably won't work. Then we'll try another, but it probably won't work either. Over and over, we'll fail. But if we stick with it, eventually we'll figure out the combination. Then, all of a sudden, the door to the safe will swing wide open, and you'll feel happy and confident again.

But you have to remember the combination. Write it down so you don't forget, because the door to the safe will swing closed again. If you know the combination, this won't be a problem.

The Exposure Model

If you want to overcome any form of anxiety, sooner or later you'll have to confront the thing you fear the most. Once you've defeated the monster and your fear has vanished, you'll feel fantastic, but you shouldn't get too complacent. Give yourself frequent booster shots of repeated exposure so your confidence will grow. If you start avoiding the thing you fear again, you may give the monster new life, and your anxiety may come back.

I told you how I overcame my fear of heights in high school by standing at the top of a tall ladder while the drama teacher stood at the bottom, waiting patiently and providing a little encouragement. After that, I loved climbing on ladders and even hiking along the edge of steep cliffs in the desert near my home in Arizona. It was always a rush, and my fear of heights seemed to have vanished entirely.

When I went off to college and medical school, I stopped exposing myself to heights. This wasn't intentional—it's just that my life took a turn in a new direction, and I never had to do anything involving heights. Twenty years later, when I was vacationing with my kids in the Havasupai Canyon in Arizona, I discovered that my fear had returned with a vengeance. Of course, if you're motivated, you can always overcome the fear by using Exposure Techniques again, but it's a lot easier just to stay ahead of the game.

I also described how my public speaking anxiety turned my first academic lecture at Oxford University into a complete disaster and how I subsequently overcame my anxiety using Image Substitution. It worked like a charm. Now I give frequent talks and presentations. I conduct psychotherapy seminars every week at Stanford and give more than twenty two-day workshops for mental health professionals around the country every year. I always speak spontaneously without notes, and every presentation is a ball. I usually don't have even a trace of anxiety before I start. In fact, most of the time, I can't wait to get started.

Let's say you've begun to overcome your shyness and you're using Interpersonal Exposure Techniques, such as Smile and Hello Practice and the David Letterman Technique. You're beginning to relax and relate to people in a more natural and effective manner. If you crawl back into your shell, your negative thoughts and feelings will begin to flourish, and soon you'll be flooded with anxiety in social situations again. But if you keep challenging yourself and pushing the envelope, your social skills and feelings of confidence will continue to improve, and pretty soon your new skills will become second nature.

The Hidden Emotion Model

Remember that anxiety is often your body's way of telling you that something's bugging you. Instead of ruminating about the symptoms of anxiety—the feelings of worry, panic, or dizziness—ask yourself if you're mad at someone or if something happened recently that was upsetting to you. Try to figure out what the problem is. When you express your feelings and solve the problem, your anxiety will generally disappear. When you look at it this way, you'll realize that feelings of anxiety or panic are not a bad thing, but an important signal that something's going on that you need to attend to.

I once treated a depressed and anxious New York stockbroker named Wilson who suffered from mild chronic anxiety and panic attacks. During his panic attacks, he'd notice his heart beating rapidly and tell himself that he was on the verge of death. Then he'd rush to the nearest emergency room. After a brief physical exam, the doctor would always send him home with the reassurance that he was just fine. To make matters a bit more complicated, Wilson was receiving treatment for a cardiac rhythm abnormality, but it wasn't a life-threatening condition and it wasn't related to his panic attacks.

Wilson also suffered from mild depression and constantly obsessed about the fact that he wasn't good enough. Although he was doing reasonably well and lived in an attractive home in a nice neighborhood, several of his friends had made millions trading stock options, and he always compared himself to them. He felt inferior and believed that there was some kind of intense, wonderful feeling that only the "beautiful" people with loads of money could experience. This belief is common in our culture. Lots of people are convinced that happiness and self-esteem look an awful lot like a new Lexus in the driveway.

Wilson could see that he based his feelings of self-worth on his success. This is the Achievement Addiction, one of the most common Self-Defeating Beliefs. He also knew that his belief wasn't to his advantage, since he was constantly beating up on himself, but he was convinced that incredibly successful people with lots of money *really are* happier and more worthwhile. Of course, he had some "evidence" for this. He believed that he'd never achieved phenomenal success, and he also knew that he'd never felt truly happy or worthwhile, so he was sure that one followed from the other.

Wilson loved to ruminate about the past, and he traced his low self-esteem to his relationship with his father. He felt like he'd had to earn his father's love by getting straight As in school and he'd never experienced unconditional love. He thought that this explained his preoccupation with success. He hoped that these insights eventually would lead to greater self-esteem, but it didn't happen. Every week Wilson's scores on the Brief Mood Survey showed that his feelings of depression and anxiety hadn't improved at all.

I used many Cognitive Behavior Therapy techniques to help Wilson challenge the thought "I'm inferior to all the people who have accomplished so much more." We tried the Downward Arrow Technique, Examine the Evidence, the Cost-Benefit Analysis, the Externalization of Voices, the Feared Fantasy, and the Acceptance Paradox, to name just a few. Wilson loved these techniques, and the sessions always seemed tremendously interesting and rewarding. But he just couldn't put the lie to the negative thoughts that were making his life so miserable, and he kept struggling with anxiety and depression.

One day Wilson had a confidential meeting with his boss and learned that the company was facing a financial crunch because of the recession. His boss told him that he was pretty sure he could save the company, but they'd all have to lower their expectations for a period of time. He explained that he was going to have to ask Wilson and all his colleagues to agree to a 20% pay cut so the company could get back in the black. He promised that when the company was doing better, he'd increase Wilson's salary. Wilson admired his boss and wanted to help the company, so he agreed.

Six weeks later, Wilson went out for a beer with his colleague, Dean, after work. Wilson asked Dean how he felt about the pay cut. Dean said that he'd flat-out refused to take any pay cut. He said that as far as he knew, all the other stockbrokers had objected to it as well. It suddenly dawned on Wilson that he was the *only* person who'd agreed to the pay cut, and he felt like a fall guy. He suddenly began to feel panicky and started obsessing about his heart. He told Dean that he wasn't feeling well and drove to the nearest emergency room to have his heart checked out. Of course, Wilson got a clean bill of health, but he continued to feel anxious and depressed.

This story suddenly cast Wilson's problems into an entirely different light. It dawned on me that his symptoms nearly always intensified right after he'd had a conflict with someone—his wife, a friend, or his boss. But he always acted nice and swept his feelings under the rug. Then the feelings of anxiety and inadequacy suddenly would flare up and start eating away at him.

I asked Wilson if he'd thought about the relationship between his feelings about the pay cut and the sudden increase in his symptoms of anxiety and depression. He said he'd never considered the possibility that there might be a connection! I also asked him if he was planning to talk the problem over with his boss, so he could say that he felt taken advantage of. This caused an instant spike in Wilson's anxiety, and he had a dozen excuses about why it wouldn't be helpful or appropriate. He said that he didn't want to rock the boat and explained that he admired his boss and thought that he was doing his best to run the company. He said that he didn't have as much seniority as his colleagues and that the crisis would soon be over anyway. He said he was sure that his boss would restore his salary as soon as he could.

I told Wilson that he was bullshitting and asked if he wanted violin accompaniment while he made excuses. I explained that he was ultimately in charge, and he'd have to do whatever he thought was right, but it seemed pretty obvious that he was conflict-phobic. I was concerned that he might not be able to overcome his chronic feelings of inadequacy and anxiety until he started sticking up for himself and telling people how he really felt. I told him that I knew it would be frightening, since he'd finally have to open up and confront the monster he'd been avoiding. Wilson reluctantly admitted that it made sense to talk things over with his boss and said he was going to do it, even though he dreaded it.

At our next session, Wilson was pleased to report that the meeting had gone much better than he'd expected. His boss seemed embarrassed and agreed to refund all the salary he'd withheld. He told Wilson how much he valued his contribution to the company and hoped they could continue to work together. Wilson experienced a sudden surge of self-confidence, and his scores on the depression and anxiety tests fell to zero for the first time. The emotional problems that Wilson and I had been working on for six months with so little success suddenly vanished. Wilson told me that he felt better than he'd felt in years.

Wilson was thrilled that he'd finally recovered but was somewhat disappointed to discover that the solution to his problems was so simple. He loved talking about his childhood and exploring deep philosophical issues during our sessions. I really liked Wilson and also enjoyed our sessions, but they never led to any improvement, much less a cure. In contrast, when we used the Hidden Emotion Technique, his symptoms disappeared within twenty-four hours.

Now, I have several questions for you. Please pick up a pen or pencil and answer them in the spaces below.

1. Wilson has finally recovered. All his feelings of anxiety, panic, and inferiority have disappeared. In your opinion, how likely is it that he'll relapse in the future? Make your prediction below. Put a number between 0% (meaning that a relapse is not at all likely) and 100% (meaning that Wilson will definitely relapse).

   I believe that the probability that Wilson will relapse is: _____%

2. If Wilson experiences a relapse and has an episode of anxiety and depression in the future, what will cause it?

   _____

   _____

   _____

   _____

3. If Wilson experiences a relapse in the future, what will cure it?

   _____

   _____

   _____

   _____

Answers

1. The answer is 100%. Sooner or later, Wilson will feel anxious and depressed again. The real question is not *whether* he'll relapse, but *when* he'll relapse and whether he'll be prepared to handle it.

2. Wilson's feelings of anxiety and depression probably will always occur when he's at odds with someone and sweeps his feelings under the rug because he wants to be nice and avoid conflict. Of course, Wilson's mind will be flooded with negative thoughts again, and you could say

that his anxiety and depression will result from his thoughts. But the real question is: What will cause the upsurge in his negative thoughts and feelings? In Wilson's case, there will nearly always be a conflict he's trying to dodge.

3. The Hidden Emotion Technique turned out to be the solution to Wilson's problems, so this will probably be the *only* technique he'll ever need to help him deal with anxiety and depression for the rest of his life. Every time he starts to get anxious, it will probably mean that he's upset with someone but hasn't expressed his feelings. The moment he addresses the problem, his negative feelings will disappear again.

Here's your last homework assignment! I want you to prepare a memo to yourself entitled "My Blueprint for Recovery." Include a description of:

- The kinds of events that typically trigger your feelings of depression or anxiety. For example, you may be especially vulnerable to failure, criticism, or rejection.
- How you usually feel when you're upset. For example, you may feel inferior, anxious, panicky, hurt, inadequate, angry, worthless, or hopeless.
- The kinds of negative thoughts you typically have. For example, you may tell yourself that you're no good and that everyone will look down on you.
- The method or methods that helped you put the lie to your negative thoughts. This is the technique you'll want to try right away whenever you get upset in the future. It may have been the Downward Arrow Technique, the Experimental Technique, the Double-Standard Technique, the Cost-Benefit Analysis, the Feared Fantasy, the Acceptance Paradox, Self-Disclosure, or any of the 40 Ways to Defeat Your Fears.

Keep this memo handy so you can read it when you relapse. Make sure you include a Relapse Daily Mood Log for yourself, like the one on page 400. Include a list of the kinds of negative thoughts that usually plague you, as well as the positive thoughts you can use to combat them. Review this memo the next time you fall into a black hole. It's like having a ladder handy, so you can climb right out again!

REFERENCES

Introduction

1. F. Scogin, D. Hamblin, and L. Beutler, "Bibliotherapy for Depressed Older Adults: A Self-Help Alternative," *The Gerontologist* 27 (1987): 383–387.

F. Scogin, C. Jamison, and K. Gochneaut, "The Comparative Efficacy of Cognitive and Behavioral Bibliotherapy for Mildly and Moderately Depressed Older Adults," *Journal of Consulting and Clinical Psychology* 57 (1989): 403–407.

F. Scogin, C. Jamison, and N. Davis, "A Two-Year Follow-up of the Effects of Bibliotherapy for Depressed Older Adults," *Journal of Consulting and Clinical Psychology* 58 (1990): 665–667.

F. Scogin, C. Jamison, M. Floyd, and W. Chaplin, "Measuring Learning in Depression Treatment: A Cognitive Bibliotherapy Test," *Cognitive Therapy and Research* 22 (1998): 475–482.

N. M. Smith, M. R. Floyd, C. Jamison, and F. Scogin, "Three-Year Follow-up of Bibliotherapy for Depression," *Journal of Consulting and Clinical Psychology* 65 (1997): 324–327.

2. R. J. DeRubeis, S. D. Hollon, J. D. Amsterdam, R. C. Shelton, P. R. Young, R. M. Salomon, J. P. O'Reardon, M. L. Lovett, M. M. Gladis, L. L. Brown, and R. Gallop, "Cognitive Therapy vs. Medications in the Treatment of Moderate to Severe Depression," *Archives of General Psychiatry* 62 (2005): 409–416. Web abstract: http://arch psych.ama-assn.org/cgi/content/abstract/62/4/409.

S. D. Hollon, R. J. DeRubeis, R. C. Shelton, J. D. Amsterdam, R. M. Salomon, J. P. O'Reardon, M. L. Lovett, P. R. Young, K. L. Haman, B. B. Freeman, and R. Gallop, "Prevention of Relapse Following Cognitive Therapy vs. Medications in Moderate to Severe

Depression," *Archives of General Psychiatry* 62 (2005): 417–422. Web abstract: http://archpsych.ama-assn.org/cgi/content/abstract/62/4/417.

3. As quoted in *Medical News Today,* July 8, 2005, "Cognitive Therapy as Good as Antidepressants, Effects Last Longer." Web link: http://medicalnewstoday.com/medicalnews.php?newsid=22319#.

4. H. A. Westra and S. H. Stewart, "Cognitive Behavioral Therapy and Pharma-cotherapy: Complementary or Contradictory Approaches to the Treatment of Anxiety?" *Clinical Psychology Review* 18, no. 3 (1998): 307–340.

Chapter 1

1. H. A. Westra and S. H. Stewart, "Cognitive Behavioral Therapy and Pharma-cotherapy: Complementary or Contradictory Approaches to the Treatment of Anxiety?" *Clinical Psychology Review* 18, no. 3 (1998): 307–340.

Chapter 4

1. J. Mendels, J. L. Stinnett, D. D. Burns, and A. Frazer, "Amine Precursors and De-pression," *Archives of General Psychiatry* 32 (1975): 22–30.

2. Hypericum Depression Trial Study Group, "Effect of *Hypericum perforatum* (St. John's Wort) in Major Depressive Disorder: A Randomized, Controlled Trial," *Journal of the American Medical Association* 287 (2002): 1807–1814. Online summary: http://www.nih.gov/news/pr/apr2002/nccam-09.htm.

3. I. Kirsch and G. Sapirstein, "Listening to Prozac but Hearing Placebo: A Meta-Analysis of Antidepressant Medication," *Prevention and Treatment* 1 (1998), article 0002a. Online article: http://journals.apa.org/prevention/volume1/pre0010002a.html.

I. Kirsch, T. J. Moore, A. Scoboria, and S. S. Nicholls, "The Emperor's New Drugs: An Analysis of Antidepressant Medication Data Submitted to the U.S. Food and Drug Administration," *Prevention and Treatment* 5 (2002), article 23. Online article: http://journals.apa.org/prevention/volume5/pre0050023a.html.

4. S. H. Preskorn, "Clinically Relevant Pharmacology of Selective Serotonin Reup-take Inhibitors: An Overview with Emphasis on Pharmacokinetics and Effects on Ox-idative Drug Metabolism," *Clinical Pharmacokinetics* 32, suppl. 1 (1997): 1–21.

I. Kirsch and G. Sapirstein, "Listening to Prozac but Hearing Placebo: A Meta-Analysis of Antidepressant Medication," *Prevention and Treatment* 1 (1998), article 0002a. Online article: http://journals.apa.org/prevention/volume1/pre0010002a.html.

I. Kirsch, T. J. Moore, A. Scoboria, and S. S. Nicholls, "The Emperor's New Drugs: An Analysis of Antidepressant Medication Data Submitted to the U.S. Food and Drug Administration," *Prevention and Treatment* 5 (2002), article 23. Online article: http://journals.apa.org/prevention/volume5/pre0050023a.html.

5. D. O. Antonuccio, W. G. Danton, and G. Y. DeNelsky, "Psychotherapy versus

Medication for Depression: Challenging the Conventional Wisdom with Data," *Professional Psychology: Research and Practice* 26 (1995): 574–585.

D. O. Antonuccio, W. G. Danton, G. Y. DeNelsky, R. Greenberg, and J. S. Gordon, "Raising Questions about Antidepressants," *Psychotherapy and Psychosomatics* 68 (1999): 3–14.

D. O. Antonuccio, D. Burns, and W. G. Danton, "Antidepressants: A Triumph of Marketing over Science?" *Prevention and Treatment* 5 (2002), article 25. Online article: http://journals.apa.org/prevention/volume5/toc-jul15-02.htm.

6. E. J. Garland, "Facing the Evidence: Antidepressant Treatment in Children and Adolescents," *Canadian Medical Association Journal* 170 (2004): 489–491.

N. Jureidini, C. J. Doecke, P. R. Mansfield, M. M. Haby, D. B. Menkes, and A. L. Tonkin, "Efficacy and Safety of Antidepressants in Children and Adolescents," *British Medical Journal* 328 (2004): 879–883.

C. J. Whittington, T. Kendall, P. Fonagy, D. Cottrell, A. Colgrove, and E. Boddington, "Selective Serotonin Reuptake Inhibitors in Childhood Depression: Systematic Review of Published versus Unpublished Data," *Lancet* 363 (2004): 1341–1345.

7. D. Healy, "Lines of Evidence on the Risk of Suicide with Selective Serotonin Reuptake Inhibitors," *Psychotherapy and Psychosomatics* 72 (2003): 71–79.

8. H. A. Westra and S. H. Stewart, "Cognitive Behavioral Therapy and Pharmacotherapy: Complementary or Contradictory Approaches to the Treatment of Anxiety?" *Clinical Psychology Review* 18, no. 3 (1998): 307–340.

9. D. O. Antonuccio, W. G. Danton, and G. Y. DeNelsky, "Psychotherapy versus Medication for Depression: Challenging the Conventional Wisdom with Data," *Professional Psychology: Research and Practice* 26 (1995): 574–585.

10. R. J. DeRubeis, S. D. Hollon, J. D. Amsterdam, R. C. Shelton, P. R. Young, R. M. Salomon, J. P. O'Reardon, M. L. Lovett, M. M. Gladis, L. L. Brown, and R. Gallop, "Cognitive Therapy vs. Medications in the Treatment of Moderate to Severe Depression," *Archives of General Psychiatry* 62 (2005): 409–416. Web abstract: http://arch psych.ama-assn.org/cgi/content/abstract/62/4/409.

S. D. Hollon, R. J. DeRubeis, R. C. Shelton, J. D. Amsterdam, R. M. Salomon, J. P. O'Reardon, M. L. Lovett, P. R. Young, K. L. Haman, B. B. Freeman, and R. Gallop, "Prevention of Relapse Following Cognitive Therapy vs. Medications in Moderate to Severe Depression," *Archives of General Psychiatry* 62 (2005): 417–422. Web abstract: http://archpsych.ama-assn.org/cgi/content/abstract/62/4/417.

11. F. Scogin, D. Hamblin, and L. Beutler, "Bibliotherapy for Depressed Older Adults: A Self-Help Alternative," *The Gerontologist* 27 (1987): 383–387.

F. Scogin, C. Jamison, and K. Gochneaut, "The Comparative Efficacy of Cognitive and Behavioral Bibliotherapy for Mildly and Moderately Depressed Older Adults," *Journal of Consulting and Clinical Psychology* 57 (1989): 403–407.

F. Scogin, C. Jamison, and N. Davis, "A Two-Year Follow-up of the Effects of Bibliotherapy for Depressed Older Adults," *Journal of Consulting and Clinical Psychology* 58 (1990): 665–667.

F. Scogin, C. Jamison, M. Floyd, and W. Chaplin, "Measuring Learning in Depression Treatment: A Cognitive Bibliotherapy Test," *Cognitive Therapy and Research* 22 (1998): 475–482.

N. M. Smith, M. R. Floyd, C. Jamison, and F. Scogin, "Three-Year Follow-up of Bibliotherapy for Depression," *Journal of Consulting and Clinical Psychology* 65 (1997): 324–327.

YOUR ANXIETY TOOLKIT

This section contains extra blank copies of some of the forms you may need. If you don't write in them, you can photocopy extras for your own personal use while you're working with the methods in this book. Mental health professionals who want to obtain a license for photocopying these and many other treatment and assessment tools can obtain further information plus an order form by sending an e-mail to: Toolkit@FeelingGood.com.

Brief Mood Survey

Instructions. Put today's date in one of the columns to the right. Then put your score on each item in the boxes below the date, based on how you've been feeling recently. Total your score in the box at the bottom. **Please answer all of the items.**	Put Today's Date Here							
Score each item like this: 0 = Not at all; 1= Somewhat; 2 = Moderately; 3 = A lot; 4 = Extremely								

Anxious Feelings

1. Anxious								
2. Nervous								
3. Worried								
4. Frightened or apprehensive								
5. Tense or on edge								
Total for today ➜								

Anxious Physical Symptoms

1. Skipping, racing, or pounding of the heart								
2. Sweating, chills, or hot flushes								
3. Trembling or shaking								
4. Feeling short of breath or difficulty breathing								
5. Feeling like you're choking								
6. Pain or tightness in the chest								
7. Butterflies, nausea, or upset stomach								
8. Feeling dizzy, light-headed, or off-balance								
9. Feeling like you're unreal or the world is unreal								
10. Numbness or tingling sensations								
Total for today ➜								

Depression

1. Sad or down in the dumps								
2. Discouraged or hopeless								
3. Low self-esteem								
4. Worthless or inadequate								
5. Loss of pleasure or satisfaction in life								
Total for today ➜								

Suicidal Urges

1. Do you have any suicidal thoughts?								
2. Would you like to end your life?								
Total for today ➜								

How to Use the Daily Mood Log

The Daily Mood Log (DML) is the most basic and important technique of all. It consists of five steps.

Step 1. **Upsetting Event.** If you want help with anxiety, describe a specific moment when you felt anxious. If you want help with depression, describe a specific moment when you felt depressed. If you want help with a relationship problem, describe a specific moment when you were feeling upset or not getting along with that person.

Write a brief description of the situation at the top of the DML. Vague, general descriptions of your problems won't work. Remember that the problem must be specific as to person, place, and time. Ask yourself, "What time of day did it happen? Where was I? Who was I interacting with? What was going on?"

Step 2. **Emotions.** Circle the words that describe how you're feeling, and rate each feeling on a scale from 0% (not at all) to 100% (the worst). Put your ratings in the "% Before" column.

Step 3. **Negative Thoughts.** Try to tune in to your negative thoughts. What are you telling yourself when you feel upset? Remember that each type of negative feeling will be associated with a specific type of negative thought. For example:

- **Anxiety, nervousness, or worry.** You tell yourself that you're in danger or that something terrible is about to happen.
- **Panic.** You tell yourself that you're about to die, suffocate, pass out, lose control or go crazy.
- **Embarrassment.** You tell yourself that you looked like an idiot in front of other people.
- **Shyness.** You tell yourself that other people will see how nervous and insecure you feel and look down on you.
- **Loneliness.** You tell yourself that you're unlovable and doomed to be alone forever.

- **Depression.** You tell yourself that you've lost something important to your sense of self-esteem.

- **Hopelessness.** You tell yourself that your problems will never be solved and that your suffering will go on forever.

- **Guilt.** You tell yourself that you're a bad person and that you've violated your own value system.

- **Shame.** You tell yourself that other people will see how inadequate or bad you are and look down on you.

- **Inferiority.** You tell yourself that you're not as good as other people or not as good as you think you should be.

- **Worthlessness.** You tell yourself that you're inherently flawed or defective.

- **Frustration.** You tell yourself that the world should be the way you expect it to be.

- **Anger.** You tell yourself that other people are self-centered jerks who are treating you unfairly or intentionally taking advantage of you.

- **Feeling trapped.** You tell yourself that you have to give in to the demands of your spouse, lover, friend, or family member.

Record your negative thoughts and estimate how much you believe each one on a scale from 0% (not at all) to 100% (completely). Put your ratings in the "% Before" column.

Step 4.   **Distortions.** Identify the distortions in each negative thought, using the Checklist of Cognitive Distortions on the bottom of the second page of the DML. Use abbreviations, such as AON for All-or-Nothing Thinking, OG for Overgeneralization, and so forth.

Step 5.   **Positive Thoughts.** Challenge each negative thought with a more positive and realistic thought. Indicate how strongly you believe each positive thought on a scale from 0% (not at all) to 100% (completely). Put these ratings in the "% Belief" column. Remember that the positive thought won't help you unless it fulfills the necessary and sufficient conditions for emotional change.

- **Necessary Condition:** The positive thought must be 100% true.
- **Sufficient Condition:** The positive thought must put the lie to the negative thought.

Now rate your belief in the negative thought again, using the "% After" column. If the positive thought wasn't effective, try again. Often you'll have to challenge a negative thought from many different angles before you discover how to put the lie to it. This is one of the most important—and least understood—ideas behind Cognitive Behavior Therapy.

Recovery Circle

The Recovery Circle will help you with Step 5 of the Daily Mood Log. Choose the negative thought that you want to work on first. Put it in the middle of a Recovery Circle. Select at least fifteen techniques you could use to challenge the thought. Put the name of one technique in each box. Be sure to include at least twelve to fifteen Cognitive Techniques, two or three Exposure Techniques, and the Hidden Emotion Technique.

The one-page list of 40 Ways to Defeat Your Fears appears on page 425. You can also review the longer list of techniques that includes the definitions, starting on page 356.

Over time, you'll get better and better at choosing techniques that are likely to be effective. The table on page 426 lists the types of techniques that are the most likely to be effective for different distortions, such as All-or-Nothing Thinking, Fortune-Telling, or Should Statements. The table on page 427 lists the types of techniques that are the most likely to be effective for different problems, such as shyness, obsessive-compulsive disorder, or depression. However, I wouldn't take these tables too literally, because the techniques that work for any individual are always unpredictable. However, once you find the techniques that work for you, they'll probably always work for you.

Daily Mood Log

Upsetting Event: _____

Emotions	% Before	% After		Emotions	% Before	% After
Sad, blue, depressed, down, unhappy				**Embarrassed,** foolish, humiliated, self-conscious		
Anxious, worried, panicky, nervous, frightened				**Hopeless,** discouraged, pessimistic, despairing		
Guilty, remorseful, bad, ashamed				**Frustrated,** stuck, thwarted, defeated		
Inferior, worthless, inadequate, defective, incompetent				**Angry,** mad, resentful, annoyed, irritated, upset, furious		
Lonely, unloved, unwanted, rejected, alone, abandoned				**Other (describe)**		

Negative Thoughts	% Before	% After	Distortions	Positive Thoughts	% Belief
1.				1.	
2.				2.	
3.				3.	
4.				4.	
5.				5.	

Negative Thoughts	% Before	% After	Distortions	Positive Thoughts	% Belief
6.				6.	
7.				7.	
8.				8.	

Checklist of Cognitive Distortions

1. **All-or-Nothing Thinking.** You view things in absolute, black-and-white categories.

2. **Overgeneralization.** You view a negative event as a never-ending pattern of defeat: "This *always* happens!"

3. **Mental Filter.** You dwell on the negatives and ignore the positives.

4. **Discounting the Positive.** You insist that your positive qualities don't count.

5. **Jumping to Conclusions.** You jump to conclusions not warranted by the facts.
   - **Mind-Reading.** You assume that people are reacting negatively to you.
   - **Fortune-Telling.** You predict that things will turn out badly.

6. **Magnification and Minimization.** You blow things out of proportion or shrink them.

7. **Emotional Reasoning.** You reason from your feelings: "I *feel* like an idiot, so I must really *be* one."

8. **Should Statements.** You use shoulds, shouldn'ts, musts, oughts, and have tos.

9. **Labeling.** Instead of saying "I made a mistake," you say, "I'm a jerk," or "I'm a loser."

10. **Blame.** You find fault instead of solving the problem.
    - **Self-Blame.** You blame yourself for something you weren't entirely responsible for.
    - **Other-Blame.** You blame others and overlook ways you contributed to the problem.

Daily Mood Log Continuation Sheet

Negative Thoughts	% Before	% After	Distortions	Positive Thoughts	% Belief

Recovery Circle

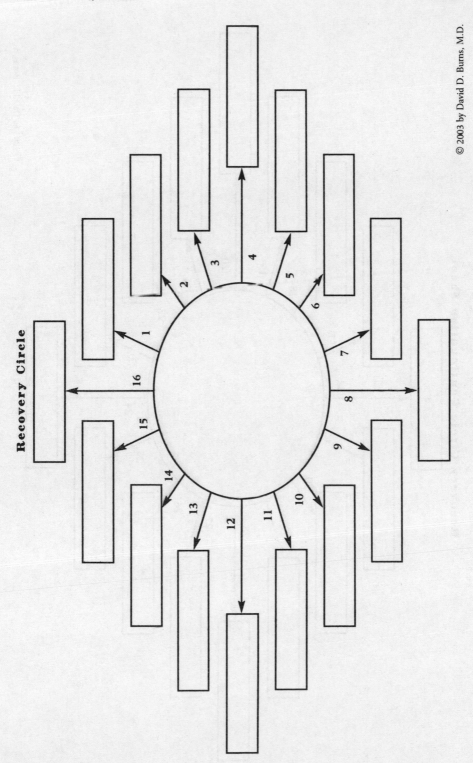

Recovery Circle Continuation Sheet

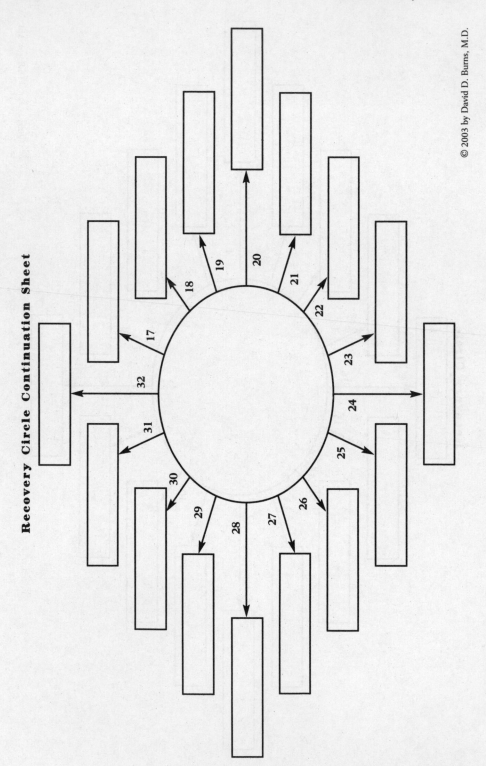

40 Ways to Defeat Your Fears

Cognitive Model	Motivational Techniques
Uncovering Techniques	20. Cost-Benefit Analysis (CBA)
1. Downward Arrow Technique	21. Paradoxical CBA
2. What-If Technique	22. Devil's Advocate
Compassion-Based Technique	**Anti-Procrastination Techniques**
3. Double-Standard Technique	23. Pleasure-Predicting Sheet
Truth-Based Techniques	24. Little Steps for Big Feats
4. Examine the Evidence	25. Anti-Procrastination Sheet
5. Experimental Technique	26. Problem-Solution List
6. Survey Technique	**Exposure Model**
7. Reattribution	**Classical Exposure**
Semantic Techniques	27. Gradual Exposure
8. Semantic Method	28. Flooding
9. Let's Define Terms	29. Response Prevention
10. Be Specific	30. Distraction
Logic-Based Techniques	**Cognitive Exposure**
11. Thinking in Shades of Gray	31. Cognitive Flooding
12. Process versus Outcome	32. Image Substitution
Quantitative Techniques	33. Memory Rescripting
13. Self-Monitoring	34. Feared Fantasy
14. Worry Breaks	**Interpersonal Exposure**
Humor-Based Techniques	35. Smile and Hello Practice
15. Shame-Attacking Exercises[a]	36. Flirting Training
16. Paradoxical Magnification	37. Rejection Practice
17. Humorous Imaging	38. Self-Disclosure
Role-Playing Technique[b]	39. David Letterman Technique
18. Externalization of Voices	**Hidden Emotion Model**
Spiritual Technique	40. Hidden Emotion Technique
19. Acceptance Paradox	

[a] This technique could also be classified as an Interpersonal Exposure Technique.
[b] Other techniques that work well in role-playing include the Double-Standard Technique, the Acceptance Paradox, Devil's Advocate, the Feared Fantasy, Flirting Training, and the David Letterman Technique.

© 2005 by David D. Burns, M.D.

Selecting Techniques Based on the Distortions in Your Negative Thought

Distortions	Cognitive Techniques										Exposure Techniques				Hidden Emotion
	Uncovering	Compassion-Based	Truth-Based	Semantic	Logic-Based	Quantitative	Humor-Based	Role-Playing	Spiritual	Motivational	Anti-Procrastination	Classical Exposure	Cognitive Exposure	Interpersonal Exposure	Hidden Emotion
1. All-or-Nothing Thinking	✓	✓	✓	✓	✓			✓	✓	✓					
2. Overgeneralization	✓	✓	✓	✓				✓	✓	✓					
3. Mental Filter	✓	✓	✓	✓	✓	✓		✓	✓	✓					
4. Discounting the Positive	✓	✓	✓	✓	✓	✓		✓	✓	✓					
5. Jumping to Conclusions															
• Mind-Reading	✓	✓	✓	✓		✓	✓	✓	✓	✓	✓	✓	✓	✓	✓
• Fortune-Telling	✓	✓	✓	✓		✓	✓	✓	✓	✓	✓	✓	✓	✓	✓
6. Magnification and Minimization	✓	✓	✓		✓	✓	✓	✓	✓	✓	✓	✓	✓		
7. Emotional Reasoning	✓	✓	✓	✓	✓		✓	✓	✓	✓	✓	✓			
8. Should Statements	✓	✓	✓				✓	✓	✓	✓	✓				
9. Labeling	✓	✓	✓	✓	✓	✓	✓	✓				✓			
10. Blame															
• Self-Blame	✓	✓	✓	✓			✓	✓	✓	✓					
• Other-Blame	✓	✓	✓	✓			✓	✓	✓	✓					

Selecting Techniques Based on the Problem You're Working On

Your Problem	Cognitive Techniques											Exposure Techniques			Hidden Emotion
	Uncovering	Compassion-Based	Truth-Based	Semantic	Logic-Based	Quantitative	Humor-Based	Role-Playing	Spiritual	Motivational	Anti-Procrastination	Classical Exposure	Cognitive Exposure	Interpersonal Exposure	Hidden Emotion
Chronic Worrying	✓	✓	✓			✓		✓		✓		✓	✓		✓
Panic Attacks	✓	✓	✓					✓	✓	✓		✓	✓		✓
Agoraphobia	✓	✓	✓					✓		✓		✓	✓		✓
Fears and Phobias	✓	✓	✓					✓	✓	✓		✓	✓		✓
Shyness	✓	✓	✓	✓	✓		✓	✓	✓	✓		✓	✓	✓	✓
Performance Anxiety and Public Speaking Anxiety	✓	✓				✓	✓	✓	✓	✓		✓	✓		✓
Obsessions and Compulsions (OCD)	✓	✓	✓	✓	✓	✓		✓		✓			✓		✓
Post-Traumatic Stress Disorder (PTSD)	✓	✓						✓	✓	✓			✓		✓
Hypochondriasis	✓	✓	✓					✓		✓		✓	✓		✓
Body Dysmorphic Disorder (BDD)	✓	✓	✓	✓	✓	✓	✓	✓	✓	✓		✓	✓		✓
Depression and Feelings of Shame	✓	✓	✓	✓	✓		✓	✓	✓	✓	✓		✓		✓
Habits and Addictions				✓				✓	✓	✓	✓				

Checklist of Cognitive Distortions

1. **All-or-Nothing Thinking.** You look at things in absolute, black-and-white categories. If you're not a complete success, you think you're a total failure.

2. **Overgeneralization.** You view a single negative event as a never-ending pattern of defeat. You may tell yourself, "This *always* happens" or "I'll *never* get it right."

3. **Mental Filter.** This is like the drop of ink that discolors the entire beaker of water. You dwell on one negative detail, such as an error you made, and ignore all the things you did right.

4. **Discounting the Positive.** You insist that your accomplishments or positive qualities don't count.

5. **Jumping to Conclusions.** You jump to conclusions that aren't warranted by the facts. There are two types:

   • **Mind-Reading.** You assume that people are terribly judgmental and are looking down on you.

   • **Fortune-Telling.** You tell yourself that something terrible is about to happen: "I just *know* I'm going to blow it when I take my test next week."

6. **Magnification and Minimization.** You blow things way out of proportion or shrink their importance. This is also called the binocular trick. When you look through one end of the binoculars, all your shortcomings seem as huge as Mt. Everest. When you look through the other end, all your strengths and positive qualities seem to shrink down to nothing.

7. **Emotional Reasoning.** You reason from how you feel, such as "I *feel* anxious, so I must really *be* in danger." Or "I *feel* like a loser, so I must really *be* one."

8. **Should Statements.** You criticize yourself or other people with "shoulds," "shouldn'ts," "oughts," "musts," and "have-tos." For example, "I *shouldn't* feel so shy and nervous. What's wrong with me?"

9. **Labeling.** You generalize from a single flaw or shortcoming to your entire identity. Instead of saying "I made a mistake," you label yourself as "a loser." This is an extreme form of Overgeneralization.

10. **Blame.** Instead of pinpointing the cause of a problem, you assign blame. There are two basic patterns of blame:

    • **Self-Blame.** You blame yourself for something you weren't responsible for or beat up on yourself relentlessly whenever you make a mistake.

    • **Other-Blame.** You blame others and deny your own role in the problem.

Common Self-Defeating Beliefs (SDBs)

Achievement	Depression
1. **Performance Perfectionism.** I must never fail or make a mistake. 2. **Perceived Perfectionism.** People won't love or accept me if I'm flawed or vulnerable. 3. **Achievement Addiction.** My worth as a human being depends on my achievements, intelligence, talent, status, income, or looks.	13. **Hopelessness.** My problems could never be solved. I could never feel truly happy or fulfilled. 14. **Worthlessness/Inferiority.** I'm basically worthless, defective, and inferior to others.

Love	Anxiety
4. **Approval Addiction.** I need everyone's approval to be worthwhile. 5. **Love Addiction.** I can't feel happy and fulfilled without being loved. If I'm not loved, then life is not worth living. 6. **Fear of Rejection.** If you reject me, it proves that there's something wrong with me. If I'm alone, I'm bound to feel miserable and worthless.	15. **Emotional Perfectionism.** I should always feel happy, confident, and in control. 16. **Anger Phobia.** Anger is dangerous and should be avoided at all costs. 17. **Emotophobia.** I should never feel sad, anxious, inadequate, jealous, or vulnerable. I should sweep my feelings under the rug and not upset anyone. 18. **Perceived Narcissism.** The people I care about are demanding, manipulative, and powerful. 19. **Brushfire Fallacy.** People are clones who all think alike. If one person looks down on me, the word will spread like brushfire and soon everyone will. 20. **Spotlight Fallacy.** Talking to people is like having to perform under a bright spotlight. If I don't impress them by being sophisticated, witty, or interesting, they won't like me. 21. **Magical Thinking.** If I worry enough, everything will turn out okay.

Submissiveness	
7. **Pleasing Others.** I should always try to please you, even if I make myself miserable in the process. 8. **Conflict Phobia.** People who love each other should never fight or argue. 9. **Self-Blame.** The problems in my relationships are bound to be my fault.	

Demandingness	Other
10. **Other-Blame.** The problems in my relationships are always the other person's fault. 11. **Entitlement.** You should always treat me in the way I expect. 12. **Truth.** I'm right and you're wrong.	22. **Low Frustration Tolerance.** I should never be frustrated. Life should always be easy. 23. **Superman/Superwoman.** I should always be strong and never be weak.

Cost-Benefit Analysis

Describe the attitude, feeling, or habit that you want to change: _____

Advantages	Disadvantages

My Fear Hierarchy

Describe your fear: _____

List the least frightening activity as Level 1 and the most frightening as Level 10.

Level	What I Fear
1	
2	
3	
4	
5	
6	
7	
8	
9	
10	

Exposure Log

Instructions. Record the date and Fear Hierarchy level you're working on. Every minute or two, record the time and how anxious you feel on a scale from 0% (not at all anxious) to 100% (intense anxiety). Describe any frightening thoughts or fantasies you have. For example, if you're riding an elevator, you may think, "The walls are closing in," or "The elevator will get stuck and I'll be trapped in here," or "I'll run out of air."

Date _____ **Fear Hierarchy Level** _____

Time	Anxiety (0–100%)	Frightening Thoughts and Fantasies

Phobia Log

Instructions. Rate your anxiety at the beginning and end of each exposure session on a scale from 0% (not at all) to 100% (the worst anxiety possible). Describe any frightening thoughts or fantasies you had.

Type of Exposure: _____

Date	Time Spent	Anxiety at Start (0–100%)	Anxiety at End (0–100%)	Frightening Thoughts and Fantasies

Five Secrets of Effective Communication (EAR)

E = Empathy

1. **The Disarming Technique (DT).** Find some truth in what the other person is saying, even if it seems totally unreasonable or unfair.
2. **Empathy.** Put yourself in the other person's shoes and try to see the world through his or her eyes.
   - **Thought Empathy (TE).** Paraphrase the other person's words.
   - **Feeling Empathy (FE).** Acknowledge how the other person probably is feeling, based on what he or she said.
3. **Inquiry (IN).** Ask gentle, probing questions to learn more about what the other person is thinking and feeling.

A = Assertiveness

4. **"I Feel" Statements (IF).** Express your own ideas and feelings in a direct, tactful manner. Use "I Feel" Statements, such as "I feel upset," rather than "you" statements, such as "You're wrong!" or "You're making me furious!"

R = Respect

5. **Stroking (ST).** Convey an attitude of respect, even if you feel frustrated or angry with the other person. Find something genuinely positive to say to the other person, even in the heat of battle.

© 1991 by David D. Burns, M.D. Revised 2001.

Pleasure-Predicting Sheet

Belief: _____

Activity Schedule activities with the potential for pleasure, learning, or personal growth.	Companion Use "self" for things you plan to do alone.	Predicted Satisfaction (0%–100%) Record **before** each activity.	Actual Satisfaction (0%–100%) Record **after** each activity.

© 2003 by David D. Burns, M.D.

Anti-Procrastination Sheet

Task Break the task into small steps that you can complete in a few minutes.	Predicted Difficulty (0%–100%)	Predicted Satisfaction (0%–100%)	Actual Difficulty (0%–100%)	Actual Satisfaction (0%–100%)
1.				
2.				
3.				
4.				
5.				
6.				
7.				

INDEX

Page numbers in *italics* refer to checklists, forms, and work sheets.

ABOUT THE AUTHOR

David D. Burns, M.D., is an Adjunct Clinical Professor of Psychiatry and Behavioral Sciences at the Stanford University School of Medicine and has served as Visiting Scholar at Harvard Medical School. Dr. Burns has been a pioneer in the development of Cognitive Behavioral Therapy, a drug-free treatment for depression and anxiety which has become the most widely used and extensively researched form of psychotherapy in history.

Dr. Burns has won numerous research, teaching. and media awards, but is best known for his successful self-help books, including *Feeling Good* and the *Feeling Good Handbook*, which have sold more than 5 million copies in the United States alone. In a national survey of American mental health professionals Dr. Burns's *Feeling Good* was the top-rated book, from a list of 1,000 self-help books, for patients suffering from depression. In addition, American and Canadian mental health professionals prescribe *Feeling Good* for their patients more often than any other self-help book.

In recent years, more than 50,000 mental health professionals have attended his training programs throughout the United States and Canada. More than 100 articles about his work have appeared in magazines such as *Reader's Digest*, *Psychology Today*, and others. He has been interviewed by numerous radio and television personalities including Oprah Winfrey, Mike Wallace, Charlie Rose, Maury Povich, and Phil Donahue.

ALSO BY DAVID D. BURNS, M.D.

We all have someone we can't get along with, whether it's a friend, boss, or family member. Based on twenty-five years of clinical experience and groundbreaking research, *Feeling Good Together* presents an entirely new theory for how we can form far more loving and satisfying relationships.

Feeling Good Together
$13.99 paperback (Canada: $17.99)
ISBN: 978-0-7679-2082-7

THREE RIVERS PRESS • NEW YORK

Available wherever books are sold.